Postmedieval Boat and Ship Archaeology

Papers based on those presented
to an International Symposium
on Boat and Ship Archaeology in
Stockholm in 1982

edited by

Carl Olof Cederlund

Swedish National Maritime Museum, Stockholm
Report No 20

BAR International Series 256
1985

B.A.R.

5, Centremead, Osney Mead, Oxford OX2 0ES, England.

GENERAL EDITORS

A.R. Hands, B.Sc., M.A., D.Phil.
D.R. Walker, M.A.

BAR -S256,1985 :'Postmedieval Boat and Ship Archaeology'.

Price £ 33.00   post free throughout the world. Payments made in dollars must be calculated at the current rate of exchange and $3.00 added to cover exchange charges. Cheques should be made payable to B.A.R. and sent to the above address.

© Swedish National Maritime Museum, 1985
ISBN 0 86054 327 7

For details of all B.A.R. publications in print please write to the above address. Information on new titles is sent regularly on request, with no obligation to purchase.

Volumes are distributed from the publisher. All B.A.R. prices are inclusive of postage by surface mail anywhere in the world.

Printed in Great Britain

Swedish National Maritime Museum Reports

with summaries in English or German language

Rapport 1   David Papp, Åländsk allmogeseglation 1800-1940.
               1971 (Reprinted by Rabén & Sjögren 1977)

Rapport 2   Arne Rydberg och Lasse Scotte, Fisket på Kråkö. 1973.

Rapport 3   David Papp och Bo Öhngren, Arbetarna vid Oskarshamns varv
               kring sekelskiftet. 1973

Rapport 4   Anders Björklund och David Papp, Sjöfartsyrken i hamnstaden
               Gävle. 1973

Rapport 5   Gunnar Nordlinder, Strömmingsfiske i Lövsele.
               Om fisket i en Västerbottensby från sekelskiftet till i dag.
               1977

Rapport 6   Anders Björklund, Splitvedsjäntor och andra arbeterskor vid
               de norrländska lastageplatserna. 1977

Rapport 7   Carl Olof Cederlund, Ett fartyg byggt med syteknik. En
               studie i marinarkeologisk dokumentation. 1978

Rapport 8   Ulla Wessling, Hivet går. Stuveriet som binäring bland
               norrländska småbrukare. 1978

Rapport 9   Anders Björklund, Lundebusar och bondesjåare.
               Ur sjöfartens och stuveriets historia i Ådalen. 1978

Rapport 10   Anders Björklund, Ulf Björklund, Jan Garnert och Björn
               Aström, Från skärgårdsbygd till fritidsdröm.
               Några drag i omvandlingen av byn Marum, Björkö-Arholma. 1979

Rapport 11   Björn Varenius, Bulverketbåten - ett gammalt fynd i ny
               belysning. 1979

Rapport 12   Carl Olof Cederlund och Sverker Söderberg. Båtar i 1600-
               talets Stockholm - om sex båtfynd i kv Hästen. 1980

Rapport 13   Ingrid Kaijser, Vraket vid Älvsnabben. Dokumentation, Last
               och Utrustning. 1981.

Rapport 14   Carl Olof Cederlund, Vraket vid Älvsnabben. Fartygets
               byggnad. 1981

Rapport 15   Per Lundström, De kommo vida ... Vikingars hamn vid Paviken
               på Gotland. 1981

Rapport 16   Carl Olof Cederlund. Vraket vid Jutholmen. Fartygets
               byggnad. 1982

Rapport 17   Ingrid Kaijser. Vraket vid Jutholmen. Last och utrustning.
               1982

Rapport 18   Gunnar Nordlinder. Singöbåtar. 1982

Rapport 19   Anders Sandström, Pansarfartyg åt Sveriges Flotta. En studie
               om flottan och striden om F-båten 1906-1909. 1984

Rapport 20   Carl Olof Cederlund (ed.), Postmedieval Boat and Ship
               Archaeology. 1985

CONTENTS

EDITOR'S FOREWORD.

This report is based on the papers presented at the third meeting of The International Symposia on Boat and Ship Archaeology, held at the Swedish National Maritime Museum in Stockholm in September 1982. It is also the first international presentation of the series of scientific reports from this museum. British Archaeological Reports has consented to produce a joint publication combining its International Series and the museum's Series of Reports.

This latter series which has been edited by the undersigned, was started in 1971 and comprises mainly reports on archaeological, ethnological and historical investigations performed at the Swedish National Maritime Museum.

Particular mention should be made of the reports 2 - 6 and 8 - 10 concerning the results of extensive ethnological and archaeological investigations along the northern part of the Swedish east coast, as well as reports 7, 11 - 14 and 16 - 17 dealing with ship archaeological and underwater archaeological development projects comprising six different investigations. All of these reports have summaries in English or German language.

The contributions to this report are presented in more or less the same order as they were at the ISBSA meeting. The themes of the sessions are used as headings for the different sections of the report. The presentation of current ship archaeological projects dealing with material predating the postmedieval age, has been placed as the final section.

The many papers from the ship archaeological field presented in this volume mirror a stage of development of the science in question. It also according to my opinion gives us useful information on important projects, source material and investigation methods.

October 1984

Carl Olof Cederlund

LIST OF CONTRIBUTORS

Paul Adam,
15 Rue du Grand Moulin
Paris, France

Béat Arnold,
Curator, Musée Cantonal d'Archaeologie,
Neuchatel, Switzerland

Michael Barkham,
Memorial University of Newfoundland,
St John's, Canada

Carl Olof Cederlund, Ph D
Head Curator at the Swedish National Maritime Museum
Docent in Marine Archaeology at The University of Stockholm

Arne Emil Christensen, Ph D
Head Curator, University Collection of National Antiquities,
Oslo, Norway

Ole Crumlin-Pedersen, Naval Architect
Director, Viking Ship Museum,
Roskilde, Denmark

Martin Dean, B Sc
Diving Officer, National Maritime Museum,
London, U K

Octavio Lixa Filgueiras,
Professor, Centre for Historical Studies,
University of Oporto,
Oporto, Portugal

Thomas Gillmer, Naval Architect
Professor of Naval Architecture (retired)
U S Naval Academy,
Annapolis, U S A

Morton Gøthche, Architect
Curator, Viking Ship Museum,
Roskilde, Denmark

Sibylla Haasum, Ph D
Head Curator, Swedish National Maritime Museum,
Stockholm, Sweden

Dan G. Harris, L commander
Maritime Museum of Gt Lakes at Kingston,
Canada

Jürgen Hausen, Dr-Ing
Lehrstuhl für Schiffbau, Konstruktion und Statik
Aachen, West Germany

Birgitta Håfors, fil mag
Head Curator, Swedish National Maritime Museum,
Stockholm, Sweden

Catharina Ingelman-Sundberg, fil kand
Curator, Maritime Museum of Malmö,
Malmö, Sweden

Hans Walter Keweloh,
Wissenschaftliger Mitarbeiter, Deutsches Schiffahrtsmuseum,
Bremerhaven, West Germany

Lars-Åke Kvarning, fil lic
Head Curator, Swedish National Maritime Museum,
Stockolm, Sweden

Jerzy Litwin, Naval Architect
Curator, Maritime Museum of Gdansk,
Gdansk, Poland

Per Lundström, fil lic
Director, Swedish National Maritime Museum
Stockholm, Sweden

Peter Norman, fil kand
Antiquarian, Central Office of National Antiquities,
Stockholm, Sweden

Eric Rieth, Dr
Attache de recherche, CNRS, Musée de la Marine,
Paris, France

Mark Redknap, BA
Curator, Passmore Edwards Museum,
London, U K

Reinder Reinders, Dr
Director, Ketelhaven Museum,
Dronten, Holland

Wolfgang Rudolph, Ph D
Akademie der Wissenschaften der DDR,
Berlin, East Germany

Prezmysław Smolarek, Ph D, Docent Habile
Director, Maritime Museum of Gdansk,
Gdansk, Poland

Hans Soop, fil lic
Curator, Swedish National Maritime Museum,
Stockholm, Sweden

Richard W. Unger, Ph D
Professor, University of British Columbia,
Vancouver, Canada

Björn Varenius, fil kand
Stockholm, Sweden

Peter von Busch, fil lic
Director, Naval Museum,
Karlskrona, Sweden

Christiane Villain-Gandossi, Ph D
École pratique des Hautes Etudes,
IVe Section, Sciences Historiques et Philologiques,
Sorbonne, Paris, France

1. THE OPENING OF THE THIRD MEETING OF INTERNATIONAL SYMPOSIA ON BOAT AND SHIP ARCHAEOLOGY.

Per Lundström

Dear colleagues, dear friends,

The first International symposia on boats and ship archaeology was held in London 1976, the second in Bremerhaven 1979.   Today we open the third meeting in Stockholm.

No doubt the earlier meetings have shown us how important it is to meet on an international basis to interchange experiences and inform each other about all important news in our science since we met last time.

I am sure that the program for this symposia will give us three days of hard work but also will give us full profit.

We open our meeting on the Wasavarvet so to say in the shadow of the Royal Warship Wasa from the 17th century and I think that the nearness of this big, marine archaeological project will be a source of inspiration for our work.

Now I wish all of you heartily welcome and declare the third meeeting of International symposia on boat and ship archaeology opened.

2. POST MEDIEVAL SHIP ARCHAEOLOGY AS A SUBJECT

Carl Olof Cederlund

With the third meeting of the ISBSA we are approaching our own time. We first met in London in 1976 to discuss boats and ships from prehistory and recording technique; the second time we gathered in Bremerhaven for the study of the medieval period and its ship archaeological objects. Now the time has come for the postmedieval period. That period is closest to us in time.

In terms of archaeological significance the material from these ships would seem to be relatively unimportant due to its low age and great quantity. But such an attitude I think is very wrong. Let me try to explain.

We in the so-called modern time, very much project our own questions and problems, on to the screen of the past – from the early stone age to the 19th century – for our own sakes and for the sake of our own time.

What is the meaning of the ship archaeological finds and remains from the postmedieval period then, in the light of our own cultural situation?

1. Primarily the shipwrecks from post medieval times are the imediate predessesors of our own vessels. They belong to the historical phase directly before our own time. This makes them important for the understanding of our own time and society. They also have considerable meaning as objects in our own time, for example as old boats preserved in museums.

2. They also are closely connected with working traditions and technical skills which still exist in our society or have only recently passed away. They are thus important for the interpretation or the revival of such valuable, living traditions in our culture, such as shipbuilding techniques of yesteryear, sailing techniques and seamanship.

As a basis for the study of these subjects, the vessels and wrecks from the postmedieval period constitute important historical material. They are evidence of past techniques and traditions which still have a meaning for us.

3. As scientific research material, carvel-built ships and the wrecks of such ships, occupy an important position. They can be seen as the fundamental tools in postmedieval technical development, economics and politics. It was these vessels that carried big sea-farers and merchandise, and were the main instrument used for warfare at sea. In this respect they can be employed as central sources for the interpretation of very important factors in the development of our society during the last five hundred years.

The boats and ships from the last five hundred years regarded as the predecessors of the vessels of our own time, give the symposium many subjects to consider and discuss:

how can we preserve the boats and ships which have survived until now "alive" - afloat and still in use?

how can we protect and economically support old preserved vessels in use? Is it possible to give them legal protection?

how can we store and exhibit old boats in museums, restore them and maintain them in a good condition?

how can we protect the wrecks of old ships on the sea bottom, not only legally but also in practice?

The boats and ships as evidence of past working traditions etc., generate other questions. This applies to both preserved vessels and wrecks. By keeping the techniques, necessary for, say, sailing a Norwegian Nordlands boat, a one-masted square rigged sailing vessel with very old traditions, you also keep an original element of the past alive.

Maybe that is the most important task of the museum researcher and ship archaeologist?

This is also relevant when it comes to sustaining old building techiques. You can learn from the aged builder of local boats, and you can also learn from wrecks which have rested on the bottom several centuries.

It is also relevant to put this aspect into the context of old seamanship in general. You can learn seamanship by sailing a schooner today and you can certainly supplement your practical knowledge by studying the remains of the sailor's real working conditions, tools and equipment in old wrecks.

The central question in this context is how the traditions of the past should be preserved, presented to and integrated in our society. The ways are many.

The scientific implications of the postmedieval boats and ships in our culture <u>might</u> be, for those of us here today, the most important consideration.

These preserved vessels and wrecks harbour a substantial and important mass of historical information, most of which is waiting to be recovered, prepared and presented.

I myself think that this is a challenge. What can be more thrilling and engaging than to be able to seek and retrieve information with which you can give your fellowmen new, qualified knowledge and understanding of history and thus improve their lives.

The scientific questions are innumerable. So I will not try to put to many of them forward. All the same I would like to make a statement of a principal character.

The big warships and the wrecks of these ships as historical objects, serve to a not so insignificant extent as national symbols. This is the case with the Wasa, and is probably also true of the Victory and other similar ships.

This is one of the reasons why they have such a strong position as ship archaeological and ship historical objects. I think they play an important role in arousing interest in ship archaeology in general with the aid of this symbolic weight. I also think that they possess a good deal of important historical information.

In Sweden the Wasa dominates the scene. I would guess that about 80 – 90% of the resources for ship archaeology in Sweden goes to the Wasa. And that has created a very positive situation in many ways.

But on the other hand the Wasa must be followed up by research along other lines, on other finds with a different character.

That is necessary if we want to give the public a differentiated and subtle picture of our past maritime life, its conditions and cultural and social implications. The latter is the responsibility of those who present the history, in different aspects, in a democracy, that is the historians and archaeologists to mention two of the categories of introducers.

Unless we ensure that the scope of our research is extensive and varied there is a risk that the view of history thus presented will be very one-sided and misleading.

Maybe our presentations here today and tomorrow – together with those given yesterday – will give a good picture of the abundant possibilities of postmedieval ship archaeology.

I will end this introduction by giving a few practical examples of what I have touched upon here. And I will be presumptive enough to use our experiences here in Sweden as examples:

Coming back to the concept of the vessels as objects of historical value, I would like to point out an investigation with the Swedish title "Bevara fartyg – att värna om kulturarvet." (In English "Protecting and preserving ships – safeguarding our cultural heritage").

It has been written by Bengt Ohrelius and Gösta Webe at the Swedish National Maritime Museum and was presented in 1978.

It deals with the stage before the situation when old ships become archaeological objects. The investigation scrutinizes the many aspects of the questions concerning preserved old vessels: why preserve and protect, what to preserve, who preserves and how to preserve?

The investigation clarifies many things concerning the care of old ships with an historical value. I think it is a useful tool for the future treatment of these questions generally.

One of the conditions for the evaluation and treatment of ship archaeological finds is the making of a systematical register of them and the mapping of them.

The information you thus collect creates a body of information which gives credence to ship archaeological material in many ways. It gives the possibility to start scientific investigations on a broad basis, or to make general statements for the care of ship archaeological finds, or to exchange information with the public.

The Swedish National Museum has compiled a register of wrecks containing among other things more than 1000 wrecks, most of which are from the postmedieval period. This is an important tool for our ship archaeological and marine archaeological work.

Coming to the aspect of the living traditions of maritime society, I would like to give one example connected with ship archaeology. One of the many aspects of postmedieval ship archaeology is its direct connection with the general public and with the society of today. Maybe we as archaeologists have not grasped this connection in its real sense.

The majority of investigations and presentations are sometimes held within a rather restricted circle of interested people - the so called scientific society. A few big projects are exceptions to this. All the same I think there is considerable interest even in the-not-so-spectacular ship finds of later times, not least a local interest, which should be met by us in a factual and in the same time qualified and engaging way.

One of the best ways to do that is to associate it with the revival or preservation of maritime traditions.

In connection with the planning of the new Wasa museum, a ship archaeological work-shop has also been planned in the museum. The public will be given the opportunity to cut their thumbs testing 17th century axes or to test the big, two-hand saw.

There will also be space for us to carry on archaeological recording work, restoration of old boats etc., under the eyes of the public. The ideal would be to be able to hold courses in boatbuilding, ship restoration, sailmaking, marine and ship archaeology etc.

Stockholm harbour will be situated just outside the museum. What would be more natural than to turn the Wasa museum into a real-life-centre of old ships and boats and of the traditions connected with them.

Well preserved local craft could, for instance, be moored to the quay of the museum. It would be very positive from the point of view of the general public if an annual Day of the Local Craft Boat in Stockholm Harbour would be held with competitions, information, public viewing of the boats etc.. Such an annual day might be a very good market place for ship archaeology, maritime traditions and culture. One has suggested that the 22.5 m long full scale replica of a medieval boat which is now being built could serve as the judges' ship at such a competition event.

The scientific approach to the subject may be exemplified in two ways.

The Archaeological Institute of the University of Stockholm has been offering courses in marine archaeology and ship archaeology for 10 years now. More than one hundred students have hitherto completed the courses. This educational work is a condition for the integration of marine archaeology in the work of museums and other similiar organizations in Sweden. The university work is also important for the establishment of scientific formulae and qualified scientific work in this field.

The plan is to include this in the regular curriculum and connect it to other institutions dealing with maritime history, not least this museum.

The wrecks of the big carvel-built ships from the post-medieval period are very characteristic Swedish marine archaeological material. There is a large number of such wrecks in Sweden and many of them are very well preserved.

The Wasa is the only one of these which has been salvaged in its entirety. To give you an idea of the many others, we have arranged a small exhibition for this symposium.

We have now passed the first stage in the development of the science of ship archaeology. During the 1960s and 70s work has been concentrated on the establishment of ship archaeological recording and investigating techniques.

This means that we now can start to collect information for the treatment and presentation of historical knowledge.

In connection with the exhibit the museum will present two development projects the reports of which now are published. Their purpose has been the development and practicing of underwater and ship archaeological techniques, especially adaptable to Swedish conditions.

3. THE ANCIENT MONUMENTS ACT AND THE SHIPWRECKS

Sibylla Haasum

I have given my lecture the title "The Ancient Monuments Act and The Shipwrecks". As it is not the law itself and its legal contents I intend to talk about I should like to give the contribution the sub-title: "The Care of Ancient Monuments and the problems connected with the finds of the big shipwrecks".

What I want to account for here really are some unsorted reflections around these problems and I will try to illuminate the situation for our Swedish maritime archaeology.

I suppose all of you know the provisions of the Swedish Ancient Monuments Act concerning shipwrecks so I will just mention that shipwrecks protected according to our law must be at least 100 years old as wrecks. As a background to my discourse you also ought to know that the costs of necessary archaeological investigations in connection with exploitation rest upon the exploiter.

We possess in this country the warship Wasa and we are very grateful for this. Wasa has meant incredibly much to Swedish maritime archaeology. Without this ship we had not arrived as far as we have done today within the maritime archaeological domain. This find has enforced a development; enforced investigation and working methods, developed techniques and preservation methods, brought about possibilities of increased economic and personnel resources and given us trained maritime archaeologists, but perhaps first and foremost; it has brought about a tremendous interest in maritime archaeology in Sweden. We are - and this I will really emphasize - immensely grateful to Anders Franzén and our National Maritime Museum for all this.

But what I want to say here is that the maritime archaeology today is so much more than Wasa and I will with this contribution try to start a discussion on the appropriate action we ought to take with all the finds and expected findings of big shipwrecks. What can we do with them, what ought we to do? And I hope to get some comparison with the way it is proceeded in other countries.

We have a great number of relatively well preserved wrecks along our coasts. We usually say like this: while the registered ancient monuments on land can be counted in hundreds of thousands the underwater ancient monuments can certainly be estimated at tens of thousands. That includes other remains too. The registers at our Maritime Museum contain today about 800 registered wrecks and about 9.000 foundering data.

We are well favoured in this country, since the shipworm - Teredo Navalis - which in other waters with higher salinity consumes sunken timber, does not exist in the Brackish sea water of the Baltic. The Baltic has in this become a goldmine for Swedish underwater archaeology and maybe the great number of well preserved wrecks is in this way something rather unique and maybe the problems are therefore not as great in other countries.

I also want to mention that we have two categories of findings; finds in connection with exploitation where the economy is facilitated by the provisions of the law and finds which have been discovered in pure research and in skindiving.

Our possibilities of carrying on research ourselves are limited on account of economic och personnel conditions and we have to take what we get in exploitation as well as by skindivers. And then the question - what shall we do with it? They are protected according to the law. I talk here only about shipwrecks. But which measures are nessecary and suitable in different contexts.

There is still much which ought to be developed within our maritime archaeology and boat archaeology.

  - we need to fill in the gaps in our knowledge referring to chronology as well as to type and boat building history.

  - we need to develop methods and techniques even more.

  - we need to develop our dating methods.

  - we need to supplement the finds and objects and

  - we need to work more with whole contexts as for ex. Foteviken. (You will hear more about that later).

Our in many ways limited knowledge makes the judgement sometimes very difficult. We must, however, learn to give priorities in connection with exploitation investigations as well as finds found in another way.

And without depriving the big shipwrecks of their value but for filling in the gaps in our knowledge we must consequently think the matter over carefully how to make the best use of our small means.

How do we then proceed with the big shipwrecks - which in fact are above all the theme of this symposium. I shall not here describe the finds we have of them just now or show pictures. You will be given an account in words and pictures of finds of current interest during today and tomorrow. I just want to try to illuminate the problems.

It goes without saying that in many cases it is not just the shipwreck in itself that will give us something. We must not disregard other values in this connection. Take for instance the Kronan (Crown) wreck which will be introduced to you later. This find has furnished us with a great many particularly valuable objects, it gives us furthermore a good insight into the "ship community", it gives us possibilities of developing techniques and methods and finally it means from a public relation point of view enormously to our County museum in Kalmar and to that whole region. And it enables us to build up a maritime archaeological activity along our southeastern coast with a planned decentralization at hand of handling maritime archaeological matters.

I am convinced that we can work with the Kronan (Crown) wreck for the coming 10 maybe 20 years if we wish to. But as I said before it is so much more we also want to do. Now our contributions concerning Kronan ought not really to be exaggerated. The investigation is done almost completely out of privately collected means.

I know that many people search eagerly for the rest of our foundered warships from that time. The search is for Svärdet (the Sword) - the ship which foundered at the same time as Kronan and which ought to lie somewhere north of it. The search is for a wreck called Resande Man (Travelling Man) - another warship from the same century foundered in the southern archipelago of Stockholm. The search is for a warship called Mars even older - from the sixteenth century - lying somewhere between the islands of Öland and Gotland. And in Scania they dream of being able to take up the remains of for example the warship the New Sword in Landskrona harbour or to investigate other similar wrecks lying along the coast of Scania (Skåne). So certainly the finds can still be many and big.

And we have a difficult exploitation matter in Scania too and that is the possible enlargement of Landskrona harbour. Here several wrecks are located and there is information of not less than some 15 founderings.

But let us relate these dreams to other wishes and put them in perspective of the wishes I have already put forward to you.

And I want to mention another find of current interest. At about 40m depth in Lake Vättern the wreck of a steamship - a paddle-steamer by the name of Erik Nordewall has recently been found. The wreck is almost completely intact. It is built in wood, oak and pine, at the engineering industry in Motala in 1836 and it became a wreck in 1856. Erik Nordewall was built at a very interesting point of time in the development of the ship-building technique; the change from propulsion by oars and sails to the new steamship navigation. This brought about great changes with respect to hull, building methods, construction techniques etc. Eric Nordewall is built exactly in this interval and for this reason it is of particular technical-historical interest. For the time being we (that means the Central Board of National Antiquities) have only granted permission to the salvage of some separate objects. The divers who found the wreckage are planning besides to make a video-film of it. But it is quite evident that there is a great interest in this wreck too and that many people want to salvage this very important find.

And we have relatively well preserved rather big wrecks of merchant vessels. Carl Olof Cederlund is going to present two of them tomorrow, both located in the Stockholm archipelago.

And personally I should like very much to find more of the smaller utility boats from the time this symposium deals with. We have certainly made quite a lot of finds of small boats, for instance at the great excavations in Stockholm, but unfortunately we have not yet had the time, money and the personnel to document and analyze them thoroughly. As regards these small utility boats there is still much to be wanted as far as research is concerned. Today we many times find it very difficult to determine their type and to date them. ·Bear in mind that we in this country cannot yet for instance derive the origin of the flat stern of some of the small boats - just to take an example.

In other words I mean that we ought to have a somewhat better balance in our boat-research.   We want to have the big shipwrecks - we need them - but at the same time we want to have more and this is today not so easy to get for instance by economic reasons.   Against the background which I have drawn up here the question is: what shall we do with the future finds of the big shipwrecks?

Let us say that we in the near future have the wrecks of a few warships more and some merchant vessels and other boats and many wishes for investigations and salvages!

Then you will have to remember - something which all of you know very well - that the real heavy expenses come afterwards with the working-up, analyses, documentation and taking care of and keeping the finds.   Then what to do?

Do we just locate and register them - and then keep them lying?

Shall we try to document them in some way?

Maybe filming is a good one.

Shall we salvage certain objects for dating and identification?

Is it for example sensible to take up more cannons out of the depths?

It is worth mentioning that we have salvaged 18 out of originally 128 cannons from Kronan.   Two of these salvaged cannons are particularly interesting.   One of them is twelve-angled and decorated with heraldic lilies, and the other one is a very old one from 1514.   Among the other cannons from Kronan there are thirtysix-pounders, a size which was not found on the Wasa.

The question is easily put - is it really advisable and desirable to continue taking up cannons?   We have besides for the time being preservation worries concerning bronze cannons.   Mustn't we begin with solving these?

Shall we salvage to avoid the risk of plundering or is this risk maybe many times exaggerated?   Can we manage this problem by increased information and co-operation?

It is evident that these questions cannot be answered uniformly - adjustments must be done in each specific case of course.

But all the same they are problems we have to grapple with and it would be interesting to have your opinions on them or on some of them.   And of course the demand for giving priority must concern all types of shipwrecks anyhow.

But much can also be done with the big shipwrecks.   We can use them for developing methods and techniques, for co-operation, for training etc.

And at the same time we must not deny the enormously great local and regional public relations significance these finds really have.   I remember the head-line of an article about Kronan quite recently, "Kronan/the Crown/ is worth every single 'öre'/cent/".   And I believe the head-line is right - but what shall we do when we besides this want so much more and is it quite right in these connections to trust completely to private means?   And are we ourselves too bad public relation persons to market "the whole maritime archaeology"?

And just think a little about the basic principle of our ancient monuments on land – we let them deliberately lie there, we preserve them, protect them and revere them.   I admit that the starting-point is not quite the same for the cultural – historical remains under water.   It is possible only for very few people to look at them; besides that they decay more rapidly than the remains on land and what's more we sometimes often need the knowledge they can give us.

In addition underwater archaeology (if we say so – it really ought not to be separated in that way from archaeology) is younger and for the time being the find of a wreck gets the feelings running high.   It does not seem to be quite so exciting to come and tell about a magnificent cairn somewhere along our coast or about a whole maritime context – as Foteviken – with a harbour, with a defense under water, shipwrecks and connecting remains on land.

Be that as it may – what I wanted to say is this:

There is a certain imbalance in our investigations and that we have to fight with it in such a way that our maritime archaeological research and the boat-archaeology won't heel over.

4. THE PRESERVATION OF THE WASA

Birgitta Håfors

Introduction

From the preservation point of view the Wasa project fell into five main categories. Those were

The hull itself
The large, disconnected components
Cast iron objects – mainly cannon balls
Sails
Leather goods

Each category was fairly extensive as was each subcategory. There were also groups of more easily handled objects, for instance smaller wooden objects like spoons and bowls which were in a very deteriorated condition.

The Hull

It was decided that the hull should not be taken apart but treated in one piece. For that purpose the pontoon structure on which the hull still rests was constructed and during the summer of 1961 the building was erected. To protect the wood from drying out immediately, plastic sheets were used and the tips of the ribs were wrapped with plastic ribbons as soon as the hull broke the water surface. During the period as the building was going up the decks were sprayed with fresh water automatically, using garden equipment, and the outer planking was sprayed with seawater by hand.

Even though the decision to treat the hull in one piece had been made, the exact formula of the preservative had not yet been decided upon. Several experts were consulted and, finally, the polyethyleneglycol (PEG) 4000 was suggested.

The function of the PEG is to diminish shrinkage of the wood on drying. The other problem – to prevent fungus from growing when the moisture level became suitable – was to be taken care of with boric acid and sodiumborate. The most desirable way of applying the fungicide was to add it to the PEG-solution and thus be able to do both the dimension stabilizing and the fungus protecting treatment at the same time.

To combine the substances in solution was my first task when joining the Wasa project in 1961. The buffering capacity of the boric acid/borate-mixture was used and it was possible to dissolve as much as 8% of a mixture of 7 parts of boric acid and 3 parts of sodiumborate in a solution containing 30% PEG 4000. On raising the PEG-concentration the equilibrium is shifted towards a mixture containing more boric acid and less sodiumborate.

When the spraying of the hull started in April 1962 it was decided that PEG 1500 was to be used instead of PEG 4000 because of the greater solubility of that molecular grade at lower temperatures. Later - in 1971 - when it had been established through laboratory tests that the PEG 600 had a greater ability to diminish shrinkage - the 1500 was substituted by this molecular grade. This was of great advantage because of the even greater solubility of the PEG 600 which became the more important as the concentration was increased.

Spraying of the hull was first conducted by hand once or twice a day, but in March 1965 an automatic spraying system was installed. This permitted the hull to be sprayed 32 times during a 24 hour period. This spraying schedule remained unchanged for six years during which period the concentration of PEG was increased from 10 to 25%. During the following eight years of conservation there was a successive prolongation of the periods between sprayings and a further increase in PEG-concentration to about 45%.

To get an idea about the efficiency of the method of spraying the solution of preservative on the wood, some laboratory tests were made and also some tests on a larger scale. Test panels which measured 1.5 x 1.5 m were built from timber from a 17th century ship, brought up by divers for that purpose. These tests mainly showed that it is not possible to accelerate the process - that a long spraying period is needed and also a long drying period. Excessively fast drying tends to draw a water soluble preservative towards the surface of the wood.

The results of the preservation process, as observed with test pieces, the test panels and on the object itself, the hull, are constantly being monitored by taking samples from the wood which are immediately divided into pieces, each representing a certain level in the wood. These pieces are put into previously-weighed test tubes and taken to the laboratory where they are analysed. The analyses gives the content of water and preservatives on the level represented by that particular piece of core. The average water content of the oak timbers from the Wasa calculated on the dry fibre weight, was 150% 1961. Today the outer planking has dried down to an average of 23% and the big timbers in the hold and on the orlop deck to an averge of about 40%. The PEG-content varies and the values range between 0 and 100%.

During the period that the hull was being sprayed by hand, 1962-1965, the RH was kept at a level of 95% by an air-conditioning unit. Another air conditioning unit, controlled by hygrostates, was brought into use in 1972 when the spraying with preservation solution was getting less frequent. To prevent the wood closest to the air outlet from drying out a diffusing device was mounted on the outlet. The RH was brought down from the original 95% to about 70%.

After the spraying of the hull with PEG 600 was finished in January 1979, it was possible to start the finishing treatment on the parts of the hull where the moisture content is in equilibrium with the RH. PEG 4000 was chosen as a surface coating. Before the treatment with PEG 4000 could start, the surface had to be cleaned from dirt and dust using sponges. The PEG 4000, as a 45% solution in water, was sprayed by hand on to the surface. This treatment had to be repeated 3 to 4 times. After drying, which took a couple of days, hot air was applied and the PEG was absorbed.

Disconnected finds

As the disconnected finds which were brought up from the Wasa had to be protected from drying out, several wooden tanks were built. The tanks were lined with plastic sheets. Everything that was brought up was put in a tank with water containing fungicide.

To be able to treat the huge mass of timber two preservation tanks were built, measuring a total of together 3.6 x 1.15 x 20 m. The temperature of the solution could be regulated and kept within a narrow range of the desired value. The solution was circulated so that an even concentration could be maintained. A ventilation system was used to concentrate the solution by evaporating the solvent (water).

The objects were placed in the tanks - in frames where necessary so as not to obstruct the circulation of preservation solution. The process was started by filling the tank with a measured quantity of water which was heated to the desired temperature. About 1.5% of boric acid/sodium borate mixture was added after which commenced the raising of the PEG concentration by adding the chosen PEG (mostly 4000 or 1500) in batches at a precalculated rate.

When the desired PEG-concentration was reached, which in the case of the Wasa's oak happened about 18 months after the process started, the solution was allowed to cool down. The preserved objects were then taken to a climatized space where they were treated by means of spraying with a solution of the same PEG-concentration as was in the tank at the end of the treatment. The spraying continued at intervals during the drying process and the RH of the climatized space was lowered from about 90% to the value (about 65%) which was going to be kept in the museum. The process took another 12-18 months.

While drying, excess PEG remained visible on the surface of the object. That excess PEG was removed by the application of hot air which leaves a protecting surface of PEG on the object.

In all, about 250 m^3 of material from the Wasa has been treated in this way.

The Leather

All leather goods as well as small wooden objects, like spoons and bowls, have been treated by freeze-drying after being impregnated with PEG 600 or 400.

Cast Iron

Cast iron articles have been reduced by hydrogen gas at high temperature and then impregnated with microcristalline paraffin wax.

Sails

The sails were found in a heap on the orlop deck and had to be excavated before treatment. As the material was very fragile the unfolding had to be done under water. After removing the rust with oxalic acid and drying the textile with alcohol and xylene, a very brittle fabric was left.

To be able to preserve the sails, it was decided to mount them on to a non-flexible backing. A glassfibre fabric was chosen for the purpose. The glassfibre fabric was painted with a acrylic-styrene polymer that was composed so that it would have the same refractive index as the glassfibre. The sails were placed on the polymerpainted glassfibre fabric and were then fastened to the supporting sheet with the aid of an emulsion of the polymer.

The separate sheets have a standard size of 1.5 x 2 m and can be mounted together to form the entire sail.

5. THE DECORATED SHIP

A small outline of the carved decoration of the warship WASA

Hans Soop

In a few words I shall try to give you a short representation of one of the most complex aspects of the warship WASA, namely the carved decoration. We will start in 1956. A short time after the ship had been found by Mr. Anders Franzén in August, the preparations for the salvaging started. When digging the six tunnels under the hull, the first sculptures were brought up from the bottom. Soon a lot of remarkable and fascinating wooden objects were spread out all over the divers' raft, exciting the imagination. There were warriors in Roman armour with grim and closed faces, small nice-looking cherubs and putti, enigmatical smiling mermaids, bearded tritons, impressive knights dressed in magnificent medieval cuirasses, wild lions with bushy manes, grotesque looking heads and bizarre mascaroons, splendid heraldic arms and escutcheons, fabulous beasts, pilasters, ornaments decorated in scroll work, grotesques and ear shell ornamentations etc. It was a fantastic and imaginative world, speaking the rich and full-flavoured language of north European renaissance art, with its mixture of classical antique forms and the remnants of the old, germanatic gothic-medieval tradition. It was a counterpart in wood to the voluminous stone decoration of palaces, burghers houses and churches in the seventeenth century capital of the newly established Swedish "great power", decorations which to a great extent still can be studied in the Old Town of Stockholm.

About 200 sculptures were found during the time of salvaging. After the WASA had broken the surface in April 1961, the divers could concentrate their work on taking up the rest of the decorations from the bottom. During the summers 1963-1967 the remaining sculptures were brought to light, and in all nearly 500 figure sculptures and several hundred ornaments of different kinds have been preserved to this day. They will all give us a good idea about the manner of decorating a big warship in the early seventeenth century.

But what did all these warriors and knights, mermaids, tritons and sea-gods represent? What did they symbolize? Where on the ship had they all been placed? To all these questions there were no immediate answers. The sculptures seemed mysterious and baffling.

Running parallel with the conservation of the water-soaked sculptures, the research upon this unique collection of art objects tried to get answers to the many questions. The restoration of the hull, which means a re-building of the ship in order to find out how she looked in 1628, gave back the most demolished parts of the WASA: the stern castle with its bulwarks, galleries and cabins, the beakhead and the railings. So, like a Phoenix, the WASA arose anew, and it became possible to find out exactly - by comparing the back side of the carvings with the construction of the ship - where each sculpture once had been placed. During this work, it became quite obvious that the decoration must have been an integral part of the architecture of the ship, and that the final stage of the restoration should be the re-placing of all the sculptures.

The work of finding the positions ran parallel with the iconographic research upon the carvings, in order to get an answer to the questions of what they represented and symbolized and what role they played on the ship. By studying the sources of renaissance artistic ideas and motifs, it soon became clear from where the artists, the wood carvers, had got the prototypes for their work. It was mainly the ancient Greek and Roman mythology, the Roman literature, history and philosophy, the Old Testament and the old Gothic-Scandinavian mythical tradition. So armoured or naked male figures could be identified with antique mythical heroes as Hercules or Peleus, sea-gods as Proteus and Thetis, Israelian kings or leaders as David and Gideon. Slender men with mantles and laurel wreaths could be identified with Roman emperors - their names actually carved in block letters at the feet of each emperor - and tall knights in Gothic armour with old mythical kings of Sweden.

It's a spectacular gallery of invented or real personages, known by name, derived from the sagas and history. During the time of the renaissance, they symbolized brilliant and glorious virtues such as bravery and courage, power and wisdom, patience and strength. At the time of the WASA, all these virtues were said to characterize princes and sovereigns. On the WASA, these representatives of virtues are paying homage to king Gustavus Adolphus, who is present on the top of the stern, in the shape of a young boy with long hair, surrounded by two griffins holding a royal crown over the head of the young king. The whole decoration of the stern means to glorify the king, to tell the world at large what an illustrious and brilliant man he is, an equal to Hercules, to king David and Gideon, and a worthy successor to his glorious forefathers and predecessors on the throne of Sweden.

Just now, the last chapter of the restoration work is to be written. It means that the sculptures will be returned to their original positions on the ship. The circle will soon be closed. In a few years, the WASA once again will appear in its former splendour.

But in one very important aspect, it will not be exactly the same ship as it was in 1628. The original colours of the hull and the carvings - of which traces still could be seen on the carvings when bringing them up from the bottom - have unfortunately disappeared during the time in the sea, and also during the time of conservation. The wooden carvings will no longer gleam of glittering gold and bright colours. That's something we must have in mind when studying the results of the skilful works of the German and Dutch woodcarvers, as they are seen in the sculpture hall or on the ship.

Fig. 5.1: The upper part of the Wasa's stern castle was decorated with the Swedish Coat of Arms which is held by two huge lions. The wooden sculpture measures 3.24 by 1.90 meters (10.6 by 6.2 feet) and consists of 19 separate pieces which have gradually been salvaged on the place where the Wasa sank. Originally the Coat of Arms was painted in the heraldic colours and gilded.

21

Fig. 5.2: The upper quarter gallery, starboard side. Part of the lower gallery.

Fig. 5.3:   Hercules. Lower stern
gallery.

Fig. 5.4:   Warrior dressed in Roman
armour. Lower quarter gallery, port
side.

Fig. 5.5: Caryatid in the shape of a
sirene. The roof of the lower
quarter gallery, port side.

Fig. 5.6: Lion mascaron. Port lid.

6. THE PLANNING OF A NEW MUSEUM FOR THE WASA

Lars-Åke Kvarning

(At the time of the ISBSA-meeting in Stockholm in 1982 the
jury of the architects' competition for the new museum had
not yet made its decision. In this paper the development
of the planning thus has been followed up to the year of
1984 to give a fuller description of the situation.)

When the Swedish royal warship Wasa, which sank in 1628, was raised
from Stockholm harbor on April 24, 1961, the event made international
headlines. The Wasa is believed to be the world's oldest identified and
completely preserved man-of-war, and is also an artistic treasure-chest; she
was embellished with 700 carvings, virtually all of which have survived.

The Wasa had been built as one of the largest ships of the navy of King
Gustavus II Adolphus, who led Sweden into an era as a major European power.
On the day of its maiden voyage, the royal man-of-war capsized and sank with
crew and guests, apparently the victim of too little ballast for its unusual
size and weight.

Almost immediately after being salvaged, the Wasa became one of Sweden's
most popular tourist attractions. Wasa exhibits crisscrossed the globe. The
guns of the Wasa fired salutes for opening ceremonies at world's fairs,
during America's Cup sailing races, and on many other ceremonial occasions.

The tourists who streamed to view the ship were received in a
provisional museum inaugurated in 1962. The ship itself was placed on a
floating pontoon structure in a cramped aluminium building that was designed
primarily for conservation and restoration purposes. Display and exhibition
facilities, a restaurant, and a film auditorium were added in the open
outdoor area adjacent to the ship. This temporary setup, to be used while
conservation was in progress, was to be replaced with a new, permanent
museum when the Wasa was restored, a job expected to take about ten years.

But knowledge of this type of project was scarce; nowhere else in the
world had the conservation of such a large wooden ship been undertaken. The
conservation and restoration took much longer than anyone expected, and it
wasn't until 1979 that the spraying equipment could be turned off and the
carvings and other decorations repositioned on the ship.

So the Wasa, now 355 years old, has been on display in its
"provisional" building for more than twenty years. The number of visitors
continues to increase and is now over half a million annually; a single-day
record of 7401 visitors was set in the summer of 1984.

With the conservation work concluded, restoration has progressed as far
as possible in the cramped quarters of the pontoon structure. The climate
in this building is also insufficient to ensure the Wasa's future
preservation. Consequently, in the autumn of 1981 the Swedish Board of
Building and Planning, which administers all state-run building projects in

27

the nation, was commissioned by the government to arrange a Scandinavian architectural contest to design a permanent Wasa museum. The building was to be erected on the site of an old shipyard on Djurgården (Deer Park) Island, so the ship would remain within the inner Stockholm harbor area. The facilities were not to exceed 6,000 sq metres with 3,425 square meters to be used as exhibition space.

The contest opened on December 19, 1981, with a deadline for submission of entries by April 5, 1982. Three hundred eighty-four entries poured in, proof of the continuing fascination of the Wasa. It proved to be the most popular architectural competition ever held in Scandinavia. The jury consisted of representatives (three) from the Scandinavian architectural associations, the museum (two), the property owners (one), the city of Stockholm (one), and the building and planning board (two).

All the entries were fully displayed, a considerable undertaking in itself. Some were released to the press, radio, and television (without the names of the contestants being revealed). The jury eventually narrowed its choices to two entries both considered in a class of their own; both were awarded first prize. One was a Danish entry with the motto, "In a hundred years the prize will be forgotten". It was designed by architects Johan Fogh and Per Følner. The other, Ask ("The Box"), was designed by Stockholm architects Ove Hidemark and Göran Månsson. However, as there were two winners, the problem of the final design of the new museum was not resolved, and in fact was further complicated by the fact that the proposed designs were to be located in different places within the former shipyard area.

The building and planning board instructed the winners to rework their designs, keeping in mind the jury's appraisals. When this was done, the designs were sent by the building and planning board for study to the Maritime Museum, to the city of Stockholm and to the board of the Royal Djurgården Park. The museum declared itself in favor of the Swedish design, as did the city, while the park board recommended the Danish design. The jury, now asked to present its views as an advisory group only, supported the Swedish design by a vote of six to three.

On April 25, 1983, the building and planning board requested government permission to go ahead with the planning of the Wasa building based on the Swedish design. According to the planning board's timetable, the Wasa could be moved into its new premises in the spring of 1989. Building costs have been estimated at 121 million Swedish crowns ($16 million). The Swedish government must now allocate the funds. A decision to plan and build the museum has been presented by the government in the spring of 1984.

The Ask design, with its suggestion of a medieval royal festival, represents unconventional architecture characterized by imagination and a sense of play. The architects themselves describe it as follows: "The museum building ought to be perceived as a composite organic shape that has derived its very special form from both its contents and its surroundings. Out of the large copper roof which serves as a common outer skin, the other architectural elements emerge: roof terraces with vegetation facing the rock, arcades at the main entrance stretching out into the park, the Wasa's masts protruding from the encasement, the ship exhibition hall's square shape suggested in the roof and in the large southern wall, the galleries that give the impression of verandas in the facade facing the water.... The building strives to be an architectural landscape."

As the jury commented on the design, "With its colors, flags and poles, eaves, bridges, canopies, and lights, it possesses a strong and joyous character that must be retained. The design's greatest merit is its gaiety, totally without the sacred element that many of the other designs have associated with the Wasa. Instead, the building is permeated by a feeling of a baroque festival. It is through these implied qualities that it so wonderfully captures the character of Djurgården."

If the facade in the Ask possesses a strong and carefree character, so does the interior. The festive atmosphere so well communicated by the exterior is definitely the impression the visitor should receive upon entering. Here, the Wasa will stand in the middle of a spacious room that houses all the activities the musuem has to offer and that amply will permit the ship to be studied from various levels, angles, and distances. It is a festive, stimulating environment totally lacking in solemn and sacred overtones, an active design that should motivate and inspire those working within it.

The first thing the visitor will encounter after passing through the entrance is an impressive overview of the Wasa. Looming twenty-five meters away and angled ideally for visitor viewing, the ship will be positioned in all its majesty. Visitors also will discover a number of additional attractions. To the right will be the visitor facilities, film auditoriums, and exhibits; on the left will be the museum shop and restaurant. The ship itself will rest with its water line at floor level, where visitors can see the underwater section of the hull, displays at the keel level, and additional exhibits at a level about halfway up from the keel and also at higher levels.

The positioning of the base exhibits will be unconventional. The idea was to ensure that the displays would always be associated with the ship, around which everything was to revolve in a direct and close connection both physically and conceptually. These exhibits will deal with specific themes, and the display groupings will be located at various levels around the ship, the levels relating to each theme in an interplay among the ship, the exhibits and the sorroundings.

To cope with the waves of tourists at peak season, the design includes three film auditoriums, with capacities of 300, 175 and 50 people. (There are now eleven language versions of the film about the Wasa). During winter, the smallest auditorium will serve as a class-room, the medium-size one will be used for temporary displays.

The design more than satisfies the museum's requirement that the visitors have an effective overall view of the ship from one side yet be able to move in closer to study it in more detail on the other side from balconies at various levels. The standing lower rig and the lower yards will be reconstructed. To give visitors a concept of the incredible volume and height of the original rig (the Wasa was 171 feet high from the bottom of the keel to the top of the main mast), the architects have placed full-sized stylized masts and yards on the roof of the building.

Support for the new building is now unanimous: the Wasa museum has the potential to be an architecturally exciting building, a superb structure for visitors, and a well-planned workplace.

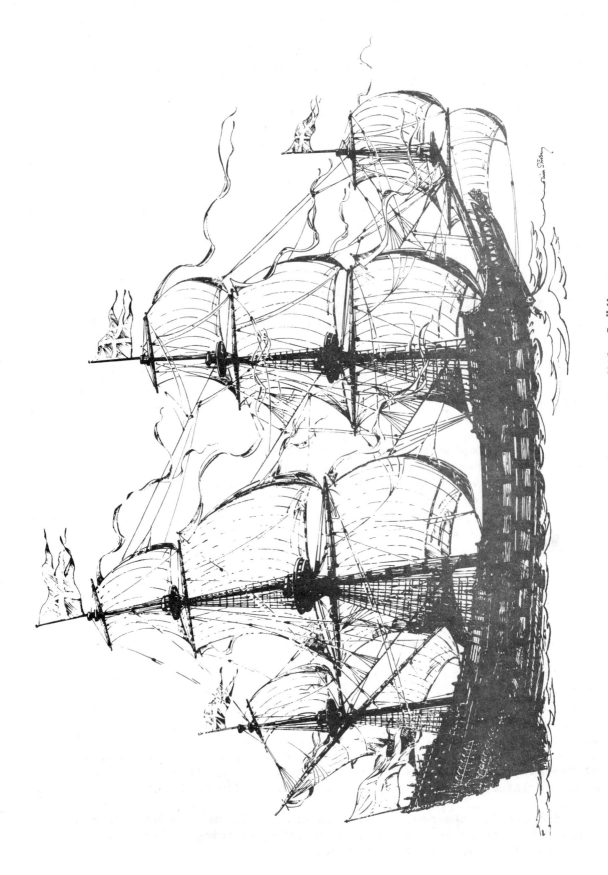

Fig. 6.1: The Wasa in its original shape.   Drawing by Nils Stödberg.

x

30

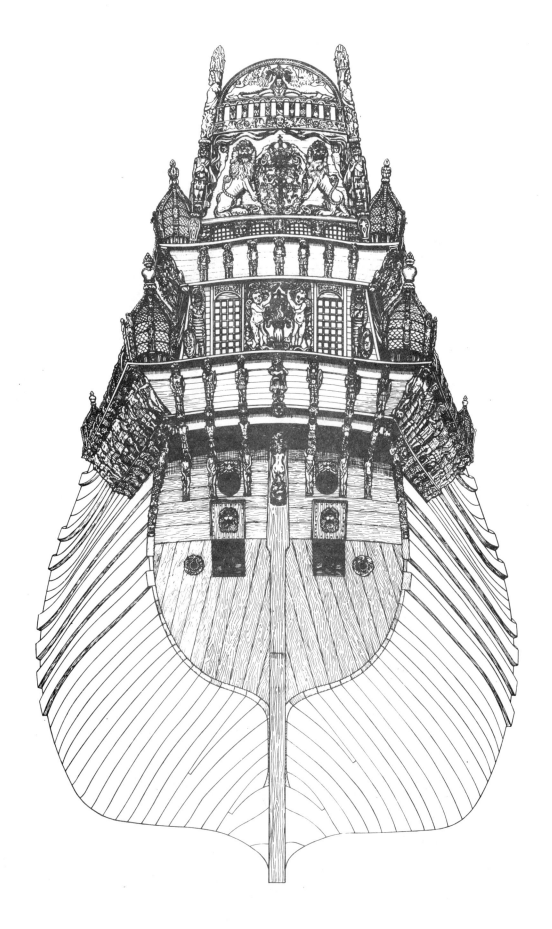

Fig. 6.2:   The stern of the Wasa in its original as well as its restored shape. Drawing by Gunnar Olofsson.

Fig. 6.3:   The figures 6.3 - 6.8 are derived from the winning design for the new Wasa Museum by the Swedish architects Ove Hidemark anbd Göran Månsson.   This figure shows the museum seen from Berzelii Park.

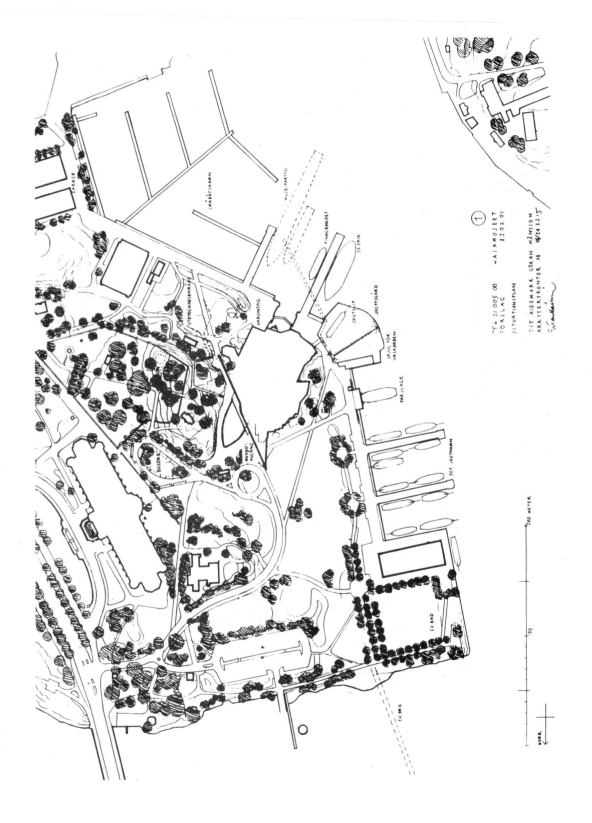

Fig. 6.4: Plan of the site of the new Wasa Museum. The museum will be situated at the waterfront where also museum ships will be moored.

33

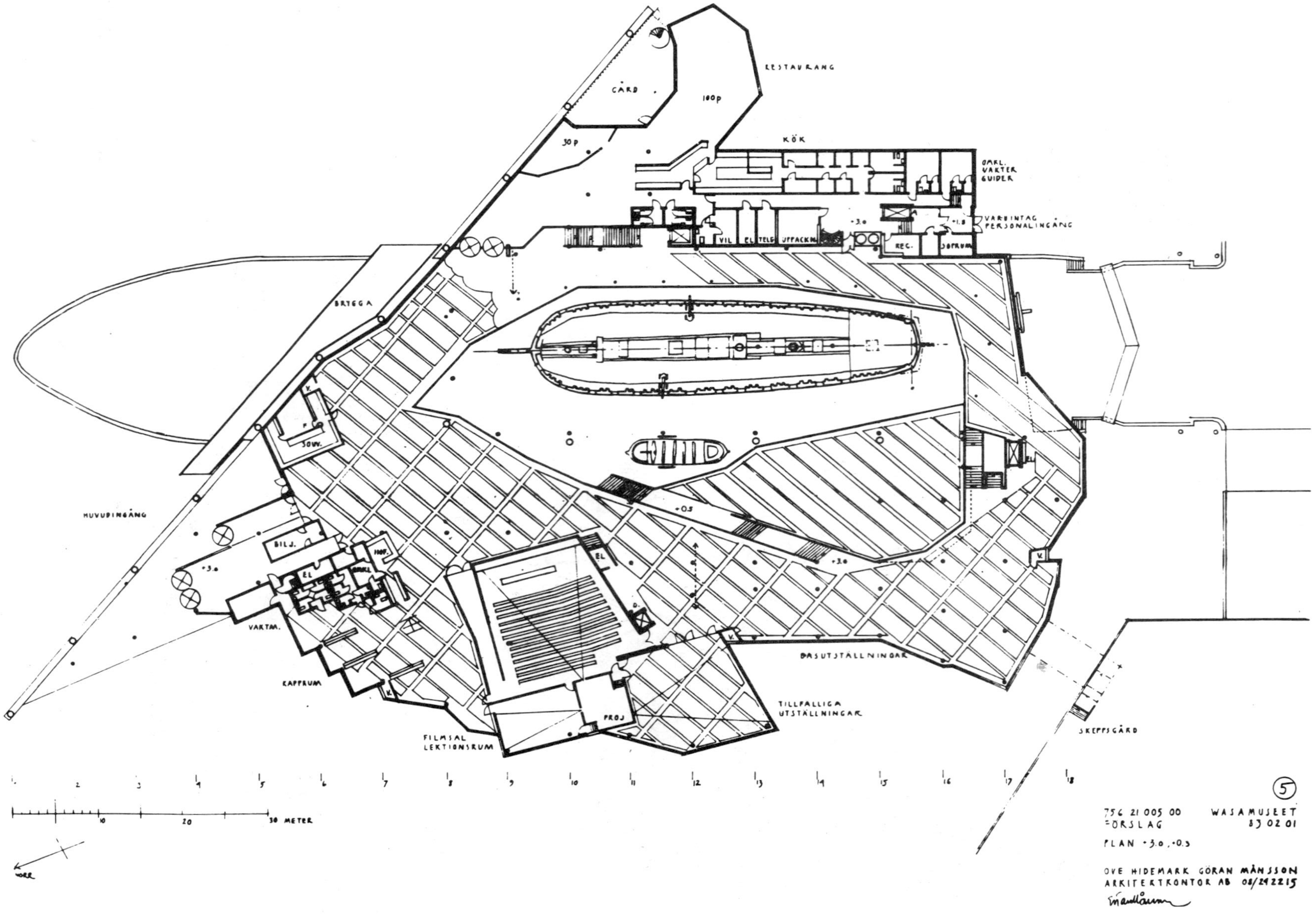

Fig. 6.5:   Plan of the building of the new Wasa Museum.

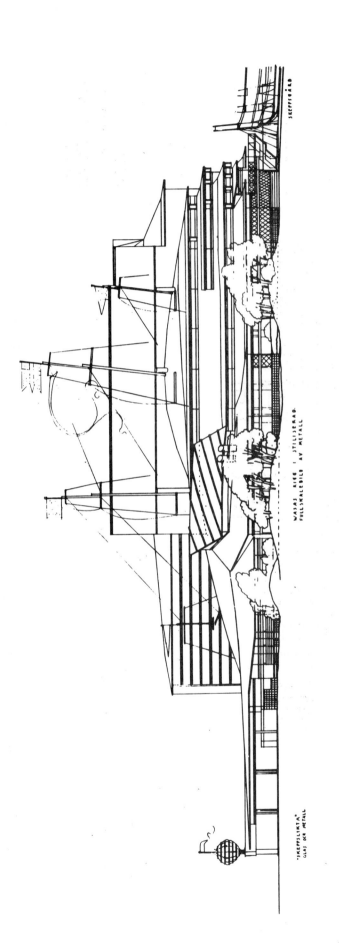

Fig. 6.6: View of the building of the new Wasa Museum seen towards northwest.

35

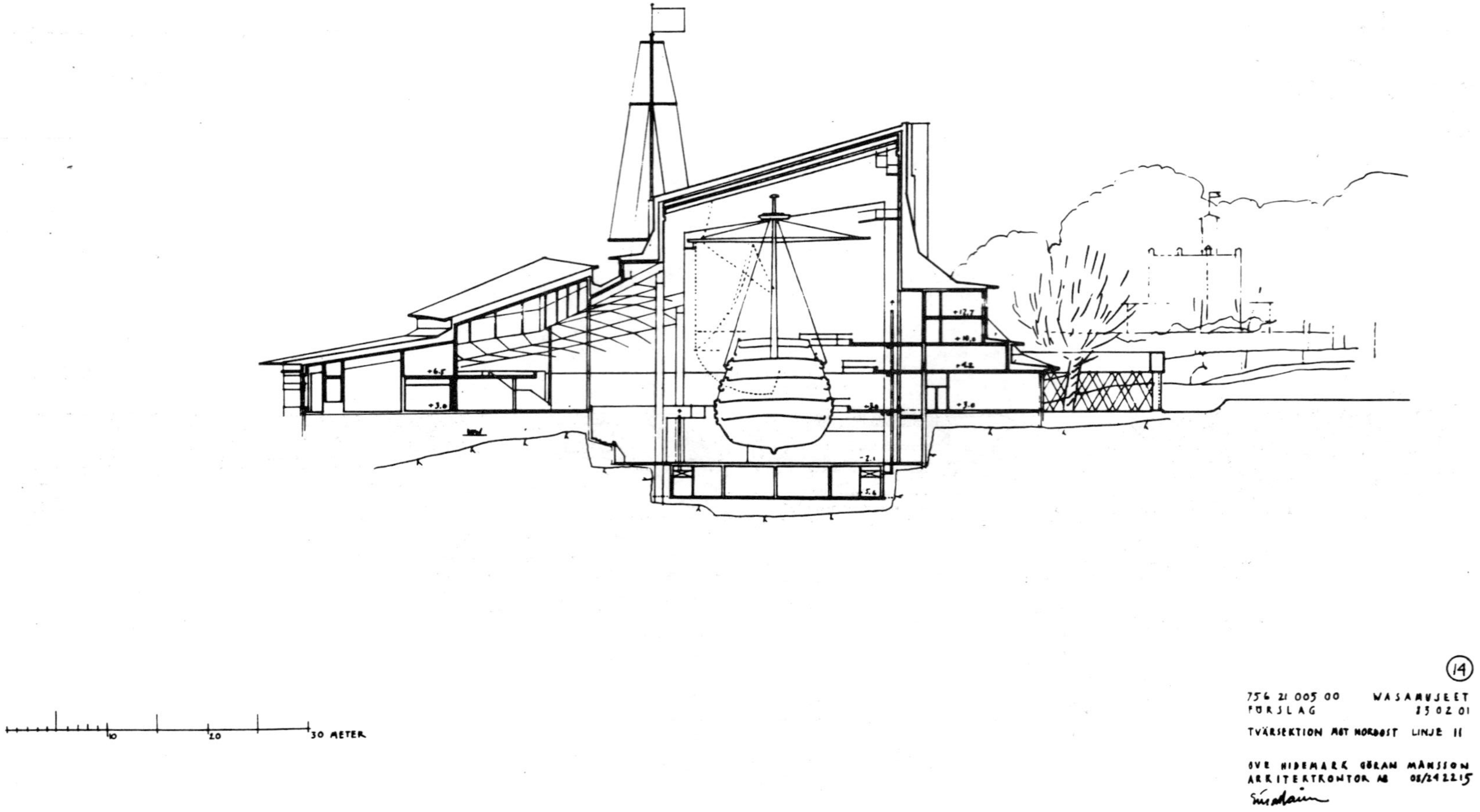

Fig. 6.7: Section of the building of the new Wasa Museum seen toward northeast.

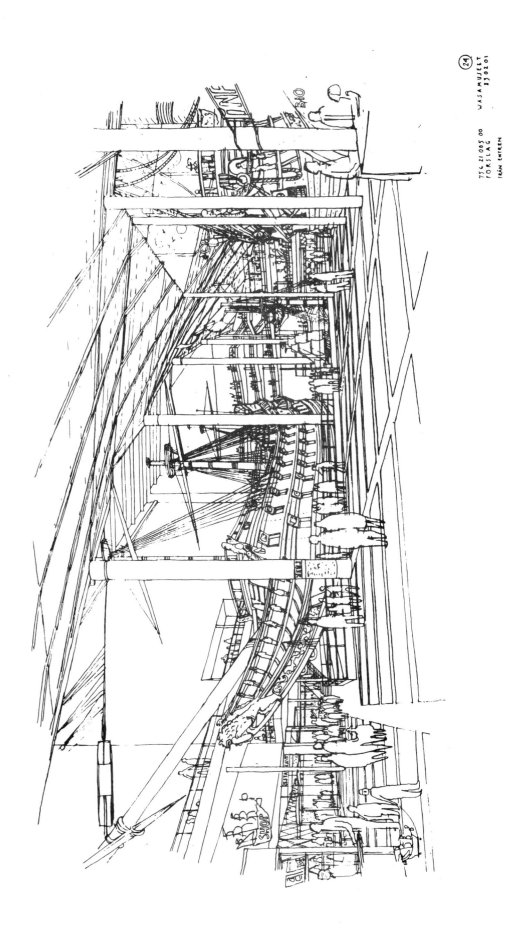

Fig 6.8: The interior of the new Wasa Museum seen from the entry.

7. THE CATTEWATER WRECK: A CONTRIBUTION TO 16TH CENTURY
MARITIME ARCHAEOLOGY

Mark Redknap

In this paper I propose to outline the results of three seasons of work
on this early 16th century wreck site, and to illustrate three of its
contributions to our present knowledge of this period of maritime
archaeology. It relies heavily on the work of many colleagues, and I must
in particular thank the following for their specialist reports: P. Boyd,
A.C. Carpenter, R. Clough, I. Friel, Cdr. E. McKee, E.C. Manley, J. Price,
K. Reilly and J. Weeks. Special thanks are due to Lieutenant Commander A.
Bax and Fort Bovisand Underwater Centre, and to B. Mortlock and M. Dean for
their archaeological direction on site.

I

The Cattewater wreck was discovered in 1973 by the dredging of deeper
channels for air-sea rescue craft in the River Plym (Fig. 7.1).   The
interest promoted by the timbers and the two fragments of guns that had been
brought to the surface led to an emergency designation order restricting
access to the site, and it became the first wreck to receive protection
under the Protection of Wrecks Act 1973.   Some work continued over the next
few years to try and relocate the wreck, which had rapidly silted over, but
not until 1976 could an intensive summer season of sea-bed survey be
undertaken (Mortlock and Redknap 1978: 195).   This continued for a further
two seasons, and during the 81 working days on site, a total of 692 man-
hours were spent underwater.

The wreck lies in the Cattewater, last reach of the River Plym as it
flows into Plymouth Sound, between the Fisher's Nose on the northern
(Plymouth) side, and Mount Batten Promontory to the south.   The Cattewater,
sheltered from all but prevailing south-west to westerly winds, remained the
principal anchorage for the medieval town of Plymouth that grew up around
Sutton Pool, and as one of the most important naval ports of the kingdom in
the 16th century she probably witnessed ship construction and fitting out.
Leland in his Itinerary c. 1535-1543 describes it as a 'goodly rode for
great shippes' (Smith 1964: 214), and the first edition of 'Great Britains
Coasting Pilot' describes its advantages and potential hazards:

'Catwater is a good Place, where ships ride that are bound to the
westward; going in, there lyeth a Buoy against Mount Batten: you sail close
by the west side of the Buoy: Being in, you must haul out a good Anchor well
over to Mount Batten side; for want of so doing many ships have drove ashoar
on the Catdown side'.   (Collins 1693: 6).   By 1548 a substantial network
of sea defences had been constructed on St. Nicholas' Isle and the Hoe,
adding to the security offered by the Cattewater anchorage.

The sea bed in this area is generally free from debris and supports little weed due to the high siltation rate. Within the breakwater the mean tidal range is 4.7m. (springs) to 2.2m. (neaps), and the current only exceeds 1.5 knots in ebbs after heavy rain. Diving was influenced by poor visibility (0-2m., rarely 4-5m.), and although the site remained divable throughout the tidal range as it was only 9m. deep, most slack tides were avoided.

The 1976 survey of the timber scattered on the sea-bed showed a concentration within the site grid that corresponded with a rise in the sea bed, and indicated that further structure may not have suffered the elsewhere extensive dredger damage. In 1977 the site was re-surveyed to confirm the absence of sea bed movement, and closed with the location and initial examination of hull structure in Area B (Fig. 7.2, southern square). In 1978 the team concentrated on completing this area and on establishing the extent of these remains.

The surviving structure lay keeled over to one side, on a slight incline rising to the north. The transverse sections (Fig. 7.3) and lines as restored are connected with a hull section running from somewhere amidships towards one end, though which end is not clear. The extent of the dredger damage was clearly defined by the splintered frame tops and twisted, broken plank ends (Fig. 7.11 and 7.12), and any stratigraphy in Area C and to its north had been extensively disturbed except where between surviving timbers. However layers 4 and 5 (Fig. 7.3) above the hull structure in Area B formed undisturbed deposits of sand and gravel with stones ranging in size from 2 - 30cm, directly associated with the wreck as ship ballast, and contained numerous finds. These included leather (shoes, straps, a purse), wood (bowl, knife handles, parrell truck), bronze (buckle, pin) lead (waste, shot), pottery, tile and textile fragments.

II

Before detailing the ship structure, it is pertinent to examine the dating evidence for the site:

1) The calibrated radiocarbon range is AD 1420-1600 (Har.-3310) using 1S.D. midpoint 1510. Dendrochronological cross-matching of the keelson with known tree-ring chronologies appeared to match in two places, giving dates for the outer rings of 1454 or 1457, but these were unacceptable when looked at visually, and dendrochronology could not help with dating.

2) The vessel is skeleton-built, with no sign of refit from clinker.

3) The keelson is paralleled by that on Rye Vessel 'A' dated to the 16th century, (Fig. 7.4; Lovegrove 1964).

4) The three guns recovered, all composite iron swivel guns, would have been considered antiquated on warships by the mid 16th century, though could have remained in use on merchant ships (Fig. 7.15).

5) The securely stratified pottery from the ship ballast is parallelled by cellar deposits in London dated AD 1495-1530 (Fig. 7.5. nos: 1,3,4).

6) The leather purse (Fig. 7.5 no. 6), pinned against a futtock by

rolling ballast when the vessel sunk, is of Tudor pattern. A similar example can be seen on a wooden carving of farmer with young pig by Niclaus Hagenower dated to the end of the 15th century (now in Badisches Landesmuseum, Karlsruhe; (Fig. 7.5 no. 7). Other leather finds suggest a date range c. AD 1490-1530.

The available evidence suggests that the Cattewater wreck sank in the early 16th century, possibly around AD 1530. Examination of surviving documentary sources has failed to identify the vessel. The present hull structure lies less than 5 m. deep at low tide, some 145 m. from the shore. Even when allowance for the rise in sea-level is made (assuming an average rise in the area of 2 mm. per year) which implies that the level in the Cattewater may have risen by approximately 1 m. since the 16th century, this cannot easily be reconciled with what we know about the best contender, the St. James, from Spain, that on 27th January 1494, during the night of violent winds and storms, lost all its rigging in Plymouth harbour and broke up on the shore (Simon Carswylle's Book, f.48, Plymouth City Records Office).

III

The Ship Structure (Figs. 7.2, 7.3 and 7.6a and b)

All the main structural elements were of oak. Ceiling planking employed mixed wood (pine, oak) and treenails were of oak or elm.

Keel (Fig. 7.11).

Uncovered for 1.35 m., beneath floor timbers (F 13-15). Seatings for the keel were visible on all the floor timbers (F 2-15). The top surface between garboards measured 21.5 cm. wide; the bottom was very heavily abraded. An addition of c.8 cm. for garboard rabbets gives a complete width of 29/30 cm. A similar timber was observed in 1973 but subsequently disappeared.

Garboard Strakes (Figs. 7.10 and 7.11).

Garboard strake (GS)1 had fractured longitudinally and sprung out of position, as had all the other strakes on that side of the keel. Treenails at regular intervals along the inboard face attached the garboard to floor timbers.

Outer Planking

All boarding planks were sawn uniformly 6-7 cm. thick, and fastened carvel fashion to all floor timbers and futtocks by treenails and iron nails. The distribution of the fastenings showed no apparent order, though iron nails were offset from treenails to avoid splitting. An exception is the close, regular setting along outer planks (P)15 and 17 (Fig.7.2) which may indicate either that the shipbuilders pitched close when they judged it necessary, or that some repairs to the hull had taken place. This combination of treenails and iron nails indicates a 'belt and braces' approach, understandable in a carvel vessel under construction shortly after

41

the adoption of the technique.   The iron nails may have been employed to attach the frames to strakes while the holes for treenails were being bored by auger.

Ceiling Planking

Less well preserved than the other members, it showed a greater range in thickness, size and shape.   Inner plank (p)4, without fastenings, may have acted as inspection hatch for the bilges (with square recess on p2 for finger grip).   Inner planking p8 and p15 probably represent a rising with bevelled edges that would have lain horizontally and vertically in the ship when afloat (Fig. 7.8).   Inner planks p6, p7 and p14 were rebated between futtocks to receive short pine planks or filling pieces to prevent material slipping down into the bilges (Fig. 7.13).   They ran horizontally along the whole length of the vessel (recovered) and indicate the upper limit of the ballast which lay above the ceiling planking in the hold (Fig. 7.14). Filling pieces have recently been found in a similar position on the mid 16th century Basque whaler mentioned by Michael Barkham in these proceedings, and on the Mary Rose.

Floor Timbers

All equally armed, with no sign of conversion from clinker.   They show progressively sharper lines towards the south (Fig. 7.3).   Sidings measured 18-22 cm.; moulded depth averaged 20 cm. and 27 cm.   Rectangular limber holes were offset to allow for the single treenail fastenings to the keel.

Futtocks

The heels of the first floor futtocks were placed between the floor timbers some 1.35 m. short of the centre line amidships (Fig. 7.2), futtock (f)3 at the southern end lying much closer (0.4 m. from centre line).   The heels were variously shaped: butt ends with waney edge (f2), bevelled one side (f16).   Several bore one or more notches of varying roundness or angularity (Fig. 7.4, below left).

Keelson   (Fig. 7.4)

Raised in 1973, its precise position within the hull is unkown, but it must have originated from around floor timbers F20-F25 (Fig. 7.2 and 7.6 a and b).   Elaborately shaped from a single piece of oak, some of its corners are waney.   The lesser keelson is sided 30 cm. moulded 27 cm. for 70 cm. at the teredoed end, and a shorter length at the other.   In-between the siding increases to 54 cm. and moulded depth increases in two steps to 33 cm., and then 40 cm.   The mast step forms a mortice in the top of the deepest section, 15 cm. deep and 33 cm. wide.   It is hard to say where the step ends and the fracture split starts (former probably not less than 76 cm. long).   A tapered eliptical hole through the first step, narrowing downwards, was probably for a pump pipe (cf. the arrangement in Kalmar ship V, c. 1500; Åkerlund 1951, pl. 16).   The flat underside is checked to fit directly over the floor timbers (14 floor timbers in the 4.6 m. recovered). These vary in width and pitch, averaging 20-28 cm. in width.   The ghost of a mortice 12.5 x 8.7 cm. between mast step and the step down to the pump hole may have held a vertical pillar or prop. Three iron bolts were spaced along the keelson, offset to the same side, through the fays on the underside. One floor timber recovered in 1973 had an iron bolt running through it, and they must have acted as tie-rods connecting keel and keelson, offset to avoid the limber holes.

Caulking material of tar and hair was used between floor timbers and outer planking. No fillets were found to seal the joins between outer planking either inboard or out.

Fracturing at the junction of the floor timbers and futtocks emphasised the weakness of this point. An attempt was made to strengthen this area by cutting 'lap-dovetails' to fasten floor timbers to futtocks (Fig. 7.4 and 7.14). These dovetails were generally 2 cm. deep, with assymetrical sets of 1 in 2 and 1 in 4, and they occur one per floor timber end, on either side. In most of the observed cases (6), the floor timber bears the recess for dovetail on the futtock, the exception being that between F26 and F27. The improved rigidity of this joint would increase the resistance to racking and hull distortion and the loosening of fastenings due to varying hydrodynamic pressure or cargo weight. The term 'lap-dovetail' has been adopted from vernacular architecture in the absence of more correct nautical terminology. One maritime archaeological parallel has now been found (the mid 16th century Basque whaler in M. Barkham's paper), an illustration of what may be a similar technique occurs in 'Détails de Construction et d'Armament des Galères' after Barras de la Penne c. 1697 (in Pâris 1976, no.2298 fig. 10; see Fig. 7.4) - although it is possible that the notches here represent spacers rather than integral keying pieces, or even illustrative error. The joint would have been wasteful of timber, and abandoned for the more economical overlapping futtock once proved reliable.

Revolutionary changes in hull form were taking place at the end of the 15th century and first quarter of the 16th century. Italian shipwrights were being employed for their internationally recognised skills, though no parallels for similar joinery have yet been recognised amongst the available Italian evidence for this period. There are clear similarities with the Basque whaler found in Newfoundland. This serves as a reminder of Plymouth's close ties at this period with Spain and SW France, and that the St. James mentioned above came 'ex partibus hispanis'.

The lap-dovetail represents one of those unrecorded small modifications in ship design that cumulatively permitted greater improvement in design, possibly as experiment or copy, by shipwrights on a merchantman of moderate size (200-300 tons) to improve strength and carrying capacity.

The extant remains are too slight to permit a convincing reconstruction of her lines, and attempts to estimate her size by comparing the scantlings of the few other known vessels are inconclusive: few rules appear to have been followed during this innovative period. However using the earliest known English method for calculating tonnage, 'Baker's Old Rule' and maximum and minimum estimates for beam and depth based on extreme profile extensions, combined with a simple doubling of the minimum keel length to mid-point of 10m., we obtain approximate figures of minimum 186 tons, maximum 282 tons burden. Small changes in the values produce considerable variation in the results - an addition of 2 metres to the keel length gives a maximum value of 317 tons - and so this calculation only gives us a rough guide.

Armament

Many of the changes in hull design at this period were due to changes in armament. The Cattewater has produced only comparatively small, quick-firing breech loaders, though the presence of larger bore stone shot (6.9 cm.) does suggest that heavier pieces may have been used. The distinction between warship and merchantman was largely a function of the artillery on board, and so for the moment we may assume that the Cattewater wreck was not naval.

Raised in 1973, the Cattewater guns have carefully trenched beds of oak (Quercus sp.; Fig. 7.15) to receive the barrels. The top surfaces had been lowered, leaving a higher platform at the rear. In the front, sections cut for the retaining rings helped retain the recoil on firing. The vertical step at the rear was reinforced by iron strapping nailed along the width of the bed and along both sides of the chamber to strengthen the abutment for the iron breech chamber and wedge-key. The step is provided with a dovetailed metal insert to take the friction of the wedge-key. The upper edges of the stock are bevelled, and off-centre low down a horizontal hole passes through the bed. A slightly longer stock at the now damaged breech end would place this hole nearer the point of balance, and it is likely that it housed a cross-bolt for swivel mounting rather than wheel carriage. On guns 1 and 2, this hole lies behind the first strip in front of the breech, on gun 3 in front of the strap at least 3.5 cm. in advance of the other position. The barrels, surrounded by retaining rings, were first believed to be a single wrapped, fire welded core with collars and rings, but X-radiography has now provided evidence of a two part inner tube held together by iron sleeves and rings. This inner barrel was constructed by at least two curved iron strips, butted together and held by nine outer rings and nine sleeves. The joins of the two inner tube plates were positioned horizontally. It could not be established whether these were barrel length or of two or more sections, each consisting of two semi-circular strips (the larger examples from the Mary Rose have inner longitudinal strips made up from one piece).

The bore of 5.5 cm. matches the smaller stone shot from the site (5.25 cm.) Two rings reinforce the muzzle end, one showing traces of an elementary foresight as illustrated in the Warwick Roll, and visible on the Danish Anholt guns and the recently found Nottingham gun. The breech end of the tube has an extra collar reinforcement to strengthen the mouth and accommodate the chamber piece. The whole tube is secured to its bed by three iron retaining straps contoured around the assembly and securely nailed. A fourth forged plate was bolted to the top of the bed at the breech end.

The breech chambers are tapered with an open end dressed externally to fit the barrel mouth. One chamber recovered from concretion during the excavation, complete with powder charge sealed by short breech plug, had parallel sides, with a reduction at the mouth to fit the barrel. Lifting handles were, as far as can be ascertained, welded at the rear only, and touch holes, plugged with twists of hemp, lay on either side of the handle base. Two iron chain links remained attached to the wedge on the complete gun.

Parallels to the barrel construction are provided by the Nottingham Castle example (A. MacCormick, pers. comm.) and fragments of two early 15th century guns from Castle Rising, Norfolk, found in the 19th century. The Anholt finds from the Kattegat, in particular the 1947 finds from the late 15th or early 16th century (now in the Danish Royal Arsenal Museum, Copenhagen: ref. No. A. 4, bore of barrel 6.35 cm.), are similar. Other examples can be found at the Swedish Army Museum; Nederlandsch Historisch Scheepvaart Museum (with bed and swivel mount); the 'Rotunda', Woolwich; Truro Museum, Cornwall and St. Michael's Mount (Lord St. Levan) Cornwall. Contemporary illustrations show swivels on the mizzen top: 'W A''s Kraek, second half 15th century, now in the Ashmolean, Oxford, and the Schlüsselfelder Nef. of c. 1503 (Oman 1963 XV–XVII). Such light defensive pieces, being quite portable, would more often appear at bulkheads of the forecastle, half deck or steerage.

Despite well documented history of the use of guns at sea in the 16th century, it is not yet possible to give anything like a definitive account of their development. Construction, shape and size is rarely documented, and these three Cattewater examples, all the same size and displaying identical manufacturing techniques that indicate contemporary construction possibly at the same foundry, form a valuable group for comparative research.

V

The ballast (Fig. 7.8)

Study of the ballast and silts around the ship structure proved useful and gave some unexpected information about the site.

Geological provenances were assigned to the stone, taking the nearest outcrops that occur along the coastline as most likely source. Commonest was local limestone, together with granite and slate, but chalk and flint (Upper Cretaceous) from Dorset or Kent/Cinque Ports, and Lower Carboniferous limestone from the Bristol/South Wales area was well represented. This variety may illustrate the practice of collecting stone from nearest sources and incompletely careening and replacing fouled ballast with fresh. A fragment of worked granite and of sandstone ashlar indicate that building material may have been used. Limestone was chief building material in the area, and granite (moorstone and dunstone) was often employed for quoins, frames and pillars.

Examination of the silt samples from four layers was undertaken (by P. Boyd) to determine whether the ballast gravel could be distinguished from the other sediments, and the nature of the sediments into which the vessel had settled. It was established that whereas 80 species of marine organisms were represented in three of the samples, the ballast gravel contained only 9 species of freshwater molluscs, and a complete absence of marine organisms. This indicates a probable source within a fairly lime rich river, at or upstream from the limit of any pronounced saline influence. The present distribution of several of the species represented seems to exclude the Plymouth region: Theodoxus fluviatilis, the commonest single

45

species, is not today recorded west of a line approximately on the Lyme Regis longitude (Dorset), a river in Hampshire or Sussex being most likely source. However at Plymouth, a centre for lime-burning, sand to be added to the lime would be taken from local rivers by the boatload, probably by landing on a sandbank at low tide, loading, and moving off at high. Building sand was certainly transported in this way, and the ballast sand could have come from a similar source.

Bone from the wreck (examined by K. Reilly) was divided into three categories: that from the ballast, that in disturbed sites but probably originating from the ballast, and that of uncertain origin. A total of 120 bones were identified as cow (Bos), 59% from the ballast. The other species - sheep/goat (Ovis capra/Capra hircus), pig (Sus scrofa) and dog (Canis familiaris) - from the ballast were few in number, and represent small joints (the dog may, of course, have belonged to the crew). No more than 3 cow individuals were represented, all below 5 years old. Butchery was evident on most of the bones - common was splitting of vertebrae and cutting of ribs into 15-20 cm lengths. The size of the cuts was limited, suitable for salting and barrelling. There does seem in some cases to be an unnecessary amount of bone that would have taken up valuable storage space. Until about 1530, when a naval victualling department was established, even naval ships often had to rely on local men at the ports where supplies were collected to provision ships. In 1512 the cost of provisioning stood at one shilling and three pence per week per man, and this had risen by 1545 to one shilling and six pence. Short measure was common, as illustrated by the letter from Admiral Sir Edward Howard, dated 1512 or 1513: 'they that receved ther proportion for ii months flesche cannot bryng about for v weekes for the barelles be full of salt, and when the peeces kepith the noumbre wher they shulde be peny peces they be scante halfpeny peces, and where ii peces shulde make a messe, iij will do but serve' (Oppenheim, 1896: 81). The Cattewater cuts correspond with such meal-sized 'peny peces', poor boney ones at that.

Examination of naval ships' registers between 1485 and 1588 shows a basic pattern of beef as the meat most generally supplied either in quarters or pipes (casks), with other references to 'flesh', or occasionally pork and mutton (Andrews 1959, 89; 249). Salt was often supplied by the bushel for the preservation of unprepared meat, though 'salte bieff redie dressed' was also supplied. Salt fish were a common provision, often red or white herring, though also cod. The ballast contained cod bone (Gadus morhua), and the presence of cleithra without heads suggests that they had been beheaded and salted (when cleithra are often left in place as a useful handhold).

Summary

This report outlines the results of three seasons of survey and excavation on this Devon wreck and the available evidence for its early 16th. century date, before describing three aspects of the examination - the structure itself from a vessel of approximately 2-300 tons, with its unusual 'lap-dovetail' joint; the armament, all light swivel guns of early composite ring and stave construction; the ballast and its contents, examined for geological, micro-faunal and osteological information.

To conclude, the Cattewater wreck belongs to a period of developing ship design bordering the revolution in naval construction taking place around 1480–1525 and the appearance of the first known English evidence for mathematically based formulae for ship lines c. 1580. As such she offers a primary source of material with further potential: the present report is based on the examination of less than 50% of the surviving structure. The remainder lies in the Cattewater beneath, we hope, protective silts until a large scale enterprise with full back-up facilities can complete excavation and save the hull from further marine degradation.

REFERENCES

Åkerlund, H., 1951. Fartygfynden i den forna hamnen i Kalmar, Uppsala.

Andrews, K.R., 1959. English Privateering Voyages to the West Indies 1588–1595, The Hackluyt Society, Cambridge.

Carpenter, A., Ellis, K.H. & McKee, J.E.G., 1974. Interim report on the wreck discovered in the Cattewater. Maritime Monographs and Reports 13, London.

Collins, Greenvile, 1693. Great Britain's Coasting Pilot, London.

Leland, J. (ed. L. Toulman-Smith, 1964). 'The Itinerary of John Leland in or about the years 1535-1543' Vol. 1, London.

Lovegrove, H., 1964. 'The Remains of Two Old Vessels found at Rye, Sussex', Mariners Mirror L, 115–122.

Mortlock, B. & Redknap, M., 1978. The Cattewater Wreck, Plymouth, Devon, I.J.N.A. 7, 195–204.

Oman, C., 1963. 'Medieval Silver Nefs', H.M.S.O. London.

Oppenheim, M., 1896. A History of the Administration of the Royal Navy Vol. 1.

Pâris, F., 1976. Souvenirs de Marine. Collection de Plans ou Dessins de Navires et de Bateaux anciens ou modernes, existants ou disparus avec les elements numeriques necessaires a leur construction, Grenoble. (facsimile reprint).

Redknap, M., forthcoming. The Cattewater wreck: the investigation of an armed vessel of the sixteenth century. National Maritime Museum, Greenwich, Archaeological Series No. 8. BAR British Series 131, 1984.

Smith: see Leland.

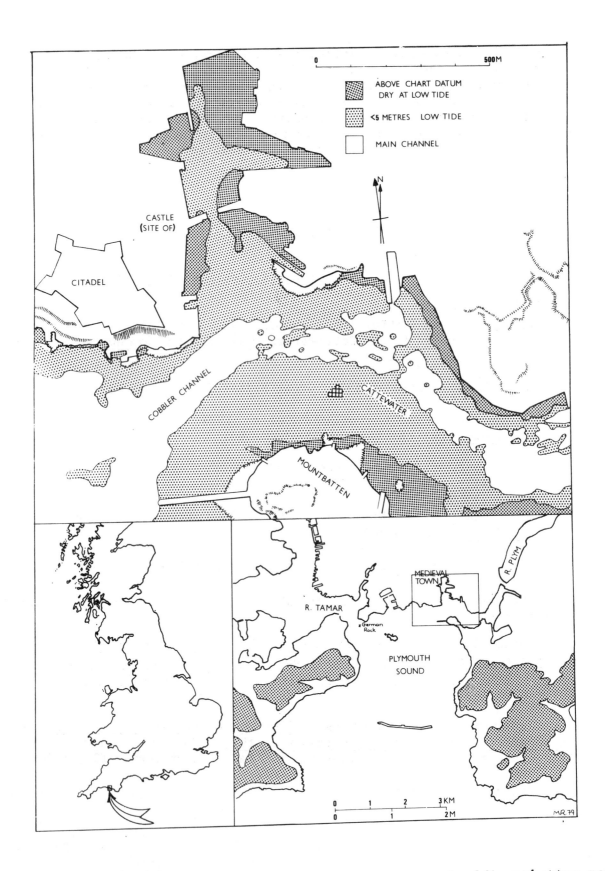

Fig. 7.1: Site topography. The 8 grid squares north of Mountbatten mark
the wreck.

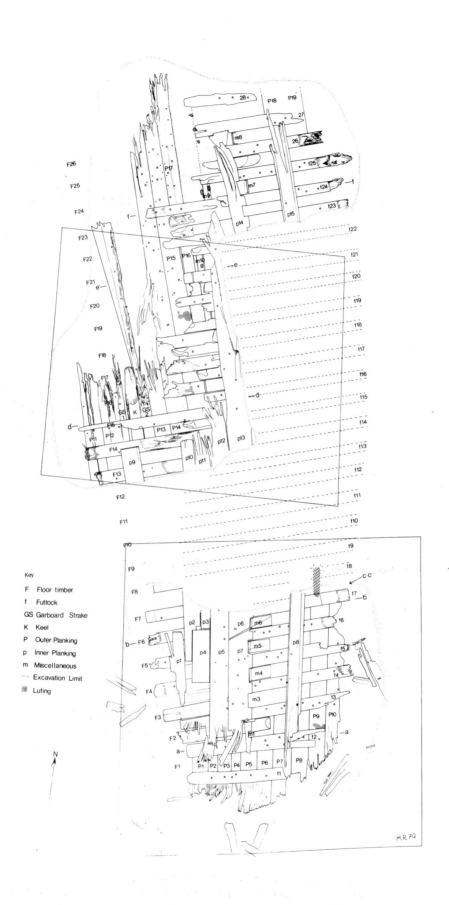

Fig. 7.2: Site plan. The southern frame has 5m. long sides.

Key
F   Floor timber
f   Futtock
GS Garboard Strake
K   Keel
P   Outer Planking
p   Inner Planking
m   Miscellaneous
--- Excavation Limit
▨   Luting

49

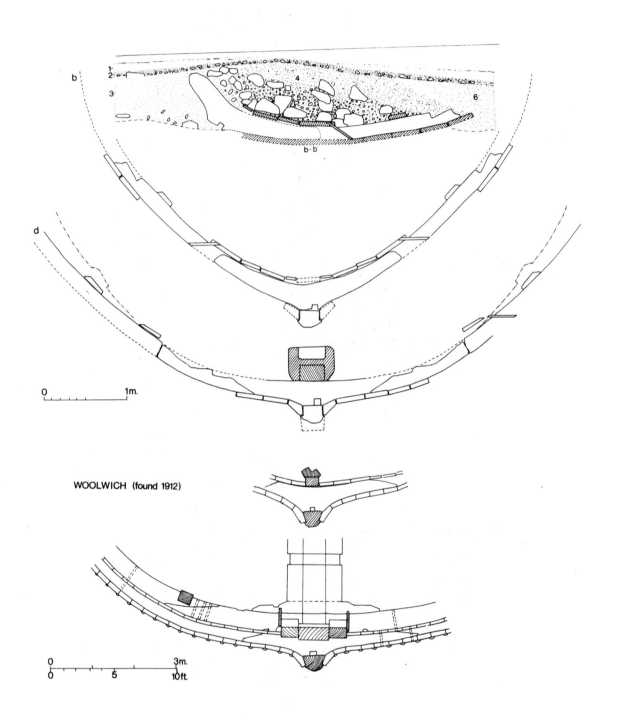

WOOLWICH (found 1912)

Fig. 7.3:   Top: site stratigraphy along profile b-b' (see Fig. 7.2).
Maximum and minimum lines are indicated on the restored profiles at b-b' (b)
and f-f' (d).   Below: sections through the ship exposed at Roff's Wharf,
Woolwich.

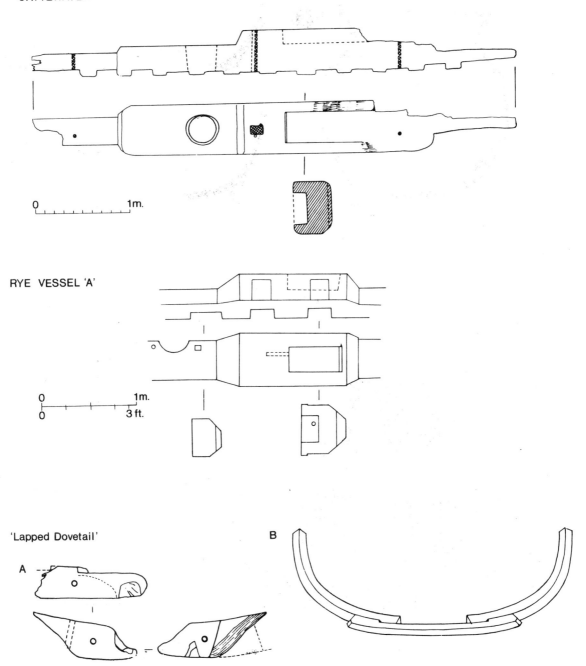

CATTEWATER

0   1m.

RYE VESSEL 'A'

0   1m.
0   3 ft.

'Lapped Dovetail'

B

A

0   50 cm.

Fig. 7.4: Top: view of the Cattewater and Rye keelsons. Bottom: A. Frame to futtock fastening - 'lap-dovetail' f-22; B. illustration from de la Penne c. 1697.

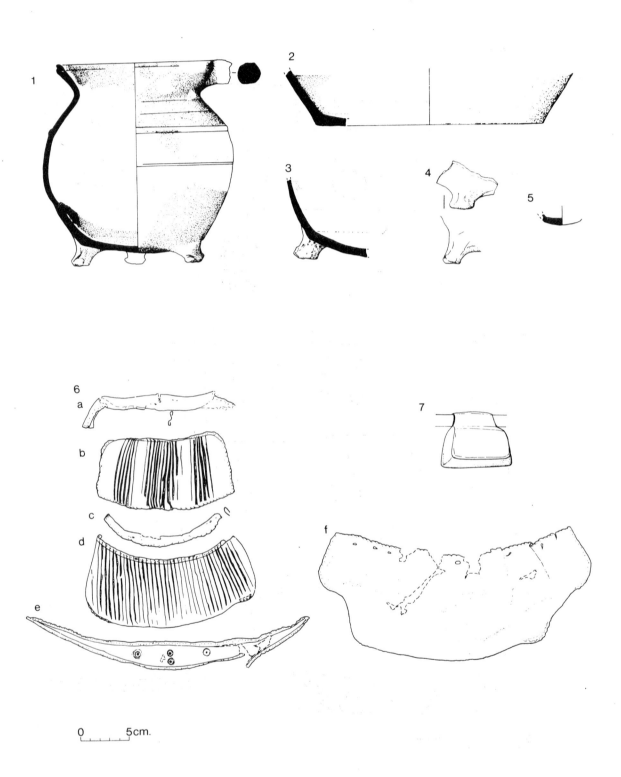

Fig. 7.5: Nos. 1, 3, 4 tripod cooking pots in sandy grey fabric and weak splashed greenish-brown glaze. No. 2, base, hard fired redware (possibly Dutch). No. 5, Siegburg mug base. No. 6, leather purse, and No. 7, line drawing of similar from lime wood carving by Niclaus Hagenauer.

Fig. 7. 6a

Fig. 7.6b

Fig. 7.6a and b: Three views of 1:20 scale model of the wreck, showing keelson replaced in possible position.   The dark area represents lost or unexposed timber.

Fig. 7.7: The first floor timbers to be found shortly after exposure in 1977. A = F4, B = p1, C = F3. Scale in 10cm. divisions.

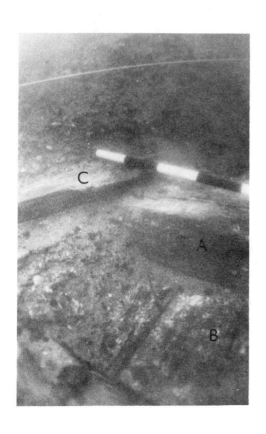

Fig. 7.8: View of gravel ballast and junction of f3 (A), P9 (B) and p8 (C).

55

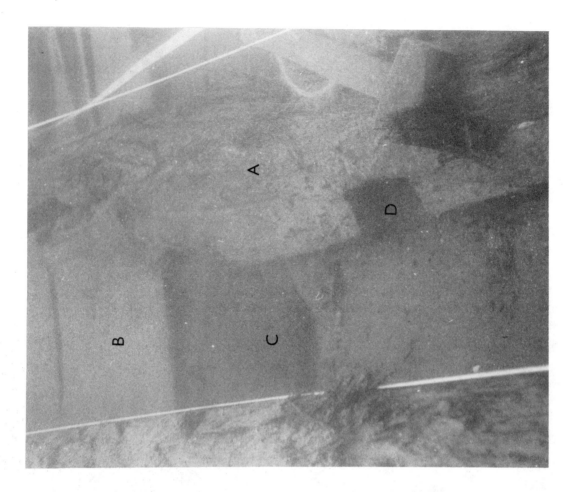

Fig. 7.10: Dredger damaged top of floor timber F15 (A) with limber hole (D), outer planking P2 (B) and garboard GS1 (C).

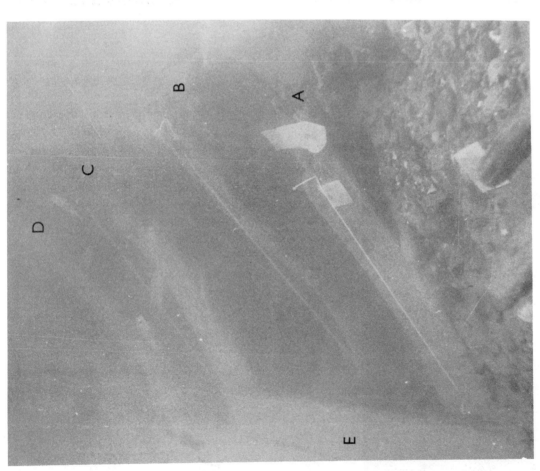

Fig. 7.9: View looking south of floor timbers F7 (A), F6 (B), F5 (C), F4 (D) and inner planking p2 (E). Unexcavated ballast at bottom of picture.

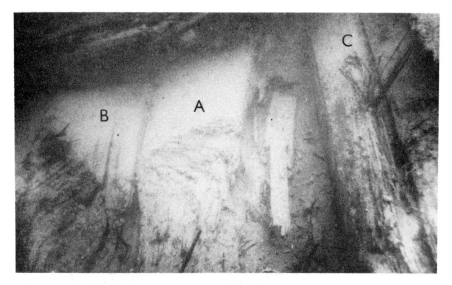

Fig. 7.11:   View looking south, of keel (A) and garboards GS1 (C) and GS2 (B) at F16.

Fig. 7.12:   F24 with horizontal treenail fastening.

Fig. 7.13:   Filling piece m4.

57

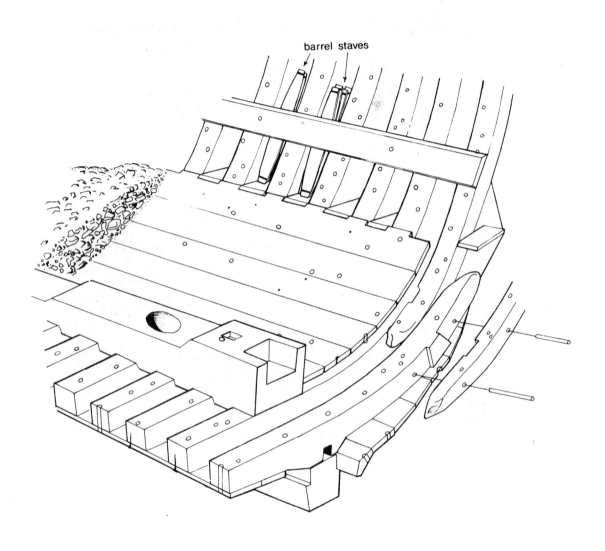

barrel staves

Fig. 7.14:   Detail of hull structure.

CATTEWATER WRECK.

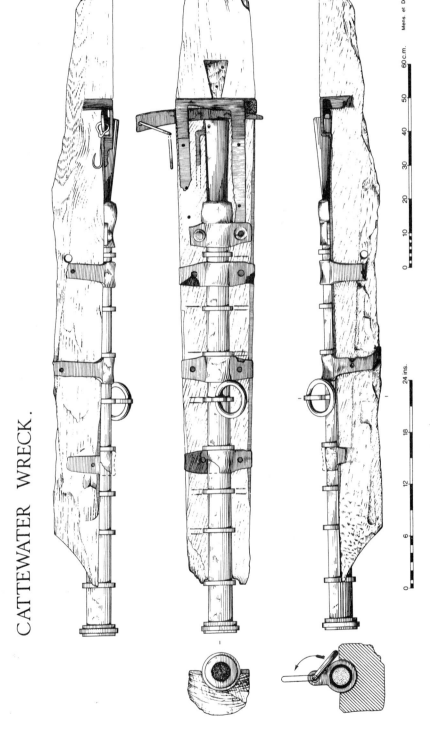

Fig. 7.15: Gun 1. Top and side views of the most complete assembly drawn by J.C. Thorn, Ancient Monuments Laboratory, Crown Copyright.

8. MERCHANTMEN FROM THE 17th TO 19th CENTURIES WRECKED IN THE BALTIC

Carl Olof Cederlund

The archaeological investigations of two wrecks of merchant ships at Jutholmen 1970 - 1974 and Älvsnabben 1974 - 1980 by the Swedish National Maritime Museum have yielded considerable information on the original ships.

The Jutholmen wreck was evidently built in the middle of the 17th century following the Dutch manner of building. The main characteristics of the structure of the ship correspond to what we, according to other sources, call a flute. It carried an export cargo of tar and wrought iron, and firewood. There is evidence to suggest that the crew had a Swedish background.

The latter ship seems to have been built around 1700 or a little later and sank around 1730. It is of the group of ships which is denoted as boejers, galiots or koffs. It carried a cargo of grain, the most important Swedish import at the time, which in this case originated in North West Germany. According to a number of indications it was a ship from Swedish Pommerania bound for Stockholm.

The following pictures illustrate the ships in their present situation and the recording performed on them (Fig. 8.1 - 8.6).

One can state that these two investigations are the two first more extensive archaeological investigations of old merchant ships built according to carvel technique in the Baltic. While a number of operations and investigations have been performed on old warships of the same building technique.

In contrast to the wrecks of warships, wrecks of merchantmen in Swedish waters are numerous. 86 wrecks of carvel-built ships have hitherto been registered in the Swedish Marine Archaeological Register from the eastern central coast of Sweden (Fig. 8.7). Most of them are from the 17th to 19th centuries, a few from the 16th.

Of these 86, 46 cannot yet be classified as to their original function. Of the others, 9 were sailing warships, 28 sailing merchant ships, 2 barges and one a composite-built steamship.

The merchant ships represent a fairly large body of archaeological material. They are evidence of the extensiveness of sea trade in the Baltic during the 17th to 19th centuries.

Trading on a bigger scale in the Baltic was to a great extent performed with carvel-built ships. They carried the essential import and export goods to and from Sweden. Swedens major export goods in the 17th and 18th centuries were iron, copper, wood and tar. These goods were because of certain politically-influenced customs-regulations to a high degree transported out of Sweden on carvel-built ships, as was the grain which was Sweden's main import for a long period.

Up to now historians have only been able to do research on this trade through written sources. The wrecks of the merchant ships described here, and which were used in this trade, represent a new source which is considerably more direct and which also throws new light onto the subject.

The wrecks of these not yet investigated merchant ships can better be described here with the help of a few illustrations (Fig. 8.8. - 8.13).

We are dealing with a highly extensive source of archaeological material, the objects of which are as a rule located such that it is very difficult to reach them for study, e.g. under water.

The wrecks often appear as big and anonymous heaps of timber and planks on the bottom, when found.

Is it at all possible to collect meaningful historical information on these objects without substantial investment of resources and money?

I think it is. We have now passed a period of initial development in our discipline - the 60s and 70s, during which time techniques for ship archaeological recording were developed. We have also started a systematic registration of wreck finds.

Now comes the second stage which involves subjecting the finds to more general study - in order to collect and present historical information.

We then need a model or a system for collecting information which gives us the basic data for a general classification of these big shipwrecks.

Much of this information could be collected in a simple, relatively inexpensive way, by amateur skindivers, coast guard divers as training etc. The main thing is that the approach to the objects is aimed at systematic collecting of ship archaeological data. The data should be brought in in such a way that it conveniently can be processed for historical examination.

Up to now we have used forms for the registration of wreck finds, making notice of the location of the site, the depth of the site, the general character of the wreck, the finds in it etc., (Fig. 8.14). This should be complemented with a new form, the one for ship archaeological registration.

This one should be designed for collecting information such as evidence of:

> the age of the ship
>
> its type
>
> its origin
>
> the traces of its building technique
>
> the shape of the hull

the type of rigging

the cargo

To obtain such information means the collecting of certain, thoroughly chosen data in the wreck, and to make different kinds of analyses of the material collected.

Most of the this information can be brought "to the surface" quite easily.

One main objective is to change our way of viewing and handling these remains - to see them as objects for the study as well as historical monuments of shipbuilding, seafaring etc., - and not only as attractive diving sites.

Technically, we have today the capability of reaching into these remains and studying them. But that which is also needed is a broad scientific grasp of the material. Of primary importance is knowing how to select the right information from the wrecks - or rather how to direct the recording work in these huge remains.

REFERENCES

Cederlund, C.O., 1981. Vraket vid Älvsnabben. Fartygets byggnad. Statens sjöhistoriska museums rapportserie nr 14.

Cederlund, C.O., 1982. Vraket vid Jutholmen. Fartygets byggnad. Statens sjöhistoriska museums rapportserie nr 16.

Cederlund, C.O., 1983. The Old Wrecks of the Baltic Sea. Archaeological recording of the wrecks of carvel-built ships. BAR International Series 186.

Kaijser, I., 1981. Vraket vid Älvsnabben. Dokumentation, last och utrustning. Statens sjöhistoriska museums rapportserie nr 13.

Kaijser, I., 1983. Vraket vid Jutholmen. Last och utrustning. Statens sjöhistoriska museums rapportserie nr 17.

Fig. 8.1: Model of the wreck at Jutholmen during the excavation season in 1973. The wreck and the surrounding bottom have been recorded by a special instrument for underwater measuring, the hydrolite.

Fig. 8.2:   The upper part of the bow of the wreck
at Jutholmen, port side. To the left part of the
stem can be seen, to the right frames sticking up
above the boardingplanks.   In the background the
foremast is visible.

Fig. 8.3:   The ship's side of the wreck at
Jutholmen had been torn down about one meter,
measured from the main deck, in connection with
salvage operations after the foundering. The photo
shows the upper part of the preserved ship's side
at the bow, port side.

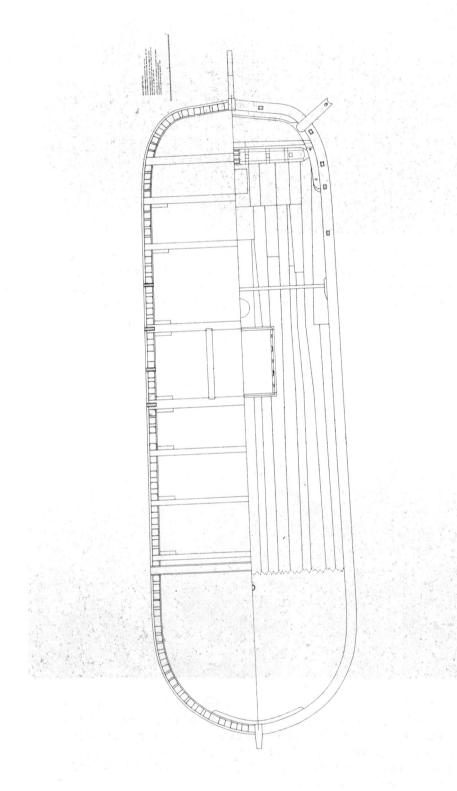

Fig. 8.4: Deck plan of the wreck at Älvsnabben according to the recording performed at the investigations at the site in 1974 - 1980. The cabin in the stern as well as the deck house aft of the main hatch were destroyed on an earlier stage and has thus not been recorded.

Fig. 8.6: The stern of the wreck at Älvsnabben, starboard side.

Fig. 8.5: The lower part of the stem and the bow, starboard side, of the wreck at Älvsnabben.

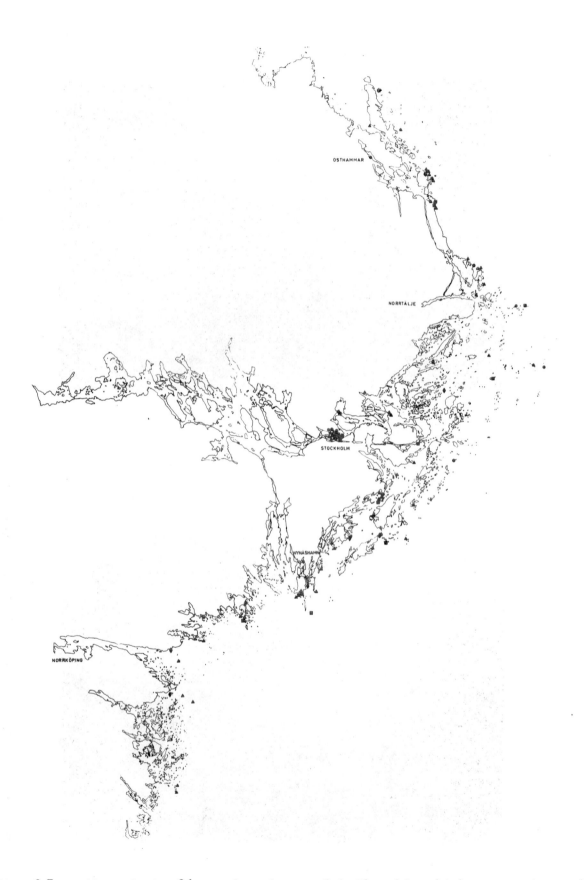

Fig. 8.7:   Map of the 86 wrecks of carvel-built ships hitherto registered
in the Swedish Marine Archaeological Register along the eastern, central
coast of Sweden.

68

Fig. 8.8: The cargo of planks in the hold of a big ship at the bottom of the harbour at Dalarö, possibly from the 17th century.

Fig. 8.9: The framing and inner planking of an unidentified wreck at Slätharan, Rödlöga, possibly from the 18th or 19th century.

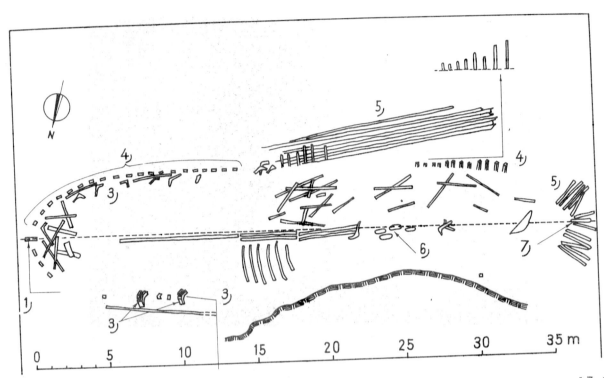

Fig. 8.10:   The site of a big, unidentified ship, possibly from the 17th century, at Högskär, East of Oxelösund.

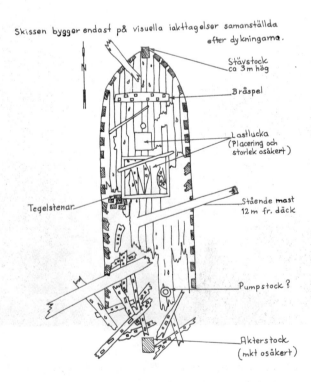

Skissen bygger endast på visuella iakttagelser samanställda efter dykningarna.

Stävstock
ca 3m hög

Bråspel

Lastlucka
(Placering och
storlek osäkert)

Tegelstenar

Stående mast
12m fr. däck

Pumpstock ?

Akterstock
(mkt osäkert)

Fig. 8.11:   The wreck of an unidentified ship from the 17th or 18th century at Garpudden, Hartsö.

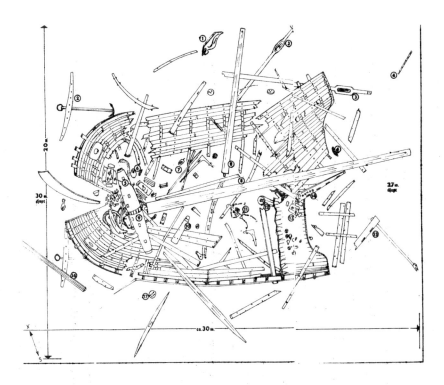

Fig. 8.12:   The wreck of an unidentified
graincarrier sunk at Huvudskär in the 1730s.

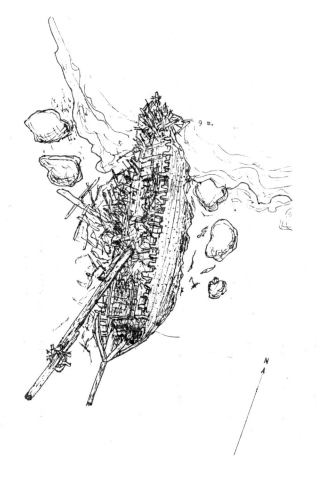

Fig. 8.13   The wreck of the brig
Margareta of Vätö sunk at Brännskär in
1898.

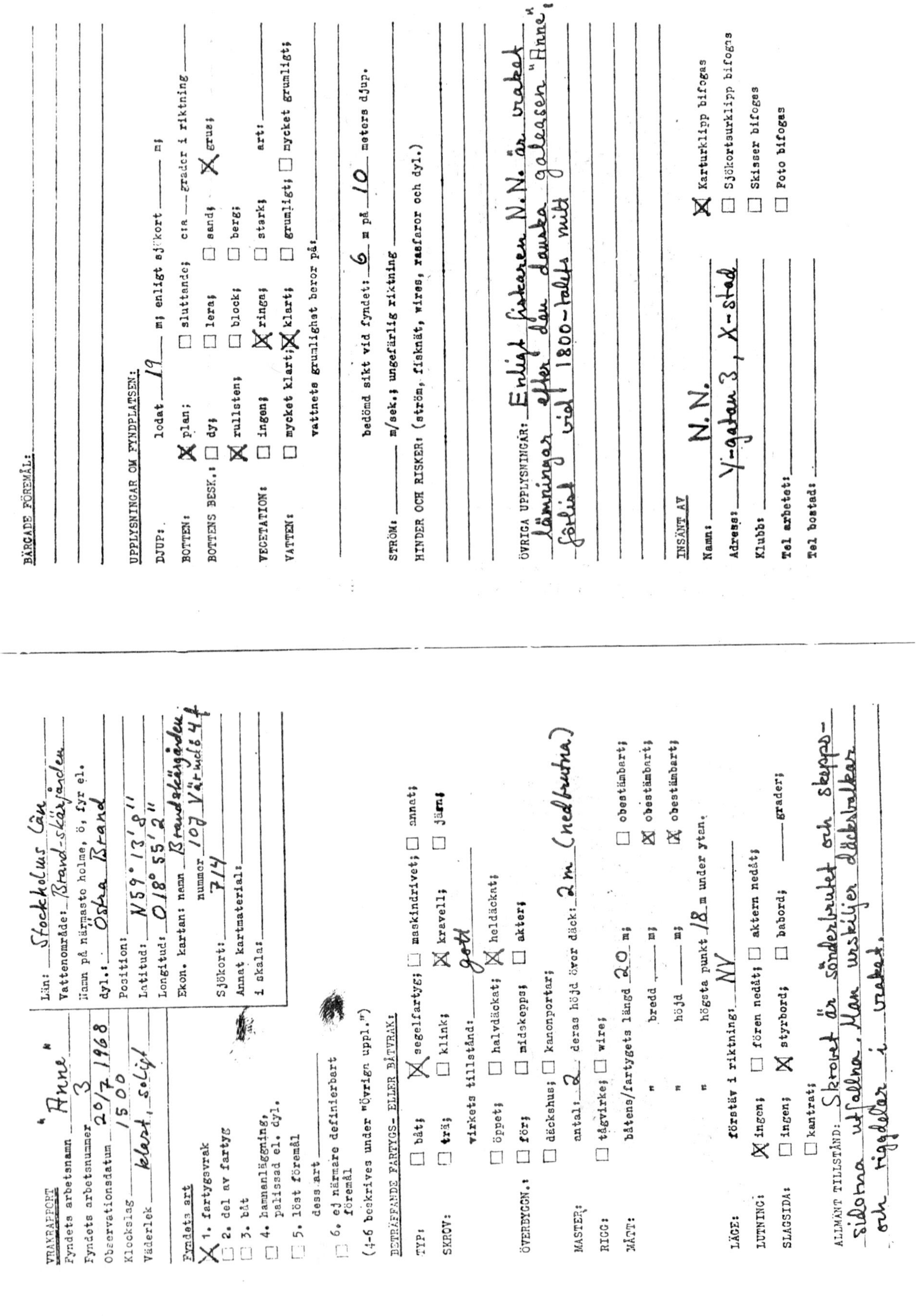

VRAKRAPPORT

Fyndets arbetsnamn _"Anne"_
Fyndets arbetsnummer _3_
Observationsdatum _20/7 1968_
Klockslag _1500_
Väderlek _klart, soligt_

Län: _Stockholms län_
Vattenområde: _Brand-skärjaclen_
Namn på närmaste holme, ö, fyr el. dyl.: _Östra Brand_
Position:
Latitud: _N 59° 13' 8"_
Longitud: _O 18° 55' 2"_
Ekon. kartan: namn _Brandstensgården_ nummer _107 Vårmdö 4f_
Sjökort: _7/4_
Annat kartmaterial:
i skala:

Fyndets art
X 1. fartygsvrak
☐ 2. del av fartyg
☐ 3. bit
☐ 4. hamnanläggning, palissad el. dyl.
☐ 5. löst föremål
    dess art
☐ 6. ej närmare definierbart föremål
(4-6 beskrives under "Övrigt uppl.")

BETRÄFFANDE FARTYGS- ELLER BÅTVRAK:
TYP: ☐ båt; X segelfartyg; ☐ maskindrivet; ☐ annat;
SKROV: ☐ trä; X klink; ☐ krevell; ☐ järn;
    virkets tillstånd: _gott_
☐ öppet; ☐ halvdäckat; X heldäckat;
ÖVERBYGGN.: ☐ för; ☐ midskepps; ☐ akter;
☐ däckshus; ☐ kanonporter;
MASTER: antal _2_ deras höjd över däck: _2 m (nedbrutna)_
RIGG: ☐ tågvirke; ☐ wire;
MÅTT: båtens/fartygets längd _2.0_ m; ☐ obestämbart;
    "   bredd _____ m; X obestämbart;
    "   höjd _____ m; X obestämbart;
    "   högsta punkt _/8_ m under ytan.
LÄGE: förstäv i riktning: _NV_
LUTNING: X ingen; ☐ fören nedåt; ☐ aktern nedåt;
SLAGSIDA: ☐ ingen; X styrbord; ☐ babord; _____ grader;
☐ kantrat;
ALLMÄNT TILLSTÅND: _Skrovet är sönderbrutet och skepps-_
sidorna utfallna. Man urskiljer dubbelbalkar
och riggdelar i vraket.

BÄRGADE FÖREMÅL:

UPPLYSNINGAR OM FYNDPLATSEN:
DJUP. lodat _19_ m; enligt sjökort _____ m
BOTTEN: X plan; ☐ sluttande; c:a _____ grader i riktning _____
BOTTENS BESK.: ☐ dy; ☐ lera; ☐ sand; X grus;
    X rullsten; ☐ block; ☐ berg;
VEGETATION: ☐ ingen; X ringa; ☐ stark; art:
VATTEN: ☐ mycket klart; X klart; ☐ grumligt; ☐ mycket grumligt;
    vattnets grumlighet beror på:
    bedömd sikt vid fyndet: _6_ m på _10_ meters djup.
STRÖM: _____ m/sek.; ungefärlig riktning
HINDER OCH RISKER: (ström, fisknät, wires, rasfaror och dyl.)

ÖVRIGA UPPLYSNINGAR: _Enligt fiskaren N.N. är vraket_
lämningar efter den danska galeasen "Anne",
förlist vid 1800-talets mitt

INSÄNT AV
Namn: _N.N._
Adress: _Y-gatan 3, X-stad_
Klubb:
Tel arbetet:
Tel bostad:

X Karturklipp bifogas
☐ Sjökortsurklipp bifogas
☐ Skisser bifogas
☐ Foto bifogas

Fig. 8.14: An example of the form used for the registration of old wrecks in the Swedish Marine Archaeological Register at the Swedish National Maritime Museum.

72

9. THE KRONAN PROJECT

Peter Norman

On the 1st of June, 1676, the Swedish Royal Ship Kronan exploded and sank in the Baltic east of the island Öland, during battle with the Danish-Dutch fleets (Fig. 9.1). The Kronan, the flagship of the Swedish fleet, was one of the mightiest ships of her day. She measured 60 metres long and 14 metres in breadth and her displacement was calculated at 2140 tons. She carried 126 guns disposed over three gun decks.

After 60 of the guns were salvaged in the 1680's the wreck was left to its destiny until the middle of this century when the man who refound the Wasa, Anders Franzén, started to search for the Kronan. Several expeditions were made, both the Marine and the Shipping Service Department participated, however, without finding anything.

In August 1980, Anders Franzén together with Sten Ahlberg, Bengt Börjeson and Bengt Grisell succeeded in locating the wreck at a depth of 26 metres, in the latitude of Hulterstad, about 6 kilometres east of Öland. Advanced technical equipment was used, including a side-scan-sonar, protonmagnetometers and a light-sensitive TV camera.

Preliminary documentation of the wreck site revealed that the Kronan had sunk deep into the seabed during the 300 years that had passed since the sinking. The wreck site is limited to an area of 50 x 40 metres, and about 40 bronze cannon could be seen scattered about together with some heavy ship timbers and various smaller objects (Fig. 9.2). Many of the guns and other objects seemed to be easy to salvage because of their accessability which, in the case of the guns, was an urgent necessity due to the problem of looters (Fig. 9.3).

During the winter of 1980 and 1981 the Kalmar County Museum was charged with full responsibility for the excavation. The salvage work was started in the middle of May the same year. The staff from the Kalmar County Museum worked with those of the men who had helped Anders Franzén the previous year to relocate the Kronan.

Several guns and a great many of the smaller objects were salvaged during the period of 14 days. Because of the lack of capacity of the salvage vessel only the smallest articles could be salvaged.

For the next few weeks the coast guard placed a bigger ship at the Museums disposal which permitted larger objects to be raised.

During the summer of 1981 financing was obtained for a test excavation. The aim was to examine the depth of the wreck site, the density of the finds, and how the wreck had sunk to the bottom. Simultaneously, objects easy to access were salvaged.

At the end of the summer of 1981, a trench was made in the stern of the wreck using an airlift. Two metres down at the bottom there were still finds hidden in the clay/loam. The layer of finds was deeper than we thought from the beginning.

During the winter it was decided that the excavation of the Kronan was to be continued in 1982. During one month five divers and archaeologists were to continue to excavate the wreck where they had started in 1981.

An exhibition of the finds in the Kalmar Castle was opened on May 15th, 1982. Nearly 45000 paying visitors have since then seen the objects, pictures, and videotapes showing the wreck site as it appears today, and the archaeologists at work.

While the exhibition opened in 1982 new dives were undertaken. The trench was enlarged in the stern of the wreck and many more finds were picked up. At the end of the summer of 1982 much of the stern had been uncovered enabling us to get an idea of how the wreck was positioned on the bottom. When the Kronan sank she came to rest on her port side, and as the centuries passed she has sunk deeper and deeper in the clay/loam and the starboard side has fallen out. An area of approximately 5 x 9 metres was uncovered in 1982. The reconstruction drawings show that the excavation work reached the very lowest parts of the stern on the starboard side over the keel and probably the lower gun deck on the port side.

In 1982 divers from Kalmar made a photo mosaic of the wreck site, a project that had taken a lot of time and which may not be finished until next year.

The position of the wreck site, 6 kilometres off the coast, limits the working schedule to the warmest period of the year. Nevertheless, a 30-50% loss in work hours must be expected due to bad weather. The wreck of the Kronan is situated in one of the most unstable areas in the Baltic, in terms of weather.

The finds which have been salvaged are recorded on the salvage vessel, where a number plate is tied to the object. Then the object is transported to Kalmar where it is washed and pre-treated; and finally sent to Stockholm to the Central Board of National Antiquities and the National Historical Museum to be properly restored. This system worked rather well during the winter of 1981 and 1982 when almost all the finds were restored.

Financing a project like this is always filled with many problems. Most of the grants have come from private donors and different funds. Some enterprise have given their support by contributing equipment, etc. And, of course, we are very grateful for all the financial and material aid that we can get. We are also very grateful to Anders Franzén for his invaluable help. The project would have lost a great deal of its credibility without his assistance.

That which interests most are the finds. They have attracted the attention of many people and, above all, they have renewed interest in 17th century history regarding research of all kinds. Some artefacts worthy of special attention are the ship's bell, still in Stockholm for restoration, an almost complete compass found in May, 1981, although another five compasses have been found since then, all of them virtually intact, some navigation instruments/tools of brass, and silver and copper coins (Figs. 9.4 and 9.5).

The wooden sculptures of the ship are well preserved because there is no Teredo Navalis in the Baltic. One of the most beautiful wooden finds is a small casket which contained 54 different objects. It probably belonged to one of the officers.

We hope to be able to continue to excavate the wreck of the Kronan and to salvage the easily accessible objects without raising the hull. The latter seems to have been blown up and destroyed. Important measurements can be made on the spot. In contrast to the hull the finds are, on the whole, well preserved and together they give a fantastic picture of 17th century Swedish society. We hope now that all the finds will stay in Kalmar and that both local and public authorities will see to it that we get a Museum where they can be housed and exhibited.

REFERENCES

Kirchoff, 1907, Seemacht in der Ostsee, Kiel.

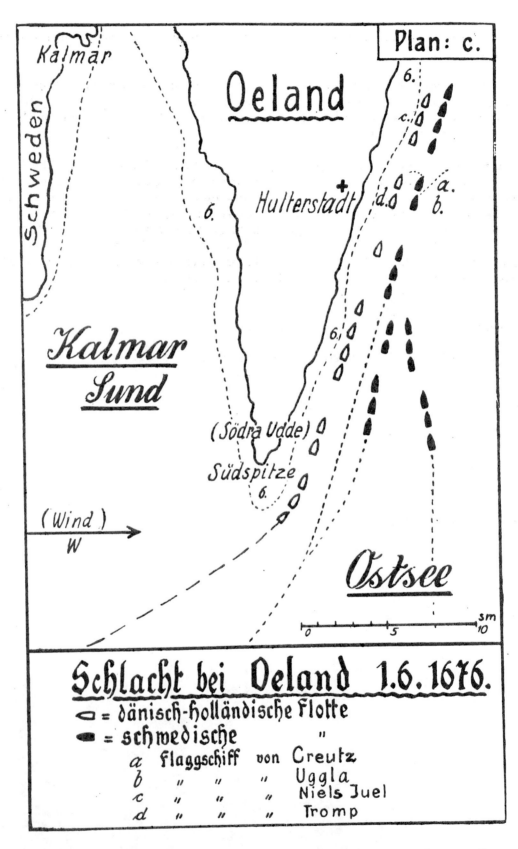

Fig. 9.1:   Map showing the order of battle on the 1st of June,
1676 between the Swedish and Danish-Dutch fleets just before
the warship Kronan blew up and sank (Kirchoff 1907).

Fig. 9.2: Perspective drawing showing the site of the Kronan. The length of the site is about 40 metres. Kalmar Läns Museum.

77

Fig. 9.3:   One of the many bronze guns found in the wreck.
Photo Kent Hult.

Fig. 9.4:   Dividers, ruler and protractor of brass, a
set of manicure tools of silver, and an inkpot found in
a small cabinet salvaged from the Kronan.   Photo, Gösta
Sörensen, Kalmar Läns Museum.

Fig. 9.5:   Sundial which also was found in the cabinet
from the wreck of the Kronan.   Photo, Gösta Sörensen,
Kalmar Läns Museum.

10. THE INVENTORY OF A CARGO VESSEL, WRECKED IN 1888

Reinder Reinders

1. INTRODUCTION

During excavations of shipwrecks in the IJsselmeerpolders, sometimes the entire and complete remains of the ships with their inventories have been found. Thus, not only the vessel's shape, construction and accommodation plan need to be examined, but also the distribution and classification of the artefacts, and in the case of cargo vessels, the cargo as well.

As to the first aspect, during the past years usable methods have been developed in Denmark and England to record data and to reconstruct the original shape of the vessel. In addition, many publications have been devoted to the innumerable objects encountered during underwater investigations of, for instance, the VOC ships Amsterdam, Batavia and Vergulde Draeck. In most cases, there was very little left of the wreck itself, or the wreck couldn't yet be raised or further investigated.

In many publications, the finds in the shipwreck have been classified according to material type, with or without description of their exact position in the wreck. Description and illustrations offer a starting-point for a more extensive study of the objects, for the draft of a typology and for the dating of a ship's wreckage. But is this all a damaged cooking pot full of tar-remains — reused as tar pot — can tell us? It seemed useful to try to classify the artefacts found in shipwrecks according to their function on board.

The intention was, of course, to start with an extensive study of literature, but the everyday activities, as usual, interfered with this plan. Instead, articles published in the International Journal for Nautical Archaeology and several recent publications served as a reference in finding out what type of classification and what standards are generally used. Unpublished sources were consulted to solve the specific question of what belongs to the ship and what to the equipment or the inventory. The objects from shipwrecks excavated in the IJsselmeerpolders formed the basis for the list of Appendix 1. In some categories, this list has been supplemented with objects that, according to written sources, should have been present, had they not been made of perishable material. The feasibility of this classification has been tested by the aid of the inventory of a cargo vessel wrecked in 1888.

2. CLASSIFICATION ACCORDING TO MATERIAL TYPE OR USE ON BOARD

According to recent publications, there appears to be a slight preference for a classification according to the various material types. Green (1977) has subdivided the catalogue of artefacts from the Vergulde Draeck into eight categories: ceramic material, non-ferrous material, miscellaneous material, organic material, tool box, ferrous material, conglomerates and coinage (Table 1). One is tempted to question several of these categories, like tool box and coinage, since these denote function rather than material type. The catalogue of artefacts in other publications do not differ essentially from Green's catalogue, but sometimes it is tried to avoid a too stringent classification, resulting in a category like navigational instruments.

Green preferred classification into material types to that related to artefacts' uses on board, as adopted by Marsden (1972) who classified the artefacts from the VOC ship Amsterdam into the following categories:

1.   parts of the ship and her armament;

2.   the ship's stores;

3.   equipment officially issued by the East India Company for use on board;

4.   the personal belongings of individuals on board;

5.   the cargo.

Marsden points out that 'no record was made of the position in the ship in which most of the objects were found'. He is sensible enough to say 'the objects seem to fall into five categories'.

For the Hollandia, Marsden (1975) uses a different classification (Table 2). The difficulty with VOC ships is that one can not always know for sure which articles in wrecked Dutch East Indiamen were the personal possessions of the people on board and which were officially owned by the Company. In contrast with the Amsterdam, no part of the Hollandia had remained intact, so that the position of the artefacts could not give any certainty about their use on board.

Another vessel of which no remains of the hull structure have been found, is the Lastdrager. Stenuit (1977) presents an inventory of finds of this ship, divided into eleven categories (Table 2). As a supplement, a list has been added of all artefacts classified according to material: brass, copper, gold, iron, lead, pewter, silver, coins, quicksilver, pottery, glass and wood.

In the VOC ships, the category equipment comprises varied objects, such as an anchor, compass, spoon, etc. This method of classification is probably based on the equipment lists of the VOC, rather than on the possible use on board. Green (1977) used these equipment lists for the following classification (apart from the one according to material type):

1.   The ship itself: its hull, masts, yards, rigging and sails;

2.   the ship's equipment and stores: including armament, spare equipment and materials for the maintenance of the ship during her voyage;

3.   the ship's provisions: these were solely for feeding and keeping the crew, officers and passengers fit and healthy during the voyage;

4.   the cargo carried on the ship for the VOC; this can be divided in three groups: specie, trade-goods, and supplies for the Company in the Indies;

TABLE 1: Classification of artefacts, according to material type (Green, 1977).

1. CERAMIC MATERIAL

> Stoneware
> Earthernware with brown or
>   green lead glaze
> Tin-glaze material
> Clay tobacco pipes
> Bricks

2. NON FERROUS MATERIAL

> Bronze
> Copper
> Lead
> Pewter

3. MISCELLANEOUS MATERIAL

> Glass
> Stone material

4. ORGANIC MATERIAL

> Wood
> Bone
> Miscellaneous: Pitch
>   and resin
> Fibres: Rope and matting
> Seeds and straw
> Timber
> Leather- Shoes

5. TOOL BOX - Iron tools and
>   wooden handles
> Precision tools
> Files
> Screwdriver blades and chisels
> Miscellaneous tools
> Wooden handles
> Miscellaneous

6. FERROUS MATERIAL
> Armament
> Miscellaneous

7. CONGLOMERATES

8. COINAGE

TABLE 2: Classification of artefacts according to their use or purpose on board ship.

MARSDEN, 1972
Amsterdam

1. Parts of the ship and her armament
2. The ship's stores
3. Equipment officially issued by the East India Company for use on board
4. The personal belongings of individuals on board
5. The cargo

CEDERLUND, 1973
Jutholmen wreck

1. Equipment of the ship
2. Objects brought by the crew for personal needs, for instance food, toiletries
3. Cargo

MARSDEN, 1975
Hollandia

1. Ship's fittings
2. Military equipment
3. Navigation and drawing instruments
4. Medical
5. Cargo and supplies
6. The treasure
7. Tableware
8. Dress and personal possessions

INGELMAN, 1976
Jutholmen wreck

1. Ship's equipment
2. Domestic objects
3. Cargo
4. Personal belongings of the officers and the crew
5. Coin finds

PERNAMBUCANO, 1979
Sacramento

1. The ship
   The ballast
   The anchors
   The armament of the ship
2. Navigational instruments
3. The cargo
4. Other finds

PRIJS DER ZEE, 1980

1. The ship and parts of the ship
2. The equipment
3. The armament
4. The cargo
5. Personal possessions

PRICE, 1974
Kennemerland

1. Ship's armament
2. Ship's equipment
3. Personal possessions
4. Cargo

STENUIT, 1974
Lastdrager

1. The ship
2. Ship's inventory stores
3. The ship's armament
4. The ammunition
5. Small arm ammunition
6. Navigational instruments
7. Cargo
8. Coins
9. Quicksilver
10. Personal belongings
11. Unrelated artefacts

STENUIT, 1976
Evstafii

1. The ship
2. The ship stores and inventory
3. Nest of weights
4. Navigational instruments
5. Ship's cargo
6. Armament
7. Personal belongings of officers, crew and passengers

STENUIT, 1977
Curaçao

1. The ship
2. The ship's inventory
3. Navigational instruments
4. The ship's armament
5. Military equipment
6. Cooking and other similar items
7. Objects issued to the crew and/or the marines
8. Personal property of officers and crew

5. personal possessions of individuals allowed by the VOC.

Despite the different methods of classification (Table 2), some elements are present in all, such as: ship, armament, equipment and stores, navigational instruments, cargo and personal belongings. The differences are due to the fact that only part of the artefacts belonging to a ship have been found and placed in appropriate categories. In the IJsselmeerpolders-area, however, it is not a matter of setting up an appropriate classification for the inventory of one specific ship; the very number of the shipwreck finds enables us to compare inventories of different ships dating from the same period, or to determine what changes the inventories of a specific type of vessel have undergone over a long period of time. This requires the establishment of a 'standard classification' that can serve as a reference to all the artefacts that have been, and will be found on board the different types of vessels from this area.

The aforementioned classifications relate, of course, to VOC ships, but also offer much information on the question of what elements constitute a shipwreck find.

3. ELEMENTS OF A SHIPWRECK FIND

The first thing to be considered is the ship itself. In the preceding lists, different descriptions have been used:

- parts of the ship and her armament;

- ship and parts of the ship;

- the ship;

- the ship itself: its hull, masts, yards, rigging and sails.

The investigation of a ship can inform us about technical questions concerning building-method, use of material, construction, shape and type; all important ingredients in the history of ship-building. The descriptions point out that it is not easy to determine what is and what is not considered to belong to the ship.

One of the most important fishing vessels of the former Zuiderzee in the 16th and 17th century was the 'waterschip' (Reinders, 1982). While investigating these ships we came upon an article that contained information on 'waterschepen' with their inventories (Hart, 1952). Judicial sales of ships in 1638 and 1736 used the following formulation to describe this ship (Recht. Arch. 2167 en 2176):

- een watership met zijn rondhout[+], opstaande en lopende want (a 'waterschip' with its spars, standing and running rigging).

[+] roundhout = spars, collective term for masts, topmasts and yards.

Then follow the ship's dimensions and its berth, plus an enumeration of the equipment present on board. The same description occurs in notarial acts concerning 'waterschepen' dating from the second half of the 17th century (Engel van der Stadt, 1951). For the investigation of ships in the IJsselmeerpolders, it seems adequate to use the same formulation: the ship with spars and standing and running rigging. Comparison with other acts is necessary to find out whether this description is universal and sufficently clear. We should bear in mind, however, that in the IJsselmeerpolders-wrecks masts and rigging are usually lacking.

The next element mentioned by almost all the authors is the equipment, although the objects included in this group may be totally different. In the first place I would like to differentiate between the general equipment, necessary to make the ship ready to sail, and the working equipment necessary to perform the function for which the ship was built (Table 3). The ship's general equipment includes anchors, sails or other means of propulsion, cordage, pumps etc. In many cases these are big objects which are permanently on board or even fastened to the ship. The objects belonging to the working equipment can give us information of the ship's function. In a cargo vessel, they may include the derricks and in a fishing vessel the nets.

It is evident that guns with appurtenances belong to the working equipment of a warship. For an armed cargo vessel however, transportation is the main function and armament is an added element. In several shipwrecks of the IJsselmeerpolders dating from before the 19th century, a small number of weapons have been found. For security's sake, people on board obviously had a weapon; this had nothing to do with the vessel's function, nor can it be considered as a personal belonging. Therefore, a separate category has been introduced: military equipment.

Furthermore the shipwrecks produce a large amount of relatively small artefacts, ranging from compasses to spoons, distinctly different from the objects classed as equipment. For this group of artefacts, we've chosen the collective term ship's inventory, divided into the following seven categories: documents and stationery, navigational equipment, tools, household effects, galley utensils, eating and drinking gear, and victuals and stores.

These categories can be subdivided into three groups of objects. The first three deal with the ship's management, the next three with comfort on board. The victuals are somewhat problematic, since there is usually little left of them. In the IJsselmeerpolders wrecks we do find jars and casks that may be considered as permanent inventory. Since the duration of the journeys on the Zuiderzee is relatively short, we suppose that the victuals were usually bought 'loose'; this was different in the case of larger ships, e.g. VOC or Admiralty, where the victuals were embarked 'encased'.

Most wreck sites produce a large amount of other artefacts and finds. First, the personal belongings such as clothes and shoes worn by individuals on board, personal tools and objects used for entertainment. The cargo vessels that sailed the Zuiderzee usually were of modest dimensions. A crew of two persons – skipper and mate – was sufficient. But we know from finds such as women's and children's shoes, that often the skipper lived on board with his family. In that case, inventory and personal belongings represent an ordinary household.

_____

Table 3:   Elements of a shipwreck find

_____

a. SHIP WITH SPARS AND STANDING AND RUNNING RIGGING

b. EQUIPMENT
      Ship's equipment   (1)   operation
      Working equipment   (2)   function
      Military equipment   (3)   armament

c. INVENTORY

   Management
      Documents and stationery (4)   administration
      Navigational equipment   (5)   navigation
      Tools   (6)   maintenance

   Comfort
      Household effects   (7)   living conditions
      Galley utensils   (8)   cooking
      Eating and drinking gear (9)   table habits

   Victuals   (10)   feeding

d. PERSONAL BELONGINGS   (11)   ship's company
   AND SKELETONS

e. CARGO, MERCHANDISE, PERSONAL   trade
   MERCHANDISE, CATCH

f. NON-RELATED ARTEFACTS

_____

(1-11) category of artefacts, see annex 1.

_____

Skeletons of crew or passengers have rarely been found. In bad weather, the vessel was obviously abandoned before it was wrecked. One of the skeletons found during an excavation in the IJsselmeerpolders belonged to a fisherman who had gotten entangled in his nets. A skeleton was also found on a cargo vessel that sunk in 1888 (to be discussed later on).

Cargo, merchandise, catches of fish or the tangible results of an expedition represent a group of artefacts or finds different from the objects that belong to inventory or personal belongings. They inform us about the function of the vessel, the products themselves and the possible trade routes. In the Zuiderzee-area we found the following types of cargo: bricks, shells, coal, compost, fish, sandstone, hides, tools and tiles.

Another group of objects, that Stenuit (1974) mentioned in the list of artefacts from the wreck site of the Lastdrager, is the one he called unrelated artefacts. These are also known in the IJsselmeerpolders. In almost every wreck we find net weights and fishing leads from nets caught in the sunken wrecks. In wrecks that lie close to the coast of the former Zuiderzee we often find refuse matter originating from nearby harbours. This matter hinders the dating of the vessel's wreckage.

Table 3 gives an outline of the elements of a shipwreck site. When we consider the ship itself as an entity and the cargo as a non-permament element, the artefacts belonging to the ship and its crew and passengers can be divided into eleven categories. Appendix 1 gives a provisional classification with examples of artefacts found in shipwrecks in the former Zuiderzee, supplemented with other sites, and artefacts described in written sources. This last element has been introduced to increase the awareness of a possible presence - among the chaos of artefacts - of ship's papers or a smoke-dried ham. A shipwreck with cargo and inventory excavated in 1976 has served as a model to test the practicability of the classification.

4. A CARGO VESSEL AT LOT H 48 IN OOSTELIJK FLEVOLAND

In 1962, during survey activities at lot H 48 in Oostelijk Flevoland, a vessel was found, loaded with shells and yellow bricks. The site is situated in the northwestern part of Oostelijk Flevoland, about 8.5 km west of the mouth of the Keteldiep. The investigation of the ship had to wait until 1976. Bottom, stem and stern, and the starboard side had stayed intact almost up to deck level, but unfortunately deck, mast, leeboards and rudder had disappeared. A few fragments of deck and bulwark and three hatches have been found in the ship's front part.

The vessel was about 20 m long and 4.5 m wide and had the following characteristics (Fig. 10.1):

    - a slightly bent stem and a straight stern;

    - a sharp bend in the bows;

    - a low wale strake, that shows little sheer, but curves up towards stem and stern;

    - a full bow and a slightly peaked stern.

The first three characteristics are generally found in vessels built in the province of Overijssel. It is, however, not easy to determine to which type of vessel our wreck exactly belonged. Some of its characteristics recall an 'Overijsselse Praam' but it lacks the angular bilge extending across the full length. On the other hand, the rear of the ship shows some characteristics of a 'Hasselter Aak' except that the vessel from Flevoland had a stem.

The main portion of the vessel is occupied by the hold, that measures approximately 13.90 by 4.00 by 1.70 m. The hold is bordered by the storage space fore and the living quarters aft, both of modest dimensions. The living quarters consist of a small cabin with two berths on either side, dimensions approximately 1.75 by 0.90 m, that could be screened off by two doors. Behind this cabin the actual living quarters were situated, where during the excavation a considerable part of the inventory has been found. Grooves in the ribs and laths on the floor indicate that corner cabinets with chests of drawers have been situated on both sides, and a window above them. Part of the living quarters is occupied by the berth-ends.

Apart from the load of shells and a small amount of bricks, the ship carried a basket containing 144 new pipes, probably on their way to be sold. They were made in Gouda. Two of them were decorated and were engraved with 'Het wapen van Deventer' (the Deventer Arms).

The hold was filled with about 40 m^3 of shells, most of the species spisula subtruncata (table 4). At the end of the 19th century these shells used to be collected especially on the North Sea beach at Zandvoort. They were used as raw material in the production of mortar. Most likely, the vessel found at lot H 48 was on its way from Zandvoort, via the Zuiderzee, to Zwartsluis in the northwest of Overijssel (Reinders, 1977). Particularly in Zwartsluis there were many lime-kilns, suitably situated for the supply of fuel from the peat-moors of Overijssel and Drenthe, and shells from the North Sea beach via Zuiderzee and Zwarte Water. The lime-kilns that produced mortar from shells were a thriving branch of industry at the end of the 19th century. Today, they have virtually all disappeared.

TABLE 4: Shell species in the cargo of the vessel at lot H 48.

Name	%
Spisula subtruncata	72
Cardium edule	16
Scrobicularia plana	+
Macoma balthica	5
Mytilus edulis	+
Donax vittatus	+
Natica catena	3
Buccinum undatum	+
Littorina littorea	+
Epitonium elathrus	+

+ small number

---

5. EQUIPMENT, INVENTORY AND PERSONAL BELONGINGS FOUND IN THE CARGO VESSEL

The preceding section dealt with the information we can obtain by investigating a vessel and cargo. This section deals with the equipment, the inventory and the personal belongings. This doesn't mean that attention was paid only to a classification according to use on board. Before being cleaned, the artefacts have been divided into different material groups, and after restoration every group has been described. A list of artefacts - 826 inventory numbers with concise information - will be published in the report of this excavation. Relatively little attention has been paid to comparative study of the artefacts. Table 5 gives the classification of artefacts according to the schedule of appendix 1.

An anchor, found in front of the bow, two back anchors, and chain-cables of different size found in the storage space fore, belong to the ship's equipment. As usual in the IJsselmeerpolders, no sails have been found, and nothing is known about the windlass since the deck had disappeared. The bilge pumps have remained in reasonably good shape. They were standing just in front of the mast, each one against a side, and extended under the ceiling down to the bottom. The large number of spare blocks in the storage space fore was remarkable. They give us a clue to the use of block on board, even with the mast and rigging missing. For disembarking and descending into the hold there were steps and a ladder; the steps could be hung on the bulwarks by means of two hooks.

In the category working equipment, far fewer objects were found; most important are an iron block and a gin-wheel. Cargo vessels for inland navigation mostly used the gig as a load-boom, to which iron blocks could be fastened. Furthermore can-hooks were present, for the loading and unloading of casks. No weapons have been found on board this ship. At least, we don't classify a cartridge case found in a drawer full of rubbish as a weapon.

Ship's papers belong to the main items of the inventory. Paper, however, is not exactly a waterproof material. Yet, fragments of a postcard and a calendar - that by the way have been classified as personal belongings - have been found, but unfortunately no ship's papers. We did find the skipper's (?) savings, 126 Dutch guilders, that could be counted as finances. Besides there were some pencils, slate-pencils, an inkwell and sealing wax in the living quarters. In spite of the fact that from this category in particular many artefacts may have disappeared, we know that most skippers were the owners of the vessel and usually kept simple accounts.

The Zuiderzee was not of such dimensions that navigation was a problem under normal conditions. Navigational equipment like an octant and dividers were therefore only found in large cargo vessels and small armed cargo vessels. Yet in the ship of lot H 48 a simple compass was encountered, gimble-mounted in a wooden case with sliding lid. A clock and a navigator's telescope were also found in the living quarters. A red, a green and a transparent glass globe probably served as elements of the running lights.

A wide variety of tools was present, used for the ship's maintenance and for simple repairs. Some of these tools were lying scattered in the storage space fore, but have probably been stored on a shelf against the stem, maybe in cupboards. Some of the objects were still in the tool box or otherwise stored. Carpenter's tools form the main category: hammers, saws, axes, files, chisels, a plane and pincers. In addition there were tools for

91

Table 5. Classification of the artefacts found in the cargo vessel at lot H 48

1. SHIP'S EQUIPMENT

Ground-tackle
  anchor, back anchors,
  anchor-chains
Cordage
  rope
Windlasses
  windlass
Pumps
  pump-casings, plungers
Aids
  ladder, stairs
Spare equipment
  blocks, bolts, nails

2. WORKING EQUIPMENT

Loading and unloading
implements
  gin-wheel, iron block,
  can-hooks, fork
Additional equipment
  fragments of a fish-trap

3. MILITARY EQUIPMENT

4. DOCUMENTS AND STATIONERY

Finances
  savings, guilders,
  2½ guilders
Writing materials
  pencils, inkwells, paper-knife,
  slate-pencils, piece of chalk

5. NAVIGATIONAL EQUIPMENT

Navigational instruments
  compass
Time measurement
  clock
Running lights
  spare globes, red, green
  and transparent
Miscellaneous
  navigator's telescope

6. TOOLS

Carpenter's tools
  hammer, files, plane, axe,
  screwdriver, chisels, pincers,
  folding pocket-rules
Materials for caulking and
maintenance
  caulking iron, making iron,
  hoes, pitch pots, pitch casks,
  pitch-mop, pitch-ladle, resin
Sailmaker's tools
  pricker, needle, marline-spike
Cleaning utensils
  heather-brush, bucket
Miscellaneous
  whetstones, grindstone

7. DOMESTIC EFFECTS

Furniture
  folding chair
Illuminants
  slush-lamp, flat candle-stick,
  tweezer, candlestick, oil lamp
Heating-apparatus
  foot-warmer
Storage
  fragments of chests, locks, keys
Furnishing
  curtain rail
Decoration
  carving, vase
Miscellaneous
  chamber pot

8. GALLEY UTENSILS

Fireplace
  cooking-range, match holder
Fireplace implements
  poker, coal-shovel
Fuel
  square of peat, peat-box
Cooking-utensils
  saucepans, bowls, cast iron
  pans, water-kettles
Kitchen implements
  ladles, fish-slice, funnel
Cleaning-utensils
  heather-brush
Miscellaneous
  coffee-mill, wooden dish

9. EATING AND DRINKING GEAR

Dinner things and crockery
  dishes, plates, sauce-bowl
  salt-sprinkler, soup-bowl
Cutlery
  knifes, fork, spoons,
  tea-spoon, cutlery-box
Drinking gear
  cups and saucers,
  jenever-glasses
Miscellaneous
  tea-pot, sugar-basin

10. VICTUALS

Supply of water
  spring-water bottle
Supply of wine and spirits
  jenever bottles, bottles
Fresh food
  potatoes, milk-jugs
Preserved food
  jars, bowls
Flavouring
  salt-pot, mustard-pot
Miscellaneous
  butter-pot, coagulant-bottle

11. PERSONAL BELONGINGS

Dress
  caps, belts, coats, trousers,
  vests, socks, buckles, buttons
Footgear
  wooden shoes, boots, shoes,
  slippers
Knitting and sewing things
  sewing-thread reel, scissors,
  needle-case
Tools
  knives, knife-case
Smoking material
  pipes, cigar-holder
Toilet-things
  razor, razor casing, combs,
  alum, mirror, shaving-bowl
Pocket money
  purse, portfolio, small change
Entertainment
  flute, skates
Books and writings
  postal items, note-book,
  fragments of almanac,
  cover of Bible
Miscellaneous
  walking-stick, pince-nez
  spectacle-frame, bric-a-brac

5. NAVIGATIONAL EQUIPMENT

Navigational instruments
compass, log, sounding lead, lode-stone, cross-stave, octant, davis quadrant, astrolabe

Time-measurement
sun-dial, sea-clock, hour-glass

Mapping material
chart, divider, ruler, chart-case

Nautical Books
nautical guide, tide-table, nautical almanac

Running lights
side lights, mast-head light, stern-light, anchor-light

Signalling instruments
bell, whelk-shell, flag, fog-horn, speaking-trumpet

Miscellaneous
navigator's telescope

6. TOOLS

Carpenter's tools
auger, hammer, saw, axe, plane, chisel, gouge, crowbar, wrench, boat-builder's bevel, file, pincers, screwdriver, adze, brace-and-bit, jack-screw, rule, bench-vice, draw-knife

Material for caulking and maintenance
caulking mallet, caulking iron, making iron, rake, pitch pot, pitch-mop, pitch ladle, scraper, paint pot, pitch, tar, resin, oakum, moss, sulphur

Sailmaker's tools
palm, pricker, needle, grease horn, serving mallet, fid, bolt rope, needle, rubber

Cleaning utensils
swab, (leather) bucket, scrubber, scoop

Miscellaneous
knife, whetstone, grindstone

Specific tools
surgeon's-, cooper's-, barber's tools

7. HOUSEHOLD EFFECTS

Furniture
couch, chair, folding chair, stool

Sleeping accomodation
berth, hammock, matress, buckwheat husks, straw

Illuminants
oil lamp, paraffin lamp, slush-lamp, gimble-mounted oil lamp, tweezer, candlestick, candleholder, sulphur match

Heating-apparatus
foot-warmer, fire-pan, warming-pan

Storage
chest, case, cupboard, drawer, lock, padlock, key, fittings

Furnishing
curtain, cushion, floor-mat

Decoration
plate, vase

Cleaning utensils
heather brush, dustpan and brusk

Miscellaneous
chamber-pot

8. GALLEY UTENSILS

Fireplace
bricks, tiles, wooden box with tiles, hearth-plate, chimney, cooking-range, trivet, pot, pot hanger, extinguisher

Fireplace implements
poker, fire-tongs, coal-shovel

Fuel
coal, square of peat, fire-wood

Cooking utensils
cauldron, kettle, cooking pot, frying pan, bucket, saucepan, pipkin, stewing pan, skillet

Kitchen implements
seave, skimmer, ladle, strainer, fish-slice, funnel, pan-holder, steelyard

Cleaning utensils
scrubber, sweeping-brush

Miscellaneous
coffee-mill

9. EATING AND DRINKING GEAR

Table-linen
table-cloth, napkin, towel

Dinner things and crockery
plate, dish, jar, bowl, salt-sprinkler, sauce-boat, soup-tureen

Cutlery
knife, fork, spoon, knife-rest

Drinking gear
can, cup, glass, mug, beaker, tankard, feeding-cup

Miscellaneous
dinner bell, coffee-pot, tea-pot, brazier

10. VICTUALS

Supply of water
cask, tap, spigot, spring-water bottle

Supply of wine and spirit
beer, jenever, wine, brandewijn, cask, bottle, stone bottle

Live stock
chicken, pig, pen, sty

Fresh food
potatoes, milk, eggs, sack, jar

Bread
bread, biscuit, flour, cask, sack

Preserved food
pork, beef, cod, cask, jar, peas, groats, fruit, sack, ham, tongue, meat

Flavouring
salt, oil, vinegar, mustard, spice, jar, bowl, bottle

Miscellaneous
coffee, tea, lemon juice, butter, dripping, lard, jar, bag

11. PERSONAL BELONGINGS

Dress
trousers, vest, stocking, sock, belt, jacket, braces, cap, working clothes, apron, uniform, casque

Footgear
slipper, shoe, boot, wooden shoe, patten, mud-boots

Knitting and sewing things
knitting-needle, sewing thread, pin, needle, scissors, needle-case

Tools and accessories
knife, weapon, boatswain's whistle

Smoking materials
tobacco-jar, tobacco-box, clay-pipe, pipe-cleaner

Toilet-things
razor (casing), shaving-bowl, alum, (fine-tooth) comb, hair-pin, perfume-bottle

Pocket-money
cent, ten-cent piece, purse

Entertainment
domino, flute, children's toys, carving, marble

Books and writings
bible, almanac, newspaper, postal items, note-book

Storage
sea-chest, kit-bag

Miscellaneous
walking-stick, jewelry, watch, glasses, trumpery, bric-a-brac

caulking such as a caulking and a making iron and hoes for raking out old caulking material. In the storage space were also casks and pots still containing pitch, a pitch mop and resin. A needle and a fid served as tools for sailmaking. Excavations of other vessels of this type produced many of the same objects, usually augmented by an auger and an adze.

Numerous artefacts were found that belonged to the categories household effects, galley utensils and eating and drinking gear. In general, one can say that life on board this ship could be reasonably comfortable despite the modest dimensions of the living quarters. The large quantity of artefacts found there even indicates that the skipper had his permanent residence on board. One of the most noticeable items is a cooking stove, placed against the stern, with a few iron pots still on top of it (Fig. 10.3). The eating and drinking gear as a whole impressed us as somewhat shabby, compared with similar objects found in 'De Zeehond', a vessel wrecked in 1886. Three pewter spoons carry the pewterer's mark with initials H K, of tinsmith Hendrik Kamphof from Zwolle, capital of the province of Overijssel (Dubbe, 1978).

In the category victuals, a sack of potatoes had 'remained', and several stone jars used for salted or pickled food as well as smaller pots for salt, butter and mustard. We are not sure about the water and beverage provisions; a real water-butt has not been found, whereas the stone bottle for spring-water and the three bottles for jenever could have been used for other purposes. On the other hand, the eleven jenever glasses found may indicate that the bottles have been properly used.

As personal belongings count in the first place the clothes and shoes found on a skeleton in the front of the ship: cap, shirt, trousers, coat, socks and boots. At hip level, pocket money was found: 1 guilder 34 cents. The savings, worth 126 guilders, were lying next to the skeleton and had probably been put in a coat pocket. In the living quarters we also found trousers, shirts, vests, a second pair of boots, and a beautiful pipe, with the exquisite inscription 'Deutschlands Friede, Deutschlands Glück, Kaiser Wilhelm brachts zurück'.

Objects indicating the presence of a woman or children on board, as was very common in the Netherlands in the 19th century, were lacking. We therefore assume that the skipper was alone on board when the ship went down, or, considering the quantity of clothes, together with another male.

Lot H 48 cargo vessel shows that a classification of objects according to use on board is practicable and yields more and different information than a catalogue of finds alone. Moreover, it stimulates the recording of find conditions during excavations. The ship of lot H 48 was especially suitable for this experiment, since it was relatively small and still more or less intact, which enabled us to relate the finds to the ship's accommodation plan. Furthermore, it was a 'young' ship with easily recognizable objects. Information from written sources, especially those concerning the VOC , the Admiralty or other organizations of the kind, can correct or supplement a classification of objects according to material type or use on board. It can also lead to a change in the sequence of categories or groups.

6. THE WRECKAGE OF THE 'LUTINA'

Information of a different nature has increased our understanding of the cargo vessel at lot H 48. In the first place, from the construction of the ship it was apparent that it had been built in Overijssel. Several objects found in the wreck indicated that the skipper had connections with this area. There were three pewter spoons, made in Zwolle, and a cask with the Zwolle Arms inscribed on it. Furthermore, the composition of the cargo indicated that the vessel was probably on its way to Zwartsluis (Fig. 10.2). From the personal belongings it was evident that there were only men on board, probably just the skipper and a mate. The skeleton of one man has been found. The extent the teeth were worn and defects in the vertebral column indicate that this man was over 50 years old and suffered from back ailment.

Two groups of artefacts facilitated the dating of the ship's wreckage; the coins and the pottery. The most recent object was a soup bowl dating from 1887. An important item was a calendar from an almanac, dated 188?. Only the last figure was illegible, but since 1 January fell on a Tuesday, the calendar was most likely that of the year 1889.

On the basis of these data, F. Peereboom (IJsselakademie, Kampen) has checked newspaper reports from the period around 1890. One series of reports corresponds particularly well with the archaeological date. These reports state that on Tuesday evening 20 November 1888 the vessel 'Lutina', with skipper Jan Kisjes, 68 years old, and his mate Reinder Tulp, 62 years old, had been wrecked. The vessel was carrying a load of shells and bricks and was on its way from Brielle to Zwartsluis. Later reports tell of efforts made to raise the vessel, but that by then it had sunk too deep in the seabed.

7. SUMMARY

Excavations of cargo vessels in the IJsselmeerpolders (The Netherlands) not only uncover ship and cargo, but in many cases also a large quantity of artefacts: elements of the equipment and inventory of the vessel, and personal belongings of the crew and passengers. The need was felt to introduce, apart from the usual classification of artefacts according to material type, another classification according to use on board. This classification has, so far, been used mainly in the description of objects from VOC ships.

A provisional classification was drafted on the basis of the objects originating from excavations in the IJsselmeerpolders. In a shipwreck find, the following elements are distinguished: ship, equipment, inventory, personal belongings, cargo and non-related artefacts. Equipment, inventory and personal belongings have been subdivided into eleven categories of artefacts.

This classification has been tested in the case of a cargo vessel loaded with shells and bricks that was excavated in 1976 at lot H 48 in Oostelijk Flevoland. It turned out to be a workable method that yielded more information than a catalogue of finds alone. In general, there is one restriction: the vessel has to be in reasonably good shape, so that the relation between the position of the objects and the accommodation plan of the ship is still evident. The hull, cargo inventory, excavated at lot H 48, presumably belonged to the cargo vessel 'Lutina', wrecked on Tuesday 20 November 1888.

ACKNOWLEDGEMENTS

I would like to thank Dr. A.H.J. Prins for the stimulating discussions on this subject, and R. Oosting, J. Samwel and K. Vlierman for their help in preparing this paper.

REFERENCES

Cederlund, C.O. & Ingelman-Sundberg, C., 1973. The excavation of the Jutholmen wreck, 1970-1971. IJNA, 2: 301-327.

Green, J.N., 1977. The loss of the Verenigde Oostindische Compagnie Jacht Vergulde Draeck, Western Australia 1656. BAR Supplementary Series, 36.

Hart, S., 1954. Het Waterschip. Amstelodamum: 153-154.

Ingelman-Sundberg, C., 1976. Preliminary report on finds from the Jutholmen wreck. IJNA, 5: 57-71.

Marsden, P., 1972. The wreck of the Dutch East Indiaman Amsterdam near Hastings, 1749. IJNA, 1:73-96

Marsden, P., 1975. The Dutch East Indiaman Hollandia wrecked on the isles of Scilly in 1743. Archaeological report. IJNA, 4: 278-300.

Pernambucano de Mello, U., 1979. The shipwreck of the galleon Sacramento, 1668 off Brazil. IJNA, 8: 211-223.

Price, R. & Muckelroy, K., 1974. The second season of work on the Kennemerland site, 1973. IJNA, 3: 257-268.

Prijs der Zee, 1980. Handleiding bij de tentoonstelling 'Prijs der Zee'. Rijksmuseum, Amsterdam.

Recht. Arch. Gemeente-Archief van Amsterdam, Recht. Arch. 2167, fol 34 en 2176, fol 230.

Reinders, H.R., 1977. Over schelpen en schelpkalk, naar aanleiding van een scheepsvondst. Bijdragen uit het land van IJssel en Vecht, 1: 47-59.

Reinders, R., 1982. Shipwrecks of the Zuiderzee. Flevobericht 197. Lelystad.

APPENDIX. 1. Classification of the artefacts of equipment, inventory and personal belongings

1. SHIP'S EQUIPMENT

Ground-tackle
anchor, bower, kedge anchor, back anchor, grapnel, windlass, handspike, buoy, buoy-rope

Propulsion
sail, mainsail, foresail, jib, cross-jack, square foresail, spritsail, oar, punting-pole

Cordage
twine, line, housing, marlin, hawser

Ballast
lead, stones

Windlasses
windlass, capstan, bar

Pumps
pump, bilge pump, plunger, pump-casing, handle valves

Boats
long-boat, sloop, oars

Aids
oar, punting-pole, tow-line ladder, gang-board, stairs, accomodation ladder, rope-ladder, boatwain's chair, boat-hook

Fire-fighting appliances
fire-engine, fire-bucket, fire-hose

Live-saving appliances
life-vest, life-belt, raft

Miscellaneous
flag, pennant, flag-staff, lamp, lantern

Spare equipment
timber, cordage, blocks, sheaves, nails, bolts, mast, rudder, sails, thimbles

2. WORKING EQUIPMENT

depends on the function of the vessel

3. MILITARY EQUIPMENT

Artillery
gun, swivel gun, mortar, breech-loading gun, carriage

Ammunition
ball, chain shot, hinged shot, scatter shot, bar shot, gun powder, powder barrel, cartridge box, sulphur salpetre

Accessories
sheet-lead, wad-hook, reamer, powder-horn, powder measure, powder funnel, lintstock, sponge, rammer, wad, gauges, bullet mould, safety lantern

Boarding implements
grappling-iron, boarding-axe, grapple

Small fire-arms
musket, arquebus, pistol, hand grenade

Small-arms ammunition
musket-bullet, wired shot

Accessories
powder flask, cartridge belt, cartridge box, musket-ball mould

Cold steel
broadsword, word, scabbard

'Stokwapens'
morgenstern, halberd, lance, pike

Daggers
kidney dagger, disk dagger

Protection
cuirasse, helmet

Signalling instruments
trumpet, drum

Miscellaneous
insignia

4. DOCUMENTS AND STATIONERY

Ship's papers
ship's log, manifest, muster-rol, note-book, case

Finances
cash, savings, cash-box

Writing materials
pencil, pen, quill-pen, inkwell, slate-pencil, slate, sponge

Miscellaneous
sealing wax, wax stamp

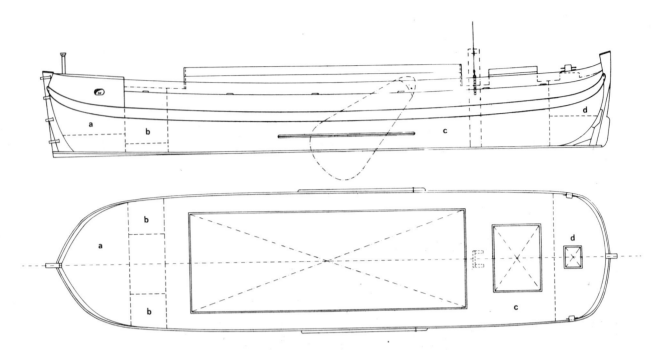

Fig. 10.1: Provisional reconstruction of the cargo vessel at lot H 48: A = living quarters; B = Berth; C = hold; D = storage space.

Fig. 10.2: Possible shipping route from Brielle via Rotterdam, Gouda, Haarlem, Amsterdam and the Zuiderzee to Zwartsluis.

Fig. 10.3: Cooking range of the cargo vessel at lot H 48.

11. ICONOGRAPHY OF THE POST MEDIEVAL SHIP

Chr. Villain-Gandossi

The paper submitted at the International Symposium on Boat and Ship Archaeology (Bremerhaven, 1979) presented illuminations from various medieval painted manuscripts located in Paris ("Bibliothèque Nationale" and "Bibliothèque de l'Arsenal"). The period covered was from the 9th to the 15th centuries. It was possible to propose a typology of these ships according to form and silhouette. The simple skiff, the ship with a mast (and either a square or a lateen sail), the vessel with superstructures, the nef-carrack, the flat bottom vessel, the coastal or river vessel, the galleys and other long boats, the ideal or imaginary boats, all were schematically drawn to the point of being often difficult if not impossible to identify definitely. The interpretation work had to proceed through multiple comparisons and confrontations, which could finally lead to an understanding of the evolution of the different parts of the ship, of the hull shapes, of its steering apparatus, superstructures, rigging, etc.

The terminus post quem of a post medieval iconography would be concentrated on the years 1480–1500 and the inquiry must go through many more different sources than for the medieval times: illuminations are no longer the main source of information and have to be supplemented by engravings, paintings, jewelry, etc.

A general look at the sources suggests, that between 1460 and 1480 the three square masted vessel begun to be widely adopted, after, perhaps, a short interim period with two masts. It is in any case obvious that the multiplicity of masts and sails is the most important innovation in the development of the first modern day vessel. One of the earliest traces of a three masted, square sail vessel is in the Florentine map of 1457.

In 1500 the main mast was still by far the biggest mast and it was made in one piece. The masts subsequently evened out in size and were made of several parts, each part having its own system of shrouds. A good example of the first step towards this achievement is shown in Fig. 11.1: the main feature of this ship, which was highly advanced for its day is the rigging which shows a much more complex and sophisticated system for the control and the orientation of the sails.

It should be noted that the artemon mast (foremast) is often absent or hidden by the main mast and sail: it is a fact that boats are often represented by the stern (Fig. 11.2).

In reality the artemon and the mizzen masts should have been introduced together. It would even have been logical to start with the addition of the artemon. It is from the bow that the sail plan began to take shape. The great single square sail on the seal of La Rochelle does not allow for the shifting of the centre of effort. When one has a waterline length of more than sixty feet, it is necessary to aid the rudder with a sail which is not a manoeuvring sail (in imitation of the little foremast of Greco-Roman merchant ships: this sail is placed very far forward, finally moving the centre of gravity;   the small mast which carries it is raked like a bowsprit).   As the increase in sail area makes manoeuvring more difficult, one has to divide the means of propulsion, enlarging the foresail, which thus becomes a driving sail. But then the vessel has too much force forward of the centre of gravity, and has a tendency to fall off the leeward.   To re-establish equilibrium and to aid luffing, one then has to place the mizzen aft, which does not have any propulsive value (and which itself be multiplied, still in the search for equilibrium, into the bonaventure mizzen; of which there are representations from about 1475).   In the documents, the foremast looks like a small mast serving to support the mainstay;   the mizzen long resembles a sort of little jigger.   The engraving of Iachopo Barbari (Fig. 11.3) shows the small top sail above of the main sail area.   The painting of Carpaccio (Fig. 11.4) also shows the disposition of the sails, at the end of the 15th century with this interesting representation of a kind of sky scraper situated above the main sail and divided into two parts.   In Fig. 11.5 a second upper sail can be noticed together on the main mast and on the artemon.   In spite of an archaic design, the same feature is shown on the map of Piri Reis (Fig. 11.6).

The multiplicity of masts could be understood as a consequence of the growing importance of ships;   in fact, the hull size did not increase immediately.

Other features of the first postmedieval ships should be emphasized: the form of the top, the importance of its defences, the shrouds with ratlines, the deadlines, the reefs on the sails, etc. If one of those must be singled out, it might be the side port holes: they appear with the first post medieval ships (Fig. 11.7). The vessel becomes a much more powerful war instrument than the galley which cannot easily accomodate guns.

A general survey of maritime iconography for all the 16th century does not suggest any significant changes in the current typology.

The three masted square sail vessels are now to be gathered in fleets (like the fleets of Cabral, Academy of Sciences of Lisbon; Fig. 11.8). Fig. 11.9 depicts an excellent example of a typical 16th century profile with large elegantly shaped superstructures on a round, rather bulky hull.

In spite of the exaggerated designs of masts and hull, the boats in Fig. 11.10 are a confirmation of the trend towards a bigger upper sail on the main mast. The anonymous painting of c. 1600 of the landing to Azores (Fig. 11.11) shows the silhouettes now characteristic of the end of the 16th century.

Finally following the discoveries, iconography begins to give pictures of exotic crafts (cf. Fig. 11.12 and 11.13), while it appears that in the mentalities of the men of the Renaissance, there are the same fantastic dreams, the same myths, the same symbols as before (Figs. 11.14 and 11.15).

Fig. 11.1: 1500 Meister der heilige Sippe, Alte Pinakotek, München.

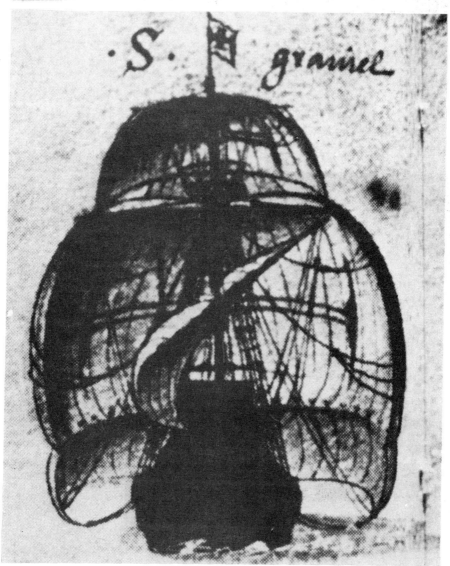

Fig. 11.2: 1497. Vasco da Gama's Log, Ministry of Information, Lisbon.

Fig. 11.3: 1500. Engraving of
Iachopo Barbari, Museo Storico
Navale, Venice.

Fig. 11.4: c. 1500. Carpaccio, Church San
Giorgio degli Schiavoni, Venice.

Fig. 11.5: 1497. Vasco da Gama'Log, Ministry of Information, Lisbon.

Fig. 11.6: 1513. Piri Reis Topkapi Saray, Istanbul.

Fig. 11.7: 1483. Bibliothèque Nationale Paris, ms. fr. 38, f° 157 v°.

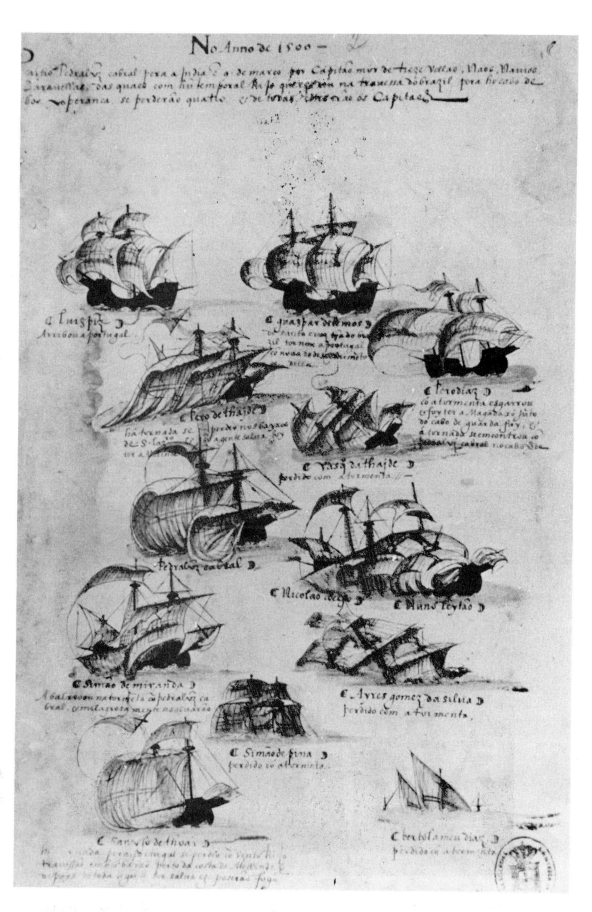

Fig. 11.8: c. 1500. "Livro das Armadas", Academy of Sciences, Lisbon.

107

Fig. 11.9: 1548. Bibliothèque Nationale
Paris, ms. fr. 25374, f° 28 v°.

Fig. 11.10: 1597. Grassi, The Genoese fleet in 1480, Museo Naval,
Pegli.

Fig. 11.11: c. 1600. Anon., Escorial, the landing to Azores.

Fig. 11.12: 1519-1522. Antonio Pigafetta, Insel Mikronesiens, Berlin, Deutsche Stadtsbibliothek.

Fig. 11.13: 1592. Théodore de Bry, Americae tertia pars. memorabilem provinciae Brasiliae continens..., chap. XXXII, page 56, Paris, Service Historique de la Marine.

Fig. 11.14: Leonardo da Vinci, Codex Hammer, formerly codex Leicester, Royal Library Windsor Castle.

Fig. 11.15: 1480 New York Pierpont Morgan Library, ms. 799, f° 234 v°.

12. SIXTEENTH CENTURY SPANISH BASQUE SHIPS AND SHIPBUILDING: THE MULTIPURPOSE NAO

Michael Barkham

From the outset it must be realized that the documents on Basque ship construction under discussion in this paper do not refer to vessels specifically built for one particular trade or function.[1] These vessels cannot be classed as ships used exclusively either for whaling or cod-fishing in Terranova, for the transport of Castilian wool to Flanders, for trade to the Indies or as warships in the royal armadas. On the contrary the ships referred to as naos or galeones in the documents could have been used to fulfil any or all of these functions. Moreover, the sixteenth century Basque merchant ship was always to a certain extent a fighting ship, as no Basque merchant would have sent his vessel unarmed on any voyage. Undoubtedly certain adjustments had to be made to convert a merchant ship into the type of fighting ship required for royal armadas, but the basic design of the vessel remained the same.

The terms nao and galeon were generic terms applied interchangeably, at least during the second half of the sixteenth century, to Basque ships with an overall length of anywhere from some 18 metres upwards. However, in spite of the same generic names being applied to small ships of 120 tons as well as to larger ships, the construction documents for Basque vessels reveal a clear difference in overall proportions between the naos and galeones of 120 to 180 tons and the naos and galeones of 180 tons and over.[2] The smaller ships under 180 tons were narrower in the beam in relation to the keel than the larger ones even though the smaller naos often fulfilled many of the same functions mentioned above.

The demand for Basque ships made by the Carrera de las Indias (the annual fleets to and from the West Indies) from 1505 onwards gradually resulted in the building of a greater number of ships per year along the Cantabrian littoral between Fuenterrabia and Santander, and the average tonnage of individual vessels increased as the century wore on.[3] At the same time, the naval requirements of the Spanish Crown were such that financial assistance was made available to shipbuilders as an incentive to increase the tonnage of their vessels.[4] These two factors, which initially stimulated the building of larger ships in the Basque country, fitted in with the general trend of expansion in commercial activity at the time (Fig. 12.1).

By the middle of the sixteenth century, if not before, a common agreement appears to have been reached amongst Spanish Basque shipwrights with regard to the most favourable proportions for the multipurpose nao. If we consider an arbitrarily chosen group of twenty-five building contracts for ships built along the Spanish Basque littoral, between Lequeitio and Fuenterrabia from 1545 to 1611, a remarkably similar set of measurements for the hull is apparent (see Table 1). One characteristic the twenty-five ships have in common is the proportion between their greatest breadth and the length of their keel. In every case the greatest breadth of the ship is always half or slightly more than half the length of the keel, the

TABLE 1: 5) Principal measurements and proportions of twenty-five Spanish Basque naos built from 1545 to 1611 (a)

YEAR BUILT	PLACE BUILT	KEEL LENGTH	BEAM MAX. (b)	OVERALL LENGTH	1st BEAMS	1st DECK	2nd DECK	DEPTH AT BEAM MAX.	UPPER DECK	KEEL/BEAM (BEAM = 1)	LOA/BEAM
1573	Zumaya	24	12						8	2	
1590	Ondarroa	25	13.5						10	1.85	
1568	Motrico	26	13						9	2.00	
1593	S. Sebastian	26	14			7			10	1.86	
1566	Zumaya	26.5	13.5	47		7.5			10.75	1.96	3.13
1596	Zumaya	27	15	43	4	7			13.5	1.8	3.07
1600	Fuenterrabia	28	14						11.75	2	
1545	S. Sebastian	28	14.5			8.5	10	11	10.5	1.93	
1573	Zumaya	28	14.5		4.5	6.5		10	15	1.93	
1583	Usurbil	28	15.5	46	4	7.5	11		12	1.81	
1584	Zumaya	28	15			7.5 to 8		10	12.5	1.87	3.07
1591	Usurbil	28	16			8.75				1.75	
1567(c)		29	15	47		9(d)			13.83	1.93	
1590	Motrico	29	15			8.75	10.5	12	12	1.93	
1574	Zumaya	29	16							1.81	
1611	Lequeitio	29.5	14.75	46		7 2/3(e)			12	2	3.12
1576	Zumaya	30	16	53		7.75	11.25		14.75	1.87	3.21
1585	Usurbil	30	16.5	50				11.5	15	1.82	2.98
1584	Zumaya	30	16.75	50			11.5(d)			1.79	3.12
1567	Lezo	31	16	51		9.5		10.5	12 5/6	1.94	3.19
1601	Usurbil	31	16						15.5	1.94	
1585	Usurbil	30.5	17.66				11.25		14.5 to 15	1.73	
1578	Orio	32.5	16.5/17	57	5	8		11	15 1/3	1.94	3.4
1577	Orio	32.5	16.75	54	5 1/3	9.5	12	11		1.94	3.18
1571	Motrico	34	17							2	

a- All measurements in codos (linear cubits) 1 codo = 57 cms. or 22.4 inches, see note 2.

b- In the building contracts manga = beam measured on the inside at the widest point.

c- According to the building contract this ship's beam was meant to be 15 codos but she was built with a beam of 15.5 codos. For the purpose of calculating the keel/beam ratio I have used the first value.

d- Given only as 'height' with no other specifications but it appears to be the depth of hold at beam max.

e- Given only as 'height' with no other specification but it appears to be the depth of hold at the first deck. However, given the late year of building it may be the depth at some other point and in this way reflect changes in Basque ship design.

average keel/beam ratio being only 1.89

If we arrange the keel/beam ratios for the twenty-five ships into seven equal interval classes, the modal class is that of ships with a keel/beam ratio between 1.90 and 1.94; a class into which eight ships fall, almost double the number in any of the other classes. This is only one of several frequency charts possible depending on the intervals and number of classes chosen but it clearly indicates the most frequent keel to beam ratios as well as the deviations from the mean keel/beam ratio (see Table II).[6]

TABLE II: Frequency of keel to beam ratios.

1.70 1.74	1.75 1.79	1.80 1.84	1.85 1.89	1.90 1.94	1.95 1.99	2.00 2.04
1	2	4	4	8	1	5

Some interesting facts about the lack of evolution of the hull shape of the Basque nao can be observed by listing the twenty-five keel to beam ratios chronologically. Table III reveals no apparent trend in these ratios and at the same time it illustrates the remarkably small variation in the keel to beam ratio of the naos over a period of time that spanned at least sixty-six years. Ships with keel to beam ratios of 1.8 - 1.82 were built in 1574, 1583, 1585 and 1596 while ships with a keel to beam ratio of 2.00 were built in 1568, 1573 (two), 1600 and 1611.

TABLE III: Chronological listing of keel to beam ratios.

Year	Ratio	Year	Ratio
1545	1.93	1583	1.81
1566	1.96	1584	1.87
1567	1.94	1584	1.79
1567	1.93	1585	1.82
1568	2.00	1585	1.73
1573	2.00	1590	1.93
1573	2.00	1590	1.85
1573	1.93	1591	1.75
1574	1.81	1593	1.86
1576	1.87	1596	1.80
1577	1.94	1600	2.00
1578	1.94	1601	1.94
		1611	2.00

In the construction agreements for these Basque ships the overall length is in many cases left to the discretion of the master shipwright who was in charge of building the vessel or, as is stated in several building contracts, to "however the stem and stern posts work out". Nevertheless, eleven documents out of the twenty-five, do specify the overall length and a LOA/ beam ratio of 3.1 to 3.2 is one that is closely followed in most cases (see Table IV). The only case where the LOA/beam ratio deviated to any considerable extent from the norm is a ship that was specifically designed for the Carrera de las Indias, built in the port of Orio over the winter of 1577-78. The LOA/beam ratio of this nao is 3.4 although her keel/beam ratio of 1.94 is in keeping with the keel/beam ratios of other Basque ships. This means that this nao for the Carrera would have had an overall length some 2.8 metres longer than other ships with the same keel and beam measurements.[7]

Of the eleven shipbuilding contracts that give the overall length only two specify at what height above the floor of the hold this length was to be measured and in both cases the height is at the extreme breadth. The similarity of measurements in Table IV gives the impression that in these Basque ships the overall length was usually calculated at the maximum width of the ship. Table IV also gives the depth of hold at beam/beam ratios of ten of the larger ships, which have a fairly constant value of close to 0.69 except for two cases.

TABLE IV: Depth at beam/beam and LOA/beam ratios of Basque naos (beam = 1).
Unit: 1 codo = 57 cms.

Year Built	Keel Length	Beam Max.	Depth at Beam max.	Depth/ Beam	LOA	LOA/beam Max.
1596	27	15	11	0.73	47	3.1
1600	28	14	10	0.71	43 at 10	3.1
1584	28	15	10	0.66	46	3.1
1567	29	15	9*		47	3.1
1574	29	16	12	0.75	46	3.1
1611	29.5	14.75			46	3.1
1585	30	16.5			53	3.2
1584	30	16.75	11.5	0.69	50	3.0
1601	31	16	10.5	0.66	51	3.2
1567	31	16	11.5*	0.72	50 at 11.5	3.1
1578	32.5	16.75	11	0.66		
1577	32.5	16.75	11	0.66	57	3.4
1573	34	17	10	0.59	54 at 10	3.2

* Given only as 'height' and not as depth at beam.

The ratio of keel length to height at the upper deck is not as uniform as the ratios already discussed since it depended on the number of decks in a ship. Ships with keel lengths roughly between 24 and 28 codos (13.6 to 15.9 metres) or from c. 200 to c. 325 tons usually had a row of beams in the hold and two full decks above. Only when the keel length and the overall length of a ship passed the 27/28 codo mark and the c. 45 codo mark respectively, and the ship reached some 325 tons, was she apparently considered long enough to carry a third deck.

These two groups of ships are give in Table V. Group I is comprised of five ships with keel lengths from 25 to 28 codos and these have keel height at upper deck (H.U.D.) ratios close to 0.38. The eight ships of group II with keel lengths between 27 and 32.5 codos H.U.D. ratios which centre around the value of 0.5. This ratio is higher than that of vessels in group I because, while a third deck has been added to the ships in group II, their keels have not been lengthened in the same proportion.

A third group of six ships with keel lengths from 28 to 31 codos is also shown in Table V. This group represents a transitional stage between two-deck and three-deck vessels. Although the keels of the ships in this group are long enough to 'carry' a third deck it has not been added, the builder having preferred to raise the level of the first deck by about one

TABLE V: Height of decks from floor of hold and keel/H.U.D. ratios (keel = 1). Unit: 1 codo = 57 cms.

Keel length	1st beams	1st deck	2nd deck	Depth at beam	Upper deck (U.D.)	Side above U.D.	Keel/ H.U.D.
Group I							
25					10		0.4
26					9		0.35
26		7			10		0.38
26.5		7.5			10.75		0.38
28	4.5	7.5			10.5	3	0.41
Group III							
28		8.5	10		11.75		0.42
28		8.75	10		12		0.43
28					12.5		0.44
29		8.75	12		12	3.25	0.41
30					12		0.4
31		9.5	10.5		12 5/6		0.41
Group II [a]							
27	4	7	10	11	13.5	2.5	0.5
28	4	7.5-8	11		15	2	0.54
29			10.5		13.83		0.48
30		7.75	11.25		14.75		0.49
30				11.5	15		0.5
30.5					15.5		0.51
32.5	5	8	11.25	11	14.5-15		0.45
32.5	5 1/3	9.5	12	11	15 1/3		0.47

a- Garcia de Palacio, op. cit., writing in 1587 gives the following deck plan for a nao of 400 tons: 4.5 1st beams, 7.5 1st deck, 10.5 (11) main deck, 14 (14.5) the jareta which can be a deck or a grating.

codo as well as that of the second or upper deck. The result was a two deck vessel with a total height to the upper deck greater than the two-deckers of group I but less than the ships of similar keel lengths in group II that had a third deck.

Two height patterns for the positioning of decks can be discerned in Table V. The first, where the initial row of beams is placed somewhere between four and five codos and the decks above at multiples of 3 or 3.5 codos, is found in most ships of groups I and II. The second height pattern is that followed largely by ships in group III where decks are placed about one codo higher than in other ships. In the case of both height patterns the height between any two levels practically always ranges from 3 to 3.5 codos (1.71 to 1.99 metres)[8] (see Table VI).

TABLE VI: Height patterns of decks   Unit: 1 codo = 57 cms.

Keel Length	1st Beam	1st Deck	2nd Deck	Upper Deck
Height pattern a):				
26		7	10	
26.5		7.5	10.75	
28	4.5	7.5	10.5	
27	4	7	10	13.5
28	4	7.5-8	11	15
30		7.75	11.25	14.75
32.5	5	8	11.25	14.5 to 15
Height pattern b):				
28		8.5	11.75	
28		8.75	12	
29		8.75	12	
31		9.5	12 5/6	
32.5	5 1/3	9.5	12	15 1/3

Some understanding of the construction of decks laid at different levels can be gained from the following extract from the building contract for a three deck ship built in Zumaya, in 1584:[9]

"The said upper deck must be a firm deck and the others as follows: the first deck below must be half-planked so that a man's foot does not pass through it, the second deck well planked and similarly the third deck [the upper deck].
- Item, all the beams, the first row and then those of the three decks, are to be placed so that from one beam to another there is a space of 6.5 palms and all of them fitted into the clamps at both ends with dovetail joints

and the ledges and carlings are to be fitted and set in with this same type of joint."

In the light of this new information regarding the design of Spanish Basque ships the following average proportions for a mid to late sixteenth century nao built in the shipyards of Vizcaya and Guipúzcoa and ranging in size from c. 200 to c. 800 tons may be put forward: 1 (beam), 1.9 (keel), 3.1 (LOA), 0.69 (depth of hold at beam). These average proportions can be compared to those of several merchant vessels of the same period and of similar tonnage (see Table VII).

TABLE VII:[10]. Main proportions of 16th century merchant ships c. 200-800 tons.

		Beam	Keel	LOA	DFD	Depth at beam d-	Tons	
1550	Venetian	1	2.17	3.1	0.5	0.5	325	b-
1575	Spanish	1	2.27	3.18				a-
1582	English	1	2.25			0.5		
1582	English	1	2.14			0.5		
1587	Spanish	1	2.1	3.2	0.47	0.7c	400	
c.1590	English	1	2.00			0.5		a-
c.1590	English	1	2.00-2.25			0.45		a-
1591	Venetian	1	2.04	3.22	0.5	0.5	500	b-
1597	Venetian	1	2.12		0.51	0.51	350	b-
1599	Venetian	1	2.1		0.56	0.56	420	b-
1550	Spanish							
to	Basque	1	1.9	3.1	0.5	0.69	200	to
1600	nao				0.58		800	
	(average)							

a- Tonnage not specified.
b- Capacity given in botte, one botta = c. 0.6 deadweight tons of 2240 lbs.
c- Depth at beam is not actually specified but because the deck pattern in this ship is identical to that of the Basque naos in group II (see Table V) we can assume it has a similar depth of hold.
d- The English dimensions give only the 'depth of hold' and do not specify whether this is at the beam or first deck above the floor. In the Venetian ships depth at the beam coincides with depth at first deck (DFD) so perhaps one can assume the same for the English proportions. However, in the Basque naos depth at beam does not coincide with depth at the first deck. The average D.B./B. ratio in the naos is 0.69, whereas the DFD/beam ratio is 0.5 or 0.58 depending on whether the ship has deck-height pattern a) or b).

While little or no difference exists between the LOA/beam ratios of the Basque naos and those of the vessels in Table VII, a difference does exist, in most cases, in their keel/beam ratios. The lowest keel/beam ratios in Table VII, 1 (beam): 2 (keel), are those of a Venetian nave (1591) and of William Borough's 'merchant ship for profit' (c. 1590), while the other ships have ratios of 2.1 or above. The keel/beam ratios of the majority of the Basque ships are noticeably lower than these ratios; although five of the twenty-four Basque naos do have keel/beam ratios of 2.00, the remaining nineteen naos have ratios closer to 1.8 or 1.9. A difference is also apparent in the depth at beam/beam (D.B./B) ratios. The higher ratio of the Basque naos indicates that they were much deeper in the hold at the beam than their English and Venetian counterparts.

The similarity of the ship proportions in Table VII, excluding those of the 'average' Basque nao, suggest that William Borough's comments on the most suitable proportions for merchant ships, made towards the end of the 16th century, did in fact hold true in several shipbuilding regions of Europe. Borough, who between 1580 and 1598 was successively Clerk of Ships, Surveyor of Ships and Controller on the Navy Board, in talking about the 'merchant ship for most profit' (keel/beam = 2.00), stated that this was the "shortest, broadest and deepest order" of ship; however, that the "mean and best proportion for shipping and merchandise, likewise very serviceable for all purposes" was a keel/beam ratio of 2.00 to 2.25[11]. Most Basque shipwrights would probably have agreed with Borough's keel/beam ratio of 2.00 but rather than setting it as the lowest possible ratio they would have set it as the highest, insisting that a ship for all purposes could easily have a keel/beam ratio of 1.8 or 1.9. At least this would have been the case for ships of over 200 tons while for ships of lesser tonnage Basque shipwrights would have accepted keel/beam ratios of more than 2.00[12].

It is evident that the greater part of the Basque ships in this study are characterized by keel/beam ratios appreciably lower than those of contemporary ships of the same tonnage for which overall dimensions are at present available. That Spanish Basque naos had short keels but a pronounced rake to compensate for this was a feature noted by writers on maritime affairs at the time[13]. Tome Cano, a pilot with some 54 years of sailing experience, mostly on the transatlantic routes between Spain and the West Indies, and author of an early treatise on shipbuilding, published in Seville in 1611, stated that in the Biscay provinces naos were built with short keels and a lot of rake and he understood this to be a measure for preventing ships from breaking as well as because of the habit of leaving ships dry for repairs[14].

If the overall measurements of some of the Basque ships can be favourably compared to those of a couple of ships in Table VII, they are in no way similar to the dimensions suggested by Tome Cano for early 17th century Spanish vessels nor to those given in the royal ordinances of 1607, 1613 and 1618 (see Table VIII). In his treatise on the building of both merchant and war ships Cano states that a merchant ship with a beam of 12 codos and a total height to the upper deck of 8.5 codos should have a keel length of 36 codos and an overall length of 49 codos. In comparison, a Basque vessel, of the type being dealt with in this paper, with a beam of 12 codos would have a keel of 24 codos at the most rather than 36 and an overall length of perhaps 38 codos but certainly not of 49 codos. These are differences of over six metres in both keel and overall length for a ship with the same beam.

TABLE VIII:[15] Main proportions of early 17th century Spanish merchant/war ships.

		Beam	Keel	Depth at Beam	L.O.A.	Tons
1607	Royal laws	1	3	0.54	3.58	238 2/8
		1	2.84	0.54	3.54	297 5/8
		1	2.63	0.54	3.56	567 7/8
		1	2.44	0.53	3.44	755
1611	Tome Cano	1	3	0.58	4.1	296
		1	2.7 to	–	–	c.300 to
		1	2.9	–	–	c.500
1613	Royal laws	1	2.7	0.5	3.45	539 1/4
1618	Royal laws	1	2.58	0.47	3.29	530
		1	2.8	0.45	3.46	198
1611	Basque nao	1	2.00		3.12	c.350

Cano's treatise clearly reflects the early 17th century Spanish move toward building ships less deep, narrower in the beam and longer in the keel as well as longer overall. But, one of the Basque ships, built in 1611, has measurements which comply with those of the earlier naos and not with those prescribed by Tome Cano. This ship would have been among the last built in the 'traditional' shape, to a certain extent in keeping with the old Spanish shipwrights' rule of thumb 'as, dos, tres', where the keel and overall length are two and three times the beam respectively[16]. Up until the early 1600s Basque shipwrights were content with building ships along lines that had changed very little since the first half of the 16th century, but the royal ordinances of 1607, 1613 and 1618 imposed major changes in ship design. The 1607 ordinances were slow to gain acceptance amongst Basque shipwrights and it was only with the issuing and enforcement of the later ordinances, together with the fact that ships not built along the new lines were forbidden to sail in the Carrera, that the new measurements for ships gradually took hold.[17]

In spite of what may appear to be rather unusual dimensions Basque naos were in great demand in Spain throughout the 16th century and, moreover, they were held in considerable esteem by contemporary experts on marine affairs. To quote from Escalante de Mendoza writing in 1575[18],

"in general they (the Biscayans) give vessels the best possible model and the most suitable dimensions, so that they can sail better and with less risk and danger; although the naos and galleons built in Lisbon for their (the Portuguese) navigations and armadas are altogether sturdier than any other ships, as is required by their trade".

Tome Cano was of the same opinion as Mendoza and he affirmed that,

"the ships that are commonly held as the best and most well built and which I regard as so are those of the provinces of Biscay and of Portugal".[19]

Elsewhere in the treatise Cano voices certain reservations about the sailing qualities of short-keeled ships and about the shape of vessels built according to the 'as, dos, tres' rule, but if it appears he did not necessarily consider these reservations applicable to Basque naos[20].

During the 16th century when Spain exerted hegemony over the rest of Europe her principal shipbuilding area for ocean-going vessels was located on the north coast of the Iberian peninsula facing the Bay of Biscay. An ample supply of essential ship construction materials, oak timber and iron, coupled with a high degree of technical skill among shipwrights and the availability of capital, enabled the Basque provinces of Vizcaya and Guipuzcoa to become the foremost shipbuilding nucleus in Spain. It can be said that on average, during the second half of the 16th century, this nucleus of shipyards on the short stretch of coast, between the border with France and Bilbao, produced each year approximately 20 ships of more than 100 tons and some as large as 800 tons, (a number of ships built for the king exceeded this tonnage).

One of the best yardsticks against which to measure the role played by Basque ships in Spanish maritime affairs during the 16th century is their involvement in trade with the New World. In a voluminous study of Seville's maritime activity from 1504 to 1650 the Chaunus made it abundantly clear that the "great infantry" of ships on the Carrera de las Indias, particularly during the 16th century, was built in the shipyards of northern Spain. They classify the involvement of these ships as follows: a minimal participation up until 1500; 80% of the total by 1520, a percentage maintained until 1580; and a decrease from then on[21]. The exact port of origin of these ships is rarely given in the registers of the Casa de la Contratacion, which controlled trade with Spanish America, but they are referred to under the generic term 'nao vizcaina'.

Corroborative evidence for the Chaunu's statistics is offered by a report on shipping in the ports from Fuenterrabia to Santander in 1571 compiled for Felipe II by one of his agents.[22] The report indicates that a total of 23 ships with an average tonnage of 290 tons were sold in Seville or Cadiz in the period immediately preceeding January 1571. Of these 23 ships 17 had been built in Guipuzcoan shipyards, the largest of 550 tons and the smallest of 80 tons.

As mentioned previously, Basque ships were also predominant in the Spanish Newfoundland cod and whaling enterprises and in the transport of Castilian wool to Flanders, and they played an important role in successive royal armadas. Prior to the armadas of the 1580's the king of Spain had no permanent Atlantic navy. He relied almost entirely upon armed merchant vessels pressed into service through a series of embargos. Whenever necessity arose he had no compunction about requisitioning merchant ships since he had, through his agents, invested royal monies in most of the larger naos. It was not until the 1580s that warships purposely built for the Spanish crown appeared on the Atlantic scene and, more often than not they were built in Basque shipyards[23]. It is not surprising to find that at least 53 of the 60 to 70 major ships built for the king between 1589 and 1598 were put down in shipyards of Guipuzcoa and Vizcaya[24].

Perhaps the simplest way of emphasizing the geographical spread of the use of Basque naos and the various functions they carried out is by noting where wrecks of these multipurpose vessels are being found today. We have documentary accounts of six vessels wrecked in harbours of Newfoundland and Labrador; one of these was the San Juan, blown against the shore in Red Bay, Labrador, during a gale late in 1565[25]. Quantities of vessels were wrecked in the West Indies. As the Chaunus have noted dozens of Basque ships serving in the Carrera, like the Santa Maria de Yciar lost in 1554[26], accidentally ended their lives either in the New World or on the outward or return voyage from Spain, as was the case of Martin de Artalequ's San Salvador. The San Salvador, of 260 tons, was launched in Pasajes in 1549, the same Basque port in which the San Juan was later built. She was used for a codfishing voyage to Newfoundland, was pressed into royal service for five months during 1554 and 1555 to patrol the route to Flanders, and later on in 1555 she was sent to Puerto Rico by the Casa de la Contratacion along with two other vessels. These three ships, under the command of Gonzalo de Carbajal, were to recover the cargoes of three treasure ships abandoned during the previous season by Cosme Rodriguez de Farfan. Far from being a profitable voyage to Puerto Rico and back, Artalequ lost both his ship and valuable cargo on the coast to Carrapateira, near Lagos in Portugal(though he did manage to swim ashore)[27]

Many other Basque ships were, of course, lost while serving in the 'Invincible Armada'. The Santa María de la Rosa, for example, which sank in Blaskett Sound off the south west coast of Ireland, and which had been located and excavated, was built in San Sebastian for Martin de Villafranca who had previously owned and comanded a series of ships on whaling voyages to Labrador[28]. In 1571 Villafranca was captain and outfitter of Jofre Ibanez de Ubilla's María Sebastiana, of 300 tons, on a Labrador whaling venture[29]. However, the venture appears to have been doomed from the outset for Ubilla was drowned when he fell off his ship at anchor in the port of Pasajes and the ship itself was lost off the coast between Fuenterrabia and Hendaye as a result of a storm that blew up when the ship was leaving Pasajes for Newfoundland.

It must be stressed, therefore, that not only on the Cantabrian coast but in the Caribbean, in Canadian waters and around the coasts of Great Britian and Ireland the remains of several sixteenth century Basque ships should be located. Because of the probability that several more of these vessels will be found a few more details about their construction might be briefly mentioned here. Apart from the principal measurements of Basque naos that have been discussed, a large number of other specifications relating to the actual building and structure of these vessels are also given in the building contracts. For example, we are told the number of beams that were to be set at each level, the distance between deck beams, the number of knees per beam and where stanchions were to be placed. To quote from a contract for a vessel of approximately 325 tons built in Zumaya in 1596[30], "the beams of the ship must have stanchions from the keel to the upper deck and between the main deck and upper deck she must have stanchions to both port and starboard."

The same ship was to be given the following wales:

"she must have the first wale at 10 2/3 <u>codos</u> and the beam at 11 <u>codos</u>, the next wale at 1.5 <u>codos</u>, the third at 2/3 <u>codo</u> and the next one at another 2/3 <u>codo</u>."

With regard to fore and stern castles we are given their height, which is usually the same as that between any two decks (3-3.5 <u>codos</u>), how far along the upper deck they were to extend and whether or not the sterncastle was to have a round-house above. Furthermore, other details such as the positioning of capstans, bitts, pump and dale, the height of the sides above the upper deck, and the number of ledges, carlings and riders are also included in the contracts. A good illustration of the type of detail provided can be found in an excerpt from a 1574 building contract for a vessel of 350 tons built in Lequeitio[31].

"Item, that from the said main deck to the upper deck there should be 3.25 <u>codos</u> (185 cms.), so that the ship's total height to the upper deck is 12 <u>codos</u> (684 cms.), and at the said upper deck she must have four deck beams amidships and, forward and aft of these, ledges with their knees; and the deck beams must have carlings; and between two deck beams, a little forward of the mainmast, she must have a large hatchway from one beam to the other ..
Item, that the bowsprit must be well fastened to the bitt.
Item, that the master carpenter must place the foremast step at the most suitable place, with seven riders, without counting the step itself."

A full discussion of the various details contained in the building contracts for Basque <u>naos</u> would be too lengthy at this stage but by way of conclusion a couple of points can be reiterated. It is eminently clear that in the cases of the ships wrecked in such disparate locations as Labrador, the West Indies, the British Isles and the Basque Country, during the second half of the sixteenth century, we are dealing with precisely the same type of vessel with identical proportions. The overall measurements of the 25 Basque <u>naos</u> built from 1545 to 1611 represent, on average, one new ship launched just under every three years, and it stands out at a glance that their main proportions remained constant over this period of time. It is also significant that these measurements are not for vessels of minor importance in terms of both trade and warfare but that they are for those ships that formed the backbone of Spain's Atlantic fleet at the time. The building contracts of Basque <u>naos</u>, along with complimentary documentation concerning other aspects of the construction and fitting out of these ships[32], go a long way in providing data for the hypothetical reconstruction of a mid to late 16th century Spanish Basque <u>nao</u>, and when used properly alongside the detailed evidence to be gained from marine archaeology, they provide an excellent source for the study and further understanding of early modern shipbuilding history.

FOOTNOTES

1. This article is based largely on unpublished documents from various
    archives in northern Spain: Archivo General de Simancas (AGS),
    Archivo de la Real Chancillería de Valladolid (ARChV), Archivo
    Histórico de   Protocolos deGuipúzcoa en Oñate(AHPGO).   Some of
    the documents referred to herein have been published in Barkham 1981.
    The author's continuing field of research is Spanish Basque Maritime
    history of the 16th and 17th centuries.

2. During the 1580's a gradual differentiation between the use of the
    terms nao and galeon appears to have taken place as the term galeon
    became increasingly associated with the new purpose-built royal
    fighting ships.
    The ton referred to in this article is that used in the documentation
    which is given as 2250 Castilian lbs. ("cada tonel de 22.5 quintales
    centenales") and a volume of eight cubic codos (linear cubits) ("cada
    tonel de ocho codos de hueco e cada codo dos tercios de vara y un dedo
    atrabesado") equivalent to 1.4-1.5 cu. m. or 50-53 cu. ft.   The
    deadweight ton of 2250 lbs. and the measurement cargo ton of 1.4-1.5
    cu. m. in use in the documents can be compared with the metric ton of
    2204.6 lbs., and the long ton of 2240 lbs., and the French tonneau de
    mer of 2158 lbs., and their volume equivalents. For a discussion of
    the relationship between these tons see Lane 1964, 213-233. Garcia de
    Palacio in his Instrucción Náutica para Navegar (Mexico, Pedro
    Ocharte, 1587) gives the codo a value of 2/3 of a vara of Castile
    (83.5 cms.) or 55.6 cms.   Veitia Linaje states that a codo is
    33/48ths of a vara of Castile or 57.4 cms. The Spanish Rule of Trade
    to the West Indies (Seville 1672, London 1702, reprinted by AMS Press,
    New York, 1977, 287).   The codo varied slightly from shipyard to
    shipyard, at least in the Spanish Basque Country, but it can be taken
    as equal to 56-57 cms. (See also note 4 in Martin 1977).   Chaunu
    (1957) refers to the ton of 1.4 cu. m. as the 'short ton' and
    differentiates it from a 'long ton' which he assigns a volume of 2.6
    cu. m.   Chaunu arrives at this value of 2.6 cu. m. using the
    following definition for a ton given by Veitia Linaje in 1672: "each
    tun being the bigness of two pipes, or eight cubical cubits, measured
    by the royal straight cubit of 33 inches such as the vara, or yard of
    Castile, has 48".   This definition of a ton is the same as I have
    found in documents and to which I refer above and yet Chaunu gives the
    ton a value almost double that which appears to be its real value.

3. In 1505 Martin de Zamudio, a burgess of Bilbao, was engaged as an
    agent by the Casa de laContratación for the purchase of Basque ships
    and artillery for use on the Carrera de las Indias. (Chaunu 1955-
    1959).

4. By royal decree of 20 March 1498 a sum of 100,000 maravedis was made
    available to those with ships from 600 to 1000 tons, to be paid to the
    owner each year the ship was ready for service.   In April 1563 this
    subsidy was extended to those with vessels of 300 to 600 tons and a
    loan of 10 ducats per ton for the building of ships of 400 tons and
    over was also offered (Artiñano y Galdácano 1920; see also Carande
    1965, 356).
    In 1567 the following Guipuzcoan shipowners received royal loans to
    build or finish their ships: Ramos de Arrieta of Pasajes 600 ducats
    for a nao of 430 tons, Marquesa de Villaviciosa de Pasajes 5000 reales

for a <u>nao</u> of 400+ tons, Domingo de Olayz of Lezo 4000 <u>reales</u> for a <u>nao</u> of 400 tons, Jofre Ybañez de Ubilla of Motrico 600 ducats for a <u>nao</u> of 350 tons (AGS, C y J de Hacienda 90-312).

5. A.H.P.G.O., partido de Azpetia, 3299, f. 44, 27 Sept. 1573
    "   "   "   , 3327, f. 15, 14 May 1590
    "   "   "   , 1899, f. cxx, 25 April 1568
    "   "   "   , 3321, f. 116, 13 March 1593
    "   "   "   , 3298, f. 498, 19 May 1566
    "   "   "   , 3324, f. 116, 17 May 1596
    "   "   San Sebastian, 420,   6 April 1600
    A.R.Ch.V., pleitos civiles, La Puerta fen., 242-2
    A.H.P.G.O., partido de Azpeitia, 3300, f. 15, 27 May 1573
    "   "   " San Sebastian, 2710, f. 58, 10 Oct. 1583
    "   "   " Azpeitia, 3312, f. 186, 25 July 1584
    "   "   " San Sebastian, 2711, f. 28, 18 Feb. 1591
    A.G.S., C. y J. de Hacienda, 90-312.
    A.H.P.G.O., partido de Azpeitia, 3318, f. 43 v., 6 March 1590
    "   "   de Vergara, 2583, f. 45, 28 April 1574
    Archivo Municipal de Zumaya (A.M.Z.), libro 208
    A.H.P.G.O., partido de Azpeitia, 3303, f. 119, 27 Oct. 1576
    "   "   "   , 3313, f. 114, 5 April 1585
    "   "   "   , 3312, f. 111, 7 April 1574
    A.G.S., C. y J. de Hacienda, 90-312
    A.H.P.G.O., partido de San Sebastian, 2709, 3 June 1601
    "   "   "   "   , 2710, 35, 5 May 1585
    "   "   "   "   , 1804, 27 July 1578
    "   "   "   "   , 1803, f. 46, 16 Sept. 1577
    A.R.Ch.V., pleitos civiles, Zarandona y Balboa fen., 167-852, f. 591

6. Six classes with the same interval value of 0.05 from 1.71 to 2.00 give the following frequencies:
    (1.71-.75) (1.76-.80) (1.81-.85) (1.86-.90) (1.91-.95) (1.96-2.00)
        2   2   4   3   8   6

7. This extra length may be due, in part, to the need for more deck space for cannon in a ship that was purposely built for service in the <u>flotas</u> to and from the Spanish American colonies.

8. In the royal ordinances of 1618 the height between decks as well as that of the fore and sterncastles is specified as 3 <u>codos</u>; Artiñano y Galdácano 1920, 300-305. Veitia Linaje gives the height between decks as 3 <u>codos</u> and the "height of the great cabbin, steeridge and round-house" as 3 1/4 and 3 1/3 <u>codos</u>; Veitia Linaje, 1702, 275-277.

9. A.H.P.G.O., partido de Azpeitia, 3312, f. 186, 25 July 1584

10. The Venetian ship proportions are from Lane 1934, 235 and 237. The 1575 Spanish proportions are those given by Juan Escalante de Mendoza in his "Itinerario de Navegación de los Mares y Tierras Occidentales" (1575) published in Fernandez Duro 1876-91, vol. V, 413-515, cited in Artinano y Galdácano 1920, 128 and 272-276. The 1582 English proportions are from Oppenheim 1896. The 1587 proportions are from Garcia de Palacio 1587. William Borough's proportions c.1590 are given by Oppenheim 1896, 126, cited in Glasgow 1964, 179.

11. Oppenheim 1896, 126, cited in Glasgow 1964, 179.

12. The author is preparing an article on Spanish Basque ships of less than 200 tons.

13. Cano 1611, edited by Marco Dorta 1964, 65-66. Anonymus, "Dialogo entre un Vizcaino y un Montañes sobre Construcción de Naves" (c. 1640), published in Fernandez Duro, 1876-91, Vol. VI, 108, cited in Usher, 1932, 197.

14. Cano 1611, 65-66.

15. For the 1607 royal laws: Museo Naval, Madrid, Colección de documentos de Fernandez de Navarrete, tomo XXIII, f. 288, doc. 47. Cano 1611, 66-67 and 90-93. For the royal laws 1613 and 1618 see Artiñano y Galdácano 1920, 287-305. For the 1611 Basque nao, A.M.Z., libro 208.

16. Cano, 1611, 62. See also Artiñano y Galdácano 1920. 120, for a discussion of this point with reference to Italian and Portuguese rules.

17. The end of the 16th and beginning of the 17th century was a crucial period in Spanish shipbuilding history. It marks essentially the changeover from medieval to modern ship design. This period of experimentation will be dealt with elsewhere.

18. In Artinano y Galdácano 1920, 272.

19. Cano 1611, 47.

20. Cano 1611, 62.

21. Chaunu 1955-1959, vol. 8, part I, 257-259.

22. A.G.S Guerra Antigua, leg. 75. For a picture of Guipuzcoan shipping in 1571 see Barkham 1977.

23. Nine ships were built by the King in Satander between 1581 and 1584 but it was really the building of the 'Twelve Apostles', from 1589 to 1591, at Guarnizo (Santander) and Deusto (Bilbao) which marked the beginning of Spain's permanent Atlantic navy. Martinez Guitian, 1935, 15.

24. Thompson 1976, 192.

25. Barkham 1982. In the summer of 1977 an expedition headed by Selma Barkham and funded by the Royal Canadian Geographical Society located several 16th century Basque whaling establishments along the north shore of the Strait of Belle Isle, Labrador. What would appear to be the San Juan was found at one of these establishments (Red Bay) in the summer of 1978 by the marine archaeology unit of Parks Canada using accounts of the 1565 disaster furnished by Mrs. B. Barkham. Since then two other vessels apparently from the same time period have been found in the harbour. As the San Juan was around 325 tons we would expect her overall dimensions to be close to: 8 metres beam, 15.2 metres keel, and 24.8 metres LOA.

26. Chaunu, 1955-59, passim. The Santa Maria de Yciar was owned by Miguel

de Jauregui, a Basque, and was named after the church of the much revered Virgin of Iciar near Deva in Guipuzcoa. She was one of three ships lost on PADRE island, Texas, in 1554. The other two ships, the San Esteban and the Espiritu Santo, may well have been similarly of Basque origin. One of these three wrecks has been excavated and in a hypothetical reconstruction Doran and Doran give the ship the following proportions: 1 (beam) 2.2 (keel), 3.1 (LOA), 0.5 (depth of hold), (Doran and Doran, 1979, 377). If the Padre Island wreck was a Basque nao, and evidence points to this, then we may reconsider these proportions in the light of measurements in Table 1.

27. A.G.S., Contadurías Generales, leg. 3019, not foliated.

28. For an account of the expedition that located the Santa Maria de la Rosa see 'The Spanish Armada. 1968-70' (Martin 1973 and 1975). The proportions of Basque naos given herein will allow for a reassessment of the dimensions of the Santa Maria.

29. A.R.Ch.V., pleitos civiles, Ceballos Escalera, leg. 229. The Maria Sebastiana may well be the same ship as the one built by Ubilla in Mortico in 1567 (see Table 1), which according to the building contract was to be of 350 toneles of 2250 lbs. each and have the measurements: 15 codos beam, 29 codos keel, 9 codos height and 47 codos LOA.

30. A.H.P.G.O., partido de Azpeitia, 3324, f. 116.

31. A.H.P.G.O., partido de Vergara, 2583, ff. 45-46v.

32. See Barkham 1981, 19-47 for a preliminary discussion of the timber, iron (anchors, nails and cannon) and masts, sails and rigging for Basque naos.

REFERENCES

Anonymous, c. 1640. Diálogo entre un Viczaíno y un Montañes sobre Construcción de Naves, first published in Fernandez Duro, 1876-91, Vol. VI: 108.

Artinano y Galdácano. G. de, 1920. La Arquitectura Naval Española en Madera, Madrid.

Barkham, M.M., 1981. A Report on 16th century Spanish Basque Shipbuilding, c. 1550 to c. 1600, Manuscript Report Series No. 422 for internal use by Environment Canada, Parks Canada, Ottawa.

Barkham, S., 1977. Guipuzcoan shipping in 1571 with particular reference to the decline of the transatlantic fishing industry, (in) Anglo-American Contributions to Basque Studies: Essays in Honor of Jon Bilbao, ed. W.A. Douglass, Desert Research Institute Publications on the Social Sciences, Reno.

Barkham, S., 1982. Documentary evidence for 16th century Basque whaling ships in the Strait of Belle Isle, (in) Early European Settlement and Exploitation in Atlantic Canada, ed. G.M. Story, M.U.N., St. John's

Newfoundland.

Cano, T., 1611. _Arte para Fabricar y Aparejar Naos_, Seville, Luis Estupinan; Ed. E. Marco Dorta, 1964, Instituto de Estudios Canarios, La Laguna, Tenerife.

Carande, R., 1965. Carlos V y sus Banqueros, vol. 1, Madrid.

Chaunu, P., 1957. La Tonelada Espagnole aux XVI et XVII siècles. (in) _Le Navire et l'Economie Maritime du XV au XVIII siècles_ (ed. M. Mollat), Paris, S.E.V.P.E.N., 1957.

Chaunu, P. & H., 1955-1959. _Séville et L'Atlantique_ (1504-1650), 11 volumes, Paris.

Doran, E. & Doran, M., 1979. "A Reconstruction of the Padre Island Ship", being Appendix E of _The Nautical Archaeology of Padre Island: the Spanish Shipwrecks of 1554_, Academic Press, New York: 375-384.

Escalante de Mendoza, J., 1575. _Itinerario de Navegación de los Mares y Tierras Occidentales_, first published in Fernandez Duro, 1876-91, vol. V: 413-515.

Fernandez Duro, C., 1876-91. _Disquisiciones Náuticas_, 6 volumes, Madrid.

Garcia de Palacio, D., 1587. _Instrucción Náutica para Navegar_, Mexico, Pedro Ocharte, facsimile ed. Colección de Incunables Americanos, vol. VIII, Instituto de Cultura Hispánica, Madrid, 1944.

Glasgow, T., 1964. The Shape of the Ships that Defeated the Spanish Armada, _Mariner's Mirror_, Vol. 50: 177-187.

Lane, F.C., 1934. _Venetian Ships and Shipbuilders of the Renaissance_, Baltimore.

Lane, F.C., 1964. Tonnages, Medieval and Modern, _Economic History Review_, 2nd Series, XVII, 213-233.

Martin, C.J.M., 1973. The Spanish Armada Expedition, 1968-1970. (in) _Marine Archaeology_, ed. D.J. Blackman, Archon Books.

Martin, C.J.M., 1975. _Full Fathom Five_, New York.

Martin, C.J.M., 1977. Spanish Armada Tonnages, _Mariner's Mirror_, vol. 63: 365-367.

Martinez Guitian, L., 1935. _Construcción Naval y Navegación en Corso Durante el Reinado de Felipe II_, Santander.

Oppenheim, M., 1896. _A History of the Administration of the Royal Navy and of Merchant Shipping in Relation to the Navy_, London.

Thomson, I.A.A., 1976. _War and Government in Habsburg Spain 1560-1600_, London.

Usher, A.P., 1932. Spanish Ships and Shipbuilding in the 16th and 17th Centuries, Facts and Factors in Economic History, Cambridge, Mass.

Veitia Linaje, J. de, 1672. Norte de la Contratación de las Indias Occidentales, Seville; English translation "The Spanish Rule of Trade to the West Indies", London, 1702, facsimile ed. AMS Press, New York, 1977.

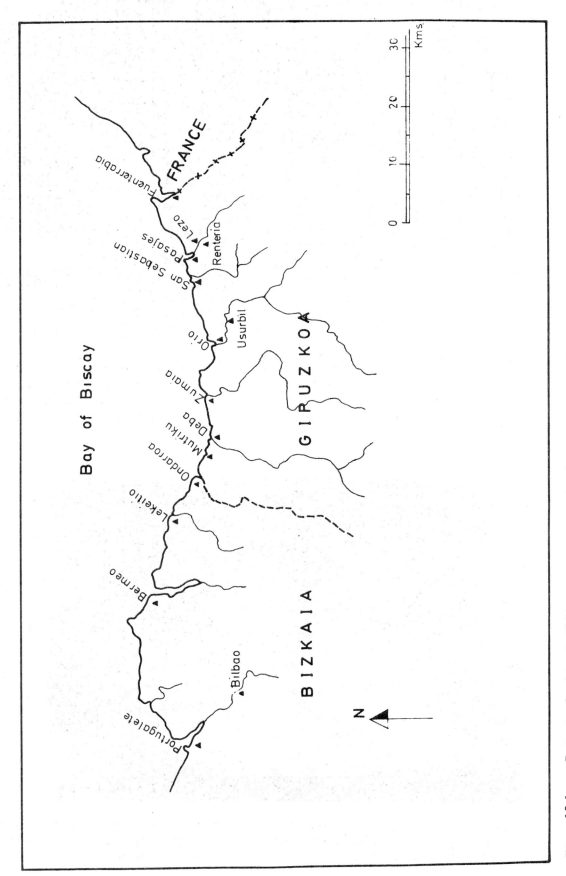

Fig. 12.1: Principal ship building centres in the Spanish Basque Country during the 16th century..

Fig. 12.2: 16th century stone carving of a Spanish Basque nao, (lintel of the house of Urasandi, Deva, Guipuzcoa). Note the single fore deck and stern castles one level above the upper deck (as specified in building contracts for these naos), also the beak-head and position of wales. (Photo: Barkham).

Fig. 12.3: This stone carving of a 16th century Basque nao is very similar to the nao of Fig. 12.2 and it displays almost all the same features, (lintel of house in Motrico, Guipuzcoa). (Photo: Barkham).

Fig. 12.4: Line drawing of the Spanish Basque nao Nuestra Senora de Conçeçion, 1611 (A.H.P.G.O., partido de Vergara, leg. 2567). Note: The spritsail topmast, a distinctive feature of 17th century ships. (Photo: Barkham).

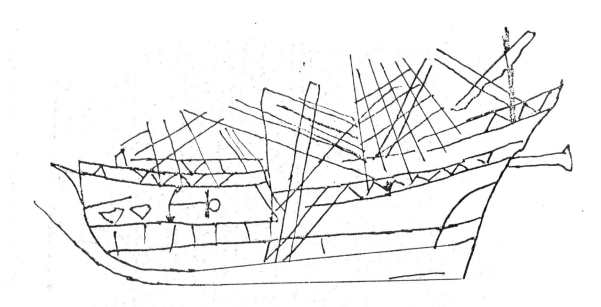

Fig. 12.5: Incised outline of a 16th century ship found on a plank of the Basque nao San Juan (Red Bay, Labrador, 1565) during the 1983 field season. It provides an interesting comparison with the 1611 sketch of the N^a. S^a. de Conçeçion and with stone carvings of Figs. 12.2 and 12.3. (Source: M.A. Stopp and R. Skaynes published in Evening Telegram, St. John's, Nfld., vol. 104, n. 166).

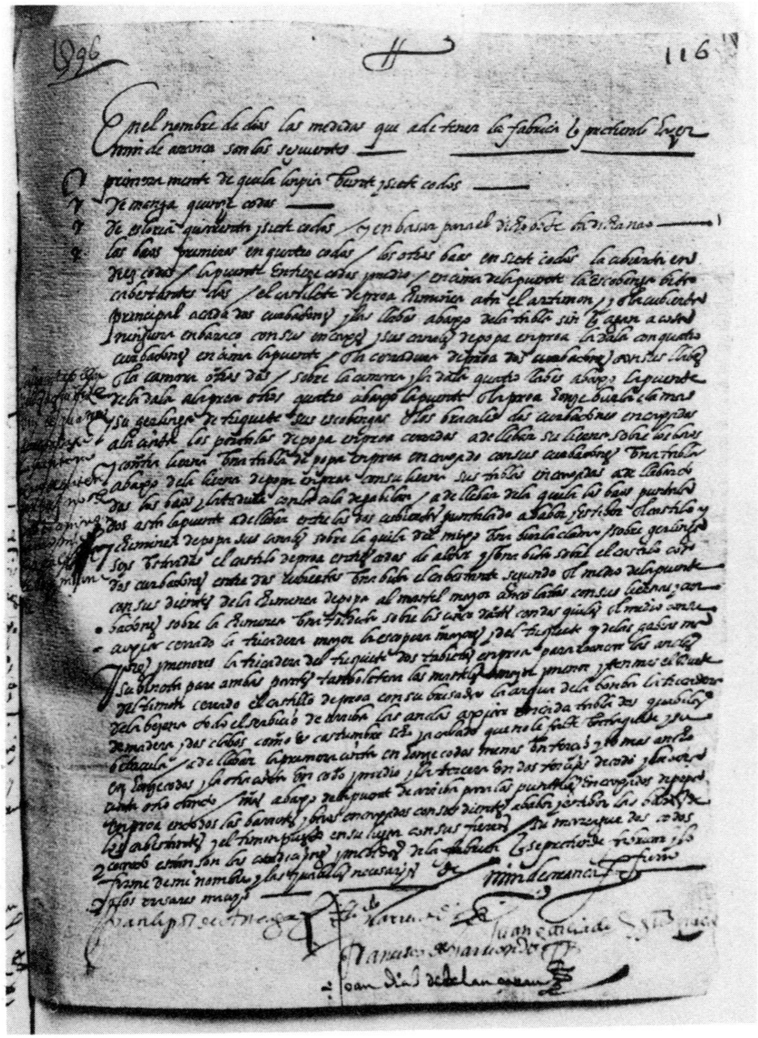

Fig. 12.7: Building contract for Basque nao of 13.5 codos beam, 26.5 codos keel, 10.75 codos height to upper deck, built in Zumaya, 1566 (see Table 1). (Photo: Barkham).

Fig. 12.6: Building contract for Basque nao of 15 codos beam, 27 codos keel, 47 codos LOA and 13.5 codos height to upper deck, built in Zumaya, 1596 (see Table 1). (Photo: Barkham).

Fig. 12.8: Longitudinal view along keelson of the Basque nao San Juan that sank in Red Bay, Labrador, in 1565. In the background are collapsed barrels for whale oil and ballast stone. (Photo: Parks Canada).

Fig. 12.9: Oblique view across the hold of the San Juan. Note keelson in the foreground and the floor timbers exposed by removal of a limber-board. (Photo: Parks Canada).

13. THE WARSHIP IN THE PAINTING FROM ARTHUR'S COURT IN GDANSK – AN ATTEMPT AT A RECONSTRUCTION

Jerzy Litwin

Through the centuries the development and wealth of Gdansk depended on close historical, economical and political connections with Poland. Through this town, situated at the Vistula river mouth, flowed for centuries a large part of Polish exports.

The close ties the city had with Poland as well as its maritime economy, are reflected in many written documents. They are commemorated iconographically, by old paintings which have been preserved until our times. These works are also useful in the study of XVth – XVIIIth century shipbuilding.

Of all the Gdansk works of art, one of the most interesting is the painting "The Vessel of the Church", which became the subject of my studies. When I started research on the ship presented on this painting I intended to:

1. carry out a detailed analysis of the vessel.

2. undertake an attempt at its reconstruction.

3. evaluate the stability of the reconstructed vessel in the version presented on the painting and in its original – presumed – version because I thought that this evaluation would confirm the absurdity of later additions to the painting.

Analysis of the warship in the painting "The Vessel of the Church"

The "The Vessel of the Church" was painted by an unknown artist on several connected panels, and its dimensions were 2.36 x 1.74 m (Fig.13.1). Researchers dated it to between the last years of the XVth century and the beginning of the XVIth century. Until 1944 the painting was in the Arthur's Court in Gdansk. At the beginning of 1945 it was dismantled and together with other valuable works of art evacuated from Gdansk. After the war only the narrowest middle board was found. This original fragment is of inestimable value for studies of the painting's content. As supplementary material, photographs of the painting, taken before 1945, may be used. Though not very clear – they facilitate interpretation of some details of the work.

In a few papers on this painting, the changes, touchings up or additions to the painting are mentioned. However, none of the authors has presented a more detailed analysis of the work.

Before 1945, the most comprehensive treatment of the warship on the painting was made by Otto Lienau, professor of the Technical University in

Gdansk, who among his other interests, undertook research on the history of Pomeranian shipbuilding. According to him, the painting dates from c.1500, while the suspicious fourth mast, flat stern and guns below the main deck are later additions. Presenting his own drawing of the warship, drawn in the same position as the one on the painting, Lienau insignificantly reduced the number of guns along the ship's side. However, he stressed that the proportions and scale of the warship in the painting have been depicted correctly. (Fig. 13.2).

The main subject of the painting is a warship manoeuvring in a port channel. In the background, on the left side, there are city walls and fortifications, which historians thought resembled the old form of Gdansk buildings. On the right side, the artist painted a high, rocky coast with contours of a city from which the ship may have been returning or which it was approaching. In the upper part of the painting the arms of East Prussia, the Jagiellon dynasty and of Gdansk are placed, arranged in the so-called heraldic courtesy arrangement.

The warship and its rigging are very interesting to a historian of shipbuilding. The hull is painted in accordance with the laws of, what is now called. frontal perspective. Accurate depiction of important structural and decorative details of the ship proves that the artist was familiar with ships of the period.

Typologically, the ship resembles a developed carrack with many details belonging to the galleons appearing at that time, for which reason it is a good example of a transitory-period ship at the turn of the XV/XVIth century. At that time, the very common carrack which was extremely common began to make room for the galleon.

The ship's planking is squarely jointed and strengthened with fender beams along the whole hull length and bonded on the after castle with vertical beams strengthening the backstays stool. The escutcheon reaches from the water line to the first castle overhang. To the escutcheon adheres the external part of the sternframe on which the hinged rudder is mounted. The rudder crosshead is lead inside the vessel.

The three-level aftercastle is relatively long and compact. On its sides and stern, on the first and second level, there are many openings through which gun barrels protrude. An interesting detail, known mainly from medieval iconography, is the side hole in which stand two sailors probably taking soundings of the port channel.

Above water level the stem is curved, with the topbearing slightly backwards. On the fore part of the two-level forecastle are placed figureheads, dragons, one on the level of the lower castle deck, the other on a level with the railing. Armament of this part of the warship is much the same as in the stern, with additional guns directed towards the stern. Above the second castle deck there is a roof supported by a wooden structure, typical for carracks from the second half of the XVth century.

It is difficult to see on the existing photographs of "The Vessel of the Church" whether there actually were any cannon in the waist below the maindeck, the barrels of which had been observed by O. Lienau. Lienau put about eight guns into his own drawing of the vessel. Seven guns were placed in this part of the ship by the artist of a rather badly done copy of the painting which is now in the collection of the library of the Polish Academy

138

of Sciences in Gdansk (Fig.13.3). Therefore I assume that there actually
were guns below the maindeck on the original painting.

The castle sides and the stern escutcheon are ornamented. The coat-of-
arms of Gdansk, East Prussia and Poland - the white eagle are depicted in a
circle. In some places they differ in small details. On large surfaces
these coats-of-arms are not entirely visible, because their central parts
are covered by dark brown areas indicating the gun ports. From these gun
barrels protrude supported by wooden beds.

The fender beams on the castle are painted in regular oblique stripes
of white, red and black. Below the stern boom, on the lower part of the
forecastle and on the stern at the lower aftercastle gun deck, white, red
and black squares are alternately painted. The railing latticework of the
upper aftercastle has been painted in a similar way.

Some details of the ship's fittings can be seen. For example, two
anchors hang alongside the left bow hawsepipe - meaning that the ship could
have four of them. Below the bowsprit a boarding grapnel is suspended and
its chain disappears on the starboard side at hawsepipe level. The ship is
towing a boat and a rope ladder hangs from the aftercastle.

The vessel has four masts. The fore-mast and mainmast are provided
with square sails and the mainsail is in the last stage of furling. Four
sailors lashing the sail are placed by the artist on the yard. The yard has
characteristic endings in the form of double hooks used for boarding. The
mizen and the bonaventure sails are triangular. On each mast there is a top
and above it a furled small sail. The masts are strengthened with shrouds
and stays (the artist painted shrouds on the port side only). The shrouds
for the main mast are secured to a special bench, and in case of the foremast - to the ship's side. The shrouds of the two after masts are probably
fastened to the deck edge. On the level of top railings the masthead
shrouds stiffening the mastheads are attached. In some places, the running
rigging is shown in more detail - this is especially true in case of the
fore- and mizen mast sails. On the mainmast top two jibs are installed with
ropes running down to the after- and fore-castles. Flags with the coat-of-
arms of Gdansk, East Prussia and Poland are flying from the mastheads.
Similar motifs are presented on shields on the tops and on the pennant on
the mainmast. The pennants are also decorated with representations of
unidentified saints and of Saint George fighting a dragon.

Some more important additions to the painting

I assume that the ship represented on the painting was painted towards
the end of the XVth century, and that in its original version the ship was
painted as a four masted vessel with one sail on each mast. During later
additions and repaintings the hull was left unchanged. Only a number of
equipment and ornamental details were added. The most controversial details
of the painting of the ship's structure are: the flat stern which extends
far above the waterline and the gun ports situated below the main deck in
the waist. The flat stern, more widely used in the XVIth century, suggests
that the painting should be dated later than 1500. In the XVth century
caravels had similar sterns but with regard to carracks and other more
advanced craft, iconography shows that such a feature was rather unpopular.
Regarding the location of the ship's artillery below the maindeck in the
waist, some light may be thrown on the subject by comparison with the ship

139

represented on the 1493 seal of Maximilian als Prafekt von Burgund. On this seal, gun ports, in the form of square openings in the ship's sides arranged along the maindeck, can be seen. Another picture of the period dated 1489, at present in the Saint Mary's Church in Lübeck, represents a similar ship to ours with four masts and with guns installed above the maindeck in the castles only.

Therefore, it may be assumed that the artillery in the waist of "The Vessel of the Church", which does not have an analogy in other iconographic sources of that time, is certainly a later addition. It may be supposed that the ship in our painting in its original form did not present itself satisfactorily at the beginning of the XVIth century, and to imitate warships of that time, appropriate additions were made. The ship bears a striking resemblance to ships depicted in a painting of the ships of Henry VI at Dover in 1520, which was done a few years after the King of England's campaign in France.

Repaintings concerned also the ship's ornamentation. Its sides on the castles above the maindeck were covered with cyclically repeated heraldic symbols. Attention is drawn to the coat-of-arms of Gdansk without a crown visible on the fore castle and on its wall on the waist side. These arms were used officially until 1457 when King Casimir IV joined Gdansk to Poland (Fig.13.4). It may be supposed that originally all heraldic shields presented the coat-of-arms of Gdansk in this form. The crowns in the city arms of Gdansk, which are shown on the edges of painted gun holes, are evidently painted much later.(Fig.13.5) Probably they appeared when the artist who did the repainting adapted symbols of the heraldic representation to the actual political situation and introduced heraldic shields with the Prussian black eagle. This first addition could have taken place after 1466, since at that date East Prussia was established.

The ship in it's original form was not armed. As late as the beginning of the XVIth century the gun ports and the guns were painted. The artist making this addition painted in a total of 59 guns on the port side and 11 guns directed along the hull axis. This, taking into account the symmetrical arrangement of artillery, gives a total of as many as 129 guns. As regards gun type, most probably the artist wanted to show breech-loadings guns. The barrels of these guns were made of pressure welded iron bars strengthened with hoops. For reasons of strength and of their loading they were supported on long wooden carriages which are easily seen in the picture. Near the centre of gravity of such a gun a fork holder was placed which was mounted in the bulwark. In effect gun barrels protruded outside the ship sides and as may be supposed, the gun ports could not be permanently closed.

The marked congestion of the guns arouses much suspicion. This is especially true with regard to the spacing of the guns placed in the corner of the forecastle, where the last port side gun may come into collision with the gun situated on the midships side. The length of the guns with carriages was about 3 metres, in the painting they seem to be too near to each other. A similar situation is visible in the fore part of the after castle. On the port side guns are shown, while on the starboard side the bulwark strengthenings are visible and guns have been omitted.

The original rigging of the ship was more modest. The present rigging corresponds to the period 1520-1530, when the armament was added and the masts enlarged. They were elongated in such a way that they are not in line with the lower masts. This is especially visible in the case of the mizzen and the bonaventure masts. This very much reminds one of extending masts with topmasts, but at that time this method was not known. This detail is proof of introduced additions.(Fig.13.6) The person making the additions did not take into account the perspective in which the ship is represented, it is possible that he did not know the principles of perspective. If he did know them he would have painted the mizzen-mast top, situated on the horizon line, in profile, and the top of the fourth mast would have to be shown as if seen from slightly above.

Because the masts were lengthened, there is not enough room in the painting for the main topmast. This element is an error in the painting's composition. Originally, the mainmast top was at, or just below, the masthead. It was the highest point in the ship. This opinion is supported by a double hoisting device used for supplying arms from the castles on which masts were placed too. The artist making the additions also painted in three sailors moving in the running rigging in positions in which it does not seem possible that they could keep their balance. One of them is seen climbing the topping line of the lateen sail yard. This line in practice would collide with the mizen masthead.

Principle of reconstruction

The problem of evaluating the main dimensions of the ship in the painting "The Vessel of the Church" can be solved through comparison with the dimensions of other known ships of that time. This method can be accepted only if we assume that the reconstructed vessel existed in reality, and was not, as can be assumed from comparative studies, an imagined ship.

Therefore, for correct reconstruction of the proportions of the vessel shown, we are left with the method of projection used by the artist centuries ago, but performed in reverse direction. The picture was painted in accordance with principles of frontal perspective in which representations may be transferred from the projected view to a drawing on a flat plane. This method was used for reconstructing the ship's profile.

The principle of copying a perspective view is quite simple. On the extension to the right of the horizon line visible in the painting is situated at point A which converge all lines drawn through transverse edges of the castles and hull of the ship (Fig. 13.7). It is also possible to determine the approximate position of the ship's axis in the plane of load waterline. Therefore, in order to transfer the ship's perspective representation to a flat plane, fulfilling at the same time the requirement for obtaining the drawing in a selected scale, the geometrically determined centres of selected transverse sections, parts of the ship structure such as rail edges, strengthenings, bracings etc., should be projected on the axis of the ship's waterline. Through the thus obtained points on the waterline axis straight lines should be drawn from point A. Taking one of the dimensions of the transferred ship silhouette in an arbitrary scale permits the reconstruction of the entire profile to be completed. The optimum solution would be to take the ship's length along its waterline but I did not have this dimension. Therefore I decided to assume one of the vertical dimensions - to be more precise, the height of the rail CD, in the fore part of the aftercastle, and from this I obtained the remaining dimensions of the ship. I carried out a few tests for different rail heights which could have been used on ships at that time. Extending the lines passing through the upper rail edge - point C and through a point D, which could determine the rail base, I obtained an area, into which, parallel to the vertical edge of the rail, the segment CD - which determined rail height in selected scale - should be put in. Next, I lead a straight line through segment CD which intersected another straight line passing from point A through the projection on the waterplane axis of the middle point of the rail. In that way point B was found, which determined the theoretical load waterplane of the transferred ship. On the drawing, this waterplane is parallel to the waterplane of the ship in the painting. By further use of the method I obtained all characteristic points outlining the ship's profile.

During the transferring an interesting dependence between the selected dimension CD and ship's length was observed. For a rail height of 1.3 m I obtained ship's length along waterline equal to 28.6 m. For a height of 1.4 m the length was 30.5 m. Increasing rail height resulted in small increases in length. Finally I decided to assume the side height of the castle part mentioned above as equal to 1.40 m. This explicitly determined the remaining dimensions of the vessel, i.e. the waterline length Kl_w _ 30.5 m, length between the stem and sternpost L_S = 32.1 m (Fig. 13.8).

Of course, I realize, that with this method some errors are unavoidable. But these possible inaccuracies during transferring of the vessel profile and selecting its dimensions are of no real significance to the concept of reconstruction and to further calculations.

Other main dimensions of the ship were selected on the basis of the ratio between ship width, keel length and hull length from stem to stern. This ratio in the middle ages was as 1:2:3. Therefore, for ship length 32.1 m, keel length could be 21.4 m and ship width - 10.7 m.

The remaining dimensions were assumed by analogy to other ships from the XVth/XVIth century, identified mainly as carracks.

The selected main dimensions of the warship may seem controversial, and the ship may seem too short. At the turn of the XVth and XVIth centuries larger ships were built. This is also recorded in Gdansk chronicles, in which building of much larger vessels is mentioned. However, the building of larger vessels is only occasional, as the building of medium-size ships are most common. The reconstructed ship could have belonged to such vessels in her original form. Her cargo capacity, calculated using the known formula, could be 292 lasts/584 tons/ and her displacement, determined after theoretical lines had been reconstructed - 829.6 T with a draught of T = 4.5 m.

The ship proportions and dimensions thus obtained confirm that the additions and changes are absurd, since for the 129 guns shown on the ship, she is decidedly too short. For comparison: "Henry Grace a Dieu" from 1545 with 21 heavy guns and 130 smaller ones was 44.2 m long, and the well known privateer "Piotzr Gdanska" (Peter von Danzig) from the early 1470s which carried 17 guns and had a crew of 350 was about 50 m long.

Determination of the reconstructed ship's stability

To solve the problem of the ship's stability it was necessary to carry out some calculations and to elaborate the moulded lines. The shape of the underwater part of the hull was transposed based on somewhat later late XVI century theoretical drawings of hulls and also based on data from excavations done in Holland. (Fig. 13.9)

Using data from the moulded lines, coordinates for the graphs of hydrostatic curves, Bonjean scale and cross curves of stability, were calculated on a computer of the Centrum Techniki Okretowej (Ship Technique Centre) in Gdansk - program 35 - TO.

Of importance for the stability calculations was the evaluation of the vessel's weight and its rigging and equipment weight as well as a calculation of the position of the ship's centre of gravity. Reconstruction of midship and longitudinal sections was attempted. (Fig.13.10) For even approximate weight calculations, determining the bulk density of the timber probably used for building the ship was quite important. I assumed that the vessel was built of oak, its decks were pine and masts and yards of spruce.

Weight calculations of the ship were carried out by graphical methods. The drawings of the hull were divided by lines drawn along waterplanes and frames. In the case of frame division, into one segment, were taken the frames and beams, knee plates, part of the planking, part of the decks and longitudinal strengthenings, part of the keel, and two halves of the frames to the right and left of the main frame in the segment. For an average frame spacing of 0.5 m, the length of the frame segment was 1.0 m.

By calculating the weight of selected characteristic segments I obtained a hull weight curve. After computing the area below the curve with a planimeter I obtained the weight of the empty hull, which was 304 T.

The abscissa of the hull's centre of gravity was computed from Simpson's formula.

Similarly I computed the weights of segments in the waterplane arrangement. In this way I obtained a second weight curve and I could compare the two results. The weight of the hull obtained from the waterplane weight curve was 298 T. For further calculations I assumed the arithmetic mean of the two values, i.e. P = 301 Tons.

The height of the hull's centre of gravity was found also from Simpson's formula, and $z_G = 5.04$ m was obtained.

Assuming identical coordinates for the hull's centre of gravity I made further calculations for each weight group of the vessel in her earlier - merchant version before repainting and later-warship version after repainting which is the vessel as depicted at present on the painting. The metacentric height of the merchant ship was GM = 0.457 m, of the warship GM = 0.186 m.

These results and characteristics of the vessel obtained from the computer were used for determining the rolling moment curves for both versions.

Conclusions

As I began this reconstruction I expected that the results of the stability calculations for the warship version would confirm the absurdity of the additions to the painting.

I think that I have carried through the task, although the stability results are to some degree subject to discussion. There are at least a few reasons for this. It must be stressed that the main dimensions of the ship were the maximum which I could assume. This is especially true of the width and draught of the warship, which are of relatively important influence for the stability of the reconstructed vessel. If a greater L/B ratio had been used (at the end of the XVth century it reaches 5 on larger ships!) the warship's stability would demonstrate much more clearly that the painter's additions are far removed from reality.

The assumed dimensions also led to the calculation of a relatively large carrying capacity i.e. 1152m³. This made possible loading of all theoretically assumed cargo, equipment and stores. Depending on the type of cargo and stores, it was possible, by appropriate arrangement, to obtain longitudinal trim and even to lower the centre of gravity of the whole ship. In this way as well the metacentric height of the vessel would increase, which for version I - the merchant vessel - with a GM = 0.457 m is near to the value of contemporary sail ships, which was normally 0.6 - 0.9 m. However, the stability of the version II - warship - is rather doubtful (GM = 0.186 m). If this is to be accepted as true and even assuming that the sides and decks were leakproof, except for the gunports which were not closed with this type of artillery, for such a metacentric height water would flow inside even at a 10° heel.

A fully rigged vessel in version I, in case of a sudden 6°B wind would have a heel of 32° and then it would stabilize at 16° heel. When danger of losing stability appeared, sail area would have to be reduced. In case of such a wind the hull itself would heel by 8°. For version I, the angle at which water would flow into the vessel is equal to 37° (Fig. 13.11)

In case of the warship (version II) the same wind would cause a heel of 53°30', and if water would not enter the ship, the heel would stabilize at 30°. For this version consecutive angles of water entry are: for midship gun ports - 10°, for hold hatch coaming on main deck - 37°, for the lowest gun port in the after castle - 52°. Therefore, judging by this calculation the reconstructed ship's stability, the ship was definitely repainted.

Work on the calculations also revealed interesting stability properties of old time ships. In some publications appear opinions that the old ships with high superstructures-castles did not have proper stability. This is not a totally accurate statement. Volumes of the aftercastle taken into account in the calculation of cross-curves of stability decidedly increase the range of the curve of righting moment levers. This could be confirmed in reality provided that the deck and castle were reasonably watertight; so that during an extreme heel no water would enter and then, after a moment, the ship would right itself, sailing at a stable heel, much smaller than the initial one.

As I have mentioned earlier, there may be a certain degree of error in the stability calculations and considerations because the dimensions of the ship and parameters of its equipment had to be assumed. This was caused by a lack of good comparative sources concerning ship structures from the turn of the XVth and XVIth century, which would have enabled correct reconstructions of the hull frames, and in effect calculation of parameters necessary for stability computations. However, I think that in the future a correction of our calculations will be possible. I hope that much information will be gained from investigations of the wreck of the "Mary Rose". It also would be quite interesting to carry out theoretical computations based on an attempt at reconstructing the "Mary Rose", whose picture was also painted in frontal perspective. A comparison of the theoretical considerations for a reconstruction of a well-preserved wreck could allow an opportunity to determine the usefulness of the method of transferring and reconstruction for studies of XV/XVIth century vessels.

Fig. 13.1: The painting of "The Vessel of the Church" from Arthur's Court in Gdansk.

Fig. 13.2:   Otte Lienau's interpretation of the warship presented on the painting "The Vessel of the Church".

Fig. 13.3:   The copy of the painting "The Vessel of the Church" in the collection of the library of the Polish Academy of Sciences in Gdansk.

Fig. 13.4:   The narrowest middle board fragment - the arms on the fore castle side.

Fig. 13.5:   The narrowest middle board fragment - the arms on the aft castle side covered by gun ports and gun barrels.

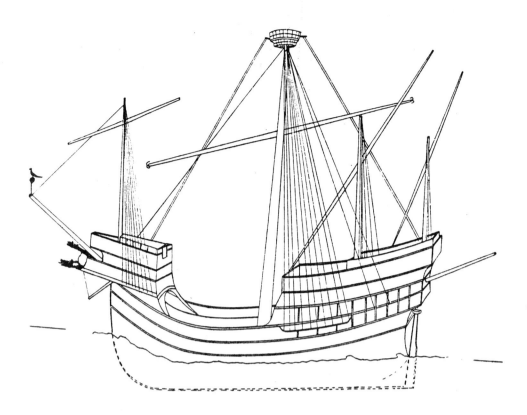

Fig. 13.6: Approximate view of the ship before additions and repainting on "The Vessel of the Church" painting.

Fig. 13.7: The principle of the ship reconstruction.

149

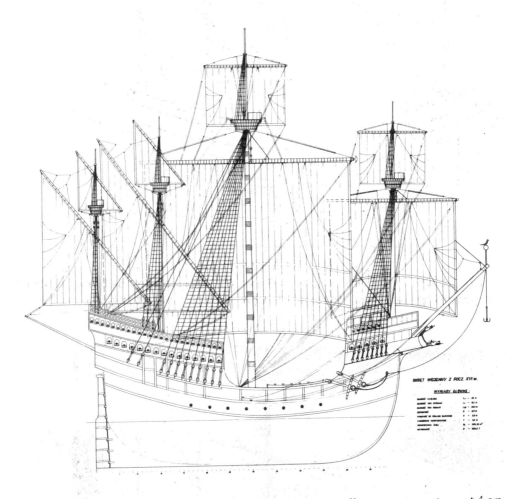

Fig. 13.8:   "The Vessel of the Church" - reconstruction
drawing.

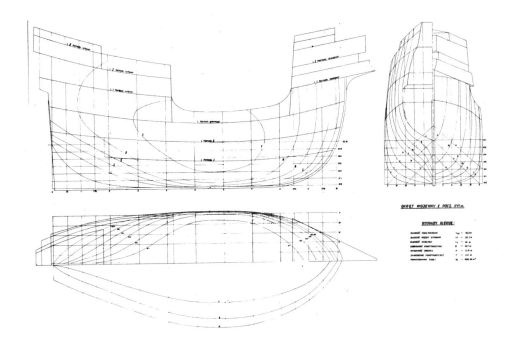

Fig. 13.9: The line drawing of the reconstructed warship.

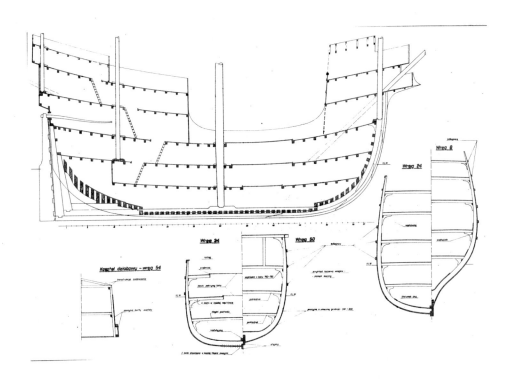

Fig. 13.10: Reconstruction of midship and longitudinal sections of the warship.

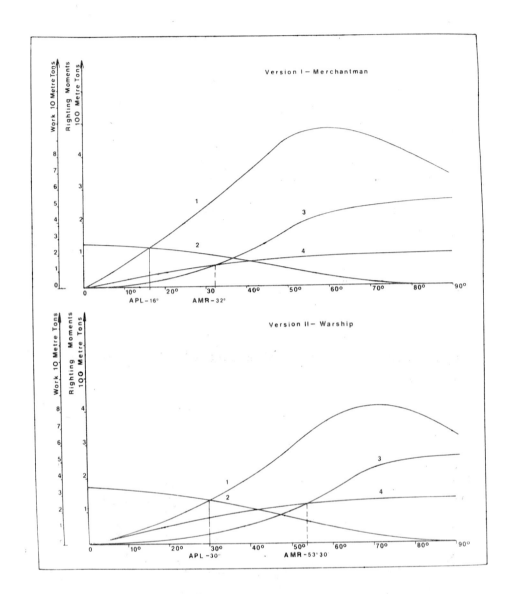

Fig. 13.11: Dynamic stability and heeling moment curves of the two versions of the reconstruction of the vessel - I) merchantman, and II) warship. 1. Static Stability Curve. 2. Heeling Moment. 3. Dynamic Stability Curve. 4. Dynamic Heeling Energy. APL = Angle of Permanent List. AMR = Angle of Maximum Roll. (10 cm)

14. DUTCH DESIGN SPECIALIZATION AND BUILDING METHODS IN THE SEVENTEENTH CENTURY

Richard W. Unger

The Dutch Republic in the seventeenth century was the envy of all of Europe. The economy thrived on the expansion of agriculture but more obviously on the growth in shipping. Dutch shipbuilders supplied the vehicles for the prosperity of that shipping. "The advantages gained by cheap and adaptable shipbuilding, and cheap and careful navigation, were summed up in the lowest freight rates in Europe, and the most extensive and efficient merchant marine" (Barbour 1930, 285). Many explanations have been offered for the great success of the Dutch shipbuilding industry. The Dutch, it has been said, bought their wood at lower prices than other Europeans and that despite the fact that all of it had to be imported from the Rhineland, Westphalia, Norway or the Baltic. The extensive commercial network, the lowest interest rates in Europe and low customs duties allowed Dutch builders to get their supplies for relatively low cost, even paying less for Norwegian timber than Norwegian shipbuilders (Barbour 1930, 269-274; Barbour 1950, 91). The lower prices were a result of the superior Dutch shipping industry which in turn depended on superior shipbuilding. The argument is circular. An explanation based on lower cost raw materials essentially begs the central question.

The Dutch industry had a massive centre in the Zaanstreek just to the northwest of Amsterdam. So many yards near each other and near a large market for their products and near sources of supply made for, so it was said, greater efficiency. Large quantities of timber as well as many other supplies were stored in the Zaanstreek which made it possible to build ships quickly and also to standardize some of the parts. But centralization can not be the principal explanation for Dutch success. Growth began in the late sixteenth century when the Zaanstreek was home for a few farming villages. Industry grew up there in the wake of commercial expansion. Moreover shipbuilding was carried on in places other than the Zaanstreek, in cities and towns large and small throughout Holland and Zeeland despite the presence of a centralized Zaanstreek industry.

Dutch builders were said to be better at the job because they were more economical in their use of wood. They were also said to be extremely neat, orderly, clean and industrious. They used cheaper wood which not only lowered construction costs but was also easier to work. Durability took second place to cost and the carpenters at times worked in poor pieces of wood just to save money. Those harder working and more productive Dutch shipcarpenters were also paid more than workers in other countries so Dutch labour costs were relatively high. The greater productivity was in part because of the use of mechanical devices, especially blocks and the wind-powered sawmill (Barbour 1930, 274, 277-278; Clément 1864-1865, part 1, 211, 295, part 2, 305-307; Colenbrander 1919, 2, 15). The greater investment on the dock, the labour-saving devices did serve to give Dutch builders an advantage though one which developed only slowly with the dissemination of the use of such devices and one for which they paid in higher wages.

Dutch shipbuilders committed themselves early to specialized design. That explanation for Dutch shipbuilding and shipping success seems much more clear and more firmly based on the evidence than any other. In the course of the fifteenth and sixteenth centuries as northern European ships were transformed. builders gradually came to appreciate the advantages of constructing vessels to do one job or set of jobs. Specialized design made the vessel more durable, more efficient and more profitable. The greatest division was between the warship carrying guns and the sailing packet. Already by the close of the sixteenth century the Dutch were building specialized cargo ships, the most important being the fluit, which carried few or no guns and had a large open hold ideal for carrying bulk goods. The type was modified too for certain trades for even greater specialization and thus greater efficiency. Other builders, most notably English ones, were slower than their Dutch counterparts to seize the opportunity created by the evolution of ship design and thus slower to pass on significant savings to shippers. Dutch cargo ships were not highly defensible but that problem was solved by having them sail in convoys protected by specialized warships whenever there was any danger of attack (Barbour 1930, 264, 279-282; Unger 1981, 233-236, 247-252). Specialization in design coincides precisely with the growth of Dutch shipping and continued along with expansion through the early part of the seventeenth century. It seems that the residual factor, technical change in ship design and to a lesser extent on the shipbuilding wharf serves as the most acceptable explanation for the dominant position of Dutch shipbuilding.

As with the success of the Dutch economy a number of different explanations has been offered for the technical superiority in shipbuilding. The location of the Dutch Republic, on the sea and with much of its land below sea level gave it a long tradition of shipbuilding. It was at the centre of the growing northern European trading pattern. Long experience with shipbuilding, made almost a necessity by local geography, gave Dutch shipcarpenters chances to improve their designs. Dutch guilds because of their openness and their ability to train highly skilled men made them an important vehicle for the development and dissemination of better ways of building ships. The competition among towns in the coastal provinces of Holland and Zeeland was an impetus to technical change since guilds limited competition in many way but never in improving design or quality of the final product (Unger 1978, especially 63-82). Undoubtedly these and other factors played a part in the success of Dutch shipcarpenters in establishing a lead over their counterparts in other parts of Europe. There is one other explanation however that appears to be promising and worthy of investigation. Dutch carpenters may have built their ships in a different way from southern and western European shipwrights.

The greatest contribution of ship and boat archaeology over the last forty years has been to demonstrate the distinction between shell construction where the strength of the vessel came from the exterior planking and skeleton construction where strength came from the internal frames. Excavations in the Mediterranean especially have shown that in the first millenium Europeans developed a unique way of solving the problem of carrying goods by water. Skeleton building was a revolutionary method, one which made it possible to build larger, more versatile and more economical ships. Skeleton building proved to be one of the most important technical advances in making possible European domination of the world's oceans. Northern European shipbuilders adopted skeleton construction in the course of the fifteenth and sixteenth centuries. They copied the designs of southern European vessels, even using visiting ships from the South as models, or learned how to build in the new style from southern shipwrights imported by monarchs like King Henry VIII of England. With the old method, clinker-building, northern carpenters built the hull first overlapping the planks to give strength and watertightness. With the new method the frames were set up first and then the hull planking was added on, pinned to the internal timbers. The hull planks with skeleton construction were thus fitted edge-to-edge rather than overlapping as before.

Dutch shipbuilders it appears did not completely adopt the new form of skeleton building. The distinguished maritime ethnologist, Olof Hasslöf, has pointed to evidence which shows that Dutch shipcarpenters first built the shell up to the waterline and then from there on built the skeleton. In pure skeleton building the frames go up before any of the hull planking while in pure shell building the hull is all but finished before the first frame is put in. Another important figure in the study of shipbuilding, Gerhard Timmerman, follows Hasslöf in seeing the Dutch method as a transitional stage between the clinker-built shell construction of the North and the revolutionary skeleton building of the South. Dutch builders compromised, so Hasslöf and Timmerman say, between the two very different approaches. There was a number of such combinations of the two methods in the late seventeenth century, combination methods which were carried on as shipbuilding traditions well into the twentieth century in parts of Scandinavia (Hasslöf 1972, 58; Hasslöf 1963, 169; Timmerman 1979, 26-27). Hasslöf's principal contention is that the change from shell to skeleton building "does not constitute an unbridgeable abyss in practice and that a gradual evolution from the former to the latter is by no means inconceivable, but precisely what we may have to reckon with, even if it has not yet proved feasible to establish the exact sequences in their varied aspects" (Hasslöf 1963, 172). Putting up frames first was not a one-time invention but rather a gradual development. Archaeological evidence has in recent years come to the support of Hasslöf to show that even in the Mediterranean, the home of the first skeleton construction, shipwrights slowly moved from building their hull first to putting up the frames before the hull. The seventh century Yassi Ada ship was built in a combination of shell and skeleton methods. Edge-joined planking of the outer hull was carried up to the waterline and then the internal frames were inserted. After that the higher hull planks were attached to the internal frames. The same progression may have been followed in a fourth century vessel also excavated at Yassi Ada. There was then a number of hybrid forms in the evolution of the skeleton-built ship. Recent excavations in northern Europe have unearthed more examples and ethnologists have found others in south Asia. The presence of edge-joined planks thus can be no guarantee that the vessel was shell-built or for that matter skeleton-built (van Doornick 1972, 140-144; van Doornick 1976, 130-131; Greenhill 1976, 63-70). Hasslöf has found that Dutch shipbuilders practised a combination method of building so it is necessary to explore what the implications for Dutch commercial success may have been from the approach of Dutch shipwrights. At the outset the accuracy of reports on Dutch building methods must be confirmed. If in fact Dutch builders only half-heartedly adopted skeleton building then their choice deserves some explanation. Moreover if the Dutch did use the hybrid approach why did they stick to it so long while all others were fully embracing skeleton building? It seems odd that one group of shipbuilders, especially highly successful ones, should adhere to aspects of an outmoded method. Were they alone in following the compromise system? Most important though is the problem of what effect using the bastard building system had on Dutch technical superiority. Perhaps the information on construction methods can help to explain the low cost of construction in Dutch yards or the speed with which ships were built or the high quality of the products. Perhaps also the building method can help explain why Dutch ship designers so early saw the advantages of specialized design and so early committed themselves to the construction of purpose-built ships.

Some historians of Dutch shipbuilding say nothing about the unique method (Barbour 1930; Crone 1939, 32 and passim; Unger 1978). Historians certainly are fallible and can easily be guilty of oversight but the failure of some to even mention a compromise approach suggests a need to look more closely at the evidence. Information for the unique procedures of Dutch shipcarpenters come from two sources: contemporary descriptions of Dutch shipbuilding by Dutch writers and the reports of French spies sent to Holland by the finance minister of Louis XIV, Jean-Baptiste Colbert. To the first category belong the two great works of the seventeenth century by Nicolaes Witsen and Cornelis van Yk. Witsen was a prominent figure in Amsterdam politics involved in a number of other projects while working on his Aeloude en Hedendaegze Scheeps bouw en Bestier which first appeared in 1671. The 1690 edition with another title was slightly expanded. While he himself knew little of shipbuilding he reported what experts told him. Witsen knew what skeleton building was. He described the procedure exactly in a discussion of shipbuilding in 1520. He copied the information from a Portugese text, a manuscript which was at his own university at Leiden. When it came to building ships in his own day Witsen did not say that frames went up first and then the planks were added. He said just the opposite. After setting out the names of all the pieces that go to make up a ship he laid down the steps for building a warship of 134 feet. The procedure at the start was exactly what one would expect for skeleton building with the keel laid down first followed by the stem- and sternposts and the transom. At that point Witsen says that the garboard strakes are to be fitted into the rabbet of the keel. Then the bottom of the ship is to be built out to the bilges. Then come the frames followed by the ribbands. Once the frames are complete up to deck level then the rest of the hull planking is to go into place (van Beylen 1970, 15-21, Witsen 1690, 88-89, 164-165). Cornelis van Yk was a professional shipcarpenter who had been practicing his trade since the age of 12. His book is more systematic and concrete than Witsen's and deals more extensively with contemporary shipbuilding. His description is similar to that of Witsen. After keel and posts the ship got a complete midship frame. Then the bottom was laid down, gradually rising up to the bilges. After that two ribbands were put in place and two more ribs built. Then a series of ribbands was stretched from post to post over the three ribs. The remaining ribs were built up from their constituent parts inside the ribbands. After that the keelson, a heavy timber fitting over the ribs and sitting on top of the keel, was lowered into place. Only then was hull planking added (van Beylen 1970, 19-20, 38-39; van Yk 1697, 67-78).

Neither Witsen nor van Yk thought building the floor first was odd. The Swedish writer Åke Rålamb in a collection of prints with explanations published in 1691 shows a ship under construction with the floor in place but with only one rib erected. He said it was a Dutch fluit being built with klampar. The bottom planks were fitted edge-to-edge but were never attached directly to each other so they needed some support to hold them in place until all the floor timbers had been fitted. Rålamb shows some small blocks of wood, the klampar, presumably temporarily nailed to connect the planks. Hasslöf found an example of a yawl built at Stavern in Friesland in 1955 in exactly that way with the entire exterior shell built up before the frames were inserted. Once the hull planks were firmly nailed to the frames then the small blocks were removed (Greenhill 1976, 66, 71-72; Hasslöf 1972,

52-53; Hasslöf 1963, 166; Rålamb 1691, 34-44; Timmermann 1979, 26-27). While the Frisian example is an interesting one it is not obvious that there is a direct connection to the method shown by Rålamb or the procedures outlined by Witsen and van Yk. A Dutch artist, Sieuwert van der Meulen, in the second of a series of 16 prints from the early eighteenth century shows a ship under construction. In this, the first stage of building the hull, there are no ribs: only keel, posts and bottom planks. Those planks are held in place by props on the ground, by clamps and blocks of wood most of which are small (De Groot and Vorstman 1980, 139). It is odd that neither Witsen nor van Yk explained how the floor was to be held in place. They did not see it as a problem worth consideration which perhaps suggests use of small blocks, also called klötzchen, knapper, knab, knaben, was at least not common on seventeenth century Dutch wharves. Above all though even if little blocks were used the attachment of the exterior planks of the floor to each other was purely temporary. Though part of the shell was built first it was not a case of shellbuilding.

The three spies Colbert sent to Holland in 1669, 1670 and 1671 included a well-trained shipbuilder, the son and ultimate successor of the chief naval administrator at Marseilles and Colbert's own son, presumably an experienced administrator with a promising future. Each went off with copious directions from Colbert on exactly what they were to do and find out. Each went both to Holland and to England. Each was to compare building methods in those two countries with those in France. Their first job above all was to find out proportions, the major dimensions of ships of all types but especially warships. Arnoul was the son of the Marseilles intendent des galères and the future administrator at Marseilles. He had also made a trip to Italy to examine shipbuilding practice there. Seignelay was Colbert's son. Both remarked on the quaint Dutch method of building the bottoms of their ships first. The Dutch, so they said, after laying the keel laid planks, ten or twelve of them, and then cut the ribs to fit those planks (Clément 1864-1865, 3, part 1, 211, 234-237, part 2, 296-300, 329; Colenbrander 1919, 12; Hasslöf 1972, 59-60, Hasslöf 1963, 170). Both observers contrasted the Dutch method with common practice in England and France. It is perhaps significant that at the end of the seventeenth century despite his close association with Dutch shipbuilding in part through his friend Witsen, Peter the Great still found Dutch methods backward compared to English ones. The compromise procedure as described by the two French agents may be what the Tsar of Russia had in mind. The Frenchmen reported on practice in the Amsterdam admiralty exclusively. Obviously the Dutch were very open to these emissaries and more than willing to share information with them. The Dutch may well have been trying to impress the French officials in the hope of getting another lucrative contract to build warships like the one for six such vessels won by Amsterdam and Zaandam shipcarpenters in 1666 (van Dillen 1974, nos. 1563, 1565-1568, 1570, 1571, 1574). It is doubtful that Arnoul and Seignelay were misinformed or for that matter that their observations applied only to warships. After all Witsen and van Yk talked about building the bottoms first and did not distinguish between warships and other types.

Bestekken or building contracts suggest that the bottoms of ships could have been built first. In two such agreements from the late sixteenth century for fishing vessels the descriptions of keel, posts, transom and the thickness of the bottom planks come in that order before the details about the frames. Van Yk reprints in full some typical contracts and they follow a similar progression from keel to posts to bottom to bilges to frames. On the other hand a 1640 bestek from Amsterdam for a ship with a full transom

157

goes from keel through posts to frames in all their parts and only then is mention made of any part of the hull planking (AA, no. 126 (1567), no. 127 (1598); van Dillen 1974, no. 497; van Yk 1697, 308-315). Of course there is no guarantee that shipbuilders proceeded in the order laid down in the bestek. It was a contract to establish the dimensions of the final product and not necessarily how the builder was to go about producing that result.

Accounts of building ships do not typically say anything about the compromise method. If the method was so odd and out of step with practice elsewhere it seems logical to expect that more notice would have been taken. No matter the approach the design was based on the shape of the central frame. It was drawing a precise outline of that frame which was the designer's most important task. Rembrandt's shipbuilder, a portrait which includes the man's wife done about 1633, was absorbed exclusively with the drawing of frames. Government officials interested in intelligence about shipbuilding like Colbert in France and Pepys in England had many questions but they did not ask about the process of building. They did not see such information as important or perhaps simply assumed that there were no differences. Thus when remarks about the building method do appear they are incidental and almost off hand (Bredius 1969, 322, Br. 408; Clement 1864-1865, for example 3, part 1, 211; Colenbrander 1919, 2, 2-7). Archaeology is not likely to produce evidence on which part went up first. Both approaches produced almost exactly the same final product. With true shell construction with frames added after the hull was in place the frames had to be notched, cut to fit precisely inside the hull planks. Wrecks of clinker-built vessels in the Ijsselmeerpolders show such notching of the frames (IJ Wreck NOP, J 137 for example). With bottom planks already in place before building in the floor timbers some extra care had to be shown in shaping the parts of the ribs but there was no dramatic difference with the floors. Any difficulty was minor. The bottom was flat and, if Witsen's advice was followed, checked with a level. Moreover the frames were built up from a number of different parts so only the floor timber fit over the planks already in place. That piece was supposed to be flat as well.

It appears that Dutch shipwrights did lay down the bottom planks first before putting up the frames with the exception of the midship one. However it is not certain that they did it for all types or at all times or in all yards. Witsen did not seem to care which job was done first. He said that the progression was really not critical and suggested that builders should proceed as they saw best. Van Yk in one case shows a small vessel under construction with the frames all up but no exterior planks in place as yet. Rålamb on the same plate as the Dutch fluit shows other ships under construction with frames up first before any of the bottom planks were laid down (Rålamb 1691, plate 1; van Yk 1697, 90, Witsen 1690, 164). Rålamb's illustration suggests that Dutch practice was considered unique and not imitated in Sweden.

Dutch shipcarpenters may have had good reason to adopt a compromise method. As in all other parts of northern Europe the skeleton system had to be imported. The first instance of building in the Mediterranean style in the Netherlands dates from 1439. The Duke of Burgundy had two vessels built for him near Brussels but needed to import Portuguese shipwrights for the job. It was 1460 before any shipcarpenters in the provinces which would become the Dutch Republic tried skeleton building. Zierikzee builders tried to construct a big seagoing ship but could not handle such a large task so a Breton shipcarpenter had to be brought in to show them how to do it. It is not clear how quickly Dutch builders went over to the new techniques. The advantages of skeleton building were greater on larger ships and Dutch yards tended to turn out few big ships especially through the first half of the sixteenth century (GAZ Register op de Charters der Stad Zierikzee, no. 224; van Beylen 1970, 7-8; van Cortgene 1551, 190). Certainly Dutch shipcarpenters did gain the skill to build in the new style but at the same time they carried on with old methods. The excavated wrecks from the Ijsselmeerpolders confirm the survival of clinker-building through the sixteenth and the seventeenth centuries. There were signs of conservatism among Dutch shipbuilders, of a reluctance to plunge into something radically new. But that is certainly not surprising especially since the costs of failure were so high (IJ Wrecks NOP 028 and P33 for example; Unger 1978, 28).

Dutch carpenters had an example of building a flat floor out to the bilges before proceeding with the rest of the ship. The cog, perhaps descended from a Celtic type, was the most important cargo ship in northern Europe in the high Middle Ages. It apparently always had a flat floor with planks fitted edge-to-edge but with overlapping planking on the sides. There is no question that the cog was shell-built. Netherlands shipwrights built such vessels from the early Christian era at least down through the nineteenth century. In the course of the seventeenth century the clinkered sides were changed to having the edges of the planks abuting but the essential form remained the same. The tjalk may have been descended from the earlier cog (IJ Wrecks NOP M40 and M93 for example; van Beylen 1970, 163-165; Greenhill 1976, 69-70, 259). Dutch shipcarpenters mastered the building of a flat bottom first long before they ever tried building with the skeleton method. When they faced the problem of how to proceed with the new imported method it would have been easiest to begin in a familiar way especially for the cog, tjalk, and other related types. Also Dutch ships continued to have flat or nearly flat bottoms throughout the seventeenth century even on the largest of ships so the analogy with the cog was a strong one. All observers mentioned the square section of Dutch ships, the sharp angle of the bilges, the almost flat floor. The box-like shape of the hold had advantages in increasing carrying capacity in cargo ships. Dutch designers built warships with the same form. The explanation always offered for the flat bottoms of Dutch ships was the shallow harbours in Holland and Zeeland. There were other advantages to the design besides not running aground when approaching a Dutch port. Dutch ships rolled less, especially important when firing cannon in battle (Clément 1864-1865, 3, part 1, 336-337, part 2, 304-305; Colenbrander 1919, 2, 12-13; Crone 1939, 35, 167-169). Whatever the reasons for the flat bottoms of Dutch ships and whatever the advantages certainly if the bottom was flat it was a much simpler process to build the bottom first before the ribs.

It is not possible to say, at least at the moment, how long Dutch shipbuilders adhered to their way of combining building styles. It is difficult to find any evidence for builders abandoning the bastard system in the late seventeenth or eighteenth centuries. The Dutch shipbuilding industry declined and all but collapsed in the eighteenth century. There was a general stagnation in Dutch trade and a drop in orders for new ships at home and especially abroad. There is strong evidence that Dutch technical superiority had been eclipsed and that Dutch builders lagged seriously behind others in Europe. Under those conditions it is hard to say whether Dutch building methods changed. Efforts were made to improve the poor state of the Dutch industry through bringing in foreign, specifically English, shipwrights to improve the competence of native builders. Contemporaries wrote books about the decline of Dutch shipbuilding and suggested ways to recoup lost ground (Anderson 1947, 218-225; van Beylen 1970, 30-31, Bruijn 1972, 18-24; Unger 1978, 42-45, 60-62; van Yk 1697, 19-21). It may well be that under pressure to modernize, to change and follow practice in England and France that Dutch builders in the eighteenth century abandoned the building of the bottoms of their ships first. Just as authors largely ignored the compromise method in the seventeenth they failed to mention any change in the eighteenth. It was much less likely for authors to say how ships were built in the eighteenth century since writers turned away from being pragmatic to being rather more theoretical. The increasing number of books on shipbuilding were written to teach shipbuilders how to become designers using compasses to draw out the shape of the ship. Even in 1586 when the master shipwright of Queen Elizabeth I of England, Mathew Baker, put together his "Fragments of English Shipwrightry" he was trying to reduce the job of ship design to drawing a proper frame or frames (Baker 1585). By the eighteenth century the effort to exploit the burgeoning knowledge of mathematics and physics made books on ship-building catalogues of proportions with tables and information on doing certain types of calculations. Officials at the highest levels wanted research done on how to use mechanics and geometry to aid shipbuilding. Scholars obliged them. The resulting books would and did have a great impact in the long run. But they say little about what shipcarpenters thought in the eighteenth century and even less about what they in fact did. Witsen had included a description of how to build a ship and he implied that builders could have too many rules to follow. In the eighteenth century such scepticism about the value of the new scientific knowledge for shipbuilders was completely drowned out (Bushnell 1664; Duhamel Du Monceau 1752; Hasslöf 1963, 175; Murray 1754; Sutherland 1711; Timmerman 1963, 19-27; Witsen 1690, 223). The lack of evidence of the use of bottom-first construction then does not prove that it was not practised. Johann Röding in his marine dictionary published in 1793 mentioned the small blocks of wood used temporarily to hold planks in place but there is not the slightest suggestion that they were to be used in the construction of the hull (Röding 1793, "knapen"). He is incorrect in translating the word into English as "forelock".

It would seem very odd that only the Dutch built their ships bottom first. If the origin of the method was building cogs then all German and Scandinavian shipwrights should have followed the compromise path. Also if Dutch builders used the method they presumably took it with them when they went off to other parts of Europe. Dutch shipcarpenters by the end of the sixteenth century were in great demand because of their superior skills. They were hired away by foreign governments, most notably by the Swedish crown for the building of warships such as the Vasa, and presumably they built in the same style abroad as they did at home (Baasch 1899, 11-12, 213; van Dillen 1974, 2, no. 1368, 3, no. 946, 1312-1313, 1316, 1637). It is certain that Dutch builders did not successively introduce bottom-first construction into every country where they worked. France is the most important and obvious example. Colbert hired large numbers of Dutch shipwrights to work in naval yards (Barbour 1930, 274; Clément 1864-1865, 3, part 1, 132-133, 199-200, 211; van Dillen 1974, 3, no. 40, 1683). The agents sent from those same French naval shipyards to Holland were amazed when the saw carpenters laying down the bottom before putting up the frames so their imported Dutch carpenters obviously did not use the bastard method when they got to France.

If the Dutch were indeed alone in building in their different way then the method itself may have imparted some real basis for the superiority of Dutch shipbuilding. But the case for explaining Dutch dominance of seventeenth century shipbuilding by their building method is not a strong one. It was certainly easier for Dutch shipcarpenters to adopt the compromise method. The transition from the old shell technique to the revoluntionary skeleton one would have been made simpler, less dramatic. But the gain would have been only a short term one. Over the long period of two or three centuries Dutch builders could have comfortably taken the next step toward building completely in the Mediterranean fashion as did so many others in western Europe. For most design practices it was really unimportant in which progression the job was done. Dutch shipbuilding gained advantages from having standardized parts for their vessels. But such standardization was practical, effective and cost-saving in any building method. There was no difference in the type or quality of wood used for building in the compromise or pure skeleton method. The Dutch were free to use lower qualities of wood and to use them more economically no matter which progression they followed. It may well be that the bottom of a ship where the planks were fitted edge-to-edge first was more watertight than one where planks were tacked onto the frames after the timbers had been erected. More important though to watertightness was the skill of and execution by the shipcarpenter. No matter which method was used the bottom of the ship still had to be caulked. It was said that Dutch builders were very good at cutting their ships in half and lengthening them by inserting new ribs between the old halves (Colenbrander 1919, 2, 14). But what made that easy was the flat floor typical of Dutch vessels and not the way in which the bottom was built. The skills required of shipcarpenters were much the same with both methods. It may be that having the men fit the bottom planks first required more effort. Greater precision may have been needed to get the planks to fit exactly but a good deal of precision was needed with the other approach too. It appears that teaching carpenters was much the same no matter the method. So with training as with most other aspects laying the bottom first meant little advantage to Dutch shipbuilders.

There were some ways that made the Dutch method technically better, ways noticed by contemporaries. There was greater flexibility in the design of the ship once building was underway. If the frames went up first their shape irrevocably established the form of the hull. But in the compromise method the shape of the hull could be adjusted while the bottom was being laid or even after it was completed. The timbers were cut to fit the planking already there, the planking serving as something of a mould to dictate the shape of the lowest member of the frame. The basic design was of course determined by the length of the keel, the curve of the posts and the curve of the midship frame. That was true no matter the approach. But once that was done if the frames went up followed by the ribbands there was no room for change by the builder. Dutch designers then worked more by eye than by theory. They saw what the ship would look like once the bottom was in place and then had carpenters shape the rest of the frames to fit the bottom (Hasslöf 1972, 59–60; Hasslöf 1963, 170). Building the bottom first decreased the number of errors in design. That made it easier to train the designers of ships, the chiefs of the shipbuilding yards, since they did not have to have the same command of theory and of mathematics as designers in France or England. Presumably there was less need to make changes or adjustments once the ship was launched. Adding extra timber to improve sailing qualities was a common practice in the seventeenth century once the crankness of a ship had been determined on a shakedown cruise. If indeed the compromise method made Dutch designers surer of their products then the approach they took to design may in fact have helped them to produce ships quickly and to produce reliable ones. They may also have found themselves better able to estimate the draught of a ship before it left the ways. That was a critical skill in the Low Countries. Not until the eighteenth century could designers reliably predict how much a ship would draw using the new scientific approach so again Dutch shipbuilders may have been better off (Perrin 1918, lxx-lxxiv; Timmerman 1963, 15-16; Witsen 1690, 302-309). The Dutch drive toward specialized design began with the herring buss in the fifteenth century which had a flat bottom. It also had a high ratio of length to breadth. The compromise method could have been easily practised and probably was on the buss. The <u>fluit</u> design grew out of experiments with the buss and it too had a flat or nearly flat bottom. It is easy to see how the compromise approach could have been carried over from one design to the other in the process of specialization. But Dutch designers appear to have used their unique method on many different types of vessels. Warships got the same treatment as fishing boats, cargo ships and inland craft. So for the critical question of design specialization it appears that choosing to build the bottom first before the frames had little if any immediate effect.

Though it would be helpful to have more substantiating evidence still it seems likely that Hasslöf and Timmerman are right. Dutch builders in the seventeenth century probably did build part of the shell of their vessels first, just to the bilges, before they put up the frames. However they were unquestionably still practising skeleton construction. The strength of the vessel came entirely from the internal frames. The planks on the bottom were certainly fitted edge-to-edge but never edge-joined as would be the case in pure shell construction. The principal conclusion which Hasslöf draws from his examination of building techniques can not be disputed. The shift from shell to skeleton construction in northern Europe was not a single event, not one revolutionary change but rather a gradual process with many intermediate steps. In fact it may well be that there was not even an evolution at all but simply borrowing from different traditions as builders tried to find the most practical and effective way to build their boats (Greenhill 1976, 70-72, 91-95, 294). But there are still some matters that are uncertain. It is not clear how common it was for builders in the Dutch Republic or for that matter in all of northern Europe to build the bottom of their vessels first or if they used that approach only for certain types or sizes of ships. It is also unclear how long the method survived in the Netherlands.

The effect of the Dutch choice of building method on their commitment to design specialization seems to have been minimal. While there were some possible savings to be reaped from putting down the bottom first in the training of designers and avoiding mistakes in construction those savings do not appear to have been great enough to explain the massive success of the Dutch shipbuilding and in turn the shipping industry in the seventeenth century. The strengths of Dutch ships and of the industry which produced them seem to have come from other sources. On the other hand the choice by Dutch shipcarpenters to retain some of the older ways of doing things, to rely on past practice does not appear to have inhibited the industry in any way. The way Dutch designers and builders put together the most profitable ships of the seventeenth century is certainly of great importance to the history of shipbuilding. The choices which those men made indicate clearly that in general and in seventeenth century industry in particular techniques changed only gradually. Maritime ethnology has proven a valuable tool in documenting the slow and often tentative adoption of new technology. However it appears that, until further information about the value of the compromise approach or the prevalence of that approach becomes available, it will be from the well-known older explanations that the reasons for Dutch commercial and industrial success in the seventeenth century will come.

REFERENCES

A.A., Archief van Adrichen, Algemeen Rijksarchief, The Hague.

Anderson, R.C., 1947. Eighteenth Century Books on Shipbuilding, The Mariner's Mirror 33 (1947), 218-225.

Baasch, E., 1899. Beiträge zur Geschichte des deutschen Seeschiffbaues und der Schiffbaupolitik.

Baker, M., 1585. Fragments of English Shipwightry, Magdalene College, Cambridge University, Pepys Library, 2820.

Barbour, V., 1950. Capitalism in Amsterdam in the 17th Century.

Barbour, V., 1930. Dutch and English Merchant Shipping in the Seventeenth Century, Economic History Review 2, 261-290.

van Beylen, J., 1970. Schepen van de Netherlanden Van de late middeleeuwen tot het einde van de 17e eeuw.

Bredius, A., 1969. Rembrandt, The Complete Edition of the Paintings, rev. H. Gerson.

Bruijn, J.R., 1972. Engelse scheepsbouwers op de Amsterdamse Admiraliteirtswerf in de achttiende eeuw: enige aspecten, Mededelingen van de Nederlandse Vereniging voor Zeegeschiedenis 25, 18-24.

Clément, P., ed., 1864-1865. Lettres, Instructions et Mémoires de Colbert.

Colenbrander, H.T., ed., 1919. Bescheiden uit Vreemde Archieven omtrent De Groote Nederlandsche Zeeoorlogen 1652-1676.

van Cortgene, J.R., 1551. Dye Cronucke van Zeeland.

Crone, G.C.E., 1939. Onze Schepen in de Gouden Eeuw.

De Groot, I. & Vorstman, R., 1980. Sailing Ships Prints by the Dutch Masters from the sixteenth to the nineteenth century (trans. M. Hoyle).

van Dillen, J.G., ed., 1974. Bronnen tot de Geschiedensis van het Bedrijfsleven en Gildewezen van Amsterdam, vol. 3, 1633-1672.

van Doornick, F., 1972. Byzantium mistress of the sea: 330-641, in A History of Seafaring based on Underwater Archaeology (ed. G. Bass), 133-158.

van Doornick, F., 1976. The 4th century wreck at Yassi Ada. An interim report on the hull, The International Journal of Nautical Archaeology and Underwater Exploration 5, 115-131.

Duhamel Du Monceau, J.R., 1972. Elémens de l'architecture navale.

GAZ, Gemeente Archief Zierikzee, Register op de Charters der Stad Zierikzee.

Greenhill, B., 1976. Archaeology of the Boat. A new introductory study.

Hasslöf, O., 1972. Main Principles in the Technology of Ship-Building, in Ships and Shipyards Sailors and Fishermen, Introduction to Maritime Ethnology (eds. O. Hasslöf, H. Henningsen, A.E. Christensen Jr.), 27-72.

Hasslöf, O., 1963. Wrecks, Archives and Living Traditions, The Mariner's Mirror 49, 162-177.

IJ, Ijsselmeerpolder Wrecks.

Murray, M., 1754. A Treatise on Ship-Building and Navigation.

Perrin, W.G., 1918. Introduction, in The Autobiography of Phineas Pett, xv-civ.

Rålamb, Å., 1691. Skepps Byggerij eller Adelig Öfnings Tionde Tom.

Röding, J.H., 1793. Allgemeines Wörterbuch der Marine in Allen Europaeischen Seesprachen nebst Vollstaendigen Erklaerungen.

Sutherland, W., 1711. Britain's Glory or, Ship-Building Unvail'd.

Timmerman, G., 1963. Das Eindringen der Naturwissenschaft in das Schiffbauhandwerk, Deutsches Museum, Abhandlungen und Berichte, 30, 5.53.

Timmerman, G., 1979. Die Suche nach der günstigsten Schiffsform, Schriften des Deutshcen Schiffahrtsmuseums, 11.

Unger, R.W., 1981. Warships and Cargo Ships in Medieval Europe, Technology and Culture 22, 233-252.

15. VISTULA CARGO-SHIPS FROM THE XVI-XVIII CENTURIES

Przemysław Smolarek

Polish boat-building and the ships it produced belong to the problems which are almost completely unknown in European literature on the subject. The aim of this article is to give a concise presentation of one specific subject, namely the types of Polish merchant river vessels from the 16th to 18th centuries. This is undoubtedly a narrow topic, if it is restricted to only one period in history and one group of ships, but such a choice is, I think, justified for two reasons. Firstly, there were ships which were typical of Vistula shipping during the period of its particularly intensive and at the same time very specific, "Polish" stage of development. Secondly, the types of ships mentioned illustrate features characteristic of native, Polish river craft in all the periods of their evolution. In this sense they might, I trust, give a certain, general view of former Polish boat-building.

Splaw shipping, its origin and character

The geographic discoveries of the close of the 15th and beginning of the 16th centuries with their concomitant economic-social phenomena, led to changes in relations in European shipping. The era of the Hansa hegemony was receding into history. The centre of gravity of trade turnovers shifted to ports situated on the Atlantic coasts. The transformations already taking place in European economy: in the West – urban development (the "demographic explosion" in the towns) and industrialization (at the expense of agriculture in Holland and England), whereas some countries regressed in their agrarian economy – intensified and increased to a growing degree, the demand for agriculturaland forest products.

The Kingdom of Poland became the main supplier of these products and many raw materials for industry, thus gaining the name of "the grainery of Europe and timber-yard for the needs of shipbuilding". Contemporary Poland boasted every predisposition to fulfil just such a role. It stretched out over a tremendous area of about million km² from Miedzyrzecz in the west, to Smolensk in the east and from the Baltic in the north to the Black Sea in the south (Fig. 15.1). Within its boundaries could be found both regions with extremely fertile soils and immeasurable and primaeval forests affording excellent raw material for boat-building. Even by the 13th century, timber and forest products were being exported from these forests. These exports gradually increased. Exports of grain, also recorded in source materials fairly early, increased successively with the growing demand abroad. Initially, this was of lesser importance than the export of forest products, but the proportions underwent a change about the middle of the 15th century. In this period, Poland's agriculture entered into a stage of intensive development, expressed in a great increase in production; this enabled the export of agricultural and stock-breeding products on a great scale. Towards the close of the 15th century, grain occupied first place on the list of goods exported from Poland.

The rivers – on which shipping and rafting had been practised from time immemorable – constituted the main export routes for Polish agricultural and forest products.   In view of the character of the cargoes, river transport was – considering the state of the roads and possibilities of carriage overland – the most convenient and cheapest means of carriage. Moreover, carriage by water was favoured owing to a well-developed network of great waterways flowing down to the Baltic (Fig. 15.1).

From all regions of the extensive kingdom, goods were carried down these rivers to the Baltic ports: down the Dzwina to Riga, the Niemen to Krolewiec, the Warta and Odra to Szczecin, but the main traffic was along the Vistula to Gdansk.   In the 16th – 18th centuries, about 3/4 of Poland's exports and about 2/3 of her imports passed through Gdansk.

In the Baltic ports, the cargoes were transferred to sea-going vessels, mainly Dutch, as they had taken the place of the Hansa in Baltic trade.   It is probably worth recalling that in 1671, de Witt stated that "the grain trade with the Baltic constitutes the source and roots of the Netherlands' greatest trade and shipping".   In effect, about 2/3 of the active capital in Amsterdam, in about 1660, was engaged in this trade.

Dutch ships predominated among those calling at Gdansk.   At the same time – let us note – towards the close of the 16th century, about 50-75% of all the ships passing from the west to the Baltic via the Sound were destined for Gdansk.   In consequence, at the turn of the 16th/17th centuries, almost 2/3 of the Baltic trade was concentrated in the port on the River Motɬawa.

It could thus be said that a kind of great grain route had formed; its one branch was formed by Poland's water-ways and the other – the Dutch sea routes.   This period was that in which Poland's river shipping was at its prime.

Who was the main representative and organizer of this shipping at the time?

This excellent economic situation was put to good use by the Polish nobility which dominated the state authorities and to which the remaining social classes were subordinated.   By means of the Sejm (Parliament), the nobles laid down the laws, including those concerning trade, shipping and customs duties.   Ensuring themselves freedom of shipping on the "navigable rivers" by law, they were able to force the professional merchants and carriers who had previously predominated on the Vistula, into the background.

The nobles were landowners for whom the peasants worked as serf labour; they thus had at their disposal the agricultural products which consitituted the basis of goods shipped to Gdansk.   The serfs carted grain to the granaries at the landing-stages (the majority of the ports also belonged to the nobles).   For the purpose of transporting the grain, the nobles built – of wood from their own forests – ships suitable for their needs.   The villeins constituted the crews of these ships.

In Poland, the period from the 16th to 18th centuries might be called the era of "gentry shipping".   In Polish literature, however, it bears a more adequate, but difficult to translate, name – spɬaw shipping, spɬaw meaning to drift, float, or ship a cargo downstream.

As mentioned, the Vistula was the main waterway for this shipping. With its tributaries, it covered a hinterland of about 200,000 km^2, the landing stages and ports being situated along these rivers. Products were brought in not only from the nearby regions, but even from more distant provinces, e.g. Volhynia, Podolia and the Ukraine. The goods were carried in stages along roads often stretching over 300 km, before reaching the ports, in summer in long caravans of carts, in winter, on sleighs.

The shipping season on the Vistula lasted from March to November. The first ships set off along the route from the landing stages at the beginning of spring, at high water. To give some idea of the traffic, I shall mention, that in the first half of the 16th century, about 1,000 ships sailed down the Vistula to Gdansk annually. In 1555 a total of 1,669 ships passed through the customs office at Włocławek, 2,000 river boats were recorded at Gdansk in 1729, whereas 1,878 in 1793. The largest number of river boats to call at Gdansk was 2,222 (in 1751). There were fewer, on average, but these figures give some idea as to the extent of boat production inland.

It is now time to pass on to the real subject of the article; let us therefore introduce the most important types of ships built to serve Vistula shipping in the 16th – 18th centuries.

Types of ships used in spław shipping

First, however, several general comments. Genetically, Polish inland waterways' craft originate from two basic prototypes; the dugout and the raft. During the centuries preceding the period under consideration, they underwent an evolution in which the development, first of the dugout and raft themselves and their mutual influence, then the evolution and mutual influence of the boats and ships originating from these prototypes, can be traced.

Such factors as, the character of the water conditions, abundance of boatbuilding materials, level of technology, organizational forms of the river shipping and the kind of transport requirements in particular stages of its development, had an essential influence on the silhouette and construction of the gradually developing merchant ships. The effect of these can be seen in each consecutive stage of development of the Vistula ships. I am sure that our readers will have no difficulty in distinguishing the influence of these factors also on the types of Vistula ships from the 16th – 18th centuries.

Undergoing a specified evolution, the indigenous types of Vistula ships did, after all, throughout their whole history, retain their basic distinguishing features, particular to floating craft in the Polish cultural area.

The specifics of these types would, undoubtedly be more distinct, if it was possible, here, to compare them, with those characteristic of the neighbouring rivers, e.g. the ships used on the Elbe, Odra, with the wiciny of the Niemen, or strugi of the Dzwina, not to speak of craft typical of the rivers running down to the Black Sea.

167

Rafts

As mentioned, timber, was one of the main goods exported from the Polish Commonwealth. It was floated down rivers in rafts.

The form and construction of the raft depended upon the type of timber to be floated and the period in history. The manner of lashing differed e.g. for coniferous round timber, baulks, oak beams or staves and split logs (Fig. 15.2).

Those rafts did, however, have certain mutual features. Their basic form was the so-called plenica, or set of several logs arranged side by side and lashed together. The basic element of the transverse lashing constituted ramiona ("arms") or cross-timbers placed at each end of the raft.

The manner in which these cross-timbers were tied or fastened to the logs or balks, depended upon the sort of wood of which the raft was built.

Thus oak beams were tied to the cross-timber by means of so-called kołacze, i.e. ropes of twisted oak twigs.

In the case of a plenica consisting of baulks, these were joined to the cross-timbers by means of wooden pegs.

A plenica of round timbers consisted of from several to 20 logs, always arranged with the younger (narrower) end pointing down river, hence they were trapezoid in shape (Fig. 15.8). These were lashed as follows: holes were burnt (later bored) in each log lying under the "arm", on each side of the cross-timber. This enabled each log to be lashed to the cross-timber with oak withes (so-called chluby). The lashing was then strengthened by fitting wooden pegs into the holes.

Several plenicas arranged one behind the other and bound together with withies and special wooden crooks (so-called rykiels) formed a pas ("belt"). This might consist of several, e.g. 3-5 plenicas. Each of these boasted its own name: the first was the głowa ("head"), the second the zagłowek ("behind the head"), the third the buchta, the fourth przedcal and the last the cal. The rule observed was that each plenica be wider than the one preceding, in consequence of which, the last (the cal) should be half as wide again as the "head".

In turn, two "belts" placed side by side and joined together, formed a płta (this will further be called a "big raft"). In such a "big raft", the left "belt" was called the "Gdansk belt" and the right - the "Torun belt". Two adjacent plenicas of neighbouring "belts" formed a glen.

For the needs of the raftsmen, each raft had a buda i.e. a simple hut of boards or dry twigs, often with a straw roof, also a second, better built, called the skarbowka ("lordly"), which had accommodation for the writer and a food store. Meals were cooked in the "kitchen", which was, in fact, a hearth built of bricks and clay and which was sheltered by a portable plaited fence (Fig. 15.3).

The "big rafts" drifted down river with the current, without any special propulsion - either oars or sails.

In view of the numerous shallows, shoals and underwater obstacles in the river, also the length of the raft, its weight and poor manoeuvrability, a fast-moving "big raft" could easily strike an obstacle. So-called opławas, igielniks, zastrzałas and zagratowniks were used to protect the rafts against impacts along the side. These were massive beams loosely tied to the "head" and other units of the rafts by means of ropes. The beams also facilitated the movement of the rafts, stopping water from entering at the side between, e.g. the first and second units etc., (Fig. 15.3).

Drygawkas served to maintain the "big rafts" in the main stream of the river. The drygawkas were hefty poles 11.50 – 14.50 m. long, similar to huge oars with relatively narrow blades, set at the head and after part of the raft (Fig. 15.3), one on each "belt", thus two forward and two aft. They rested on siodło ("saddle") and moved between wooden pins. The siodło was a naturally bent semicircular curve, attached to the first and last of the cross-timber, convex part upwards, into which the pins were driven, in turn.

If the stream was too slow, or the river was shallow, long poles called laski ("sticks") terminating in ferrules were used to pole the rafts; where it was necessary to stop the rafts this could be carried out in two ways: by means of a grot or sryk.

The "big rafts" usually set out in the spring or autumn, when the water in the rivers was at its highest. They usually travelled "en masse", forming a so-called kolej ("train").

At the head of such a group of rafts (kolej) was a pilot (retman) in a dugout, with a pilot-mate (retmanczyk). They were very well acquainted with the river, but the Vistula, unregulated, frequently changed its mainstream. It was thus the task of the pilot to find the most convenient channel in the particular year and month. His experience enabled him to "feel" the river, he was able to estimate the depth from some distance, from the course and colour of the water, deftly marking the stream with poles. A specific signal system thus came into being incidentally. For example: a kołbiegany, i.e. straight pole indicated the deep water, a koł łamany or partly fractured pole, warned against danger. If the pilot raised his paddle in his left hand, for example, this meant that the left side of the river was unsafe, whereas striking the water with the paddle at the right side of the dugout indicated that the water was deep on that side. The removal of the pilot's hat and raising it above his head meant that the raft was on a safe course and that following craft could carry on their way.

Rafts could be floated down to Gdansk without cargo, as timber, but they frequently carried forest products such as pitch, wax, tar, potash, etc. The "big rafts", "belts" and single plenicas carring cargo to Gdansk, thus acted not so much as rafts in the sense of floated lumber, as also – or rather – transport craft.

Single rafts were floated along Polish rivers in such a character – as a means of transport – in prehistoric times.

Later, with the development of inland shipping trade, they found increasing application in the carriage of goods down river. In the Middle Ages, when timber and forest products were exported in particular, the use

169

of the raft also as a means of transport could be said to be a natural phenomenon. Literary sources mention that Hungarian copper which had been forwarded in transit through Poland since the Middle Ages, was also carried from the country's southern boundary to the Baltic, along the Dunajec and Vistula on rafts.

In time wider application of simple improvements which enabled the carriage of goods which could not tolerate moisture, on rafts, was introduced. One such improvement was the placing on the rafts, of platforms or floors of planks, on joists. Vertical posts were set up in the corners of this rectangular floor. These enabled the stretching – from post to post – of a planking housing, protecting the floor on all four sides. This was called a kokoszka. The additional lining of the floor with straw matting enabled the carriage, in this chest-like container, of such cargoes as e.g. grain. A raft with similar construction can be seen in Issak van den Blocke's painting from 1609 (Fig. 15.4). This was one of the ways which led to the transformation of the raft into a craft with built-up sides. Another factor favouring such evolution, was the forming of rafts of deal planks, reinforced not only with cross-timbers, but – among other things – with an additional couple of cross-pieces (progi). There were also, of course, other paths which led to the transformation of the raft into a ship, but we shall not discuss these in this article.

The komiega.

One of the types which developed from the raft, was the komiega. It would seem to have appeared, or gained popularity during the period of the great intensification of exports of agricultural products from Poland. In the 16th century, written sources still contained the expressions: strues alias comiegi or rates vulgo comiegi.

The komiega resembled the raft – to the end of its days – in many respects: construction, names of particular parts, operation etc. One could say that it was, as it were, a raft, the four sides of which had been built up with planks. Or that the komiega gave the impression of a great floating chest or container for the carriage of grain. The location of the centres in which the komiegas were built would suggest that it might have originated from the river Bug basin; it was, at any rate, popular in this region.

Completely flat-bottomed, it was trapezoid in horizontal projection, similar to the plenica ("single raft"): it was slightly narrower at the "head" than the cal ("stern"). In the 18th century, the komiegas built on the Bug were about 16 - 19.50 m. in length, 7 - 9 m. wide aft and 5 - 7 m. wide at the "head" (Figs. 15.5 and 15.8).

Their loading capacity was substantial, being about 15 to 35 lasts.

The crew of a komiega built on the river Bug consisted of 6 - 9 men and a "foreman". During its trip, a komiega drifted with the current. The crew was distributed similarly to that on the raft: some of the men were positioned in the rear and some forward. They operated the massive drygawkas mentioned in the description of the raft. The main drygawka (located in the fore part) was about 9 m. long, the drygawka calowa (located in the after part) – about 7 m. (Fig. 15.5). The primary task of the crew was to maintain the komiega on its proper course – in other words to steer the craft. If it became necessary to pole the vessel, so-called <u>laski</u> i.e. long, strong sticks terminating in ferrules, were used.

Similar again to the rafts, the <u>komiega</u> was built for a single run down river to Gdansk with grain. On arrival, the craft were sold as building material or firewood. Occasionally the local merchants or carriers purchased them, for their own transport requirements or as port lighters.

After the partitioning of Poland, this type disappeared. Another craft which competed with the <u>komiega</u> to a certain extent, had, in any case, already appeared on the horizon. This was the <u>galar</u>.

The <u>galar</u>.

This type was particularly popular in southern Poland, in the region of the uppper Vistula and its tributaries. Being of very old origin, it would, however, have seemed to have been of local or regional use. Later, when the Vistula <u>spław</u>-shipping first flourished, it occasionally operated as a lighter, accompanying the flotilla of merchant ships.

Its importance in the <u>spław</u> gradually increased, but in the 18th century, until about 1780, the Vistula customs records included entries concerning a small number of <u>galars</u> arriving at Gdansk as independent merchant or trading vessels. With the exception of the years 1748, 1763 and 1764 the number of <u>galars</u> noted as trading craft in the Motława port rose from a few in number to several score (fewer than 100 annually). From the 1780's, however, the number of <u>galars</u> arriving at Gdansk increased distinctly and rapidly; in the 19th century, this type of vessel became the most common river vessel in Poland. One striking fact is that almost simultaneous with the commencement of the successful career of the <u>galars</u>, the <u>komiega</u> suddenly began to disappear, as has been mentioned above.

What were these crafts like, what were their advantages and faults, to what can their widespread popularity be ascribed?

First, it should be mentioned that the <u>galars</u> were different both as regards construction and size. They did, however, boast specific common features which distinguished them from other types. The names of the particular parts of the <u>galar</u> are similar to those of the <u>komiega</u> and raft, e.g. "head", <u>cal</u> etc.).

They were flat, broad and low and - similar to the raft and <u>komiegas</u> - trapezoid in horizontal projection. As compared with the <u>komiega</u> they were longer, narrower and lower. There was also a distinct difference in the "head" and <u>cal</u>, the waist being curved outward (Fig. 15.8).

At the close of the 18th century, i.e. when it began its career in Vistula shipping, the <u>galar</u> was 19-21 m. long, 5.70 m. wide aft, 4.40 m. wide in the fore part and had sides about 0.80 m. high.

The bottom was raised at both ends, the rise in the bow being slightly more prominent. Massive planks of soft-wood were used for the bottom. Elements called <u>progi</u> ("balks") formed the transverse framing. They were made, wherever possible, from naturally-grown bends, the longer horizontal pieces constituting the floor-timbers, whereas the shorter, made up the upright side-frame. These side-frames supported alternatively the starboard or port side. An additional side-frame or knee was sometimes used to strengthen the opposite side of the vessel.

The planking generally consisted of two broad strakes, perpendicular to the bottom, laid edge to edge, occasionally overlapping. The stern part was closed by a flat, upright transom; the bow could also be terminated in the same manner. As a rule, however, the line of the bottom was sloping to the height of the upper sheer. At this height, a strong, transverse beam closed and joined the two sides.

The framing was attached to the bottom and sides by wooden pegs driven in from the outside and wedged from the inside.

A keelson constituting the main longitudinal binding was set on the floor timbers and ran along the ship's axis of symmetry; this was joined to the floors by iron pins.

The bottom and side seams were caulked with moss. After fitting in the strips of moss, the seams were covered with thin slats then held by means of žabki – special nails with two points. The whole ship was then coated with tar or pitch.

The galar was operated by a foreman (przednik) and 4 - 9 men. The name of the types of galars depended upon the number of crew members, e.g. a "six" (szostkowy) or a "nine" (dziewiatkowy). The method of operating a galar was an extension of the system applied on the raft and similar to that on the komiega. This is illustrated in Fig. 15.6, showing a "nine". The drygawka's fit into tholes.

The draught of a galar without cargo was barely 0.10 m. (!). It could carry between 9 and 13 lasts (this was, by the way, the smallest load capacity of all the Polish cargo vessels operated in 18th century Vistula spław shipping). With such a load, the draught of the galar was about 0.74 m. Thus, at maximum load, the bow of the craft rose only a few centimetres, above the surface of the water. (So even in light winds, these craft could be fairly risky to travel in).

The low draught of the craft and its construction indicate that it was designed for specific water and operational conditions. In fulfilling its functions on the upper Vistula, in shallow waters, it was a manifestation of the concrete economic-social situation which arose in the Polish Commonwealth at the time of the partitions and later, under foreign annexation, in the 19th century. It became, namely, a cheap means of transport, adopted by the provincial, indigenous traders, who began to compete with the nobles on the one hand and professional river carriers on the other, along the Vistula route.

The byk.

In the formal sense, the so-called byk/"bull"/constituted the consecutive link in the evolutional chain of the group of craft discussed. In this sense, it could be defined as a transitional stage between the raft-shaped craft and the river-ships sensu strictiore.

In the second half of the 18th century, the byk had a length of about 21 - 24.50 m. Being longer than the komiega and galar, it was simultaneously narrower and higher, with an aft width of about 4.40 m., head width of about 2.50 m., a side height of about 1.28 m.

The load capacity of the byk was from 13 to 20 lasts, the draught at full load being calculated as 0.86 to 0.96 m., that of an empty ship being 0.13 – 0.16 m.

The two ends of the flat bottom of the ship have more distinct rockers than in the galar – particularly forward. The after part continues to be square cut, but the "head" although terminating in a blunt bow – what one might call "bull's forehead", – tends towards narrowing of this part of the hull as can be seen. At the same time, the sides are curved distinctly outward. It can be seen from the illustration (Fig. 15.7), that the high fore constituted successful protection against spray or flooding. It was even topped – similar to the stem of a true ship – by the top of the "head"-frame.

An upperwork for stores, tools and sleeping quarters appeared in the after part. Similar to the raft, this bore the name buda/"hut"/ the names for the bow and stern were also the same as those used on the raft. The cargo occupied the middle and forward part of the craft.

The more elongated shape of the hull, better lines and stern upperworks, favoured the adoption of a different method of operating than on the raft, komiega and galar.

There was a crew of 6 – 12 men, these consisting of oars-men and a steerman, the former being situated only in the fore-part of the ship. As opposed to the men operating the komiega and galar, their task consisted mainly in setting the ship in motion. They rowed in a sitting position, facing away from the direction of travel. The steerman acted as the operator-navigator proper, observing the water channel from the "bridge" /pochoda/, raised in the after-part, athwart the longitudinal axis of the vessel, above the upperworks. The design of the "bridge" enabled the steerman to operate the rudder, which continued to be a drygawka. It was no longer set loose, between pins, but on a strong bolt, driven into the block secured to the aft edge of the upperworks.

The byk could, on occasion, take advantage of the wind as a means of propulsion and even return to its home landing stage from Gdansk.

A second group constituted river vessels sensu strictiore. These included primarily the szkuta, dubas and koza (Fig. 15.9).

Having passed through a long term of evolution, during the period discussed here, these ships gradually formed certain "classes", with characteristic measurements, carriage capacities and number of crew required to operate them.

The table presented here, gives the characteristics of these "classes".

As can be seen, the smallest – the koza – was built in two "classes"; the initial craft was the "eight" and the second larger – the "ten".

The next type, the dubas, was also built in two classes called the "twelve" and the "fourteen".

173

The largest type, the szkuta, was divided into three classes: the "sixteen", the "eighteen" and the "twenty".

As is not difficult to surmise, the names originated from the number of men constituting the crew of oarsmen. Simultaneously, however, the names indicated, as it were automatically, the size and carriage capacity of the given vessel.

On analyzing the Table in greater detail, a certain system and correlation can be perceived in the gradual increase in size and load capacity of the individual types and classes. Let us then just point out that the smallest type included in the Table - the koza-eight, had a length of about 17 m., and could carry from 10 to 13 lasts of cargo. The largest type, on the other hand, the szkuta-twenty, was about 38 m. long and had a cargo capacity of 36 - 38 lasts. Mention should, however, be made of the fact that the Table refers primarily to ships built on the River San, which is a fairly shallow tributary of the upper Vistula. In other regions of the country, particularly on the central and lower Vistula, vessels with a load capacity exceeding 40 lasts were built. The measurements of these units also differed slightly.

From the technical point of view, the szkuta, dubas and koza had certain mutual features. They were thus flat-bottomed, beamy for their length and fairly low. (The widening of the hull was probably one of the features distinguishing the ships built in the grain-exporting era from the earlier versions of the szkuta or dubas). The stern was closed by an upright transom, the bow, on the other hand, being relatively pointed. The maximum width was attained more or less amidships. They were oar-sail propelled and steered by means of a pałakowy rudder, etc. Thanks to their shapes, features and propulsion, these craft could be operated both up and down river.

Having these and other mutual features, these types also differed. Due to shortage of space for a detailed description of and discussion on all the types and classes mentioned, we shall restrict ourselves to a concise presentation of only one type - the szkuta.

The Szkuta.

The ship known in the 16th to 18th centuries as the szkuta, originated from an ancient prototype used on Poland's inland waterways and which, gradually taking shape with the evolution of the Vistula shipping, passed through successive stages of development. Not only did its shape and construction develop, the names of the craft also underwent certain mutations. The oldest source records refer to it under the general name of the "Vistula ship". The Latin texts assumed the name scapha, which finally turned into szkuta in Polish.

According to written and iconographic sources from the 17th to 18th centuries, the szkuta was flat-bottomed, fairly slim and low. In horizontal projection it was spindle-shaped with a truncated stern and pointed bow. Longitudinally, the lines of the bottom and sheer ran parallel. The bottom was raised both forward and aft, the former being greater than the latter. The cross-section was classic in form with straight, flared sides (Fig. 15.10).

174

Type	Clear Length in metres	Breadth in metres	Moulded depth in metres	Draught in metres empty	Draught in metres loaded	Cargo capacity in lasts maximum	Cargo capacity in lasts minimum	No. of crew
Szkuta								
The twenty	37.80	8.19	0.95	0.42	1.05	38	36.67	20
The eighteen	34.02	7.56	0.95	0.38	1.03	36.67	33.33	18
The sixteen	30.24	7.56	0.95	0.34	0.97	32	20	16
Dubas								
The fourteen	28.35	7.25	0.95	0.32	1.05	26.7	20	14
The twelve	24.57	6.93	0.71	0.21	0.84	20	16.67	12
Koza								
The ten	20.79	6.30	0.71	0.21	0.74	16.67	13.33	10
The eight	17.01	5.98	0.71	0.21	0.74	13.33	10	8

The flat bottom was arranged from about 50 massive, broad pine planks each about 11 - 15 m. in length and 5 - 10.5 cm. thick, laid edge to edge. The seams were caulked with so-called zuja, i.e. strips made from animal hair, covered with laths and held in place by means of skobliczki (twin-pointed nails).

Floor-timbers 20 - 31 cm. wide, fitted fairly tightly, fastened to the bottom by means of wedged wooden pegs, later iron nails, constituted the transverse structures. These floor-timbers were made of natural bends, usually oak: the shorter arm of the bend, extending the timber on one side, constituted the side-frame. The extension of the floor-timber onto the opposite side was a so-called kwarek, i.e. knee, also made of naturally curved oak.

The sides of the szkuta were built of overlapping planks, 9.50 - 13 m., in length and about 5 - 8 cm. thick. The first, stronger strake, called the podwalinka ("foundation"), was made of oak, L-shaped in section. Its horizontal part, constituted the outer bottom plank, whereas the upright part constituted the first strake of the planking. The upper strakes were usually of pine. The top strake was thicker at its upper edge or strengthened from the outside by an oak wale. The side was completed by a plank secured flat to the top strake and wale.

The planking was fastened to the frames originally with wooden pegs, then forged iron nails. The strakes were nailed together with rivets about 15 cm. long, with washers on the inside. The seams were caulked with moss from the outside and targan from the inside.

The stern part terminated, as mentioned, in a transom consisting of several, e.g. 4, wide planks 5 - 13 cm. thick. The bow, markedly raised, was bound by an oak stem bent upwards and backwards and stylized.

The main longitudinal bracing of the bottom was a keelson, 15 - 23 m. long and 26 - 52 cm. thick. Another, similar member, with a special casing for the mast-step usually rested on this.

Amidships, beams connecting the sides, running immediately at the mast and simultaneously constituting a support for this, played the function of the main transverse bracing. Similar cross-beams were used to join the sides in the bow. The fore deck was set on such a beam; the crew's quarters were situated below this deck.

A superstructure (buda), with the skipper's cabin, accommodation for possible passengers, food stores and galley, was set up in the stern.

As the whole of the midship part was designed for cargo, the oars-men were situated in the fore part of the craft. In the szkuta-twenty, there were ten on each side. They sat on benches with their backs to the ship's course and worked long oars called pojazdy, which were set in wooden thole-pins.

Oars were usually used on the runs down river, the driving force of the wind being used on the return trip up river.

The 11 - 23-metre pine or fir mast, set in the maststep and held by a clamp or partner, was rigged by a fore-stay (7.8 cm. thick) running from the top to the bow and a so-called obceje (5.2 cm. thick), as well as thinner, one-inch karnaty, running from the top of the mast to the sides of the vessel.

The mast carried a yard 9.5 - 19 m. long, raised and lowered by means of a line called a trarew. A linen sail, leeched at the edges, was tied to the yard by means of robands. The sail was manoeuvred by means of braces and sheets.

The helmsman steered the ship from the "bridge" raised immediately in front of the superstructure or buda. The steering gear was a combination of the stout drygawka and a stern-rudder. A vertical stock, called a słupiec was attached by hooks in the centre line on the transom. Its lower end reached the edge of the hull bottom. At this level, a 15 - 23-metre blade, directed backwards and submerged in the water, was set horizontally in a stock. An element consisting of two parts (the so-called pałak and hamulec) was fixed at a distance from the end of the blade. This element was gently bent in the direction of the ship, towards the helmsman on the "bridge", its two parts being fastened by a rope (Fig. 15.11). Below the fastening, the element was set on the head of the stock, which also gave it the necessary support.

It is not difficult to recognize the drygawka in this element. In the szkuta-type craft, the drygawka was unable to fulfil its role. In view of the numerous shallows in the Vistula and its tributaries, the classical stern-rudder with its blade reaching into the water below the hull, or with a shorter blade, but not reaching sufficiently far back, would also have been unsuitable. Hence the symbiosis of these types, which I have called a pałak-rudder.

During a voyage when the ship was under sail, the cloth might have obscured the helmsman's vision as he moved about the high "bridge". In order to remedy this, he was able to raise the lower, middle part of the sail with a rope called a tryska.

On returning from Gdansk, up river, the wind was not always favourable; and currents could prevent oared-propulsion. It was then necessary to simply tow the vessel against the current. A thick line called a polka served for this purpose. Normally stowed on the fore deck, alongside the capstan and anchor, if required, it was raised by means of an auxiliary line to about half the height of the mast. The oars-men, wearing special braces, walking in file along the river bank, towed the vessel.

Lighters.

When speaking of rafts, I mentioned numerous navigation obstacles on the Vistula and its tributaries.

If a ship grounded, attempts were first made to push it off by means of poles. If this did not help, the men proceeded to 'slamowac', i.e. positioning of another vessel in the current, so that the current would wash away the sand from beneath the grounded vessel.

There were such situations in which the simplest method was to part discharge the cargo. For this purpose, suitable craft usually accompanied the flotillas proceeding down river were used. This could be a special type of auxiliary vessel, a small kozka, galar, or larger plank-built boat.

177

In the 18th century, lighters, i.e. special auxiliary craft, were built with overlapping planks. They were small units, about 5.40 - 10.80 m. long, with a crew of 2 - 4 men. Some of them were simply smaller versions of cargo vessels, while others brought to mind the large types of fishing boats.

The czołno.

Apart from the lighters, the flotillas sailing down to Gdansk also included the hollowed-out czołno. These fulfilled various auxiliary and pilotage functions. As regards the latter, they were described when discussing the raft. Let us then just mention here that the manner of piloting cargo vessels, although - generally speaking - fairly similar, differed slightly from that of the rafts. This resulted, among other things, from the fact that the cargo vessels were faster than the large rafts and easier to control.

The auxiliary functions consisted, among other things, of maintaining, with the help of the czołno, communications, during the trip, between the individual ships of which the flotilla consisted, by sailing up to the river bank or going ashore to settle various matters, without having to hold up all the ships, or directing them to the shore.   In case of accident or emergency, the czołno was used to bring assistance from nearby villages, etc.

Such czołnos or log-boats were usually made of pine, poplar and sometimes but rarely, beech or oak. They were made by hollowing-out, or sometimes hollowing-out and scorching trunks. The shapes differed locally. Generally speaking, they resembled the log from which they had been made - they were thus long, narrow and low, narrower to the fore.

They were more or less flat in cross-section, in some cases slightly rounded.   The sides were usually straight, perpendicular to the line of the bottom.   The stern was rounded, blunt or straight cut, but raked backwards. The bow sloping outward from the bottom was usually more pointed.

When hewing out the inside of the hull, the ends were not hollowed out and a bulkhead or strengthening ridges were left across the bottom.   The bulkhead could be situated to the fore of the dugout, in the central part, or to the rear.   The sides of the boat were relatively thin, whereas the bottom was thick and heavy.

The czołno (dugout) had no rudder.   It was propelled by paddle, which simultaneously served to steer the craft.

The dugout, dated to the late 16th or early 17th century, recently raised from Lake Głebokie south of Gdansk, had similar features (Fig. 15.12).

As we remember, the dugouts, together with the rafts, belonged to the oldest prototypes in the northwest territories occupied by the Slavs.   In the Polish interior, they played a highly essential role: as river ferries, fishing vessels in local shipping, for the transport of goods over greater distances and communications.

It might be worth mentioning here, that in the 18th century, dugouts were still used in trade on the River Dzwina and the shipping of goods to Riga, in the north-eastern of the Polish Commonwealth. In the 19th century, various sizes of dugouts and those enlarged by extending the sides with planks, were operated in the eastern regions.

To come back to the Vistula and its tributaries, it should be noted that one can easily perceive features indicating that in their shape and construction, various, native Polish types of plank-built boats and ships originate from the dugout, i.e. single or paired logboats.

The Decline of the Spław Shipping.

In the second half of the 18th century, the "Royal Republic" entered a period of social and economic reforms. Matters related to the development of shipping and river trade were among those which occupied a prominent place in publicism and the work of the Sejm (parliament).

The aim of the reformers was to bring about significant changes in the character of trade and the organization of river shipping in Poland. The era of the "gentry shipping" was approaching its close and with it, the types of trading craft which served it. The general tendency was for shipping to be taken over by professional merchants and carriers. They would be interested in other types of ships, more economical, designed for use on various waterways (including canals), to carry various cargoes and besides, not requiring large crews.

The taking up of a great enterprise aimed at connecting the Vistula with the Niemen, Dnieper and Odra, thus creating an extensive system of waterways connecting the Baltic and Black Seas, became one of the manifestations of these aims in Poland, in the second half of the 18th century. The clearing of rivers, their dredging, regulation and primarily, the building of canals, was to serve this purpose. These aims resulted in the building, in the years 1765-1784, of the Oginski Canal connecting the Niemen and Dnieper; in 1784, a second canal – the Royal Canal – connecting the Vistula and Djnepr was opened. The course of political events put a stop to the materialization of the third project – the building of the Vistula-Odra canal. This plan was fulfilled by the Prussians after the 1st partitioning of Poland.

Now, Polish ships were able to cross to neighbouring rivers along these canals, and vessels characteristic for the River Odra and the eastern rivers were able to sail into the Vistula and its tributaries.

Of those ships which sailed into the Vistula in the second half of the 18th century, the odrzanka (German: Oderkahn) was to play the most important role. Being unable to describe all the new types, let us devote some attention to this one. The odrzanka was already operated on the Vistula in the 1770's. Having undergone certain adaptations in local yards, it became common under the name of the berlinka. The drawing from 1796 (Fig. 15.13a-c) presents a ship which differs distinctly from the indigenous Vistula types. As opposed to the latter, the berlinka represents a double-ended type. In its proportions, it was then long and narrow, also decidedly higher than the szkuta, dubas or koza. It was spindle-shaped in horizontal projection, with an elongated, pointed bow and stern; in cross-section, it was similar in form to ____/. A feature of the longitudinal projection was the raised stern and bow. Its measurements were: clear length of about 32 to 38 m., width 3.20 - 3.80 m., inside height - about 1.30 m., draught empty - about 0.20 m., loaded - about 0.85 - 1.05 m. As compared with the Polish vessels, the load capacity of the berlinka was not very great, being only from about 6 to 10 lasts. It was oar-sail propelled, with a 4 - 6 man crew.

At the beginning of the 19th century, the Vistula saw the introduction of the first steam-ships - symbolizing the birth of a completely new era.

Concluding our comments, it should be stated that the Poles were not able to fulfil their programme of reforms in river shipping, develop a system of waterways, improve the types of ships and adapt them to the new requirements - and gain the advantages expected from these undertakings.

The reforms in trade and shipping were only one fragment of a huge reconstruction programme of the whole state, undertaken by Poland in the second half of the 18th century. Disquieted by the progressive character of this programme and the spirit of the new Constitution passed on 3rd May 1791 in Warsaw, Russia, Prussia and Austria negotiated an alliance, the purpose of which was to destroy the Polish state and seize its territory by force. This criminal plan was carried out in the three consecutive partitions of Poland. In consequence, when Europe stepped into the 19th century, with its tremendous transformations in economy, industry and transport - Poland disappeared from the map of the world and on her extensive territories arose powers which were to change the fate of our continent. Polish soil was divided by the boundaries of the annexing states, the governments of which delibrately blocked the natural and proper economic and social development of the occupied territories. Customs houses defending the incompatible trade interests of Berlin, Petersburg and Vienna, were set up on the rivers, cut across by artificial frontiers. One of the results of such relations and the general backwardness of the country which followed, was the decline of shipping of the Polish rivers and regression in boatbuilding serving this shipping.

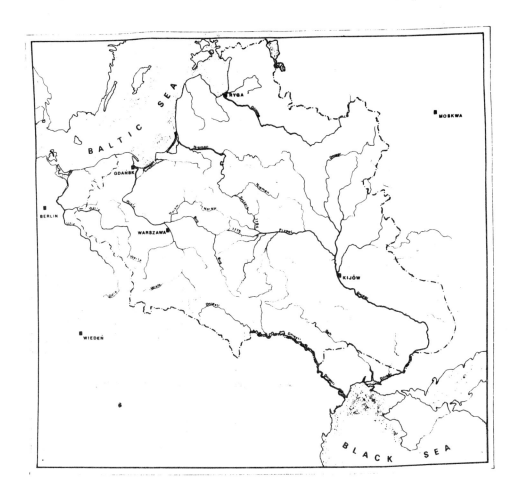

Fig. 15.1: The Kingdom of Poland and the network of its great waterways in the first half of the 17th century.

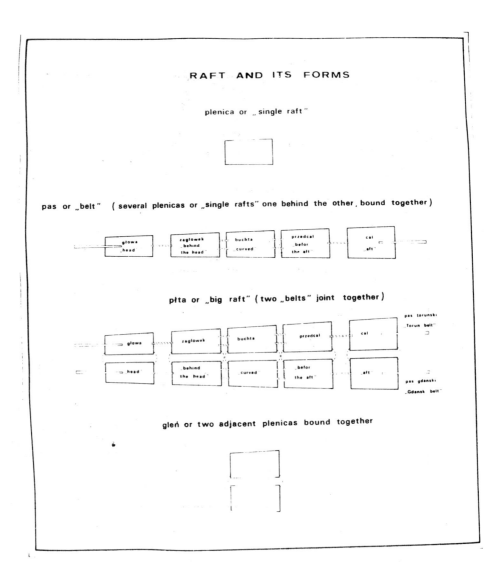

Fig. 15. 2: Raft and its forms.

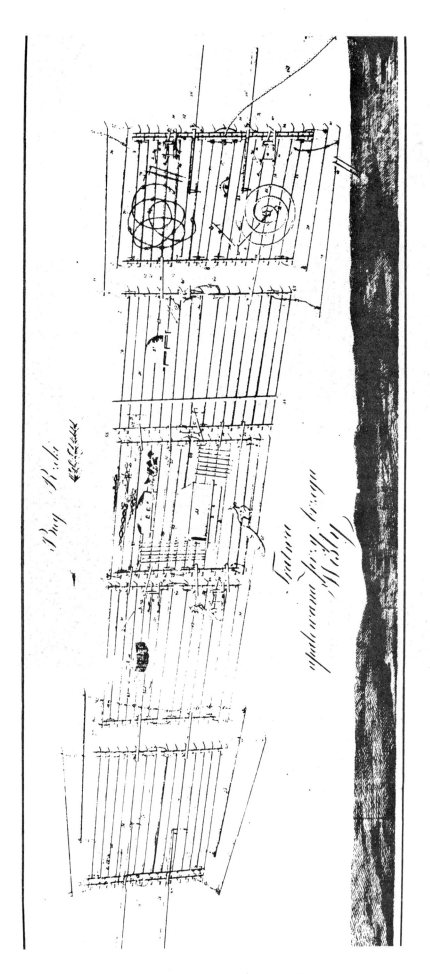

Fig. 15.3: A "big raft" from a drawing by Haczewski (c. 1835).

Fig. 15.4:   Detail of painting by Issak van den Blocke (from 1609) showing a planking housing erected on vertical poles on a raft (a <u>kokoszka</u>) in which goods which could not tolerate moisture could be carried.

184

Fig. 15.5:   Engraving from 1770 showing the structure and the manoeuvering by the crew of a komiega.

Fig. 15.6:   A galar, so-called "nine".   Drawing by F.A. Lohrmann (1770).

Fig. 15.7: A <u>byk</u>, from a drawing by F.A. Lohrmann (1770).

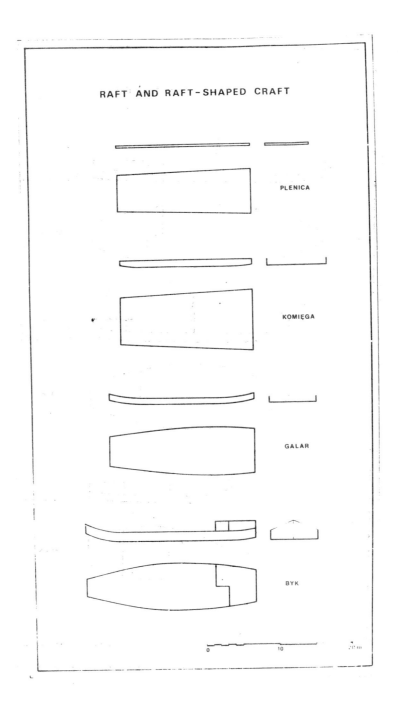

Fig. 15.8: The shape in horizontal and vertical projection of rafts and raft-shaped craft in Poland.

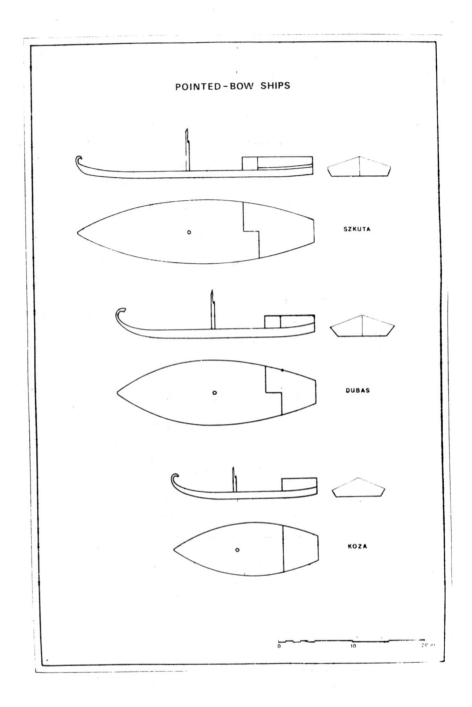

Fig. 15.9: The shape in horizontal and vertical projection of different types of pointed – bow river craft in Poland.

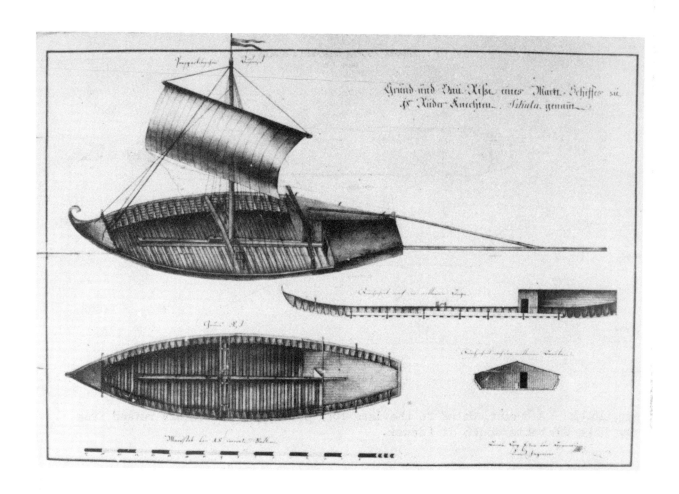

Fig. 15.10, 15.11: Engravings showing the structure and the manoevering of a szkuta, a flat-bottomed, fairly slim and low vessel with a truncated stern and pointed bow.

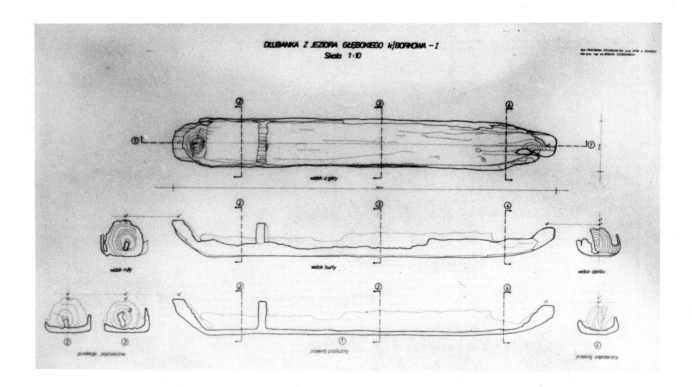

Fig. 15.12:   A dugout, dated to the late 16th or early 17th century raised from the Lake Głebokie south of Gdansk.

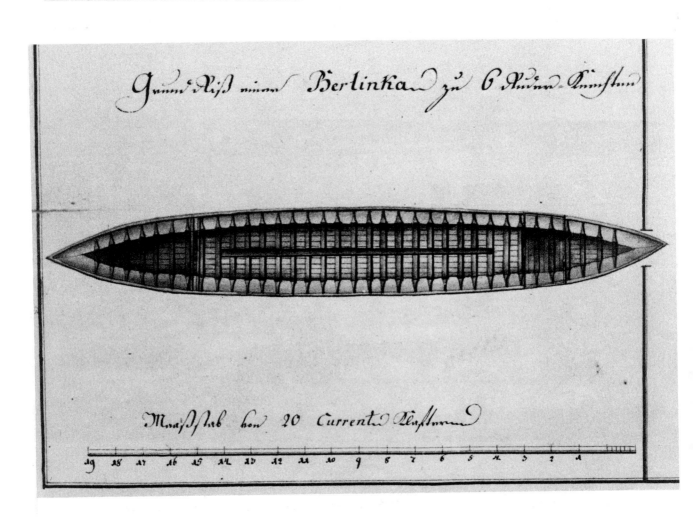

Fig. 15.13a:

190

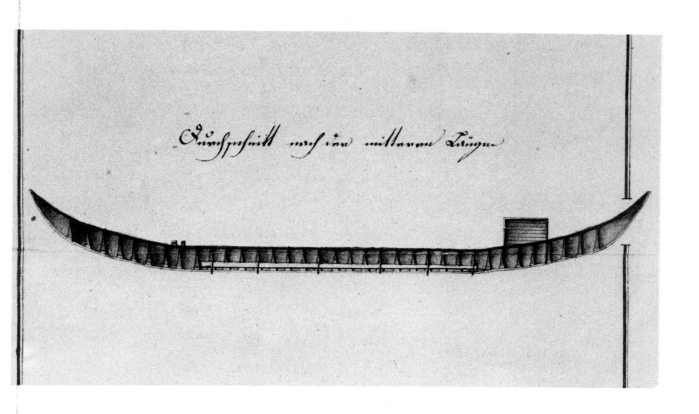

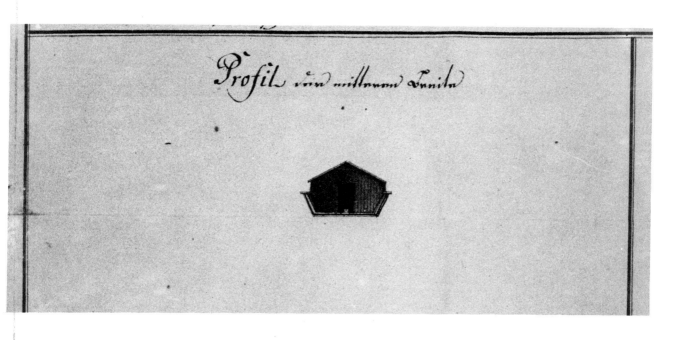

Fig. 15.13:   a - c.   Drawings from 1796 showing the structure and shape of a berlinka (German - Oderkahn) in horizontal plan, longitudinal section and cross-section.

16. THE "BOOK OF ALL TAGUS BOATS, INCLUDING CARGO AND PASSENGER, AS WELL AS FISHING CRAFT"

Octavio Lixa Filgueiras

The "Book of all Tagus boats, including cargo and passenger as well as fishing craft" is a small album of 20 engraved plates measuring 200 by 152 mm, each of them numbered and depicting a different type of craft, plus a title page, numberless, and slightly bigger: 200 by 161 mm. The book does not include any text other than the legends to the illustrations.

The title page shows, inside a plain frame, the title, both in Portuguese and in French, the author's name and status – João de Souza, professor of Naval Architecture and of Design at the Midshipmen's Company (Academy) – and other bibliographical references: na loie de José da Fon.<u>ca</u>" (at José da Foncesca's shop), "o Arsenal (at the Arsenal), "L.<u>xa</u>" (Lisbon), "Silva direx" (direxit). No date is given. On the bottom left of plate one, however, the following is shown: "Ramalho f. (fecit; made) in 1785"[1]. This engraver's dating has occasionally been taken for that of the publishing itself, but there is no evidence to support this claim[2].

The number of known copies, six[3], tells us of the rarity of the first edition which the Câmara Municipal de Lisboa (Lisbon City Council) has now printed and published in facsimile[4]. Its rarity is further increased by the fact that there is no notice of other contemporary Portuguese works on the same subject. Admittedly, the earthquake of 1755 and the exile of the Royal Court in Brazil, from 1806 to 1821 led to irreperable losses of books and other documents, which prevent us from achieving a better, precise, knowledge of developments of the day in terms of river activities.

Even if it possesses neither the comprehensiveness nor the technical quality of such works as "Plusieurs sortes de Bâtiments Hollandoises", by Groenewegen (1789), or Différents sujets de Marine" by the Ozanne brothers (1770?), the book has great cultural significance and may possibly be related to the period of drastic changes that the training of naval officers in Portugal was then undergoing.

Joao de Souza (Pather), "a master draughtsman", was appointed Professor of Design and Naval Architecture (two separate chairs) on the 19th of March, 1783, six days before the opening of the studies at the Royal Midshipmen's Academy (Royal Arsenal)"[5]. He held these chairs for many years, as certain documents, dated 1802, still bear his signature as professor[5]. And the first professor of those chairs he certainly was, since the Academy, whose "creation was a very important step to the Portuguese midshipmen's Academic and professional education", though chartered on the 5th August 1779, by the Queen D. Maria I, and already installed in 1780 at the Colégio Real dos Nobres (The Noblesmen's Royal College), was not established at the Casa des Formas of the Royal Naval Arsenal until 1783[6].

In such a context, this collection of engravings, with their Portuguese and French legends, seems to have been intended for a wide audience in spite of its short explanatory notes.

Paradoxically, the plates are almost wholly reproduced (the exception being the "falua" plate[8]) in a German work, the "Marine General Dictionary", by Johan Heinrich Röding (1794-1798)[7] where, however, the legends are restricted to the Portuguese names of the boats ... [8]. Up to now, no explanation has been advanced as to their appearance in this "classic". Two important points have been brought to my attention, regarding this matter: in spite of his recognized, punctillious character,[9] Röding does not acknowledge the book nor its author[10], probably meaning that he was not aware of them[9]; on the other hand, and considering that many of Röding's sources remain unknown, the omission of the "falua" plate suggests that he might have had access to a disperse set of engravings and not the complete, original[9] work. This hypothesis is somehow confirmed when we compare the original plates and their German copies: the already mentioned absence of the explanatory notes on the German copies is strange, particularly if we keep in mind that the original plates also carry a French version[11]; again, and notwithstanding their considerable accuracy and neat detailing, the copies engraved by A. Stöttrup are not always as faithful to the original as could be expected - as a matter of fact, the specimens drawn by Joao de Souza and engraved by Ramalho may be regarded as exceptionally expressive, if not always technically perfect. Indeed, Souza's sketches provide the means to identify numerous vessels and to infer the typological characterisation of others, even if the live works are never shown. This actually is one of their most positive features. It is only regrettable that our author has not left a similar work on all Portuguese vessels of his time.

Even so, and assuming that he has not failed to record any other significant specimen of the Tagus boats[12] (a safe guess, as he also includes some models that, although not native to this river, were frequently found on its waters - cf. Plates 1, 13, 14, 15, 16 and 20), Souza puts within our reach some indispensable material to appraise, with reasonable accuracy, the deep alterations that would follow soon afterwards, particularly those issuing from the economical development policies undertaken in the second half of the 19th century[13].

I am sure that there is no need to emphasize the economical relevance traditionally held by fluvial navigation and fishing, as this has been extensively dealt with in some remarkable essays, but allow me to bring forward the great variety and speciousness of functions that these crafts deployed, as pointed out in the legends, and the large number of the nautical types recorded. Both are enough to realize the significance of such activities as supporters of the life in the capital of the kingdom and the wide basin of the Tagus river. To illustrate this, I propose a selection of extremely elucidative maps (Fig. 16.1-16.4).

Proceeding now to the analytical study of the book, the first thing to do is to classify the models, according to their uses and the conditions under which they operated and distinguish those models belonging to Tagus harbours from those that, although moored there, came from outside (Cf. Table I). Another approach would be to separate them into groups according to the characteristics of the hull and their nautical archaeological connotations, as attempted in Table II. Comparing both maps, it becomes

Nº	BOAT NAME	SEA & RIVER BOATS		RIVER BOATS	
		SPECIFIC OF EXTERIOR HARBOURS	SPECIFIC OF ESTUARY HARBOURS	ESTUARY SAILING	INTERIOR SAILING
1	IATE PORTUGUES	★			
2	BARCO CACILHEIRO			★	
3	BARCA D'ALDEIA GALEGA			★	
4	FRAGATA D'ALCOCHETE			★	
5	BARCO DOS MOÏNHOS			★	
6	BARCO DE RIBA TEJO				★
7	BATEL D'ÁGUA ACIMA				★
8	BATEIRA DE PORTO BRANDÃO		★	★	
9	BARCO DE MOYOS			★	
10	FRAGATA			★	
11-A	FALUA			●	
11-B	CATRAIO			●	
12	ESCALER A REMOS	●			
13	LANCHA DO ALTO	✱	✱		
14	CAÍQUE	✱ ★			
15	BARCO DE SESIMBRA	✱			
16	BARCO DA ERICEIRA	✱ ★			
17	BARCO DE CASCAIS	✱ ★			
18	MULETA		✱		
19	BATEL		✱		
20-A	SAVEIRO DA COSTA	✱			
20-B	SAVEIRO DO TEJO	✱			

★ CARGO BOATS
● CARGO / PASSENGER BOATS
✱ FISHING BOATS

Table I

I: PLANKED CANOES / MESOPOTAMIAN TYPE	KEEL BOATS / MEDITERRANEAN TYPES			
	II: OLD TYPE	III: VERNACULAR BOATS		
		DOUBLE ENDED	WITH FILLING CHOCKS	TRANSOM AFT
7 20-A 20-B	6 18	2 3 5 8 9 13 15 16 17 19	2 3 5 8 9 13	4 10 11-A 11-B 14

Table II

clear that the adoption of so many different hulls cannot only be due to the uses that awaited the vessels or to the conditions under which they operated: on the contrary, as we shall see it is mainly from a cultural point of view that we must explain the reasons for such adoptions (Fig. 16.5).

Let us begin with the planked canoes of Mesopotamian type[15]. They belong to an age-old nautical family of which a great number of specimens may still be found in Iraq and Portugal. In my country, most of these are located in the central zone of the Western coast, namely in the Ovar - Aveiro - Ilhavo area. This ancient home of the "Turduli Veteri", where South Iberian people moved to after the destruction of Tartessus by Carthage, was the meeting point of boats belonging to these migrating peoples. The intercourse between Tartessus, Crete and Ugarit may possibly explain the origin of this heritage of ours[16].

The well known migrating disposition of varinos, aveiros and ilhavos i.e., Ovar, Aveiro and Ilhavo natives) was strongly attracted by the opportunities to work that they found along the Tagus, both as fishermen and as boat-builders. After some periodical stays, these hard workers settled in colonies, as they did, in our own days, at Vila Franca de Xira or, in the 18th century, at the Caparica Coast, whose specific boat was sketched by Souza: the saveiro da costa (litt. Coast saveiro, i.e., the Caparica Coast shad boat) shown in plate 20-B (Fig. 16.6). The name that it now carries in that area, meia-lua (half-moon) (Fig. 16.7) corresponds to a variation of the barco do mar (sea boat) or of the xavega boat, predominant further North on the coast, from Lavos to Vieira de Leiria. This engraving (Fig. 16.6), even if it is one of the least accomplished, leaves no doubt as to the identification of the model. I add the plans showing its present design (Fig. 16.8): the differences between them are minimal (e.g., the disappearance of the earlier prow covering and of the rigging and the replacement of the rudder by a lateral oar). There is some evidence, however, that as late as 1893 the oars were not the sole means of propulsion and that either a rudder or a steering oar were then indifferently used[17]. The same source elucidates that "at high tide they (the meias-luas) used to carry their catch up the river, to Trafaria or even to Lisbon"[17] which may be the reason why they appear in Souza's book.

As to the saveiro do Tejo (Tagus shad boat)[18] very defectively depicted in Plate 20-a (Fig. 16.9), it probably corresponds to the enviada (tender), a larger craft of a type close to the Aveiro mercanteis (merchantmen) (Fig. 16.10) that, benefiting from calm weather and the Spring monsoon, "used to sail along the sea coast from Aveiro to Lisbon, loaded with wood, salt and oak or willow bark employed in the treatment of the nets; with a crew of not more than 2 or 3 men and having on board, as sole nautical instrument, a rude and imperfect compass"[19]. After selling the cargo, and often also the boat, the owner would go back home, carrying with him "the sails and the product of this curious trade"[19]. Known along the Tagus as varinos (Figs. 16.11 and 16.13), they were used for sardine fishing off-shore and for loading and unloading vessels calling in the estuary[19]. This model is an ancestor of the modern varino (Figs. 16.15 and 16.16)[20] of which we have the excellent plans prepared by Rafael Monléon (1890) (Fig. 16.11). Comparing the former varino to Plate 20-A, small differences are noticeable: on the latter the shape of the prow is less curved and graceful, and the rig is still the original, a high lug-sail, instead of the fore-and-aft rig characteristic of the South type[21].

The omission of the fishing _bateira_[22)] (Figs. 16.13 and 16.28) in Souza's book strikes as unexpected: these boats, which were very often carried, together with their crews, on the _enviadas_, went forward by their own means[19)], either upstream or down the coast as far as the Sado, Algarve or even South Spain[23)], for great was the mobility of these fishermen, so great that they are occasionally named, after it, as "sea gypsies".[24)]

Finally, we shall deal with the _batel d'agoa a'ssima_ (upstream boat)[25)] of Plate 7-A, 7-B (Fig. 16.12). Their raked bow, ending in an agressive peak and revealing their flat bottom [26)] (7-A) make them little different from the _barco d'agua acima_, alias _monaio_, alias _culé_,[27)] their corresponding model in the following century (Figs. 16.14 and 16.15). Could they be the remotest example of this type of craft? They were built to sail to the harbours up the river Tagus, even to those that were away from the river bank and could only be reached through ditches or minor river shunts. From such ports they would carry cork, fruit and other goods down to Lisbon, either to the city or to the ships on the estuary[28)]. As for the rig, while the _batel_ has either a lateen sail with a strongly fore-raked mast or a sprit sail and fore sail.

To understand the importance of the planked canoes of Mesopotamian type along the Tagus, we only have to consider that, as late as 1860, they still accounted for 29.8% of all river craft: 431 units out of a total 1143! (Cf. Table III).[29)]

Although sailing along the Tagus, just as the batel did, the _barco de Riba Tejo_[30)] (Upper Tagus Boat) of Plate 6 (Fig. 16.17) belongs, together with the _muleta_[31)] (Figs. 16.18-19), to a quiet different nautical family. Their basic structure is based on a normal skeleton frame with a keel. In order to make good use of shallow draught, it has a concave bottom and the keel is level with the bottom (Fig. 16.20). Hence their need for lateral stablizers – the _pas de borda_ – for sailing. A Mediterranean origin, dating back to the classical age, has been suggested for this peculiar hull.[32)]

Notice must be taken that both fishing and cargo boats have similar general characteristics. Even the normal rig does not differ except for the single fact that the _muleta_ has a small fore sail. Only for trawling do they use some complementary sails to move to leeward[33)] (Figs. 16.19 and 16.20). The display of this full rig was in the origin of an understandable popularity that survived after they had faded away at the beginning of our century.

The _barco de Ribatejo_ carried bulky cargo – bales of hay, cork, etc. – and the _muleta_ used to fish outside the estuary, the catch being then removed to other small craft that would be awaiting at the mouth of the river to carry it to Lisbon[33)].

Proceeding to the keeled boats of the traditional Mediterranean type, we shall distinguish the double ended from the aft transom ones and, among the former, those with filling-chocks from those without them.

The double ended boats are predominant [34)] (Plates 2, 3, 5, 8, 9, 13, 15, 16, 17 and 19), the aft transom ones being less than a half of their number [35)] (Plates 4, 10, 11A and 11B). In the 19th century the former have faded away almost completely except for one specimen – the _cangueiro_.

198

RIVER HARBOURS	AVEIROS *	BATEIRAS	BARCOS	BARCOS DE MOÍNHOS	BATEIS	BOTES	FALUAS	FRAGATAS	TOTAL
ABRANTES	190								190
ALCOCHETE	8		6			1	5		20
ALDEA-GALLEGA	3		3		1	35	9		51
ALHOS VEDROS			1			1	1		3
AMORA						4			4
ARRENTELLA						2			2
ALCANTARA	4					2			6
ALFAMA	3					16			19
BARREIRO			1			19	2	1	23
BOA-VISTA	24			1		4		8	37
BELEM						28			28
BARQUINHA	75								75
CONSTANÇA	51								51
CAES NOVO						1			1
CHAMUSCA	5								5
CAES DO SODRÉ	13		3			85		20	121
CAES DO TOJO	30		1	33		12		28	104
CAES DA PEDRA	22		1			88	1	38	150
CASCAES			1		3				4
CACILHAS						30			30
FUNDIÇÃO						13		3	16
JUNQUEIRA						1			1
MOITA			4			6		9	19
PAÇO D'ARCOS		4	3			1			8
PORTO BRANDÃO			1		4	21			26
LAVRADIO	2		1						3
PAMPULHA			1			11		2	14
SAMOCO						1			1
TRAFARIA						5			5
PRAIA DE SANTOS						2		1	3
TERCENAS								1	1
RIBEIRA NOVA	1					73			74
TERREIRO						5			5
SEIXAL						43			43
SOMMA	431	4	27	34	8	510	18	111	1143

* INCLUDING ALL THE DIFFERENT BOATS OF THIS BREED   Table III

PLATE	18TH CENTURY	MAIN USE	19TH/20TH CENTURY	DOC.
2	BARCOS CACILHEIROS	SHIP LOADING & UNLOADING	FRAGATA	4
8	BATEIRA DE PORTO BRANDÃO	TRANSPORT / STONE	CANGUEIRO	6
9	BARCO DOS MOYOS	TRANSPORT / SAND	CANGUEIRO	6
3	BARCA D'ALDEIA GALEGA	TRANSPORT / WOOD	BOTE DO PINHO	M/M
-	------------	TRANSPORT / SALT	BOTE DE 1/2 QUILHA	M/M
5	BARCO DOS MOÎNHOS	TRANSPORT / FLOUR		
4	FRAGATA D'ALCOCHETE	TRANSPORT / FIREWOOD	BOTE DO PINHO	M/M + 9
10	FRAGATA	CARGO BOAT	BOTE FRAGATA	9
11-A	FALUA	CARGO & PASSENGERS	FALUA	8
-	----	CARGO & PASSENGERS	CANOA CACILHEIRA	2
11-B	CATRAIO	TRANSPORT / PASSENGERS	BOTE CATRAIO	1
		COASTER	BATEIRA	17
13	LANCHA DO ALTO	MARITIME FISHING	CANOAS	M/M
15	BARCO DA ERICEIRA	MARITIME FISHING & PILOTS	CANOAS	11, 16, M/M
16	BARCO DE SESIMBRA	MARITIME FISHING & PILOTS	CANOAS	11, 16, M/M
17	BARCO DE CASCAIS	MARITIME FISHING & PILOTS	CANOAS	11, 16, M/M
19	BATEL	RIVER FISHING	BOTE PEQUENO	M/M

PLATES: Nº FROM JOAO DE SOUSA BOOK
DOC. : Nº FROM OP. CIT. PINTO BASTO
M/M : FROM MARITIME MUSEUM ARCHIVES

Table IV

In the above mentioned major group, almost all the boats incorporate a filling-chock; and, despite some distinctive peculiarities between them, these are not enough to make any typological subdivisions. On the contrary, everything leads to the idea of a type so adaptable that it can perform a multitude of tasks - from transport in the estuary and coasting [36] (Plates 2, 3, 5, 8 and 9) to fluvial and sea fishing and pilots' service [37] (Plates 13, 15, 16, 17, 19). Their uncontroversial vernacular feature comes out of a design where the prow and the stern shapes are outstanding and where round forms prevail[38] (Fig. 16.21). It is most elucidative to compare the illustration showing the barco do moinhos (mills boat)[39] (Fig. 16.22) with those showing two country models typical of the 19th century: the bote cacilheiro[40] (Fig. 16.24) and the faulua.[41] (Fig. 16.23).

Finally, as to the large variety of their names, these were mainly chosen after their home harbour or after their specific uses; and - we must keep this in mind - the same name being indifferently given to several models. Let us consider now the boats in the book and those of the 19th century with similar functions (Table IV).

The 19th century boats, divided into these groups ("transport/coasting/fishing), have been ordered from larger to smaller sizes, according to data from the Lisbon Maritime Museum archives and then compared with their equivalents in Souza's book.

Some curious conclusions may be drawn: the word cacilheiro points to the home harbour - Cacilhas. The specimens bearing this name in those two different ages [42] are not related and have not the same functions. The barco cacilheiro[43] (Plate 2) (Fig.16.25) will be replaced by the grande fragata[44] (Fig. 16.27) with no connection at all with the fragata in the book[45] (Plate 10), (Fig. 16.26).

Another name for unrelated models is bateira: it was given either to small fishing boats from Aveiro (Fig. 16.28), or to the ancient stone transport boat from Porto Brandão[46] (Plate 8), (Fig. 16.29) or even to the fragata de fora da barra (offshore frigate) (Fig. 16.30) for coasting[47] that was used later on.

Falua[48] (Plate IIA) (Figs. 16.36 and 16.23) seems to evoke the idea of fast transport - eventually, fast passenger transport.

Also the usual passenger transport in this area is mostly associated with the words catraio and catraiar[49] (Plate 11B).

Completing these short comments on the "Tagus" craft hulls I would like to mention a small group of sea-going craft.

The Iate Portugues[50] (Plate 1), (Fig. 16.31) a kind of two masts bateira[51], was the largest of our purely coastal craft and had Setubal for its last home harbour, as suggested by the designation Iate de Setubal (Figs. 16.31, 16.32 and 16.33).

The caique[52] (Plate 14) (Fig. 16.34) either a fishing boat or a coaster, native to Algarve,[53] was different from its modern equivalent (Fig. 16.35) on account of its very curved prow; lack of boards steps (boards salience); too high settie-sails and slightly raked masts. The Caravela of the age of Discoveries having been occasionally identified with the Algarve caique[54], the following doubt arises: the last reference to

MAIN SAIL	MAST LEANING	SECOND SAIL	MAST LEANING	FORE SAIL JIBS	E	18TH CENTURY	D	19TH/20TH CENTURY
LUGSAIL	AFT	------	------	------	20	SAVEIRO		------
"	VERT.	------	------	------			12	SAVEIRO
" (AFT)	AFT	LUGSAIL (FORE)	AFT	------	2	B. CACILHEIROS		------
LATEEN	FORE	------	------	------	6	B. RIBA TEJO		------
"	AFT	------	------	FORE SAIL	7	B. AGUA ACIMA	3	B. AGUA ACIMA
"	FORE	------	------	JIB	8,19	MOLETA + BATEL		------
" (FORE)	FORE	LATEEN (AFT)	FORE	------	3	B. ALDEIA GALEGA		------
					5	B. MOÍNHOS		------
					15	BB. CESIMBRA,		------
					16,17	ERICEIRA, CASCAES		------
" (Y/M)(FORE)	AFT	" (Y/M)(AFT)	AFT	------	4	FRAGATA ALCOCHETE		------
SETTEE	AFT	------	------	------		------	2	CACILHEIRO
							9	B. DO PINHO
							M/M	CANOAS
" (AFT)	AFT	SETTEE (FORE)	AFT	------	1A,14	FALUA, CAÍQUE	8	FALUA
" (FORE)	AFT	" (AFT)	FORE	------	11B	CATRAIO	15	CAÍQUE
" (FORE)	AFT	SPRIT SAIL(MIZEN)	AFT	------			16	CANOA DO ALTO
SPRIT SAIL	VERT.	------	------	FORE SAIL	9	B. MOYOS		------
"	FORE	------	------	------	7A	B. AGUA ACIMA		------
					10	FRAGATAS		
"	AFT	SPRIT SAIL(MIZEN)	AFT	JIB		------	1	CATRAIO
GAFF SAIL	AFT	------	------	FORE SAIL	8	BATEIRA	4	FRAGATA
							5	VARINO
"	AFT	------	------	FORE SAIL + JIB		------	6	CANGUEIRO
							M/M	B. MEIA QUILHA
" (AFT)	AFT	GAFF SAIL (FORE)	AFT	INNER + OUTER JIBS *	1,13	YATE + LANCHA	17	BATEIRA
"	AFT	------		FORE SAIL+JIB+FLYING JIB		------	18	HIATE
" (AFT)	AFT	GAFF SAIL (FORE)	AFT			------		

Y/M : MAST & YARD COUPLED TOGETHER (A. MOORE, p. 142)
E : ENGRAVING NUMBER (J. SOUZA)
D : REF. PINTO·BASTO (Nº); OR MARITIME MUSEUM OF LISBON DOC.

* PAASCH PL. 11-A

Table V

<u>Caravelas</u> being found in a document dated 1738[55]), it is difficult to explain why only 47 years later this name was replaced by <u>caique.</u> And for no apparent reason at all!

I shall finish with a table showing the rigs of Tagus boats, both in 1785 (Fig. 16.36) and in the next period (Table V). The side views of the latter (Fig. 16.37) are reproduced from Manuel Leitāo op. cit, by kind permission of the Author.

I suppose the importance of the book by Joāo de Souza is evident; its analysis having been done in the essential, I propose it as a homage to all of you and particularly to the organizers of this III Symposium and our hosts.

O Caderno de Todos os Barcos do Tejo

Notes

1. Cfr. Luis Chaves, <u>a</u>, <u>b</u>; and <u>c</u>-II pp. 161/180, 181/194.

2. Id. <u>c</u>-II pp. 181/182.

3. Lisbon Maritime Museum; General Library of the Navy (Lisbon); National Museum of Archaeology and Ethnology (Lisbon); Lisbon City Museum (Municipality of Lisbon); and two more sold by antiquarian book-sellers.

4. Celebrating the "Tagus Week".

5. Very kind information by C. er A. L. Porto e Albuquerque, through doc. ref. due Rear Adm. A. Teixeira da Mota.

6. Cfr. A. L. Porto e Albuquerque, II-2nd, p. 356.

7. Very kind information by Dra. M. E. Lavoura. There is a facsimil. ed. by Uitgeverij Graphic Publisher, Amsterdam (1969).

8. But including a short mention of the boat in the Portuguese - German Index: "Ein Fahrzeug auf dem Tejo" (III, p. 64). This is also the generic presentation of the Portuguese boat engravings: "Tab. XXXIII-XLIII, Fig. 260-278. Auch Fig. 280. Portugiesische Fahrzeuge auf dem Tejo" (IV, p. 28).

9. Dr. Boye Meyer Friese, Altonaer Museum (Hamburg), by very kind colab. of R. Burmester. But the <u>catraio</u> and the <u>falua</u> are depicted side by side on the Plate II (Joāo de Souza Book) - or Röding reproduced only the former. We cannot understand why!

10. Dr. M. Burger, Deutsches Museum (Munich), by very kind colab. of R. Burmester.

11. The A. "has read everything, but he knows very well how incomplete and inaccurate most of these sources are, and therefore he has gathered oral information for nearly every language treated; <u>I therefore had to seek information from foreigners, who were professional seaman</u> ..." (C. Kruyscamp, <u>Preface</u> of fac-simil. ed. of Röding Dict. p. XVII). In fact

his Glossary (<u>Index</u>) is more accurate than the engraving's interpretation.

12. I have detected only one omission: the <u>bateira</u> from Aveiro (cfr. next note 20).

13. The railway; first installed in 1856, had great impact on regional economy and was the source of alterations on the Tagus traditional water transports.

14. Cfr. Bibliography: Baldaque da Silva, J. Gaspar, Lacerda Lobo, A. Silbert.

15. <u>Book</u> Plates 7, 20-A and 20-B.

16. Cfr. O.L. Filgueiras, <u>a</u> and <u>b</u>.

17. A.J. Pinto Basto (13).

18. <u>Book</u> Plate 20-A.

19. L. Magalhaes, p. 61.

20. A.J. Pinto Basto (5); "Marinha do Tejo", p. 381.

21. A.J. Pinto Basto, (12) presents a <u>saveiro</u> with the original lug-sail - besides the different stem curve the other divergency is the oarlocks of which there is evidence.

22. "Marinha do Tejo", p. 325.

23. L. Magalhaes, p. 60.

24. In <u>Club das Donas de Casa</u> (magazine, see Bibiliography).

25. <u>Book</u> Plates 7A and 7B.

26. Id. 7A.

27. A.J. Pinto Basto (3) and Lisbon Maritime Museum Archives.

28. A.J. Pinto Basto (3).

29. "Marinha do Tejo" p. 381.

30. <u>Book</u> Plate 6.

31. <u>Book</u> Plate 18; cfr. Baldaque da Silva <u>a</u> p. 399, and <u>b</u>; A.J. Pinto Basto.

32. Cfr. The Monléon coloured picture "Roman and Carthaginian ships" at the Madrid Maritime Museum (Room V); and Ramalho Ortigāo, p. 16.

33. Fore sails - <u>toldos</u>, <u>muletins</u>, <u>varredoura</u>, <u>cosinheira</u> (e.g. 6 or 7 sails); aft sails - <u>varredoura de cima</u> and <u>varredoura de baixo</u>. Cfr. Baldaque da Silva, app. 299/301 and 399.

34. Book Plates, 2, 3, 5, 8, 9, 13, 15, 16, 17, and 19.

35. Book Plates, 4, 10, 11A and 11B.

36. Book Plates 2, 3, 5, 8, 9.

37. Book Plates 13, 15, 16, 17 and 19.

38. E. Rieth pp. 34/35; E. van Konijnenburg pp. 30 and ff.

39. Book Plate 5.

40. "Marinha do Tejo" p. 248.

41. Id. pag. 261.

42. Book Plate 2 and A.J. Pinto Basto (2).

43. Book Plate 2.

44. A.J. Pinto Basto (4).

45. Book Plate 10.

46. Book Plate 8.

47. A.J. Pinto Basto (17).

48. Book Plate 11-A; for the recent model cfr. A.J. Pinto Basto (8), and "Marinha do Tejo" p. 261.

49. Book Plate 11-B; for the recent model cfr. A.J. Pinto Basto (1), and "Marinha do Tejo", pp. 247/248.

50. Book Plate 1.

51. A.J. Pinto Basto (18).

52. Book Plate 14.

53. A.J. Pinto Basto (15).

54. A. Iria.

55. Quirino da Fonseca II, p. 158.

Acknowledgements

The English version of this paper was prepared by Leonor Filgueiras and revised by Alexandre Vasconcelos.   The tables were organized with the collaboration of Miguel and Carlos Filgueiras.

REFERENCES

Baldaque da Silva, A.A. 1891a.   Estado Actual das Pescas em Portugal, Lisboa..

Baldaque da Silva, A.A. 1895.   "Da muleta de pesca", Revista da Arqueologia e Arte Moderna, Lisboa.

Chaves, L. 1940a.   "Barcos do Tejo", Revista municipal, Lisboa.

Chaves, L. 1941b.   "Barcos das aguas estremenhas", Boletim da Comissão de Fiscalizacão das Aguas de Lisboa, Lisboa.

Chaves, L.   1961c.   Lisboa nas auras do Povo e da Historia, Lisboa.

"Ciganos do Mar"   1965.   in Club das Donas de Casa, Abril, Lisboa.

Filgueiras, O.L. 1975a.   "Comentarios Técnicos da Tese do Moçarabismo Nautico", Memorias do Centro de Estudos e Marinha, Lisboa.

Filgueiras, O.L. 1977b.   "The Xavega Boat, a Case-Study on the Integration of Archaeological and Ethnological data", Sources and Techniques on Boat Archaeology, Greenwich.

Gaspar, J. 1970.   "Os portos fluviais do Tejo", Finisterra, Lisboa.

Gronewegen,   G.   1789.   Vier en Tachtig Stuks Hollandsche Schepen/Plusieurs sortes de Batiments Hollandoise, bij. J. Van den Brink Rotterdam (ed. fac-sim., s/d.).

Iria, A. 1963.   As Caravelas do Infante e o Caique do Algarve, Lisboa.

Kruyscamp. J.   cfr. Rôding, b.

Lacerda Lobo, C.B. de, 1812.(1794).   "Memoria sobre a decadencia das pescarias em Portugal", Memorias Economicas da Real Academia de Sciencias, Lisboa.

Leitão,   M.   1978.   Boats of the Lisbon River, the Fragata and related types, Greenwich.

Magalhäes. L. 1905/1908.   "Barcos da Ria de Aveiro", Portugalia – II, Porto.

Moore, A.   (1925)   1970   Last Days of mast & sail, 2nd. Ed. Devon. "Marinha do Tejo" 1860.   Archivo Pitoresco, Lisboa.

Paasch,   1937.   De la quille a la pomme du mât – Dictionnaire de Marine, Français, Anglais, Allemand, Espagnol, Italien,   Paris.

Pâris, A. 1882/1908.   Souvenirs de Marine Conservés,   Paris.

Pinto Basto, A.J.,   1893.   "As embarcaçoes que navegam no Tejo", Revista do Exercito e da Armada,   Lisboa.

Porto e Albuquerque, A.L.,   1979.   "A Academia Real dos Guardas Marinhas",   Historia Naval Brasileira, Rio de Janeiro.

Quirino da Fonseca, 1978 (1932). A Caravela Portuguesa, Lisboa.

Ramalho Ortigáo, 1943 (1897). "O Culto da Arte em Portugal", A Arte Portuguesa, Lisboa.

Rieth, E., 1978. "Embarcations et Navires de la Méditerrannée Française", Ex-Voto Marins de Méditerranneé, Paris.

Röding, J.H., (1793/1798). Allgemeines Wörterbuch der Marine, Hamburg .

Röding, J.H., (1969). facsimil (with a Preface by C. Kruyscamp) ed. by Viteverij Graphic Publisher, Amsterdam.

Silbert, A., 1978. Le Portugal Méditerraneén a la fin de l'Ancien Régime, XVIIIe. début du XIXe. siècle, Lisboa.

Souza, J. de, (1785?). Caderno de Todos os Barcos do Tejo, (Lisboa).

Van Konijnenburg, E., (1895/1905). L'Architecture Navalle depuis ses origines, Bruxelas.

Vichot, J., 1968/1971. "L'Oeuvre des Ozannes", Neptunia, Paris.

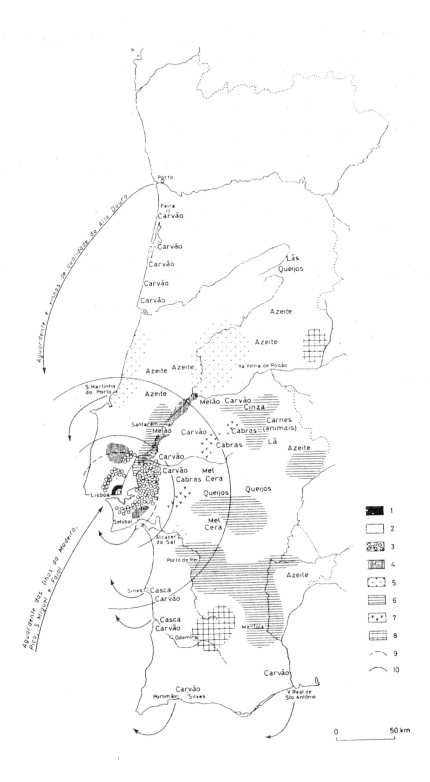

Fig. 16.1:   Land economic organization from Lisbon – pre-railway times
(Fig. 5, op. cit. by J. Gaspar): 1. Vegetables/milk; 2. Wine/milk; 3.
Firewood; 4. Vineyard (large scale production); 5. Wood; 6. Wheat; 7.
Barren wasteland, where not even coal can be produced due to the distance it
is from the Tagus; 8. Seasonal pasture land for transhumant livestock; 9.
A 7 leagues limit inside which glass factories were forbidden (1562); 10.
A 10 leagues limit, by Lisbon authorities, for town meat (1564) and wheat
(1574) supplies – this limit follows along the river up to Abrantes; idem,
20 leagues, for "meat, wood and other provisions" in 1705.

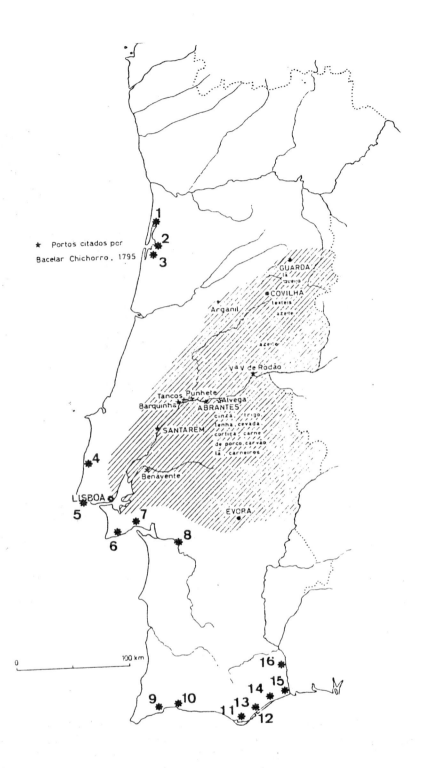

Fig. 16.2:   Tagus hinterland drainage area (ref. Lisbon) - end of 18th
century (Fig. 1 in op. cit. J. Gaspar, completed with the localisation of
the following exterior harbours: 1. Ovar; 2. Aveiro; 3. Ilhavo; 4.
Ericeira; 5. Cascais; 6. Sesimbra; 7. Setûbal; 8. Alcâcer do Sal; 9.
Lagos; 10. Portimäo; 11. Faro; 12/13. Olhäo; 14. Tavira; 15. V.R.
Santo Antônio; 16. Alcoutim.

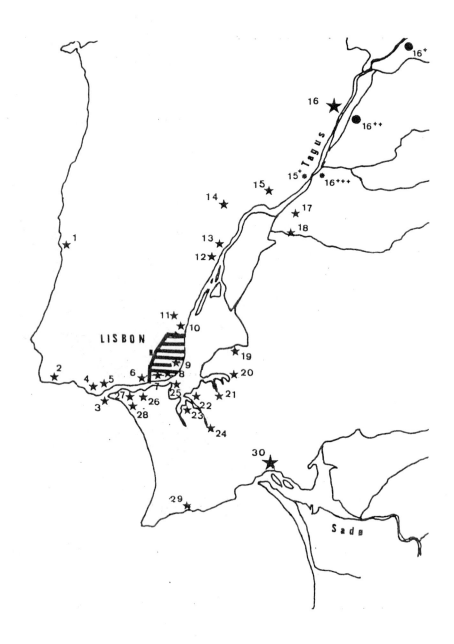

Fig. 16.3: The Tagus harbours up to Chamusca, and the localization of the
exterior harbours near Lisbon: 1. Ericeira; 2. Cascais; 3. Bugio; 4.
Oeiras; 5. Paço D'Arcos; 6. Belém; 7. Praia de Santos; 8. Cais do
Sodré 9. Alfama; 10. Sacavem; 11. Fonte da Talha; 12. Alhandra; 13.
V.F. Xira; 14. V.N. da Rainha; 15. Azambuja; 15+. Valado; 16.
Santarém; 16+. Chamusca; 16++. Almeirim; 16+++. Muge; 17. Salvaterra
de Magos; 18. Benavente; 19. Alcochete; 20. Aldeia Galega; 21. Moita;
22. Barreiro; 23. Seixal; 24. Coina; 25. Cacilhas; 26. Porto Brandão;
27. Trafaria; 28. Costa da Caparica; 29. Sesimbra; 30. Se túbal.

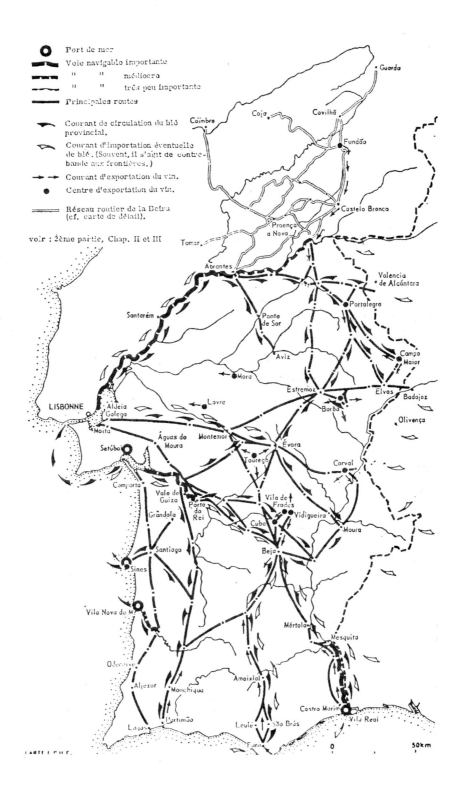

Fig. 16.4: Roads, water transport and trading currents in Alentejo (end of 18th century; map 15 in op. cit. by A. Silbert).

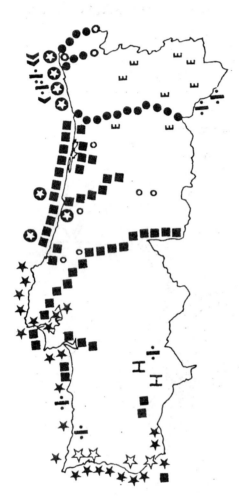

●	Germanic tradition
ш	Box-like river <u>barcas</u>
÷	Rafts
O	Local craft
≽	<u>Masseira</u>
■	Middle East tradition
✪	Povoa boat
✫	<u>Calão</u>
✶	Aft transom craft
I	Merida influence

Fig. 16.5: Distribution of the Portuguese traditional boat types (20th century O.L.Filgueiras).

Fig. 16.6:   Saveiro da Coasta (Caparica):   Plate 20 in João de
Souza Book, repr. by Röding.

Fig. 16.7: <u>Meia-Lua</u> (Caparica): photo O.L. Filgueiras.

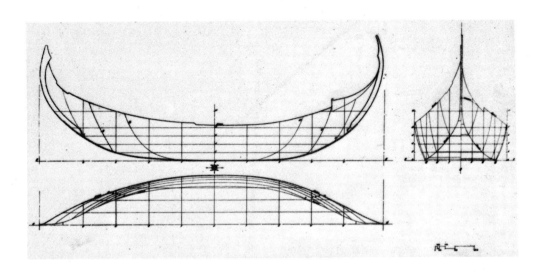

Fig. 16.8: <u>Meia-Lua</u> (Caparica): plans by J. Carvalho.

Fig. 16.9: Saveiro do Tejo: plate 20 in João de Souza <u>Book</u>, repr. by Röding.

Fig. 16.10:   Barco Ilhavo: Lisbon Maritime Museum model   (Col. Seixas).

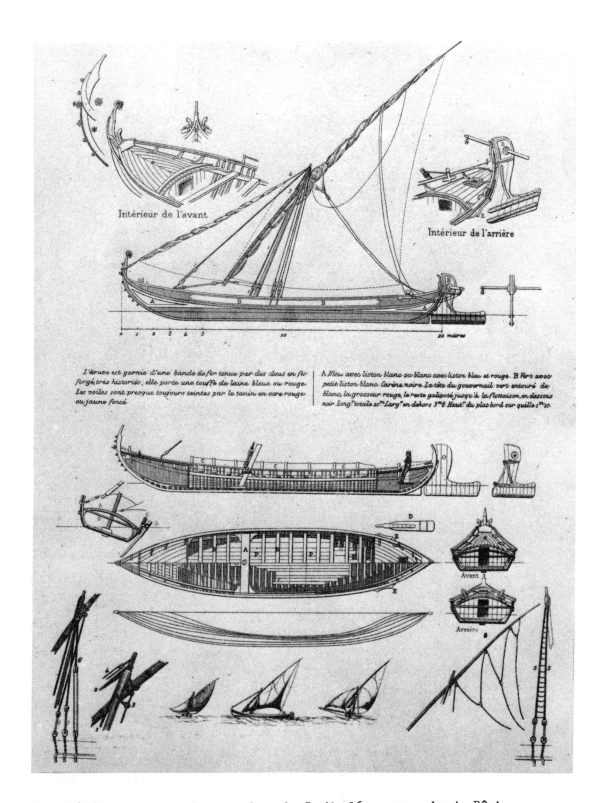

Intérieur de l'avant

Intérieur de l'arrière

L'étrave est garnie d'une bande de fer tenue par des clous en fer forgé, très historiés, elle porte une touffe de laine bleue ou rouge. Les voiles sont presque toujours teintes par le tanin en ocre rouge ou jaune foncé.

A Bleu avec liston blanc ou blanc avec liston bleu et rouge. B Vert avec petit liston blanc. Carène noire. La tête du gouvernail vert entouré de blanc, la grosseur rouge, le reste galipoté jusqu'à la flottaison, en dessous noir. Long.e totale 20m Larg.e en dehors 3m.8 Haut.e du plat bord sur quille 1m.20.

Fig. 16.11: Varino do Tejo: plans by R. Monléon, repr. by A. Pâris.

Fig. 16.12:   _Bateis d'agua acima:_   plate 7 in João de Souza _Book_, repr. by
Röding.

Fig. 16.13:   _Saveiro, Alijo, Sávara:_   from "Marinha do Tejo",   p. 325.

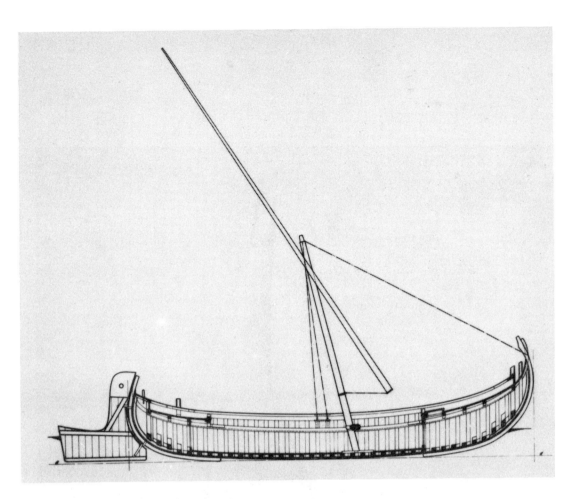

Fig. 16.14: _Monaio_ or _Culé_: plans by J. Rodrigues dos Santos, Lisbon Maritime Museum Archives.

Fig. 16.15: _Varino_ (19th century model) & _Monaio_: from "Marinha do Tejo" p. 381.

Fig. 16.16: <u>Varino</u> (19th century model): photo taken 1961 (O.L. Filgueiras).

Fig. 16.17: <u>Barco de Riba Tejo</u>: plate 6 in João de Souza <u>Book</u>, repr. by Röding.

Fig. 16.18: <u>Muleta</u>: plate 18 in João de Souza <u>Book</u>, repr. by Röding.

Fig. 16.19: <u>Muleta</u> - photo taken at the beginning of the century.

MULETA, bateau de pêche et de charge portugais

Mulets trainant leurs filets à la dérive

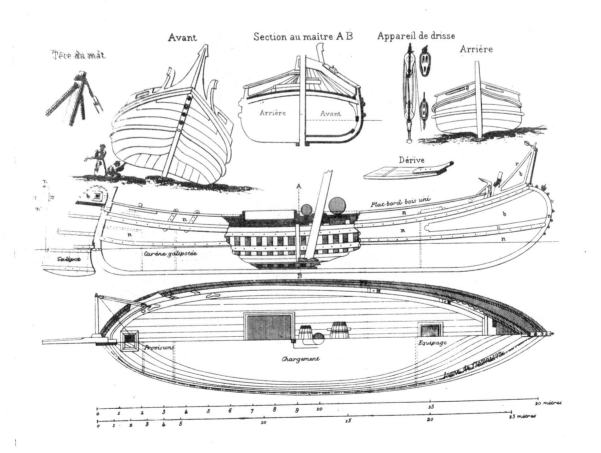

Fig. 16.20: <u>Muleta:</u> plans by R. Monléon, repr. by A. Pâris.

223

bateau XVIIe s.

Fig. 16.21:   Bateau, 17th century (in op. cit. F. Rieth).

Fig. 16.22:   Barco dos Moinhos: from "Marinha do Tejo", p. 69.

Fig. 16.23: <u>Falua</u>: from "Marinha do Tejo", p. 261.

Fig. 16.24: <u>Bote Cacilheiro</u> and <u>Catraio</u>: from "Marinha do Tejo", p. 248.

Fig. 16.25: <u>Barco Cacilheiro</u>: plate 2 in Joǎo de Souza <u>Book</u>, repr. Röding.

Fig. 16.26: <u>Fragata</u>: plate 10 in Joǎo de Souza <u>Book</u>, repr. Röding.

Fig. 16.27: <u>Fragata</u>: photo taken 1961 (O.L. Filgueiras).

Fig. 16.28: <u>Bateira</u>: planked canoe/Mesopotamian type, from Aveiro (O.L. Filgueiras). (10cm)

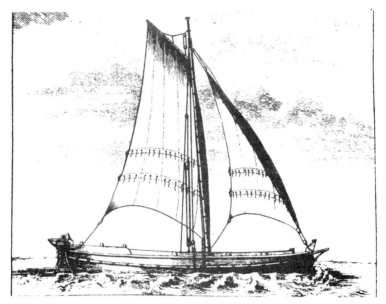

Fig. 16.29: <u>Bateira</u>: plate 8 in João de Souza <u>Book</u>, repr.
Röding.

Fig.17. Bateira

Fig. 16.30: <u>Bateira</u> (19th century): plate 17 in op. cit.
A.J. Pinto Basto.

Fig. 16.31: <u>Hiate</u>: plate 1 in João de Souza <u>Book</u>, repr.
Röding.

Fig. 16.32: Iate: Lisbon Maritime Museum model (Col. Seixas).

Fig. 16.33: _Iate_ (right) and _laitau_ (left): photo O.L. Filgueiras.

Fig. 16.34: <u>Caique</u>: plate 14 in João de Souza <u>Book</u>, repr. Röding.

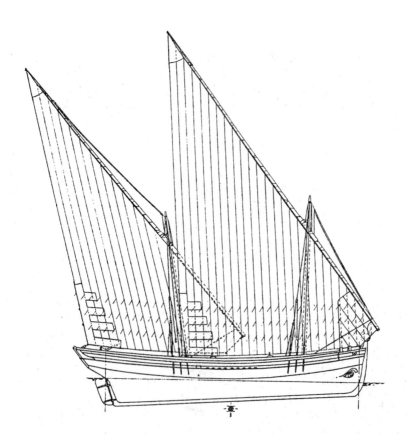

Fig. 16.35: <u>Caique</u>: side view reconst. by Alfredo Barroca.

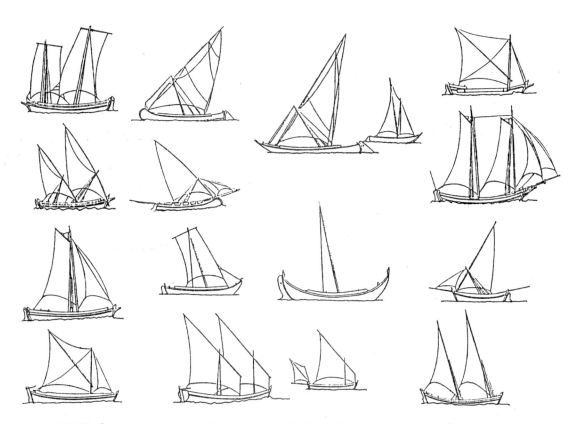

Fig. 16.36: Boats of the Tagus recorded by Joao de Souza (O.L. Filgueiras).

Fig. 16.37:   Boats of the Tagus, 19th/20th century   (M. Leitao).

17. AN AUTOMATIC METHOD FOR BOAT DESIGN

Paul Adam

It has been around 20 years since the Bremenhaven cog, the Wasa warship and the Roskilde boats were found or excavated ... and their plans have still to be drawn.   The reason is that the plans are considered to be the final stage of the salvage work and therefore are delayed with the hope that with time more information will emerge enabling them to be drawn with greater accuracy.

But perfectly exact plans are impossible: boats are continuously changing with the waves they ride, with the years they spend on or below the surface of the water.

The difficulty could be overcome if each hull could be represented by several plans showing the full span of possible variations.   Unfortunately, the corresponding load of work would be too big for the traditional ways of the naval architects, unless hull design could be automated.

I cannot pretend that the computing/design method, briefly presented in this paper, brings about the right solution, but I can state that surely the solution can only be found in such a direction.

The method used in this paper is half way through the final one which will be used in the book I am preparing on this topic.   The design is done by hand on the basis of results given by computer print-out, the final aim being, of course, to have everything done by computer.   But whether the design is done by hand or automatically, the basic computation method is exactly the same.

All is based on the formula "du verre d'eau" (cf. the Introduction of my book "Systèmes Economiques et Histoire," published in 1980) which, in its simplest form, reads as follows:

$$x = X \left(1 - e^{-Ky^B} \right)$$

and which serves the purpose of computing the line of a section (Fig. 17.1).

- x and y are the usual coordinates (see graph):

- X is the vertical asymptote with which the line of the section tends to merge;

- K and B are non-dimensional parameters.

The computation programme combines the following steps:

1 - Each <u>section</u> is determined:
  - by its maximum width and height, i.e. the coordinates of the point P.max in the attached graph, and

  - by the parameters K and B which allow calculation of the curve from the point P.max down to the lowest point of the section where it meets the axis of the hull, P.o in the attached graph.

2 - A <u>hull</u> is therefore a succession of sections which should follow one another in a well-faired manner, i.e.:

  - all points P.max and P.o, for all sections, should be faired so as to obtain a good-looking profile for the deck and hull lines, horizontally as well as vertically;

  - the parameters B and K for all sections should also be faired so that the hull surface would be automatically faired.

The computation or computation/design procedure can arrange the broad above- mentioned steps in any order required by the kind of work undertaken (it can be used to compute a new hull or, conversely, to find out the parameters which would allow to compute an already existing hull) and, at the same time, making the best of the constraints given at the start.

The nautical archaelogical application of this method leads to the following steps:

1 - starting from the available material, tentative determination of the shape of some sections and of the profile (hull and deck lines);

2 - in most cases no sure and unique solution will be found, therefore, through a trial and error process, only possible when the many necessary computations are automatically made, a "family" of possible solutions should be searched for and defined.

CONCLUSION

More complete details and explanations will hopefully make this automated drawing method fully understandable, and manageable, for the archaeologists whose cooperation is indispensable. While the architect makes his best with the lines, the archaeologist who knows the site, who has touched, carried and measured the wood, must be able to intervene and should follow and discuss the lines derived from his excavation and salvage work. Neither the architect nor the archaeologist could work in isolation.

An automated drawing method would also allow scientific treatment. For the time being, tank tests are difficult and not very useful because they can only apply to one single hull; modifications to the design have to be followed by new complete tests. Conversely, systematic mathematical treatment and classifications would allow extrapolations as well as much more efficient and much faster further work.

In the following the method is applied on plans of a few old ships and the results are presented: The Cheops boat Fig. 17.2-17.4; the Nydam ship Fig. 17.5-17.7; the whaleboat of Mystic Seaport Fig. 17.8-17.10; the Marsala Punic ship Fig. 17.11-17.14; the model of the nao from Mataro Fig. 17.15-17.17; and the Roman Cargo ship at Madrague de Giens Fig. 17.18.

Each old ship is given a short introduction.

REFERENCES

Adam, P., 1980. Systemes Economiques et Histoire.

Ansel, W.D. 1978. The Whaleboat, U.S.A.

Fox, U., 1937. Racing, Cruising and Design. London.

Frost, H., 1981a. The Punic Ship Museum, Marsala. Mariner's Mirror LXV.

Frost, H., 1981b. Lilybaeum, The Punic Ship: Final Excavation Report, Accademia Nazionale dei Lincei, Roma.

Jenkins, N., 1980. The Boat beneath the Pyramid.

Winter, H., 1956. Die Katalanische Nao von 1450, Magdeburg.

Note: Although the computations in this paper are intended to be exact, the basic data and the drawings are not necessarily so.   Dimensions are in millimetres unless otherwise indicated.

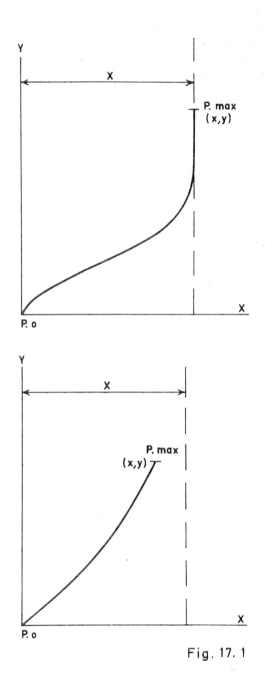

Fig. 17.1

Fig. 17.1:   Reduction of a computer print-out.

236

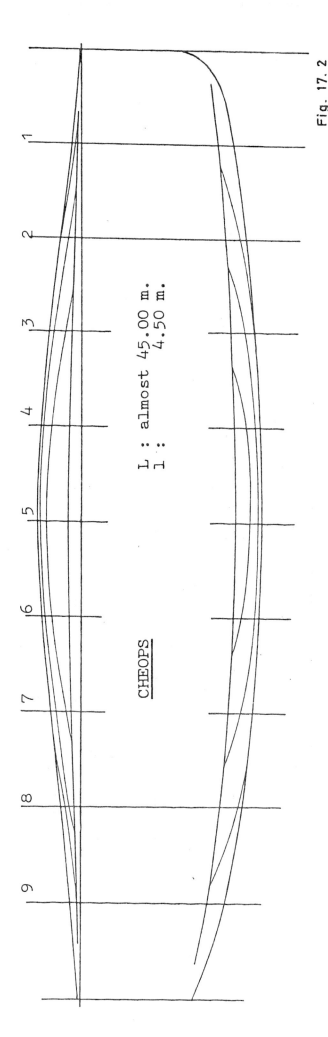

CHEOPS

L : almost 45.00 m.
l : :   4.50 m.

Fig. 17. 2

Fig. 17.2-17.4: The Cheops boat was found in one of the boatgraves beneath the Cheops pyramid. It has been dated to c. 2600 BC and is built primarily to be used on the Nile. The lines of the boat have been taken from a sketch of the profile in Jenkins 1980. The sketch is so imprecise that many different interpretations are possible. The profile and the parameteres selected here can be modified (cf. the example of the section 5, dotted line, computed with a higher value of K), giving different lines for each modification. The possible variations are so numerous that the actual hull should eventually be obtained.

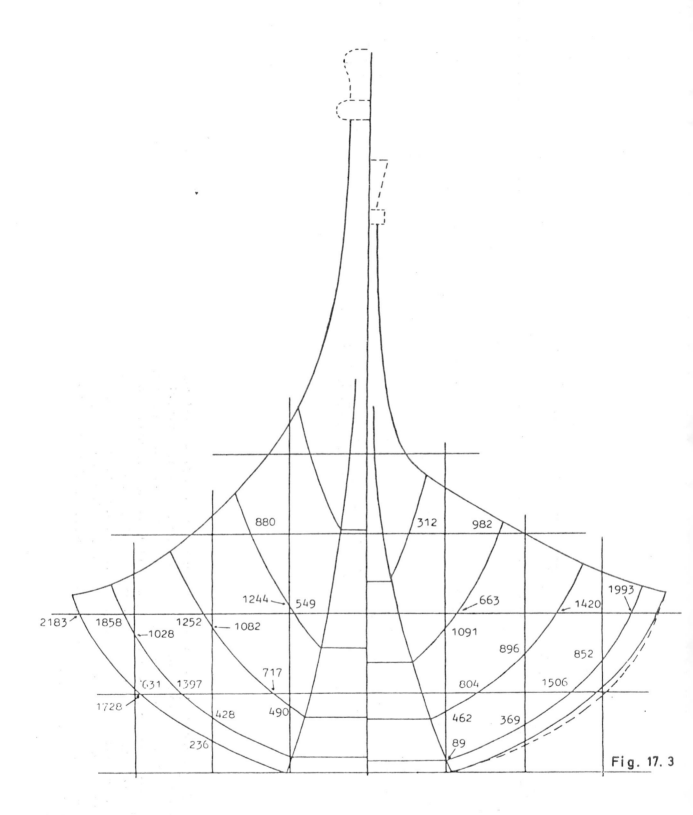

Fig. 17. 3

238

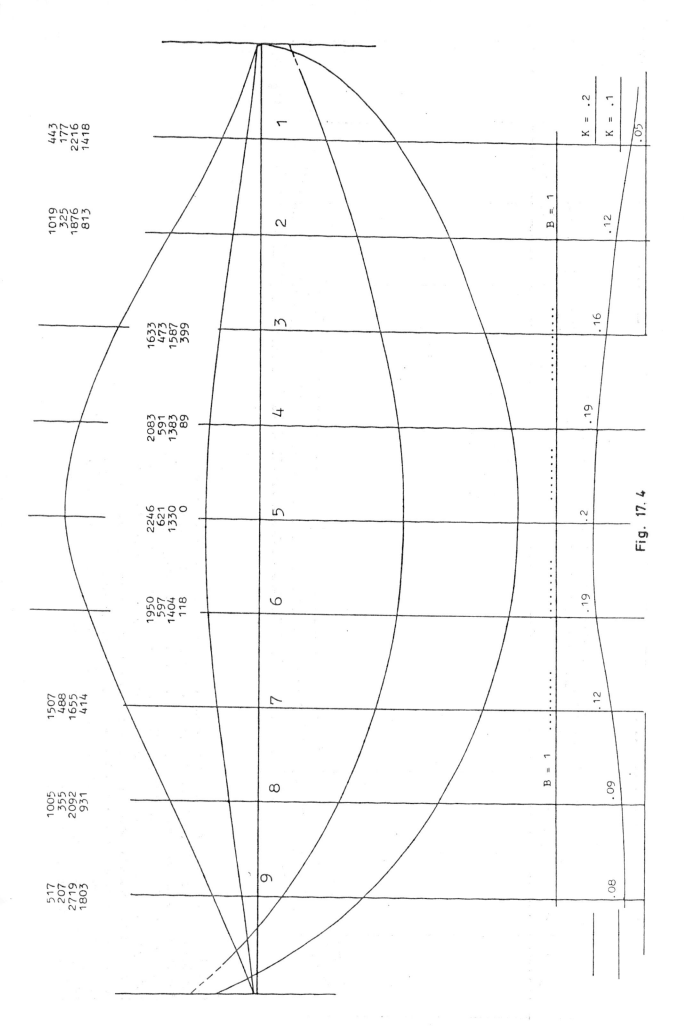

Fig. 17.4

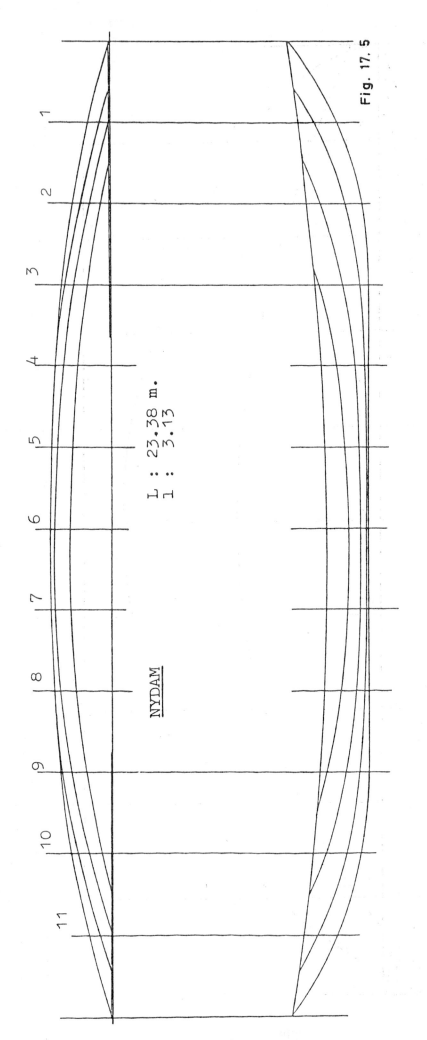

NYDAM

L :: 23.38 m.
1 :: 3.13

Fig. 17.5

Fig. 17.5-17.7: The Nydam boat was found and excavated in a peat bog near the border between Denmark and Germany in 1864. It has been dated to c. 300 BC and is a long rowing vessel. Here is presented lines of the ship published by Uffa Fox (Fox 1937, 120). More recently the lines have been redesigned taking into account the shrinkage of the wood (Akerlund 1963). This is a typical case where slight successive modifications of the profile and of the parameters could allow many different transformations of the first set of lines. The Nydam ship is a full member of the "flat bottom family" and for all such hulls, the lines for the parameters K and B show a well recognizable general shape.

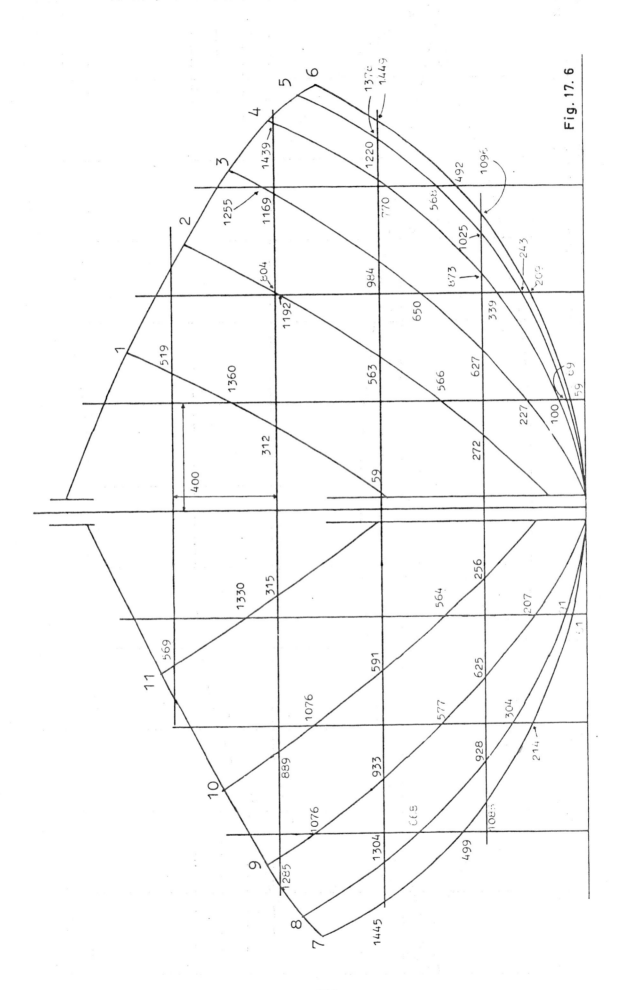

Fig. 17. 6

241

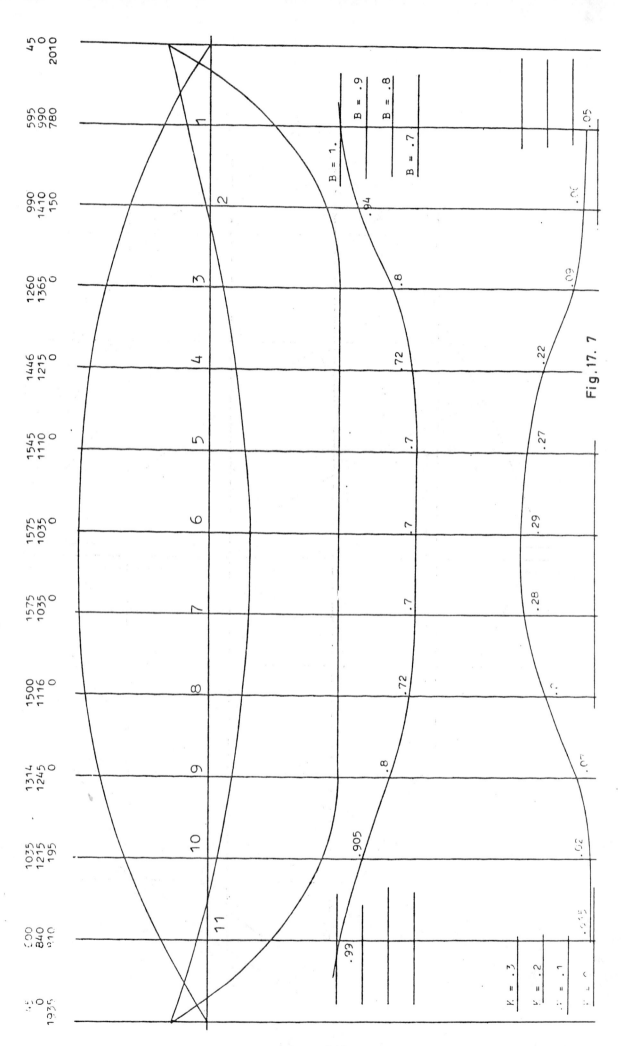

Fig. 17. 7

242

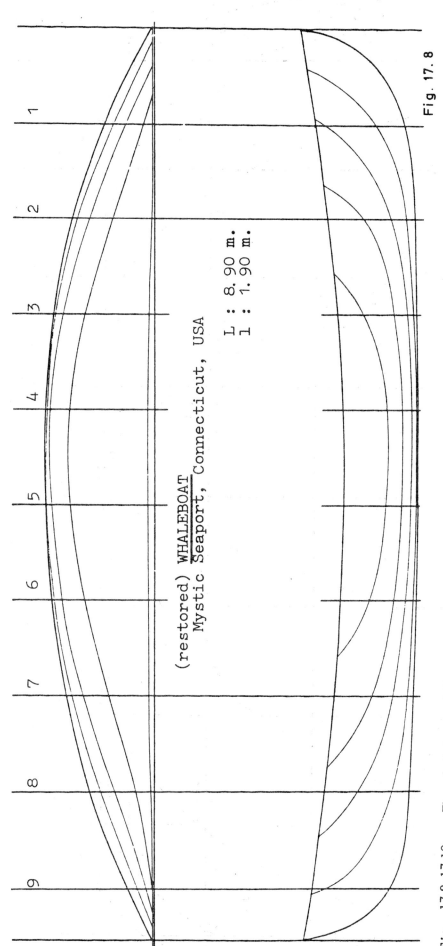

(restored) WHALEBOAT
Mystic Seaport, Connecticut, USA

L : 8.90 m.
l : 1.90 m.

Fig. 17.8

Fig. 17.8-17.10:   The whaleboat of Mystic Seaport is a light rowing boat
for whale hunting.   The lines have been taken from Ansel (1978).   The
vessel has a round hull and is not flat-bottomed.   It belongs to another
family than the boats mentioned above.   The similarity of the lines for the
parameters K and B should nevertheless be noted as being a link with the
previous family of hulls. Has the restoration exactly respected the
original lines?   Certainly not!   In any case the reproduction of the
design in the above mentioned book and its photocopy, used as a basis for
the computations, have certainly introduced further distortions.   Slight
distortions which would imply modifications of the lines, modifications which
might be taken care of by slight changes in the profile and the parameters.

243

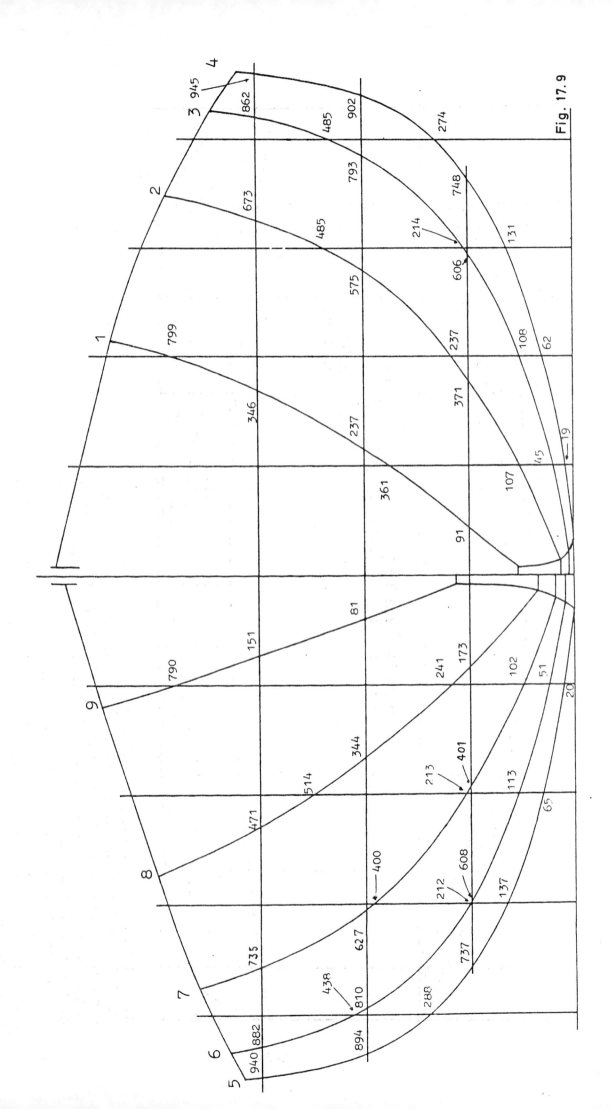

Fig. 17.9

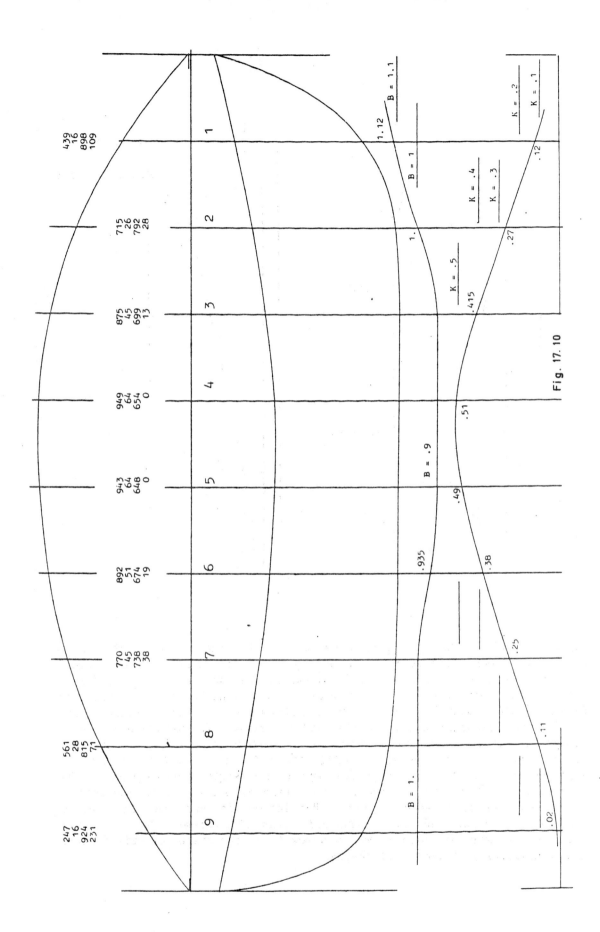

Fig. 17.10

245

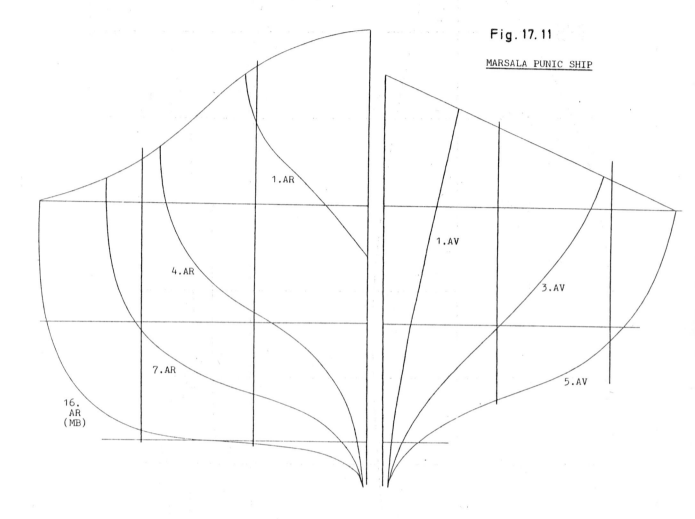

Fig. 17.11

MARSALA PUNIC SHIP

1.AR

1.AV

4.AR

3.AV

7.AR

5.AV

16.
AR
(MB)

Fig.17.11-17.14:   The Punic ship excavated at Lilybaeum, near Marsala in Sicily, has been dated to the 3rd century B.C.   The lines have been taken of the reconstructed ship by Carol Greene in the museum of Marsala (Frost 1981a).   The reconstruction of the ship in the museum has been described in Frost 1981b.   The S-shape of the sections in the ship requires more complicated computations than in the earlier cases.   The parameters K and B cannot be kept the same from the top to the bottom of each section, at least not amidships.   The necessary modifications in the computations are not explained here as they would go far beyond the length of this paper.   The figures 17.11-17.14 give an idea of the intricacy which can be encountered when the method is pursued further.   But let us add that these intricacies can often be organized into systematic classifications, significantly reducing the haphazard variety which seems to be the characteristic feature of any collection of boat hull shapes.

Marsala Punic Ship

Sections for the modified stern

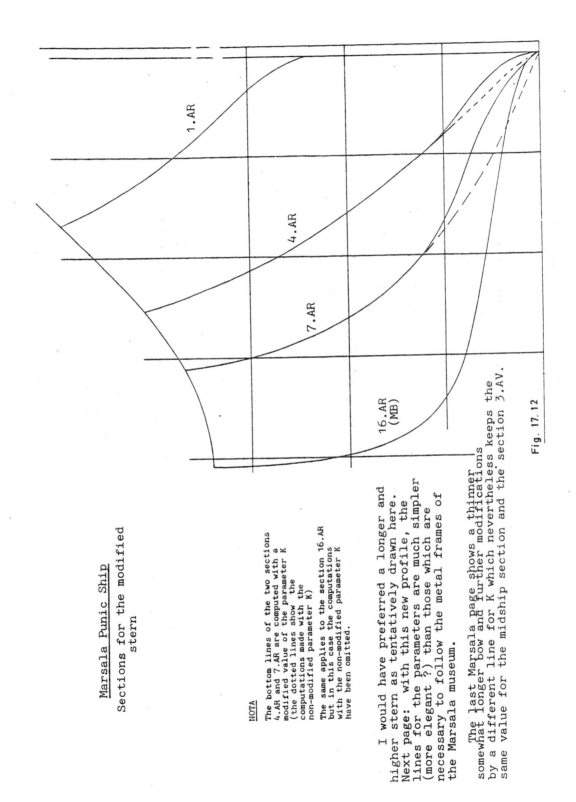

NOTA

The bottom lines of the two sections
4.AR and 7.AR are computed with a
modified value of the parameter K
(the dotted lines show the
computations made with the
non-modified parameter K)

The same applies to the section 16.AR
but in this case the computations
with the non-modified parameter K
have been omitted.

I would have preferred a longer and
higher stern as tentatively drawn here.
Next page: with this new profile, the
lines for the parameters are much simpler
(more elegant ?) than those which are
necessary to follow the metal frames of
the Marsala museum.

The last Marsala page shows a thinner
somewhat longer bow and further modifications
by a different line for K which nevertheless keeps the
same value for the midship section and the section 3.AV.

Fig. 17.12

247

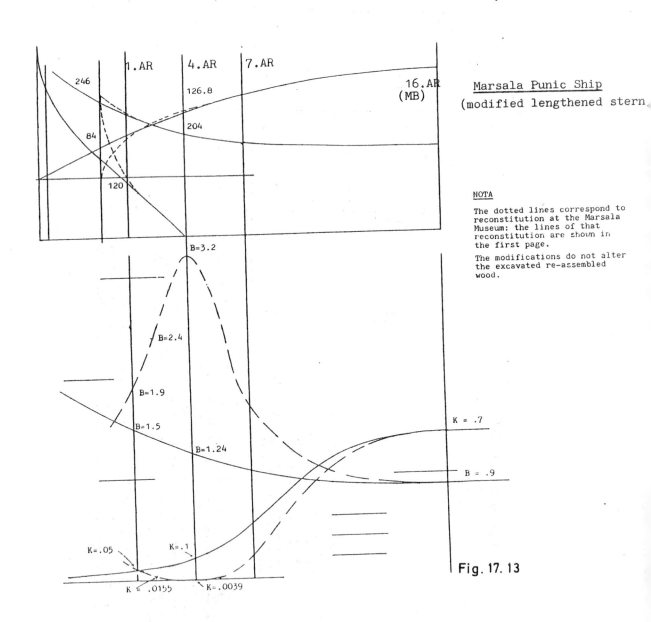

1.AR 4.AR 7.AR

246 126.8 16.AR (MB)

84 204

120

B=3.2

Marsala Punic Ship
(modified lengthened stern

B=2.4

B=1.9

B=1.5

K = .7

B=1.24

B = .9

K=.05 K=.1

K ≤ .0155 K=.0039

Fig. 17. 13

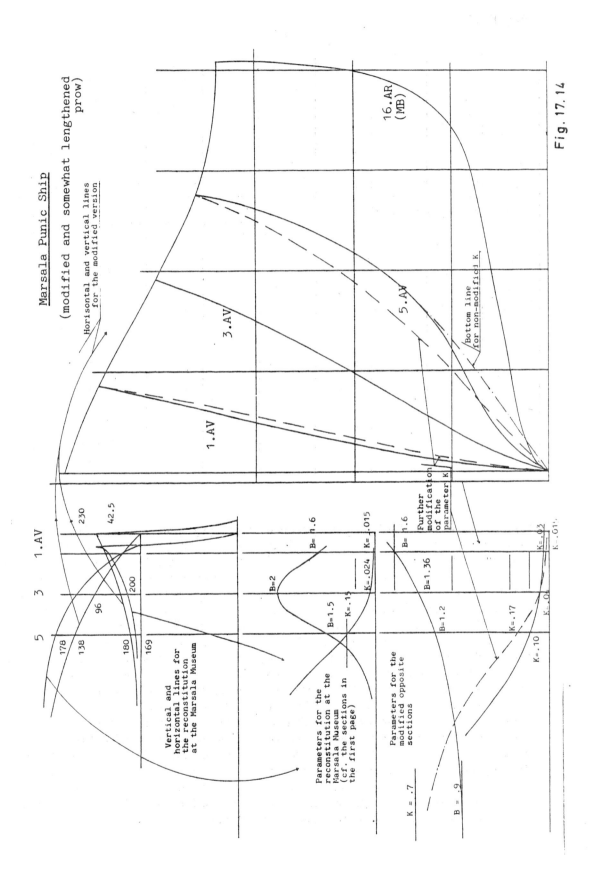

Marsala Punic Ship

(modified and somewhat lengthened prow)

Horisontal and vertical lines for the modified version

3.AV

1.AV

5.AV

16.AR (MB)

Bottom line for non-modified K

Further modification of the parameter K

Vertical and horizontal lines for the reconstitution at the Marsala Museum

Parameters for the reconstitution at the Marsala Museum (cf. the sections in the first page)

Parameters for the modified opposite sections

5   3   1.AV

230

42.5

178

138

96

200

180

169

B=2

B=1.6

B=1.5   K=.15

K=.024   K=.015

B=1.6

B=1.36

B=1.2

K=.17

K=.10   K=.04

K=.03

K=.01

K = .7

B = .9

Fig. 17.14

Fig. 17. 15

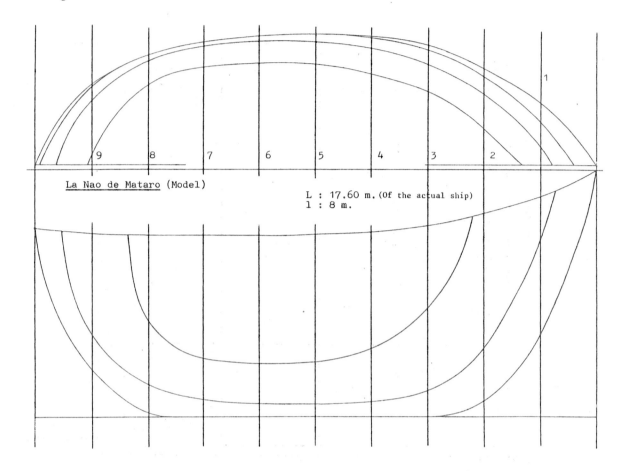

La Nao de Mataro (Model)

L : 17.60 m. (Of the actual ship)
1 : 8 m.

Fig.17.15-17.17:   The model of the nao from Mataro at the Catalonian coast is dated to the late 15th century AD (Winter 1956).   The length of the original ship can be estimated to c. 17.6 m. the breadth to 8 m.   The lines of the "Nao the Mataro" are, in my opinion, very inelegant... I was therefore happy to find that my method did not follow such lines without "humps".   If the "humps" are eliminated from the line for parameter B, they automatically reappear on the line for parameter K.   Furthermore, section 8, which is the only one describing a noticeable S-shape, can only be computed with a modification of parameter K at and around this section... which helps to accentuate the inelegant character of the design.   The lines which have been taken of the model show in other words a rather awkward set of lines, i.e. a ship whose sailing capabilities might have been far from exceptional.   Furthermore the "abnormal" S-shape of the section 8 must have been caused by an error made by the model maker.   The wooden planks of the original full size ship should have obliged the shipbuilder to avoid such a discrepancy.   It must be added that the profile of the model is designed at a non-distorted scale.   All other designs in this paper look somewhat clumsy because of an exaggerated width and height compared to length, a design trick which allows to draw fairer lines.

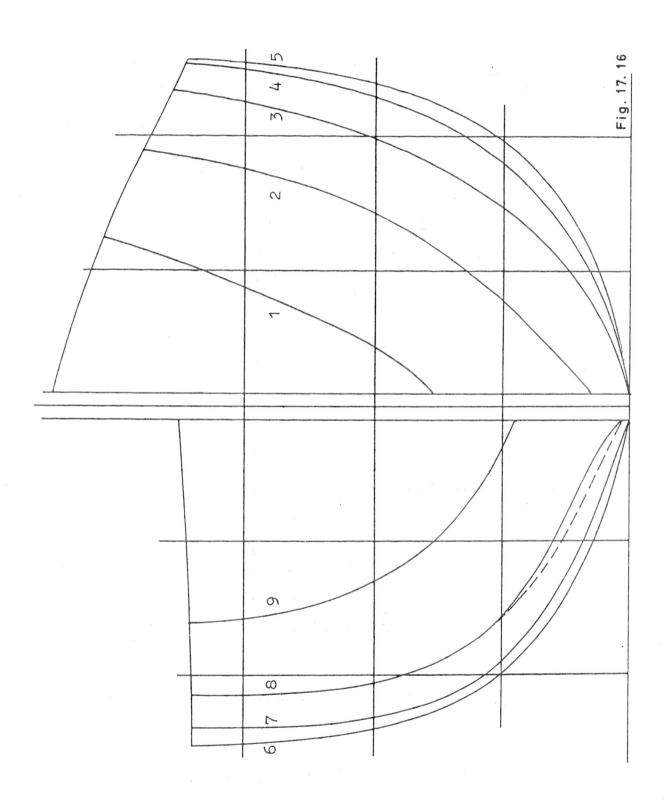

Fig. 17. 16

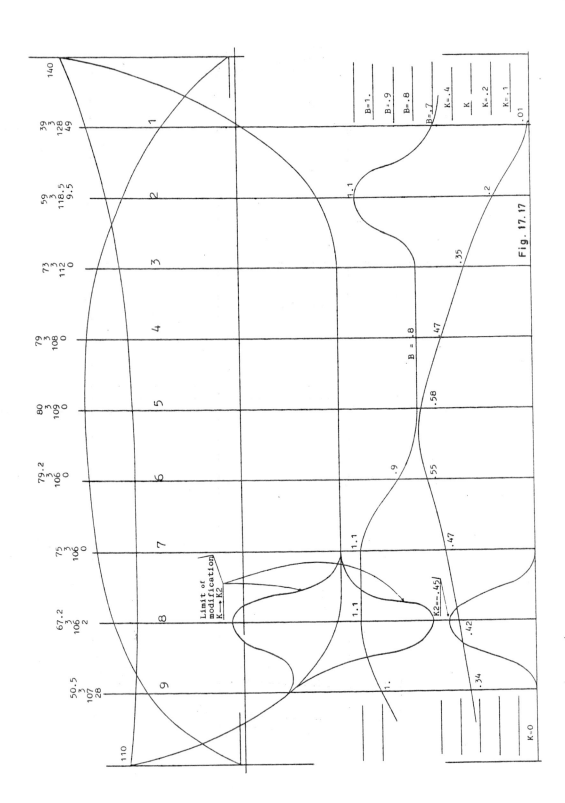

Fig. 17.17

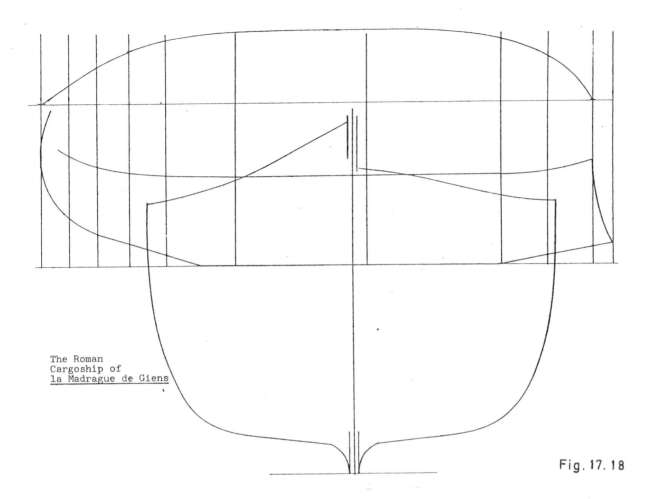

The Roman
Cargoship of
la Madrague de Giens

Fig. 17. 18

Fig. 17.18:   A sketch of the Roman cargoship excavated at Madrague de Giens
by P. Pomey is sufficient to show how different could be a good design.
But such statement would need justifications requiring many more pages than
can be used for this presentation.

18. EVOLVING SHIP DESIGN TECHNOLOGY REVEALED IN WRECKS OF POST MEDIEVAL SHIPS

Thomas Gillmer

This paper has relatively little to say about examples of ship design technology actually exposed in wrecks of post-medieval ships. It is rather pointed toward making a case for archaeological awareness of such examples.

In considering the evolution of ship technology there is much convincing evidence as well as simple dialectic that there is a stream, continuous in the time of man, where progress prevailed. At the center of the stream is the tide of progress however sluggishly it was moved by ingenious hands, and toward the outer edges there was and are the backwaters where can still be seen some of the efforts of the past. This progress in the mainstream center, I believe, has dealt with the concept of bettering performance of ships, first in propulsive techniques (whether sails, oars or mechanical systems); as well as performance which includes safety and reasonable habitability across oceans of unpredictable nature.

It is only in the latter course of this stream of shipbuilding progress where it has widened to a broad and powerful flow to provide the transport of mankind, with his wealth and disputes, that rational ship design has assisted.

Very broadly, ship design is the art of the shipwright with his instincts, craftsmanship and knowledge that enable him to fashion a boat (or ship) capable of performing and keeping the sea. This concept of ship design is most abstract and its essence is skilled craftsmanship with applied knowledge. It is interesting that nearly the whole of shipbuilding history was led by this broad concept of ship design and that only for approximately the past 350 years has there been any other kind.

In the more narrow, definitive sense, ship design is the predetermined formulation of the ship's structure and configuration. The process has its beginnings and, properly, its summation before ship construction begins. By its nature it is conceptual and its key is predetermination. The process must be a rational one and one whereby its practitioner is held accountable for his product. It is only in this way that through practice and record can genuine technical progress be established; where the right procedures illuminate the wrong; where successes as well as failures become recorded and where acquired knowledge correctly identifies the best approach. We cannot leave this definition so simply without also properly saying that the whole process of modern ship design is replete with theory. The recognition of ship design as a process apart from shipwright, ultimately to be called naval architecture, occurred in Europe somewhere and very gradually during the end of the 17th century and the beginnings of the 18th. However its practice is frequently accomplished still in shipyards in close proximity with the working shipwrights.

We must return to the earlier and more general sort of ship design that prevailed for so many centuries and marched so slowly along with humankind marking his progress with other technology. Being concerned here with evolving ship technology I hope I may be excused for suggesting that nautical archaeology does not exist as an end in itself. I see it as a basic source in the process of identifying the evolutionary stages of ship technology. Historians must leave it to others to study the treatment and preservation of ship timbers, techniques of salvage, and other technology. When the ship itself is revealed from its remains and shown with its proper place, my curiosity concerning its structure and shape then reaches its peak.

It is the shape of the hull that is of first concern in revealing the ancient shipwright's ability to create a capable sailing vessel and in this an insight to sailing qualities can be helpful. If it might be allowable, for sake of example, to reach back beyond the confines of post-medieval time it is most interesting to look at the shape of the ship's bottom in some boats of shell-first construction. The characteristic is found in the structure of the wreck of the oldest ship found, as well as in the wrecks of the ships in the museum at Roskilde and even in the bottoms of ships still built in the Persian Gulf and others.

Originating in the earliest of external keel-built ships a fortuitous bottom shape, sometimes called a "hollow garboard", provides a superior quality of sailing that is not present in more recent and plainer "round ships". Or is it in those with flat or near-flat bottomed hulls. The characteristic is clearly present and easily identifiable in the semi-restored wreck called the Kyrenia ship of the 4th century B.C. found close to the north shore of Cyprus. The wooden remains of this ship provide an exceptional opportunity to study and appreciate the quality of early classical shipbuilding. It more importantly provides our best index and bench mark from which to measure historic development of ship construction. The quality of construction in this example is very high and it is typical in the ancient method. The method is generally known as shell-first contruction. Most significantly however this elegantly built ship shows the first existing example of an external keel, however old its use may have been at the time (Fig. 18.1).

The keel of the Kyrenia ship is shaped and installed in the best practice of wooden structured ships, ancient or modern. Its section proportion of height to breadth is approximately 2:1 with a generous rabbet at the top for the garboard strake. The rabbet is clearly and skillfully cut with a slight outboard angle. The floor timber above the keel with its limber chock provides the exact slope and flare of the garboards and first bottom planks. The Kyrenia ship thus has an excellent "built-down" keel with a hollow-like run in the best tradition of fast sailing vessels even of the 18th and 19th century. The same characteristic prevails in fast sailing yachts today, in the most exaggerated form recognized as the "keel-fin". This is, no doubt, a hull shape or form characteristic that has been "discovered" and "rediscovered" on untold number of occasions by shipwrights in many places and times since the Kyrenia ship and quite likely before. So we know it has been a feature among some sailing vessels for at least 24 centuries. More recent examples than the 4th century B.C. Kyrenia ship are the majority of lap plank ships of the Norse. The Kyrenia ship, at least provides the earliest bench mark for this hull style feature (Katzev 1980 and 1981).

To describe the advantageous contribution to the quality and performance of sailing provided by this hollow, built-down area adjacent to the keel, I will only briefly point out the physical phenomena. As we all know, a sailing vessel moves through the water most usually at some angle relative to the wind direction. (We will ignore the single and most uncomfortable situation of sailing directly before the wind). On all other courses the wind will produce a leeward component, tending to move the vessel to the side while at the same time it is going forward. This sideward drift or "leeway" is dependent on many factors quantitatively. The strength and angle of the wind contributes most siginificantly; the sails' shape and effectiveness, the amount of heeling angle the ship takes, etc., are all parts of the equation. The final result is that the course sailed is not the same as the course steered and, on our acompanying diagram, the difference in these courses or angles is the "drift angle". Obviously the smaller the drift angle, the better the progress in the intended direction of sailing. But also if we try to narrow the drift anlge too much as we steer we will reach the no headway condition; the sails will not remain airfoils, the hull drag will become larger than the useful drive of the sail and the vessel will "fall off" a bit. Without going further into the physical phenomena it may be simply concluded that to continue sailing with the optimum speed and progress along the ship's track, there is some <u>drift</u> angle always existing. To achieve optimum progress, particularly with a relative wind forward of the beam, is to measure the ship's sailing performance and windward ability. So with the drift angle in mind let us consider the extended keel area in the ship's bottom. This centerline protrusion, with gently rising hollow surfaces adjacent, moving through the water at a small "drift" angle is much like an aircraft wing moving at an angle of attack in an airstream. There is produced a "lifting" component of force. In the case of the ship, this component is lateral, toward the <u>up-wind</u> direction. The obvious conclusion we are presented with is that, at least since the 4th century B.C., it has been possible for ships sailing, "on" or "off" the wind, to experience a superior quality of windward sailing due to the exceptional feature of built-down keel or hollow garboards.

I do not believe that the ancient shipwrights who built the Kyrenia Ship or similar ships of that time or earlier had any particular understanding of the contribution of this feature to sailing quality. I further think that a great number of the classic sailing ships had this very same faeture in bottom structure. It was not the result of deliberate planning in sculpting of hull shape to produce a better able boat. The hollow garboards were the result of the method of construction, the sequence of planking and framing the hull. Consequently we cannot attribute an early sense of "design" planning, at least in this very significant and contributive hull shape feature.

The hollow garboards in early vessels, built in the well-identified <u>shell-first,</u> edge-fastened manner, resulted quite naturally in such shape because of the difficulty in twisting planks unsupported by frames from a near-horizontal bottom surface to the vertical surface of the stem or stern post surfaces. This same difficulty quite likely contributed to the profile of the bow and form of the stem in many ancient ships. The planks adjacent to the keel that began flat in the bottom must continue with little twist and run out farther forward producing a full and extended bow form. A finer entrance, or sharp waterline requires an up-curving stempost and a gradual turn in planking, hence the built-down keel in <u>shell-first</u> built ships.

257

In the long progression of external keel-built vessels, and the gradual exchange of <u>shell-first</u> construction for <u>frame-first</u> or skeletal construction there was much variation in the overall hull form. There also was very little improvement in the quality of sailing performance. During this exchange, there was a gradual trend to larger capacity hulls, more heavily timbered structure, more complex sailing rig and multi-mast arrangement, but there seems to be no evidence over these long ages toward rational improvement of hull design.

Here we must pause to recall the notions of "design" as mentioned at the outset of this paper. Thus far the change in shape and style and complexity of ships has been regarded only in the broad sense of ship design. Either from historical or archaeological evidence there is nothing that can be identified as "ship design" in the definitive sense which assumes a rational determination.

We cannot do better at this point when considering shipbuilding of the post-medieval period than consider the definitions and limitations of naval architecture proposed by Fredrik Henrik Chapman in 1775. His thinking clearly is applicable not only in his own time but generally historically and currently today. A ship can have no less attention to its planning and design and basically needs little more. I would like to categorically repeat Chapman's five requirements for knowledge in shipbuilding and as I understand them (Chapman 1775). He wrote:

1. That a ship with a certain draught of water should be able to contain and carry a determinate lading. (Determination of displacement in the design process).

2. That it should have a sufficient and also determinate stability. (Determination of a ship's safe and intact stability).

3. That it should be easy at sea, or its rolling and pitching be not too quick. (Design to provide a ship with acceptable motion in a seaway).

4. That it should sail well before the wind, and close to the wind, and work well to windward. (Design to provide a ship of acceptable sailing or propulsive performance).

5. That it should not be too ardent, and yet come easily about. (Sailing vessel design to provide that it be well-balanced and easily tacked. This later provision is obviously applied only to sailing craft).

These words of Chapman, which were probably the earliest definition of naval architecture may serve as most useful guide for examining the shipbuilding of prior centuries and can be very little improved upon in executing the design of a sailing vessel of any age including the present. Only a moment's reflection on the five requirements makes it apparent that four of the five deal with providing safety and sailing performance. All of them infer that the requirements be predetermined in the design process. It should be emphasized that they all predominantly deal with the ship's hull configuration. By remote inference we must assume that the structural strength be adequate as well.

It is realized that it is most difficult in examining the remains of ships from archaeological ship finds to ascertain any of these requisite characteristics or whether they are revealed at all. Some finds, where the hull is to a considerabled degree intact, will reveal the performing qualities of the ship and perhaps speak plainly about stability and possibly even the windward ability and balance. Tests have been made in this diretcion for some ship remains in the form of construction of models, replications, etc. The accuracy of conclusions rest on the depth and quality of the experiments and the results should be studied with these restraints in mind.

However, there would seem to be very little in a wreck of an antique vessel that would reveal whether the hull configuration, including its structure whole or in part had been predetermined by a rational design process. Nor is it the intention here to attempt to identify any such instances. It is important however to observe, and identify where possible, when such characteristic properties may exist and to what degree. Marking the wrecks, for quantity of ballast stones relative to its size; noting reference marks for draft and signs of waterline erosion marks; identifying locations of mast steps and alignments with mast partners in deck; and recording all of the indicators of ship employment. All these make for more revealing reconstructions. These occasions will be the small milestones that mark the evolvement of ship design. Whether or not the ship "design" was drawn in graphic projection, lifted from model or otherwise predetermined, is not in itself of great importance.

Ship design in its strictest, most disciplined sense requires that the methodology used be evolved from acceptable physical theory. It strongly suggests that the displacement be calculated by some form of mathematical procedure, most practically that advanced by Newton and Leibnitz in the early 18th century. It requires that the stability be determined and described in terms of metacentric theory, likewise involving the calculus. Ships so designed are not easily identifiable with any probability. The determination of design source of a modern ship would be doubtful without the most extensive examination and with the help of many detailed blueprints of the vessel.

So when we look for evolving ship design technology we must be relaxed in our definition of design. We must regard design in the broader abstract sense and at the same time be aware of evidence of refinement and improvement contributing to growth and capability. This is functional history.

Again, I must ask to be permitted to step back a bit to medieval Europe to pick up a thread or two that I see as critical to the shipwright's task. In early medieval years, 1025 more precisely to date a wreck, was a time when shipwrights of the south of Europe were apparently using a newer technology. The earliest remains of a ship indicating a sequence of frames-first assembly or skeletal construction raised 1977-78, Srece Liman, Turkey, revealed the new trend that, to say the least, was a slow and gradual one (Steffy 1982). However this approach to building from the inside out instead of from the outside in can only be viewed as a very large milestone in the ship construction progress. All of the archaeological evidence of the preceding three millennia indicates firm dedication of shipwrights to the idea of building a sculpture of planked skin, with fastened edges by laborious systems.

With no frame erected first on a centerline backbone there are few if any arrangements to control the concept of hull shape. Using planks fastened by edge would seem a method with material controlling the builder who was much constrained in his choices of hull form. He was able to build only to imprecise dimension and, to a degree, strive for proportion, significantly length and beam.

A shipwright in the world of Alexander or in the empire of Caesar did not know with any degree of accuracy at what draft his ship would float when launched. His confidence in how it would perform under sail, or how far it would heel to a wind was based solely on previous experience with a like vessel. This sort of craft does not have much room for progressive growth.

So we must regard the movement toward <u>frame-first</u> construction as an evolutionary development ultimately to provide the means of rational design.

It would be evident early in use of <u>frame-first</u> construction that the method provided a ship with inherent symmetry. I am told by the restorer and reconstructor of some of the significant early Mediterranean wrecks that a common feature among them is lack of symmetry about the longitudinal axis, not as a result of age or erosion, but because of dissimilar assembly of planks port and starboard. With the easy establishment of symmetrical <u>frame-first</u> the surface of the hull must be held to symmetry. The pre-detrerinate and symmetrical form of the ship's hull made possible by the <u>frame-first</u> emplacement is the cornerstone for development of ship design, through the post-medieval age to the twentieth century. This system ultimately embraced design in its broadest as well as its most precise sense.

There were, and are, many factors controlling the design of ships that have little to do with Chapman's thinking on the architecture of a seagoing vessel. Most significantly these things are (perhaps in order of significance) the hull shape imposed by economic requirements, and political fulfillments. The economic requirements need little explanation. The understanding is universal that wide full ships deliver much bulk cargo and the greater the volumes the greater result the profits. There is little here that gives priority to speed and manoeuverability. The ultimate in this concept of economy are sailing barges, with many degres of compromise to preserve a necessary minimum of seaworthiness. There is precious little to be discovered in the bulk cargo transport relating to growth of the technology of ship design. There is much relating to transport law and rules of measurement for tonnage and taxation.

The ships created for public or governmental purpose are of course predominantly war vessels and their evaluation is a more complex and perplexing study than can be undertaken in a short paper such as this. Warship design is in a special category and singleness of purpose.

It was pointed out previously that the hollowed or concave curvature of the bottom surface of the ship's hull is an advantageous characteristic in sailing, particularly on the wind. Also that the pre-medieval and ancient boats of the Mediterranean had such shape because it was the result of the <u>shell-first</u> planking technique.

In post-medieval ships we are aware that the basic shipbuilding methodology has turned to the <u>frame-first</u> system of assembly particularly in the larger ships. And also it is a matter of history that in these post-medieval centuries the marked trend was toward larger and fuller and more complexly rigged vessels. The simple logic that bigger was better seemed to be proved in that larger ships were able to go to sea for extended periods, carry more profitable cargoes and even sail faster (though less efficiently) than their smaller ancient predecessors. As the frame-first system of building became refined the shape of the frames were "designed" by elaborate geometric procedures that resulted in hull forms that were only remotely related to good sailing performance. The hollow garboards of earlier shell-first structures seem to have been lost. The bottoms near the keel were flat or nearly so. The rise in the bilges was gradual and full, swelling to the fullest near the waterline.

It is tempting to be convinced that the dominant, prosperous shipwrights of the 16th and 17th centuries were so preoccupied with rules of geometry, in the fullness of hold, masting and rigging that they were blinded to the real requirements of sailing vessels. It is not until the 18th century that there is evidence of basic improvement.

It is the "age of enlightenment" that the more elegant architectural drawings show refinement in geometrically drawn sections. They also, at last are showing controlled configuration. It can be seen in examples of early 18th century ship's sections, the experimentation of various deadrise angles, and in many the redevelopment of a hollow in garboard planking. This can be interpreted as controlled and predeterminate hull shape in the planned ship's frame shape. Solid examples of rational design.

Where this hollow garboard form is found in a wreck of a post-medieval ship or boat one can be sure that it was put there intentionally by a reasoning shipwright. We can reasonably hope that he was also proudly aware of his ship's superior weatherly performance.

It is notable that elegant draughts of Chapman identify themselves by this hollow garboard characteristic. His handsome designs of frigates, privateers and yachts, all vessels requiring speed and weatherly performance show body plans whose sections are hollow for the whole length of the keel. This man was a designer of vision and it was ship's hulls like these that were in the mainstreamn of evolving and advancing ship design.

I am much persuaded to look for evaluation of ship design among the smaller "working classes". The evolving ship which has survived through all the years has done so in a process somehow akin to Darwin's Theory: one of natural selection. "The survival of the fittest", to overwork a phrase, is most appropriate. The selective process is at work continually in the evolution of working ships, and is particularly evident among shipwrights creating the smaller, less ostentatious craft. Those people were closer to the environment of their product, and worked empirically with more economy and efficiency (Fig. 18.2). So ultimately the thread of good design prevailed among the carriers of small commerce, privateers and smugglers perhaps, whose boats competed not only with their sisters but with the sea directly. In turn it follows from this sort of "laboratory" development that the losses and failures are relatively small financially and are either successfully reproduced or abandoned for something better.The successes and advancements are further developed and ultimately observed and acquired by the builders of bigger ships, "filtering up" as it were. This is perhaps contrary to a common assumption of the school believing in moving only with the establishment.

261

In the ultimate analysis, I believe that those features which most likely improved ship performance and ship safety are more naturally predominant and prevailing among the characteristics of evolving commercial and private ship design. There are again those that Chapman, here in Stockholm, said must guide all naval architects.

An example of evolving ship technology is noted in an excavation recently in the United States of a small American armed brig. The vessel identified as the Defence, 170 tons, was sunk in 1779 by a British Navy Squadron together with some other continental Navy vessels in Penobscot Bay, now in the State of Maine, U.S.A.

In 1975 an archaeological project under the Maine State Museum proceeded to uncover the remains of one of this ill-fated Penobscot expedition. They soon discovered the Defence to be an 80-ft. vessel, about 40 to 45 percent intact in the hull. She was found to be in an upright position with a port list of about 15°. The overburden was removed revealing a vessel of finely modeled hull. Her construction is traditional with rather more closely placed frames than customary in this type of ship. Her deck was gone but the silt-filled hull was well-preserved from below the port chain plates to just below the starboard waterline (Symonds 1979). The hull shape is easily identified from the midsection shape and the forward bow form. This hull was clearly an early example of an American type called a "Virginia built" hull.

"Virginia built" was a term synonymous with "Chesapeake built" and described as often lightly structured but sharp-ended hull of extremely sharp deadrise. They were noted as vessels of exceptional performance and speed (Fig. 18.3).

Existing records show that this vessel was built in Beverly, Massachusetts in 1778 as one of twelve privateers, never apparently to have been close to Virginia or the Chesapeake. This archaeological evidence of the shipbuilder's recognition of the sailing qualities of Chesapeake vessels of this style and bottom form reinforces the quest for historical design technology. It also reinforces colloquial points of view among American historians on the possibility of the migration Northward from the Chesapeake of shipbuilding techniques and style, which has long been arguable among the ethnically inclined historians.

The emphasis on ship performance is evident in the Penobscot ship, and it is an example in an age of awakening ship technology.

Sailing performance and windward ability, essential goals in progressive design technology, depend largely on ship's bottom shapes, with surfaces generating pressure differential on opposing sides. There are other factors of evolving ship design rather less related to sailing performance and more to the practical side of ship operation.

Stability is measured in a ship by both its geometry and gravitational force; more strictly, by the separation of the buoyant and gravitational forces. Buoyant force is the result of the ship's immersed geometry or hull form below the water, gravitational force as a function of its weight distribution. A ship's stability can only be affected or manipulated by the shipboard sailors to the extent that they can change the weight or loading. The loading is often evident in the wreck of a sunken ship where it comes to rest. Its distribution is often confused but it is worth a considerable amount of study and care if determination of the cause of the ship's loss is of interest.

Of the ship's weight, its ballast is the most significant but probably its most uninteresting part. It is there exclusively to provide adequate stability and it should be located in the lowest part of the ship. The type of ballast is quite as important as its location, in that, in its greater density, less volume will be required for its placement.

The "adequate" amount of ballast in a ship is not an easy or frequently possible determination. Merchant ships as well as warships had stowage plans that utilized their regular cargoes, ship's stores, and equippage as functional ballast. Beyond this and when merchant vessels were with light or minimum cargo some considerable attention and provision required real ballast. This historically has been, with few exceptions, in the form of stones. Such ballast is obviously economical and very available. It was better than sand or gravel in its adaptability. Its weight, generally greater, than that of customary cargoes or the variety of ship's stores, made it more effective. There was in most ships even from antiquity some stone ballast. This, obviously indicates an awareness of the need to offset the force of wind in the sails and of high super-structure. Such awareness apparently was not always intuitive. The findings of ballast among wrecks or indeed its identification in the wreck's site is difficult. It has been more often in wrecks of later centuries of the post-medieval period suggesting rational evolutionary trend in ships. However, it cannot be credited as such a positive predeterminate, therefore, design factor with overwhelming confidence. It would be helpful to have more analytic study of wreck sites with the ballast factor in mind, with a comparison to the ship's displacement.

An awareness of comparative ballast effectiveness is most helpful in an analytic study. As indicated in the foregoing stone and beach rock are most frequently found in wreck sites and obviously was for ballast purpose. Stone compared to common metal such as iron is only about 25% as effective on the basis of weight. Iron in the form of excess or old cannon on warships was not uncommon as ballast. Iron billets or pigs were being gradually adopted in some of the smaller, faster sailing vessels by the late 18th century. Such usages as this is prime evidence of evolving ship design technology.

The storage of water and wine casks in the lowest holds is evident ballasting, such liquids being only a little less in density than stone.

The amount of ballast in a sailing vessel beyond the weight of ordinary or neutral cargoes of densities similar to the ship's structural woods can be roughly stated in limits relating to the ship's displacement. The center of gravity of an unballasted sailing ship without cargo or neutral weighted cargo is located normally a little above the level of flotation. Such location is too high for the conventional form of ships to insure adequate stability. Indeed at such condition the ship might easily be lost. Ballasting to lower the center of gravity, as well as raising the waterline in sailing vessels of 17th and 18th century to the point of adequate stability amounted to added weight near 25% of the final weight (displacement) of the ship. This quantity of required stone or beach rock is substantial and in the evidence existing among most wrecks of late post-medieval ships it is not present in any such quantity in photographs of, or

reports of the contents of the finds.   It is of course difficult, for lack
of knowledge of its precise shape to determine the ship's total weight.   If
the ship can be identified as it often can through documentation the weight
can more readily be approximated.   Ballast in small, fast brigs and
schooners in the smuggling trade or privateering in late 18th century often
equaled or sometimes exceeded the above figure of 25%.

It has been suggested with intended emphasis that the historic
sequences of shell and frame assembly in shipbuilding have had some
significant bearing on evolving ship design technology. It is worth
summarizing this involvement. It seems evident from the series of wrecks
found in the Mediterranean as well as Northern Europe that the shell-first
system was the earliest of the two systems. The system was used at least as
long as the Old Kingdom of Egypt or about 2700 B.C. It was used and
developed in refinement throughout the millennia. The change to skeletal
construction took place gradually apparently with the earliest known example
dating early 11th century A.D. The establishment of this system as the more
conventional to predominant usage took place over the years of early
medieval and into post-medieval. Certainly it was into the mid to late
postmedieval years, the 18th century when the full advantages of frame-
first building sequence was fully exploited. It was this enlightened age
with its resolutions of naval power and world colonization that brought
emphasis to serious and responsible shipbuilding utilizing the best
scientific foundation. Ship design separated from shipwrightry as the
dominant and controlling direction. The shape of a ship, its nonlinear
dimensional criteria, and its capacities could by that time be largely
predetermined (Fig. 18.4). The determined amount of a ship's displacement,
and thus its precise mark of flotation; its stability and power to carry
sail, as well as knowledge of its performance under sail were in the hands
of the shipwright before an axe was swung or a saw lifted during the last
two and a half decades of the 18th century.

So, I believe that it can be safely agreed upon that the post-medieval
period in Europe embraced a time of design evolvement and refinement in
shipbuilding technology.

In the archaeology of shipwrecks it is suggested with some resolution
that there should be an increased awareness toward recognition of factors
with their effects some of which have been described in this discussion.
They are not as visible as the artifacts of more common historic disposition
but they are far more useful in our discovery of the evolution of the ship
(Gillmer 1981).

REFERENCES

Chapman, F.H., 1775. Tractat om Skepps Byggeriet; (Translation by Rev.
James Inman 1794), Stockholm.

Vial du Clairbois, 1776. Essai Geometric et Pratique sur L'Architecture
Navale, Malassis, Imprimeur du Roi & de la Marine, Paris.

Katzev, M., 1980. INA Newsletter, Vol. 7, No. 1.
A Replica of the Kyrenia Ship.

Ibid., Vol. 8, No. 2, 1981. A Sailing Model of the Kyrenia Ship.

Symonds, C.L., 1979. New Aspects of Naval History. Nautical Archaeology in Penobscot Bay. David C. Switzer. 4th Naval History Symposium, Annapolis.

Gillmer, T.C., 1981. Signposts Toward the Origins of Ship Design. Fifth Naval History Symposium, Annapolis.

Steffy, J.R., 1982. IJNA, Vol. 11, No. 1, The Reconstruction of the 11th Century Serce Liman Vessel. London

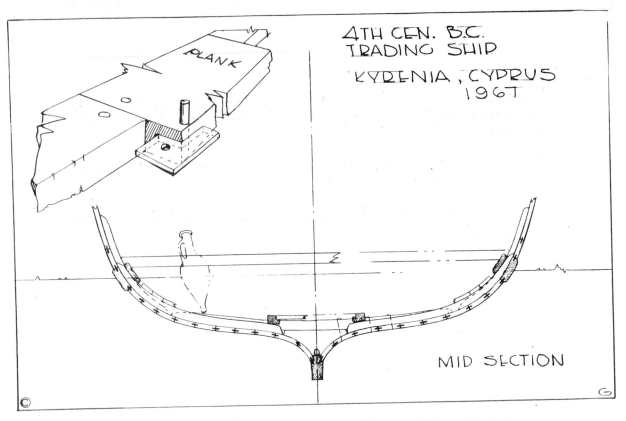

Fig. 18.1: Midsection of the 4th century, B.C., Kyrenia Ship which shows a very handsome and capable section of a fine sailing vessel. Particularly notable are the hollow garboard areas adjacent to the keel. This configuration is a natural result of the deep external keel and the morticed shell construction.

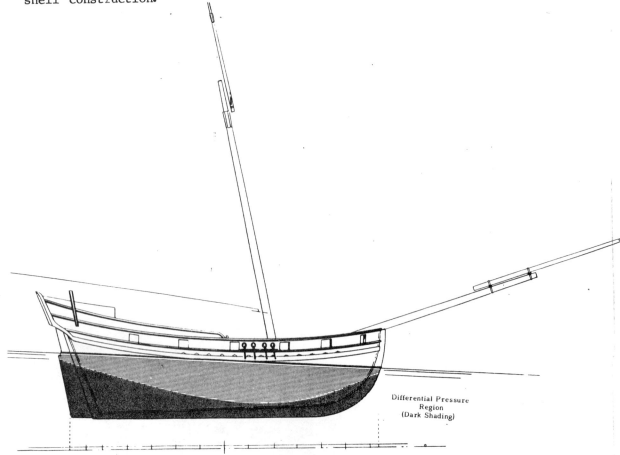

Fig. 18.2: The hull profile of this Bermuda sloop is typical of the many smaller new world vessels being developed in the early 18th century. They were of deep-keel with a marked drag high deadrise and hollow garboards particularly in the after sections. The darker shaded portions above the keel indicate the advantageous pressure differential area generated while sailing.

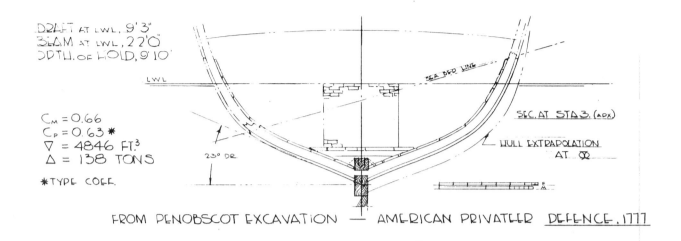

DRAFT AT LWL, 9'3"
BEAM AT LWL, 22'0"
DPTH. OF HOLD, 9'10'

$C_M = 0.66$
$C_P = 0.63$ *
$\nabla = 4846$ FT³
$\Delta = 138$ TONS

*TYPE COEF.

LWL

SEA BED LINE

SEC. AT STA 3. (APX)

HULL EXTRAPOLATION
AT ⊗

23° DR

FROM PENOBSCOT EXCAVATION — AMERICAN PRIVATEER DEFENCE. 1777

Fig. 18.3: An archaeological example of design technology is indicated in the section of this excavated privateer of the American Revolution. Note the high deadrise angle of her nicely molded bottom with a slight hollow carrying through the middle body garboards.

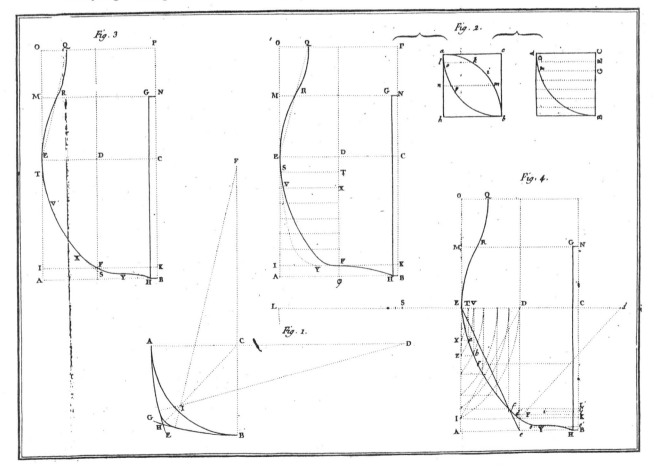

Fig. 18.4: This plate of drawings from the Vial du Clairbois book, Architecture Navale, Paris 1775 indicates a developing concern in the geometry of a large ship's midsection to create a hollow garboard underbody.

19. MODERN SHIP STRENGTH CALCULATION - A MEAN FOR THE RECONSTRUCTION OF WOODEN SHIPS

Hardly is there an issue of the International Journal of Nautical Archaeology that comes out or conference or even meeting of scholars in the field of underwater research held without the announcement of newly recovered wrecks of boats or ships. The sites are spread all over the world, but very seldom have complete ships been found, like the WASA, which can be viewed at the WASAVARVET in Stockholm. Normally, only sections or merely parts of a boat or a ship have survived such as beams or planks, belonging to a ship's bottom or side. Environmental conditions, the position of the sunken ship and the length of time that it has spent on the bottom of sea, lake or river are of great importance for the extension and state of preservation of the remains of a shipwreck, if there are any remains at all.

One means of discovering the missing parts of a ship's construction is through old plans, the earliest of these dating from the late 17th century, although most are from the 19th century. But finding the plans belonging to a ship under investigation is nearly as difficult as searching for the wrecks themselves, as we at Aachen University have learned in our daily work which now and then consists of making an expert's opinion on inland ships of more than twenty years of age.

In order to be able to restore recovered ships, which as originals are of inestimable worth for the history of shipping and the history of mankind, including the missing parts further sources of information are required:

    written sources - descriptions of ships and shipbuilding,
                reports of voyages and naval battles,

    prints and paintings, and - from the last hundred years -
                photographs and films,

    models and sculptures,

    the technical knowledge and workmanship of old
                shipbuilders,

    the methods of construction in some so called
                underdeveloped parts of the world.

All these sources are considered in reconstructing a ship of earlier ages, but there are cases when all these references are either absent or lead to contradictory statements. In these cases - and in some others too - a strength calculation may help to arrive at a reliable solution.

The field of investigating and calculating a ship's strength is a relatively recent one in ship technology, compared with the subjects of this meeting. Following a suggestion made by Edward J. Reed, the chief constructor of the British Admiralty in 1870 (Reed 1871), a ship is to be considered as an irregular loaded box-girder, which is carried itself by the buoyancy according its distribution.

Let a ship floating in still water be subdivided into several parts by vertical cuts (Fig. 19.1a) and let further these parts be free in the vertical direction, then it is easy to see that every part will be in separate equilibrium following Archimedes' principle. Fig. 19.1b shows this schematically: the fore and aft parts display a tendency to sink lower than the middle ones, as there is less buoyancy at the ship's ends. The weight of fittings, provisions and cargo is usually found concentrated at some part of a ship. Wherever this concentration is the downward motion of that part of the vessel is obviously considerably exaggerated (Fig. 19.1c). In some cases this causes or accentuates an excess of weight over buoyancy, while in others this brings the weight up to a level almost equal with the buoyancy.

For a ship at sea similar conclusions can be drawn, as at sea the distribution of buoyancy changes continually. For this reason, two more situations besides that of a ship floating in still water must be considered: i.e. the two extreme positions of support: the ship on a wave-crest and the ship in a wave-hollow, whereas the length of the wave is assumed as to be as great as the ship's length.

The downward motion of separated parts under excess of weight over buoyancy is not due (the ship lies in water as is shown in Fig. 19.1a), because of the rigid construction of the ship. Nevertheless, the prevention of vertical displacement causes strains and stresses in the ship's body, which can be calculated provided that all details of the weights and buoyancies and their positions through ship's length are given.

Fig. 19.2a and 2b show the distribution of weight and buoyancy respectively over the ship's length. The superposition of the curves in Fig. 19.2a and 2b gives the load distribution shown in Fig. 19.2c. The curve in Fig. 19.2c - the curve of the irregular distribution of loads - has to be integrated twice according to usual mathematical methods. The first integration produces the distribution of shearing forces (Fig.19.2d) and the second one the distribution of bending moments (Fig. 19.2e), both through the length of the ship.

The investigation of transverse strength also requires knowledge of the load distribution, but for the ship's section. Obviously, in the radial direction the pressure of the surrounding water acts upon the ship's body, trying to compress the empty hull. The draught of a ship being loaded increases and as a result water pressure increases too. Inside the hull, the weight of the cargo counteracts this pressure. The load distribution as well as consequential shearing forces and bending moments too depend on the superposition of external water pressure and the weight of the cargo. Assuming that the load distribution is given, the transverse strength parameters can be calculated in the same manner as the parameters for the longitudinal strength investigation (double integration to obtain the shearing forces and bending moments respectively), even if more sophisticated methods are in use.

A measure for the overall strength of a ship can be found if longitudinal and transversal strength are taken into account as well and if "open" ships like Viking boats are to be considered, torsional strength.

Using these calculations much better utilization of the building material can be achieved which is one reason for its introduction just about the time that iron, which was relatively expensive, became important for shipbuilding. On the other hand the methods described above are only suitable for material as homogeneous as iron or steel, so applying them to wooden ships can entail some problems.

Bending moments and shearing forces (longitudinal and transversal) cause strains and stresses in different directions, which have to be taken up by beams and girders, by struts, plates and planks, out of which the ship's body is built up. How far these members are capable of doing so depends on their dimensions, as well as the species of wood used and its material properties. Accordingly, mathematical formulae for calculating the stresses in the ship's structure or in a single beam, only contain quantities which depend on the dimensions of the structural members (section modulus for instance) and values characteristic for the material used. As long as materials are used for which a linear relation between strain and stress exists, the so-called Hooke's Law, upon which all methods of strength calculation are based, - iron and steel for instance - these characteristic values (Poisson's ratio and Young's modulus) are constant for all types and directions of load and all levels of stress, beneath the yield point at least.

In contrast to iron or steel, wood is a non-homogeneous anisotropic material, as a result of which Hooke's Law loses its validity. The mechanical properties of steel are always the same whereas the mechanical properties of wood are different corresponding to different types of load - tension, pressure, bending - and according to the angle between fibre flow and the direction of load. For example, when this angle is zero i.e. when grain and load are undirectional the tensile strength of oak or beech, is about twenty times greater than when they meet at right angles (Kollmann 1951 and 1955). Thus, special attention must be paid not only to the type of wood, but also to how the timber is cut or sawn and to how beams or planks are assembled within the ship's structure.

Another difficulty that arises as a result of the building material used, is the natural limitation imposed by the height of trees. Today's welding techniques allow the construction of large steel panels or extremely long girders without any weakness at the welded joint. The width or length of wooden constructions however were limited by the length and width of the tree unless strong gussets were fitted between two or more wooden beams. Concerning evaluations of these connections in wooden structures, you can study suggestions made in the second half of the 19th century especially in England (White 1877).

Namely a beam consisting of two connected parts, behaves, when longitudinal pressure is applied, like an undivided beam of the same length and area. However, if tensile forces are applied the joint will not hold at all unless it is strengthened by employing more sophisticated lap joints. As this irregularity might prove deficient, the mechanical properties will be diminished according to the stability of such a connection and the type of load.

The argument that suggestions made by modern-day builders may not be used for building methods found in old shipwrecks is disproved by Fig. 19.3 in which examples of keel lap joints out of a manual from the beginning of this century are shown (Brix 1921). Fig. 19.4 shows a keel lap of a Roman ship. Sunken in the 3rd century A.D. it was recovered - or at least the remains of it - from the harbour of Monaco (Benoit 1961).

Everyone who knows a little about stress and strain will understand that the Roman method of lengthening the keel is better than the modern methods and its diminution factors will be better, too. The solution shown here is the most expensive and therefore you will not find this lap joint in modern constructions.

From what has been said so far it is clear that a strength calculation of a ship made of iron or steel is an extensive task, but a task without any problems. The investigation of a wooden ship remains a complicated project, involving a number of problems, more than are mentioned up to now. The investigation of a recovered wreck or a ship found in a burial chamber on the other hand normally presents fewer difficulties than an attempt to calculate the strength of a ship, which is only represented as a model, sculpture or in a painting.

A recovered ship enables the measurement of the outer form of the vessel for the purposes of making a body-plan. When a ship is recovered it is possible to measure the dimensions of the structural members, which are to be used for the determination of the section modulus. Besides this, there is another advantage in investigating a recovered ship: it is possible to determine the building material used even if the wooden parts are hidden beneath the sand of a desert, the water of a lake, a river or the ocean or under a layer of mud in marshy country for hundreds or thousands of years.

Such a determination of the building material might also be possible even if there are no recovered items of the ship's structure to be found. The building material used is normally stated in old specifications laid down by the admiralty or private owners. The region in which a ship under study is built may also help to determine the type of wood, as there are regional standards to be found for the use of only a few different species of wood for shipbuilding purposes.

Once the building material is specified, the material properties and the characteristic values should also be established. But there are specified types of wood about which nothing is to be found in books about wood technology, especially if the wrecks were discovered in or around the Mediterranean Sea. There, acacia, cypress, fig or cedar are the most common types of wood found as building material for ships or parts of them.

Dendrological investigation and material testing to discern the mechanical properties and characteristic values are very expensive and not of general interest, as today these types of wood are not used for building or shipbuilding purposes. It would be nearly impossible, even to get a specimen for testing. But there are several imponderables in such an investigation. So one more might not be detrimental at all, and for these technically "unknown" species of wood the known mechanical properties and characteristic values of wood today in use can be employed, if only the latter is related to the unusual type of wood. In place of the properties of acacia Nilotica the known values of the false acacia will be used, the American cedar may replace the cedar from Lebanon, although different climates may cause differences.

These replacements may be accepted, as even if the material used is well known timber with well known mechanical properties, the results remain doubtful. Differences in the range of 100% or sometimes even more are not unusual in testing timber with modern machinery. The mechanical properties of the timber are subject to a considerable number of influences such as the age of the tree, environmental conditions (climate, nature of ground), moisture content, number of limbs or branches, appearance of pest attack and others, like the curious influence which is attributed to the season, during which the tree is cut (Kollmann 1951 and 1955).

Knowing the sort of material, its mechanical properties – with certain reservations – the kind of lapping beam and planks, all items needed for a strength calculation are given besides the distribution of weight and buoyancy. For determining the distribution of weight, the weight of the ship's body, fittings, ballast and armament, along with the weight of the provisions and cargo and the weight of the people on board must all be taken into consideration. Assuming that the ship is recovered completely, the weight of the ship's body can be calculated from the dimensions of the timbers and the specific weight of the wood used. In some cases fittings, armament and cargo can still be found in the wreck or nearby, provided they have not decayed in water, sand or mud. Tiles and other earthernware were found in Roman ships, for instance, while cannons and ammunition were discovered in the WASA. However, only the distribution of these items over the ship's length is to be determined. But normally most of the equipment and cargo has disappeared, often the armament too, and weight and weight distribution have to be estimated according to the size of the wreck. Ships which sank more recently can often be identified by name and origin, so that it may be possible to find some documentary references from which the weight of the cargo can be established.

As to the distribution of the cargo and provisions contemporary descriptions and primarily knowledge of the existence of "logical" loading conditions are the most reliable guidelines. These latter are called "logical" as there is only a small range of possibilities available for loading a ship safely, limited by stability and manoeuvrability, (errors and faults of the captain and crew not included).

From the estimation of the weights of the ship, equipment, armament and cargo the aggregate weight is determined and consequently the necessary buoyancy can be worked out. Together with the measured or estimated form of the outer hull, the draught of the ship and the distribution of buoyancy can be calculated. The load distribution follows as is described earlier.

All those who criticize the proposed procedure of calculating the ship's strength because of a number of instability factors should realize that there are some factors which may neutralize each other. On the other hand, several calculations with different assumptions can and must be made to increase the value of the results obtained.

The practicability of such a calculation shall be demonstrated using the boat found beneath the pyramid of Cheops near Giza, Egypt, as an example, a ship 43.4 m in length and with a breadth of 5.9 m. As these calculations were made in 1976 they might differ slightly with the details given in Nancy Jenkins' famous book which was published in 1980 (Jenkins 1980).

Because of its fineness – the ship has a length-beam-ratio of 7.35 – there is no doubt, that only the longitudinal strength might be critical and thus its calculation is by far of greater interest than the calculation of the transverse strength.

Although this ship, beyond all doubt, was used for religious purposes, in construction and building technique it seems not to be different from ships used for economical reasons. Ships like the recovered boat from Cheops' pyramid might be used for the voyages to Byblos, which are verified at least for the time of King Sahure about 100 years later than Cheops. For the intended calculation it is supposed that the ship was appointed and fitted out for the transport of goods.

A lines-plan of the ship was published by Björn Landström in 1970 (Landström 1970). Fig. 17.3 shows the body-plan and Fig. 19.5 the displacement curve belonging to this plan (Hausen 1979).

Out of the cross-section and other sectional views given also by Landström the approximate quantity of wood used could also be determined. By substituting the specific weight of American cedar the weight of the ship's body could be established. The equipment estimated to be necessary in Egypt's old kingdom was added according to its supposed mass and position. For burial or other religious purposes the ship might have been towed by other vessels and the oars - five pairs were found in the boat-pit - might have been there for symbolic reasons as Nancy Jenkins supposes. As a merchant ship more than ten oarsmen, five on each side, were required, let us say, 20 to 25 on each side.

After estimating the weight of oarsmen and crew a load distribution as is shown in Fig. 19.6 can be worked out for the empty, fully equipped ship (Hausen 1979). Additionally, Fig. 19.6 shows the load distribution for the ship carrying a cargo of about 30 tons stowed away in the ship's hold. Here, the curves of the load distribution have been prepared for the integration, i.e. the distribution of mean values is shown compared to the real distribution shown in Fig. 19.2c.

Fig. 19.7 gives the bending moments for the empty and the loaded ship as well resulting from the double integration of the curves in Fig. 19.6. The maximum bending moment for the ship with cargo is by far higher than that for the empty ship. Naturally, the worst possible load condition must be considered when calculating the stress from these bending moments. The maximum longitudinal bending moment is to be withstood by the ship's longitudinal structure, as there are the keel-planks, five side-planks on every side and three longitudinal girders, the central and side shelves as Nancy Jenkins called them. Fig. 19.8 published in Landström 1970 and Jenkins 1980 as well - gives more detailed information about the boat's midship structure. As there is, however, a lack of information about the degree to which these girders have been lapped - whether the beams of 26 m in length were cut out of a cedar tree in a whole or were made up out of two or more pieces by lapping them together - the latter and more critical was supposed. Consequently 10% of the area of the members under compression stress and 37.5% of the area of the ones under tensile stress was deducted.

The maximum bending moment causes compressive stress in the keel-planks and the lower side-planks and tensile stress in the longitudinal girders and the uppermost side-planks as well. Both compressive and tensile stress are very low compared with the ultimate strength of cedar, but the safety load factors have to be much higher for wooden structures than for steel structures because of the instability of the mechanical properties obtained from material testing. Moreover, ultimate strength estimations must be

274

reduced by about 30%, if the timber under consideration is always in a wet environment as is the case here with the planks under compressive stress.

In evaluating the stresses, it must be remembered that only the longitudinal stresses resulting from the longitudinal bending moments of the ship floating in still water have been calculated. For ships remaining on rivers and lakes - this condition corresponds to the still-water-condition - longitudinal stresses resulting from the transverse bending moments, from torsional moments and from local loads must be added. Under usual circumstances the longitudinal stresses caused by the longitudinal bending movements are assumed to constitute the major portion of the total longitudinal stresses and therefore the magnitude of the other stresses is generally only estimated.

Had this ship been used for voyages to Byblos or another place along the coast of the Mediterranean Sea, two other conditions must also be calculated as was mentioned earlier i.e. the ship on a wave-crest and the ship in a wave-hollow. The bending moments in these conditions are roughly about twice as great as those calculated for the ship floating in still water. This means that the stresses resulting from the bending moments are in turn twice as great, but still far lower than the ultimate strength for compression and tension respectively.

Nevertheless, the ships were strengthened, when they were used for long distance and seagoing voyages, as can be seen for instance, on the walls of the famous tomb of Queen Hatshepsut in Deir-el-Bahari. Fig. 19.9 (reproduced from Busley 1919) shows one of these ships, which are thought to have plied the legendary coast of Punt somewhere along the south coast of the Arabian peninsula. To strengthen the ship for the open sea a strong rope runs the length of the ship supported on several posts, as was the manner which was used about 5,000 years later, when in the second half of the 19th century American river steamers were strengthened by means of a "hogbeam", Fig.19.10 (Busley 1919).

Although, as has been proven here, this type of strengthening device was unnecessary, a calculation was made for a ship floating in calm water fitted with such a rope, to find out whether it was able to withstand the stresses occuring and if it led to a substantial reduction in the tensile stresses in the longitudinal girders of the ship's structure. To determine this the arrangement of rope and posts as shown in Fig. 19.9 is theoretically applied to the ship under consideration, the ship found near the pyramid of Cheops. While the number of posts is of minor interest for the intended calculation, the height of the posts and accordingly the position of the rope, is very important.

As can be seen from Fig. 19.9 the posts are as high above deck as the men standing upright, whereas the rope runs considerably lower on a ship from a sculpture from the tomb of King Sahure (5th dynasty).

Estimating a height of 1.7 m above deck, a rope diameter of 5 cm and a longitudinal distance between the end posts of 40% of the ship's length, the tensile stress of the rope can be computed using material properties of hemp (as given in engineering handbooks published in the middle of the last century, as nowadays the fabrication of hemp-rope is more sophisticated and imparts much better mechanical properties). While the tensile stress in the rope amounts to about 15% of the ultimate tensile strength, the reduction of the tensile stress in the longitudinal girders, the shelves, will be about

25% compared to the stress caused by the bending moments of the loaded ship without such a rope.

Naturally, a rope running above the deck can only be of any value in cases where the deck structure of the ship is tension-loaded, as is always the case in ships, where fore and aft body are falling out so extremely. A rope might also be of interest in a ship-bottom, if keel and keel-planks are lapped several times, which, as is said earlier, considerably weakens the members, when they are under tensile load. When the wrecks of Grand Congloue were recovered floor timbers were found each with a hole of nearly 4 cm in diameter situated on the same position. Fig. 19.11 shows the reconstruction of the bottom-part by Benoit (Benoit 1961). Under compressive strength the bottom structure seems to be strong enough as lapping causes no reduction in strength. Thus, a rope which can transmit tensile forces turns out to be a very good, light and cheap solution, as the tensile stress in the keel is reduced considerably. The extent of decrease in strain and stress depends on the arrangement of the rope within the bottom structure and on the material used.

The performance of a strength calculation has proved that, from the constructor's point of view, the ship found beneath the pyramid of King Cheops was as good and seaworthy as any ship built more than 4,000 years later. In fact, regarding the poor quality of the wood used in ancient Egypt the above ship was probably even of better quality than wooden ships of the 17th or early 18th century, when the British Admiralty searched for timber all over Great Britain for months simply to build one ship. More than that, the Egyptian shipbuilders knew that for the purpose of sea transport they had to strengthen their ships. This was done by running a strong rope the length of the ship from stem to stern, thus relieving the deck structure of load as it was regarded as too weak for its intended task.

In calculating the strength of a ship completely recovered, i.e. the Royal ship of King Cheops, there are some uncertainty factors, and if the ship has partially disintegrated the degree of uncertainty grows.

Normally, the possibilities of reconstructing the missing parts are greater the more parts are missing. However, even in the extreme cases, in which no parts are recovered or no parts could be recovered owing to the other appliances mentioned in the beginning, some questions relating to a reconstruction can be answered by making a strength calculation. Therewith at least can be eliminated reconstructions like those made for Queen Hatshepsut's "Great Obelisk Lighter" carved on the walls of the Queen's tomb in Deir-el-Bahari as well. It depicts the transport of two mighty obelisks lying on a barge, which is being towed by thirty rowing boats. Fig. 19.12 shows the barge as portrayed by Landström with his restoration in stippled lines (Landström 1970).

In the opinion of several authors, this ship which was originally built for the transport of two obelisks from the quarries near Assuan to Thebes, should have had a displacement of about 2,650 tons based upon the supposition that two obelisks, 30 m in height each weighing a total of about 750 tons were to be transported. This ship measuring more than 60 m in length and about 25 m in breadth should have been built without transverse frames as Herodot mentioned in describing Egypt that in this country, ships were built without any frames.

Meanwhile it is known that the sculptures in Deir-el-Bahari show the transport of two other obelisks of 57 m in height (Habachi 1957), weighing a total of about 4,800 tons provided that they possess the same proportions that those of 30 m in height have which were found in between two pylons at Karnak, the place of the main sanctuary of Amun, Mut and Chons. A ship having such capacity has to have a displacement of about 7,300 tons, which means a length of about 100 m and could not have been built without transverse frames. Even the shorter one of only about 60 m in length must have had transverse frames as can be shown by a calculation of the transversal strength.

REFERENCES

Benoît, F., 1961. L'épave du Grand Congloué à Marseille. XIVe Supplément à "Gallia", Paris.

Brix, A., 1921. Praktischer Schiffbau - Bootsbau. 6. ed., Berlin.

Busley, C., 1919. Schiffe des Altertums. In: Jahrbuch der Schiffbautechnischen Gesellschaft, 20, 187-279.

Habachi, L., 1957. Two Graffiti at Sehel from the Reign of Queen Hatshepsut. In: Journal of Near Eastern Studies, 16, 88-104.

Hausen, J., 1979., Schiffbau in der Antike, Herford.

Jenkins, N., 1980. The Boat beneath the Pyramid. London.

Kollman, F., 1951 & 1955. Technologie des Holzes und der Holzwerkstoffe. Vol. I & II, Berlin.

Landström, B., 1970. Die Schiffe der Pharaonen. Gütersloh.

Reed, E.J., 1871. On the Unequal Distribution of Weight and Support in Ships, and its Effects in Still Water, in Waves, and in Exceptional Positions on Shore. In: Philosophical Transactions of the Royal Society, 2, 413-465.

White, W.H., 1877. A Manual of Naval Architecture. London.

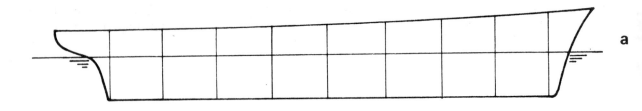

a

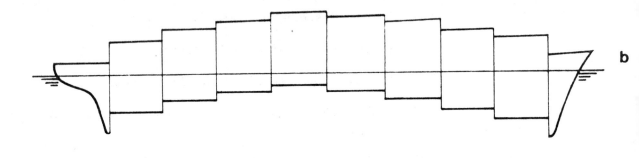

b

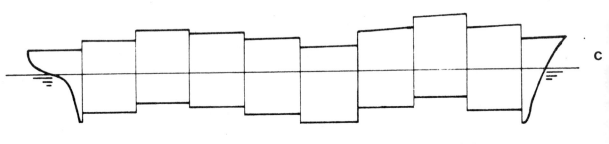

c

Fig. 19.1a - c

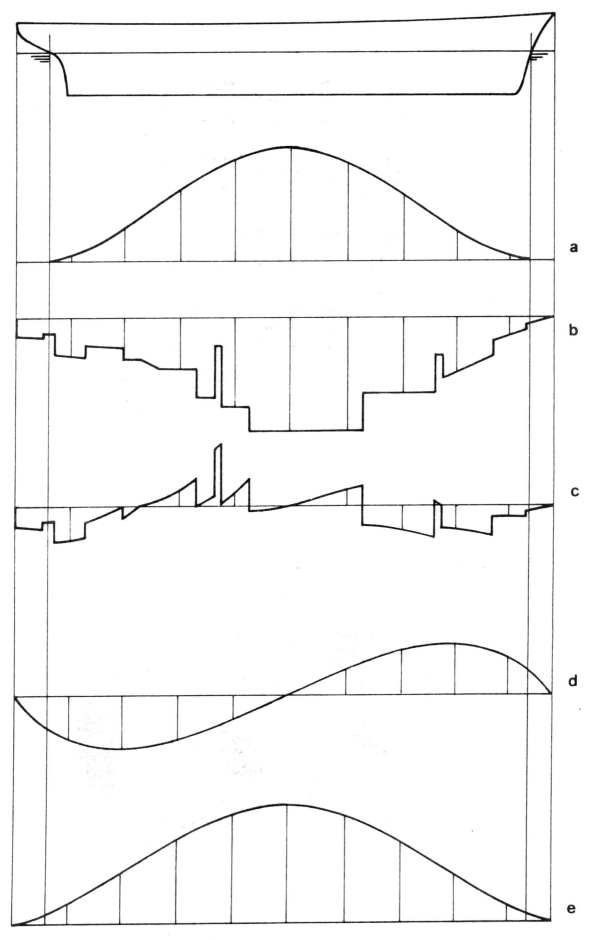

a

b

c

d

e

Fig. 19. 2 a-e

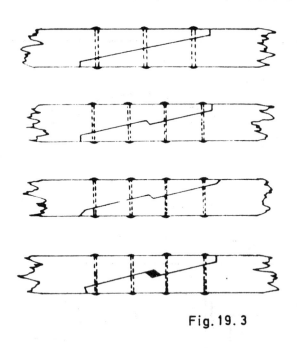

Fig. 19. 3

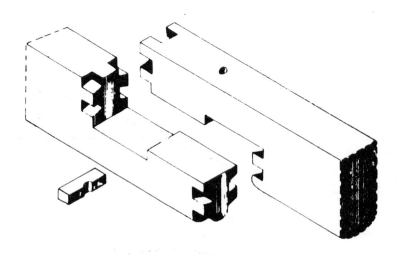

Fig. 19. 4

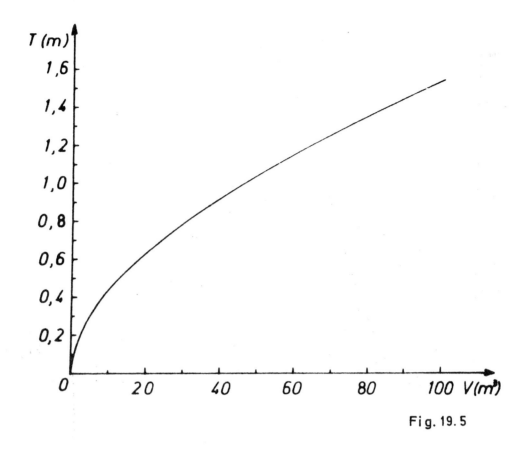

Fig. 19.5

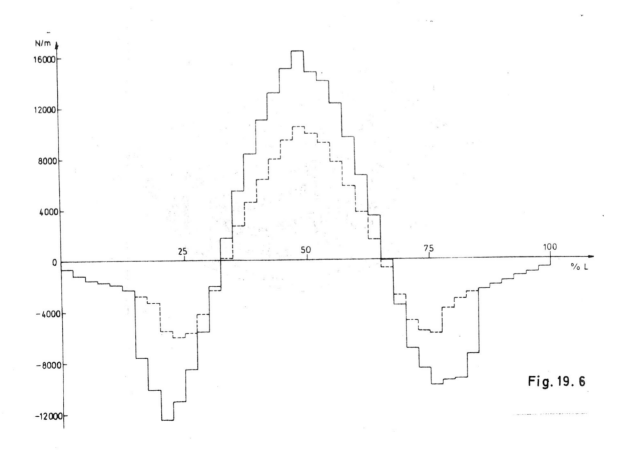

Fig. 19.6

281

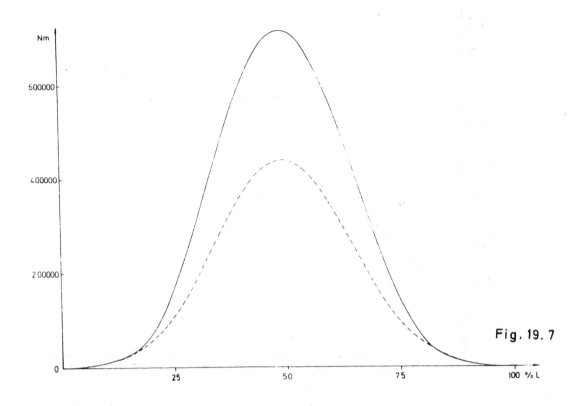

Fig. 19. 7

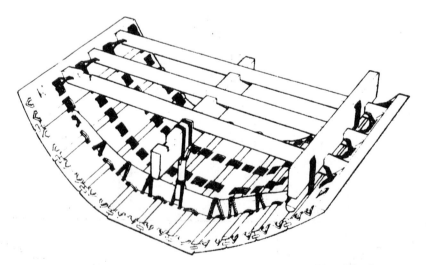

Fig. 19. 8

282

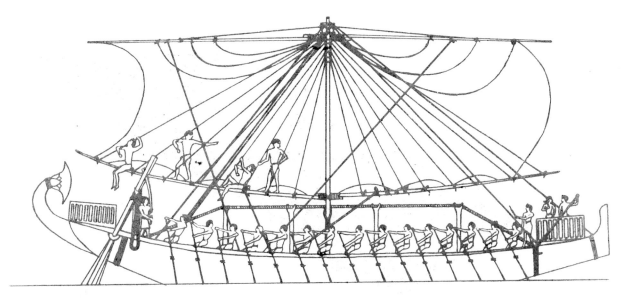

Fig. 19. 9

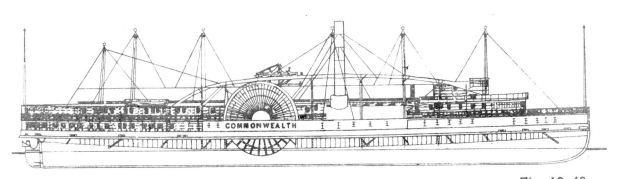

Fig. 19. 10

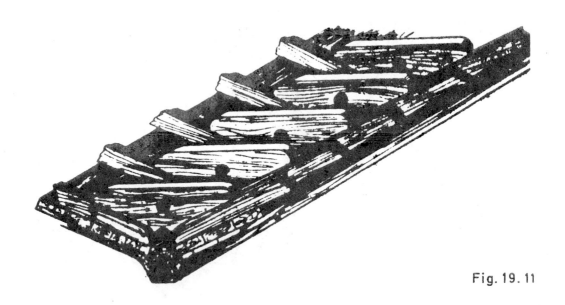

Fig. 19. 11

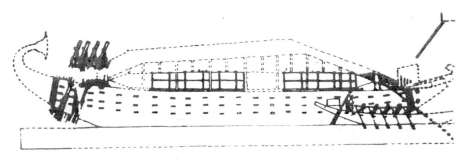

Fig. 19. 12

20. FROM LOGBOAT TO PLANKBOAT - SOME TRADITIONAL CRAFT OF SWITZERLAND

Béat Arnold

At the beginning of this century, the traditional inland water transport system on the Swiss Plateau was very much in use and logboats could still be seen on lakes Zug and Aegeri (Fig. 20.1).

Eighty years later, all that remains are a few wrecks aground on the shore. Since 1974, we have been trying to set up the plan of the last surviving evidence of this system and, when possible, to save them (Fig. 20.8).

In central Switzerland, the logboat tradition was still very much alive in the 19th century on lakes Sempach, Hallwil, Luzern, Zug and Aegeri (Fig. 20.6 a and b).   Unfortunately though, the fishermen, who were the main users of logboats, were forced to replace them with plankboats because of lack of raw material and its high cost. This transition was at first made either by adding a strake on a tree-trunk of a smaller dimension (lakes Zug and Luzern), or by assembling a few planks together (the Bretter-Gransen of lake Aegeri - Fig. 20.6b), some of which are carved out of large beams in order to obtain curves as close as possible to the logboat model (called Gransen - Fig. 20.6a and b).   At present, these Planken-Gransen are in use in those areas where previously logboats were used in the middle of the 18th century.   This boat type has its planks sawed and the sides, which have an almost vertical inclination, are much appreciated by fishermen, as it makes it easier for them to pull up their nets.

These boats are steeped in tradition first appearing in Switzerland in the middle Neolithic (a flatbottomed logboat made out of linden tree, from Auvernier NE 1973 - Fig. 20.3).   Other craft of this type date from Bronze age (Auvernier NE 1975, Bevaix NE 1879, Douanne/Twann BE 1975) and from Iron Age (Bevaix NE 1917).

The transition from logboat to the plankboat in the area studied, probably took place first during the latter age or maybe since the late Bronze age.   The constraint imposed by the raw material (the dimension of the trees) greatly diminished with the introduction of plankboats such as the Gallo-Roman boats of celtic tradition, as those of Bevaix NE 1970 and Yverdon VD 1971.   These craft are also characterised by their flat bottom that rises and narrows at each extremity.

Such craft, with a punt end, are present throughout the Middle Ages and still bob nowadays on the waters of the Rhine and the Aar, and also on numerous bodies of water in eastern Switzerland.   They are called Weidling (or Waidling; Fig. 20.1 and 9).   Their sides are no longer vertical and can reach an angle close to 60°, the bilge-strake (no longer made of half a logboat) are formed by two planks.   Planking and framing were first secured with iron nails, which were replaced in the bottom by treenails, especially on transport-craft.

The following boats are attached to the Weidling group:

- the neyeu of lake Neuchâtel;

- the Grosse Nauen, Ledi-Nauen, Jasse of lakes Luzern and Zug (Fig. 20.4 and 10);

- the Ledin (or Lädine) of lake Zürich (and Walenstadt);

  - On lake Boden the small Eisboot should be mentioned with two skates that enable it to move on ice.

The following boats have their stern ending with a more or less vertical plank:

- The nâcon (or boc) of lake Neuchâtel;

- the arlequin on the Doubs river;

- the Bocke of lake Thun (and Brienz), where the plank is so low that it nearly forms a punt-end.

On the Boden lake both the bow and the stern end as a pyramid: the bottom rises and ends in a point.   In this group we find the Lädine (or Ledin, Lödi, Leede), Halblädine, Segner (or Seggner, Seegner, Segmer), halbe Segner, Zuggarnschiff.   These transport and fishing craft are also characterized by their trapezoidal sail, the long side being at the top of the mast and by rudder or Tür which is fixed at larboard, this asymetric arrangement being unique on the Swiss lakes.

On lake Brienz, the small fishing boats also have a pyramid prow but it is dropped, and the stern ends with a plank (Fig. 20.7a-b and 11).

Before examining the craft of lake Neuchâtel (as well as those of lakes Bienne/Biel and Morat/Murten) it is necessary to draw attention to the presence of carpenters who had come from the Mediterranean, specially to build war galleys on the Léman (lake Geneva) during the 13th, 14th and 16th centuries.   These galleys, adopted and adapted by the indigenous people, attained their apogee by the construction of the brigantin and the barque du Léman at the end of the 19th century.   These craft, built on a keel, and having two lateen sails, will have influenced the evolution of the small native boats (Fig. 20.5a).   They have influenced the shape most probably of the stem on the barque pour la pêche au grand filet du Léman and of the galère of lake Neuchâtel (Fig. 20.8).

Several documents of the 16th and 17th centuries show drawings of a nau, an indigenous boat having a flat bottom that rises rapidly to end in a sort of small slanting stem.   Little by little this boat has changed and has been replaced by the cochère.   Its stem extended to the more or less flat bottom.

Most of the craft of lake Neuchâtel are attached to this group: grande barque, barque des marmets (or barquettes), galère (mentioned above), loquette or liquette, canardière.

The craft on the Swiss Plateau underwent very little development for two thousand years and the brigantin and the barque du Léman are exceptional cases. Thus, the building of warships on the Léman during the 18th century by carpenters from lake Boden left very few vestiges.

The nâcon of lake Neuchâtel was built by carpenters having come especially from the shores of lake Thun. The study of a nâcon, sunk offshore near Cudrefin VD, has on the other hand, shed light on the close ties that exist between the nâcon and the big lighters of the Sâone.

The study of new wrecks of the 19th and 20th centuries will surely bring to light other elements of a vast network of influences (shown only by details of construction) which, no doubt, originated from the emigration of carpenters from other waterways.

REFERENCES (limited to the boats of Switzerland)

ASSP. Annuaire de la Societé suisse de Préhistorie et d'Archéologie.

CAS. Cahiers d'archéologie subaquatique.

HA. Helvetia archaeologia.

IJNA. International Journal of Nautical Archaeology and Underwater Exploration.

Logboats

Amman, B., Furgler, A., Joos. M. & Leise-Kleiber, H., 1977. Der bronzezeitliche Einbaum und die nachneolithischen Sedimente. Die neolithischen Ufersiedlungen von Twann 3, Bern.

Arnold, B., 1976a. La pirogue d'Auvernier Nord 1975 (Bronze final), contribution à la technologie des pirogues monoxyles préhistoriques. CAS 5, 75-84.

Arnold, B., 1980a. Bevaix NE 1917: un monoxyle celte et des courbes hydrostatiques. ASSP 63, 185-199.

Arnold, B., 1983. Les derniéres pirogues monoxyles de Suisse centrale HA 14, 55-56, 271-286.

Keller, F., 1869. Ueber den Einbaum. Indicateur d'antiquités suisses 2, 33-35, pl. 4.

Messikommer, H., 1902. I. Die Einbaum-flottille in Ober-Aegeri am Aegerisee, Canton Zug; II. Die Herstellung des Einbaumes, speciel] von Ober-Aegeri; III. Die Fischerflotte von Walchwyl am Zugersee. Corr.-Blatt d. deutsch. Gesell. f. Anthropologie, Ethnologie und Urgeschichte 23/5, 36-38.

Gallo-roman boats

Arnold, B., 1974. La barque gallo-romaine de la baie de Bevaix (lac de Neuchâtel, Suisse). CAS 3, 133-150.

Arnold, B., 1975. The Gallo-Roman boat from the Bay of Bevaix, lake Neuchâtel, Switzerland. <u>IJNA</u> 4, 123-126.

Arnold, B., 1977. Some remarks on caulking in Celtic boat construction and its evolution in areas lying northwest of the Alpin arc. <u>IJNA</u> 6, 293-297.

Arnold, B., 1978. Les barques celtiques d'Abbeville, de Bevaix et d'Yverdon. <u>Archéologia</u> 118, 52-60.

Bonnet, F., 1982. Les ports romains dÃventicum <u>Archéologie suisse</u> 5, 127-131.

Egloff, M., 1974. La barque de Bevaix, épave gallo-romaine du lac de Neuchâtel. <u>HA</u> 5, 19/20, 82-91.

Weidmann, D. & Kaenel, G., 1974. La barque romain d' Yverdon. <u>HA</u> 5, 19/30, 66-81.

Lake Léman

Cornaz, G., 1976. <u>Les barques du Léman.</u> Grenoble, (4 Seigneurs).

Lake Neuchâtel

Arnold, B., 1976b. Le nâcon de Cudrefin (La Sapine), barque du XIXe siècle (lac de Neuchâtel, Suisse) et quelques remarques concernant les bateaux celtes. <u>CAS</u> 5, 105-120.

Arnold, B., 1980b. Navigation sur le lac de Neuchâtel: une esquisse à travers le temps. <u>HA</u> 11, 43/44, 178-195.

Eastern Switzerland

Clerc, J.-L., 1942. La marine suisse. <u>Formes et Couleurs</u> 4/3.

Haerry, A., 1918. Zur Geschichte der schweizerischen Binnenschiffahrt. <u>Schweizerland</u> 4/10, 519-526.

Mitzka, W., 1933. Deutsche Bauern- und Fischerboote. Grundfragen aus einem Sachkreise der Volkskunde. <u>Wörter und Sachen</u> 6, Heidelberg.

Lake Boden

Bloesch, P., 1979. Die vom "Schiffmacher" Johannes Strasser aus Gottlieben für die Republik Bern 1665/66 erbauten Kriegsschiffe. Ein Beitrag zur Kenntnis des Bodensee-Schiffbaus im siebzehnten Jahrhundert. <u>Schriften des Vereins für Geschichte des Bodensees und seiner Umgebung</u> 97, 29-52.

Leidenfrost, J., 1975. <u>Die Lastsegelschiffe des Bodensees. Ein Beitrag zur Schiffahrtsgeschichte.</u> Sigmaringen (Thorbecke).

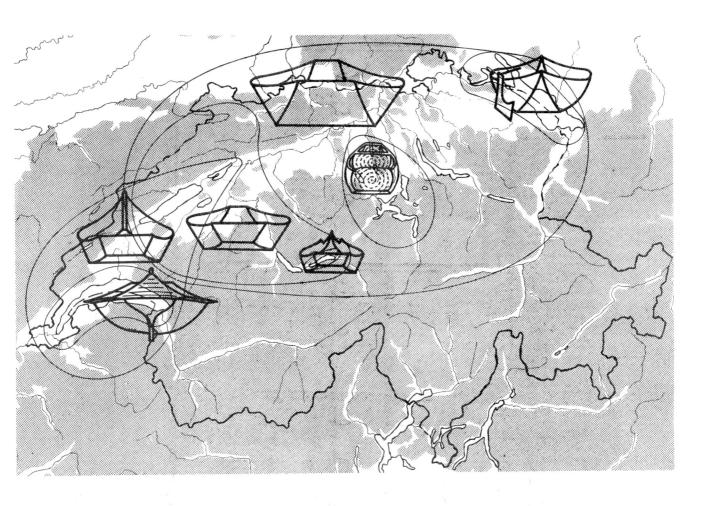

Fig. 20.1:   Craft, seen from behind, from the Swiss Plateau at the end of
the 19th century. In the western part of Switzerland, **the** flat bottomed
craft with a stem **are** predominant. There are also keelboats on the Léman.
In Central and Eastern Switzerland, archaic flatbottomed craft with a punt-
end at both extremities are still found (Weidling type). In the west, the
craft are sometimes fitted with a plank at the stern. In the east, on the
lake Boden, the two extremities end in a pyramid. Lastly, in Central
Switzerland, the logboat tradition lasted right up until the middle of the
20th century.

Planken - Gransen vom
Zürichsee ZH

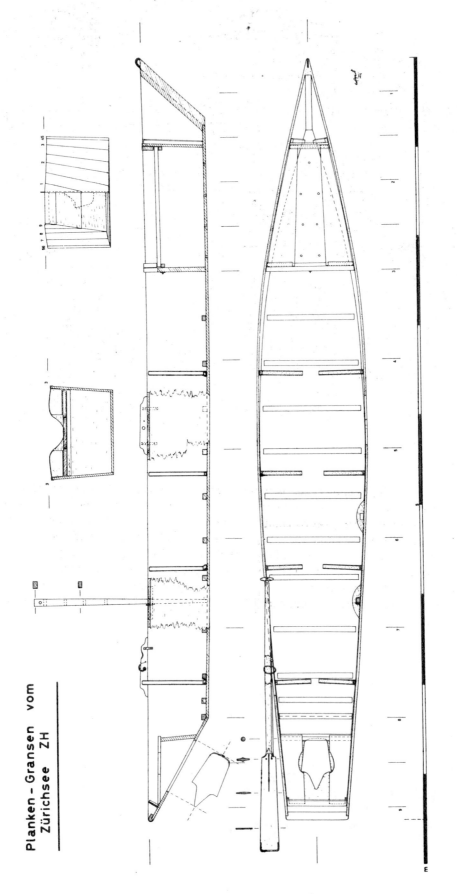

Fig. 20.2: The development from logboat to plankboat can still be seen today through some fishing boats of lake Aegeri ZG such as the logboat called Gransen (first quarter of the 20tth century), the Bretter-Gansen built in 1948 (having a hexagonal cross-section and a bottom made of two big carved beams) and the Planken-Gransen (a fishing craft that now spreads across the area where the use of logboats was still frequent at the end of the 18th century; fig. 20. bb; after ARNOLD 1983).

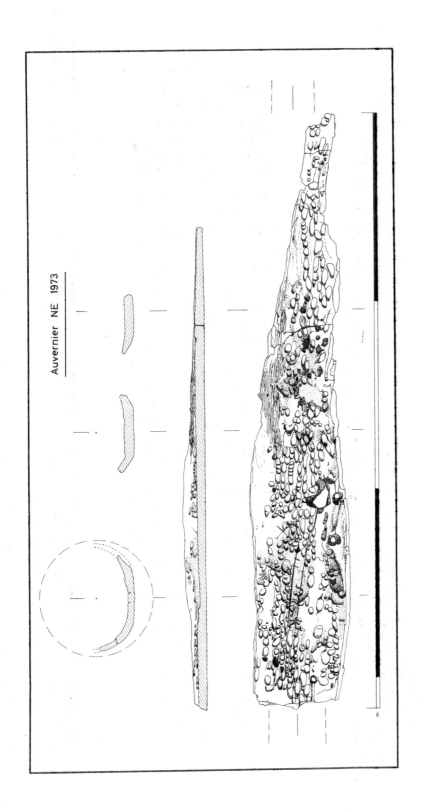

Auvernier NE 1973

Fig. 20.3: The logboat of Auvernier NE 1973 is carved out of a soft wood, in this case out of a lime tree as is the case for the majority of the early and late Neolithic craft. Contemporaneous with the classical Cortaillod (c.3800 B.C.), this logboat is characterised by a flat bottom (ARNOLD 1980b, fig. 2).

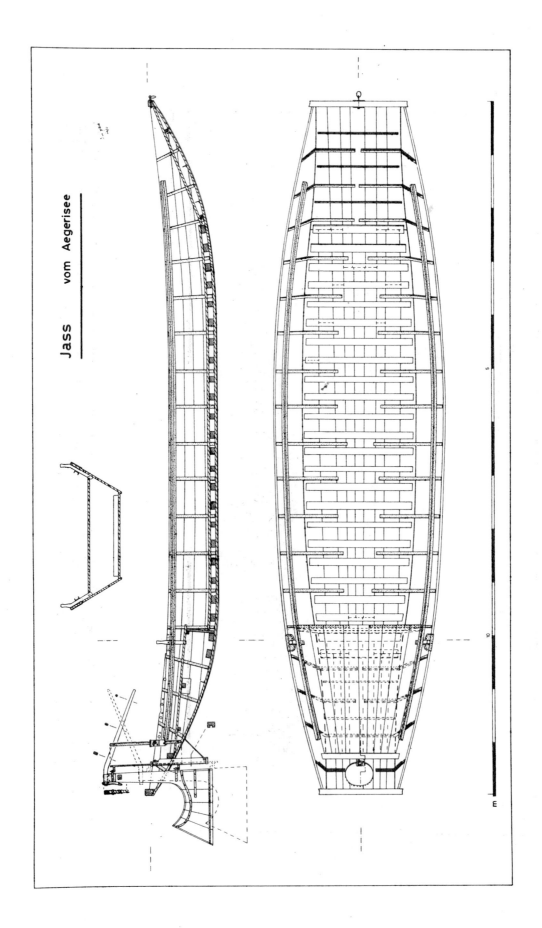

Jass vom Aegerisee

Fig. 20.4: Jass, of lake Aegeri ZG, used for all kinds of transport (hay, wood, construction material, passengers). This boat dates from the beginning of the 20th century and is linked to the Weilding group.

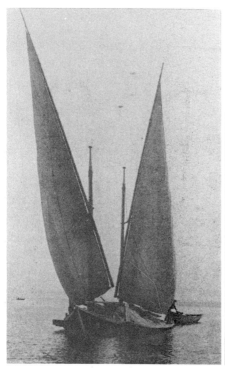

Fig. 20.5a and b: The barque du Léman built on a keel (begin. of the 20th
century).   Fig. 20.5b: the Neptune, in 1974, during its reconstruction.

Fig. 20.6a: August 1976:   the last logboat of Switzerland (type Gransen) on
the shore of lake Aegeri ZG.

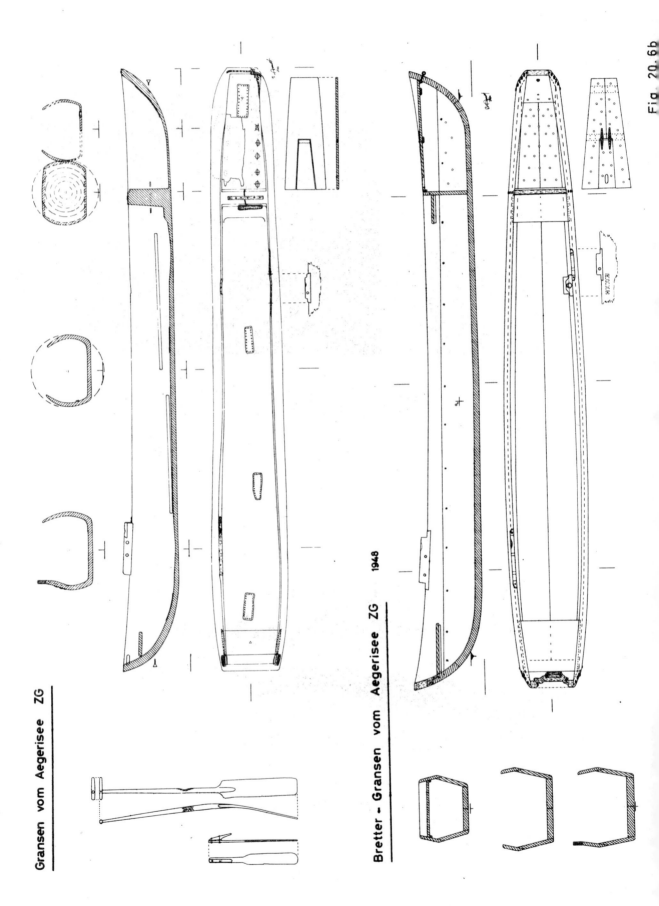

Gransen vom Aegerisee ZG

Bretter - Gransen vom Aegerisee ZG   1948

Fig. 20.6 b

294

Fig. 20.7a and b: Fig.7a: fishing boat of lake Brienz BE, and a detail of its carved prow (see fig. 20.11).

Fig. 20.8: Flat bottom craft with a stem: the galère and the canardière (foreground) of lake Neuchâtel.

Fig. 20.9: _Weidling_, on the river Aar (Aarau, 1976).

Fig. 20.10: _Jass_ of lake Aegeri ZG, with its elaborate rudder (see fig. 20.11).

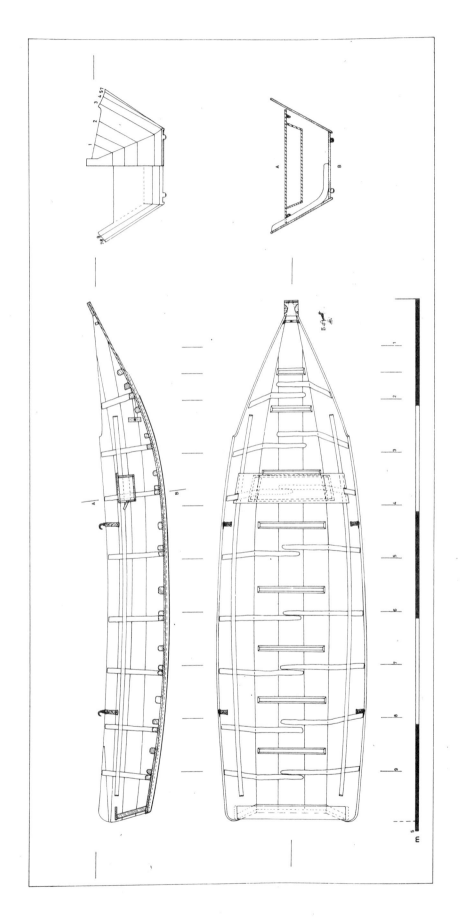

Fig. 20.11: The small fishing boat of lake Brienz BE has a pyramid prow but it is dropped, and the stern ends with a plank.

21. "SANDSKUDER" – VESSELS FOR TRADE BETWEEN NORWAY AND DENMARK IN THE 18TH AND 19TH CENTURIES

Morten Gøthche

The map of Denmark shows the country as a kingdom of many islands of various sizes, grouped to the east of the mainland Jylland, which is the only part connected to the continent.   Between the islands are belts and sounds, and many narrow fjords penetrating deep into the land.   Todays Denmark is a highly developed technological society based on an efficient land-based system, connecting the many islands by bridges and a great number of ferries.

In former days all these sounds, belts and fjords held the kingdom together, as it was much easier to go by boat or ship than to travel on bad roads.   It was also much easier to take a heavy load from one town to another by ship than taking it over land by horsedrawn carrier.   Therefore most of the towns were located near the sea with a small jetty or pier, where ships and boats could load and unload their cargoes.

In the shipping between the provinces and the capital as well as between the provincial towns, different kinds of small vessels, such as jagt, galease and galiot were in use.   The cargoes consisted of meat, fruit, firewood and different kinds of groceries.

Another trade of considerable importance was the trade between Denmark and Norway, the so called "skudehandel".   Part of this trade connected towns near the belts, and the islands Samsø and Laesø in Kattegat with the area around the Oslo Fjord in Norway.   The cargoes here mainly consisted of grain to Norway and timber back to Denmark (Fig. 21.1).

A very special part of the "skudehandel" between the two countries in the dual monarchy Denmark-Norway was the trade between the open northwestern coast of Jylland and the southwestern part of Norway.   Here, local farmers brought the surplus of grain and animal production to Norway and returned with timber to this part of Jylland, which was very poor in wood.   This trade differed from the provincial trade elsewhere, because it took place outside the towns with their privileges – and without a pier or jetty, as the vessels were landed directly on the shore.   This actually gave name to the vessels in this particular trade "sandskude" – (sand vessel).

Following the mercantilistic ideas, the central power tried to concentrate trade to the towns by giving privileges to the merchants.   For many years farmers were not allowed to do any commercial trading with their own goods or vessels.   It was, however, very difficult for the central government to control the trade between these two parts of the kingdom, and it often ended in conflict between the inhabitants of the towns and those of the coast land.   Thus, the coastal people sent their complaints, very well formulated, to King Frederik the Third, who in 1666 granted them the rights to carry on this trade.   In 1670 this was confirmed by King Christian the Fifth.   Now the shoremen could do their trading legally and without paying the normal consumption taxes. Instead, they had to pay the so-called "skudeskat" on the sand vessels. Of course they still had to pay the normal customs duties for their vessels like everyone else in the provincial trade.

Primarily they traded their surpluses of grains such as barley, rye, oat and peas from the land behind the sanddunes, but also meat, salted or dried beef, butter, eggs, cheese, wool etc., were traded in exchange for wood or timber for housebuilding. Also, iron bars, iron stoves, stoveplates and ironpots were part of the cargo returning to Denmark. The value of the export of agricultural products was considerably more than the value of the import of timber and iron.

The sand vessels departed from various places on the north-western coast of Jylland; from Ringkøbing in the South to Skagen in the North. The most important places were Klitmøller and Vigsø, secondly Stensbjerg, Thorup Strand, Slettestrand and Tranumstrand. The places in Norway were Kristiansand, Arendal and Mandal, but also Øster Risor, Langesund, Farsund, Flekkefjord and Stavanger. Many sand vessels went as far as Bergen on the west coast of Norway. The sailing season was from the beginning of March to the end of July with 4-5 trips during the season.

We do not know exactly how old this trade was, but it has been claimed that before 1600 it was mainly the Norwegians in particular from the Lindesnes area, who took part in the trade (Vigeland 1936, 20). From the middle of the 17th to the beginning of the 19th century, we know for sure that the trade was mainly carried out from Denmark. 2/3 of all sand vessels were built in Norway and 1/3 in Denmark, of Norwegian wood of course.

In the complaints from the middle of the 17th century the skippers of the sand vessels tried to give the impression of being poor people, who had to carry this trade due to poor fishing and farmland in order to survive. But during this period they became wealthy merchants with large farms, precious clothes and fine furniture. This wealth culminated at the. end of the 18th century, and up to the war between England and Denmark-Norway it declined. Klitmøller, one of the largest places during the period, had eleven sand vessels and one galease in 1772, five sand vessels and three galeases in 1799, and in 1805 one sand vessel, four galeases and one schooner. Because of the blockade from 1807-14, Norway needed grain more than ever, and the King asked the skippers of sand vessels to transport the necessary grain to Norway. After the war, the term "sandskude" disappeared completely and a presumably new fleet of well known types such as "jagt", "galease" and "slup" began taking over.

Another important event changed the historical patterns. After the opening of the Limfjord to the North Sea due to a storm in 1824, the concentration of the "skudehandel" shifted over to the Limfjord, where the towns took over a large part of the trade - but the old trade going directly from the shore never died out completely. In the Northern part of the North-West coast at Løkken, a new trade arose and continued up to the beginning of this century.

From written sources we know a good deal about this particular trade, and a natural question arises: What did these sand vessels look like? The question is difficult to answer, because nobody seems to have given a detailed graphic presentation of this ship type at the time it was in use.

In publications on the sand vessels trade, a crude ship portrait painted on the face of a grandfather-clock, located in Vester Vandet church, keeps showing up (Krogh-Jensen 1967, 49). The clock was given to the church by the skippers of sand vessels from Klitmøller in 1754. The 4½ m high clock shows that the donators were of high social status in this small community. The little painting gives the impression of a larger merchantman of that time. It is rigged with three masts - the fore and main mast with square sails and the mizzen with a lateen sail (Fig. 21.2). From the same time we know of some sketches of different ship types (Møller 1981, 60), and among these there is a type mentioned as a "skude", rigged similarly. If we can trust the artist, we can be sure that the painting is of a "skude", but maybe not a "sandskude".

In the archives, in the custom records, we find a statement from 1754 about these vessels: "Skudernes takkelage ere af 3 slaette staenger med råsejl og klinkbygning og fahrer alle på Norge." This means that the rigging of these vessels incorporated three polemasts with square sails, clinker-built and all of them sail in the Norwegian trade. From that period we know of a ship type with three masts and square sails, the "krejert". From the customs records we also know that a krejert the "Sankt Jørgen" was once registered as a skude. Another vessel, the "Christiane Elisabeth" was called various terms such as skude, galease, brig and finally slup during the period 1798-1818. This is a reminder of the problems defining the correct terminology of these types of ships.

In 1750 the whole fleet of sand vessels had to be remeasured. From the documents, we can get various kinds of measurements; the length, width and depth, and we get an idea of the capacity of the sand vessels. The document shown in Fig. 21.3 indicates the tonnage in "kommercelaest" of every sand vessel before the remeasuring. The third column is very peculiar: here the tonnage is reduced by the so called "one sixth moderation". From 1672 all Danish-Norwegian vessels should have their official tonnage fixed at only 5/6 of their actual tonnage in order to strengthen their position against the foreign tonnage. This was of course kept secret, and was only known by the official measurer in Copenhagen. The idea was that the vessels sailing in the provincial trade at that time were to fixed 1/6 less than the true tonnage by the authorities at their first call at Copenhagen, and therefore never got the benefit of the alteration, but in the case of remeasuring in 1750-54, the authorities used the opportunity to adjust the tonnage of all sand vessels. The numbers in the fourth column show the difference between the original tonnage and the adjusted one.

In connection with the remeasuring there were many complaints from the skippers of sand vessels. Here again we get some information about the shape and construction of the sand vessels. The nearly identical complaints state that the stem and stern curved underneath the vessel, which made them very sharp in the fore- and aft-ends. This meant that they could not load very much of the cargo under the cabin and the galley. One of the complaints tell us even more about the shape; that they were all built on (a) keel and very much like the Dutch flute (Dutch cargo ship type of that period with a very narrow deck).

Finally there is a description of the area Thy from 1802 (Aagaard 1802, 31). Here the author gives a description of the trade from the shore. About the construction of the ships he tells us, that they were built with a special construction to be able to resist the hardship of running directly onto the shore. The secret is that the sand vessels were built with treenails (especially of wood from the juniper tree) instead of iron fastenings, which made them very flexible. The vessels were not, as normally assumed, flat bottomed, but built on a keel. Further more the author tells that these vessels were able to carry 300-400 "tønder" (barrels) of oat. The description also gives us an idea of the conditions for the sand vessel trade; it was not without risk, especially when the sand vessels landed directly on the shore, it had to be fine weather. Coming from Norway, they did not dare to land on the shore fully loaded, so they unloaded half of the timber cargo at sea before they sat on the sand. After landing on the shore they had to unload the rest of the timber in a hurry and quickly get ready to take in the new load of grain. Sometimes, if a storm was approaching, they had to leave with only half of the cargo on board, sometimes without any cargo at all.

Out of season the sand vessels were pulled up high between the sanddunes, where they could not be reached by the sea. In spring the vessels were launched and loaded on the very same day. After the hard work of taking the vessel to sea, they could be caught in a storm again. When taking up or setting out there had to be 30-40 men to do the work - with rollers and ropes as the only tackle for the job.

If we try to sum up the facts about sand vessels, we now know that they were clinker built on a keel and did not possess very sharp lines. Instead of iron fastenings, they had treenails, which gave them their flexibility. They had a cabin aft and a galley in the fore or visa versa, and between here the hold. The stem and stern curved in under the vessels in a way, which left no room for cargo beneath the cabin and galley. We have also been told that the shape of the sand vessel was similar to that of the Dutch flute. The length of the sand vessels were 40-45 feet (12.2-14.7m). They were c. 12-14 feet (3.6-4.2m) wide and c. 4-6 feet deep (1.2-1.8m). For calculations of the tonnage, the measurer used the "Amsterdamfod", which is about 11 Danish inches, or more exact: 28,3133 cm. The length of the hold was 20-30 feet (6.1-9.1m). The capacity was 6-8 kommercelaest (after reducing the true tonnage by 1/6). A kommercelaest equals 2 registered tons of the system used today. In another way, they could carry 300-400 barrels of oat.

About the rigging we know, according to the clock-painting and written sources that some sand vessels carried three masts and a square sailrig. We also know that some sand vessels were called various names besides "skude" such as krejert, galease, brig and slup. As some of these ship types had two masts, this may also have been the case with some of the sand vessels.

THE WRECKS

Whenever we were notified about a wreck find on the North-West coast of Jylland, we hoped for a sand vessel. In 1976 an interesting wreck turned up, and the present author was sent to record the find.

After a storm in early January 1976, several parts of the wreck had been washed ashore at Klim Strand, one of the old centres of this trade. These pieces were presumably from a wreck, first noticed during the summer of 1973, and known by the local fishermen as "Tjaereskibet" (the tarvessel). At the same spot a fisherman from Thorup Strand had caught ship's timbers in his trawl. These originated from a small clinker built vessel with oak planking. The planking was held together with treenails made of wood from a juniper tree. The frames and planking were held together with treenails of oak. The transverse joints of the planking were scarfed. The vessel had been built on a keel, and was decked. She must have been 30-40 feet long. About 65% of the vessel had been preserved, but unfortunately not the keel nor the stem – or sternposts (Fig. 21.4).

It was decided to record the various parts of the wreck accurately enough for a model of each section to be made. In this way it would be possible to fit the models of the various pieces together just like the archaeologist assembling the broken pieces of a jar.

The most important tool for recording was the "measuring-table". It consisted of four poles driven into the ground. Straight boards were then nailed horizontally to the poles, so that it formed a rectangle. Then, each separate part in turn was placed underneath the "table" with the inside upwards. The recording was made by measuring several sections across the planks and normally alongside a frame. Even the position of the broken or dressed ends of planks and ribs, as well as joints, treenails, spikes, marks etc., were recorded, and many black/white photos were taken (Fig. 21.5).

Afterwards a drawing of each piece was made in the office, showing the pieces in plan and with several cross-sections in 1:10 scale and with details in 1:1 of treenails, spikes etc.,. Then a montage of all plans and sections of the wreckpieces was made in order to find the proper place for each part in the original vessel. In this way it was possible to obtain a good impression of the size, shape and structural lay-out of the vessel. She had been 10-12.5 m long, double-ended and very beamy fore and aft, but with sharp lines below the waterline, and prominently curved sheerline (Fig. 21.6).

As already mentioned, the vessel had been decked, which can be seen on the notches in the deck-shelves for deckbeams. One of the deckbeams had gone through the planking. This may have been a hollow deckbeam leading the water overboard from a pump, placed next to it. We can also see small rectangular holes just above the deck-shelf – scuppers to lead the water away from the deck. Finally two ironbolts were located just aft of amidships, maybe used for fastening the shrouds supporting a single mast with a square sail.

The preliminary reconstruction of the midship section show a beamy vessel, built on a keel with very little rise of the bottom (Fig. 21.7). The clinker built vessel had 16 strakes from keel to gunwale amidships and one more aft. But here a peculiar feature appears: the lower strakes are a normal clinker built construction, but the 13th and 15th are placed inside the upper edge of the previous strakes. From the Skagerak-area of Norway and Sweden, we know of boat types with the uppermost strake fitted in the same way, so that the strake underneath forms a projecting fender. But this – using a carpenter's term – "one on two" – construction has not been recorded before here.

A painting from 1886 of "Familiens Lykke" of Lønstrup, gives us the impression of a hull, very similar to that of the "tarvessel" from Klim (Fig. 21.8). It is double-ended too, and with a nearly vertical stempost. The final reconstruction, based on the wreckpieces assembled will give us a more certain answer, though. The "Familiens Lykke" of Lønstup has a common "jagt-rigging", of fore n' aft rigging with the mast placed well forward of amidships, while the "tarvessel" shows traces of a mast step amidships and probably a square sail. There were no associated finds to date the Klim-wreck, and no other dates for the vessel are available by now.

OTHER WRECKS

Over the years several wrecks have turned up along the north and west coast of Jutland. Some of them are said to be sand vessels, and some of them may well have been so. From Løkken, we have a report of a row of frames on the shoreline originating from a small carvel built vessel. This may be the remains of an old "jagt", a ship type, which took over from the sand vessels and was used in this area into the beginning of this century (Fig. 21.9a).

From the same place another wreck was observed, where only stem and sternpost were visible, including a rabbet for a clinker-planking. The planking had been cut into stem- or sternpost in steps, not as in normal practice with a straight rabbet line (Fig. 21.9b). This could be a sand vessel too, but the same construction appears in the "slup", which is another ship type used in the area during the end of the period.

A wreck found just over a year ago at Nors Å - not very far from Klitmøller, an important village in the beginning of the period, gave us another hope of finding a sand vessel. Just like the "tarvessel" from Klim Strand, she was clinker built with treenails of juniper, here both in the planks and in the frames. Unlike the "tarvessel", she had butted joints in the planking instead of scarfs. This vessel had oak planking, but frames of fir (Fig. 21.9c). The presence of the so called Norwegian spikes, factory made, connects the wreck to the period just about the turn of the this century, but she could be much older. The spikes originate from a newer carvel planking, nailed directly on the outside of the clinker planking. A typical example of giving an old vessel a new life by putting it into an envelope. The wrecks from Loken and Nors Å could both be of the "sandskude" or the "slup" type. In both cases the building-tradition is similar to that known from the southeast coast of Norway in the 19th century.

CONCLUSION

All these different kinds of testimony lead to the conclusion that the sand vessel was a simple, local craft, especially built for this particular "farmertrade", rather than being a large merchantship with a lofty rigging, as indicated on the painting of the Grandfather-clock from Klitmøller. The Klim Strand wreck shows traces of a mast position amidships, probably to carry a single square sail. These simple types of vessels with one mast stepped amidships and with one single square sail can be seen on several town prospects from the 17th century. Perhaps this type had a longer life in this far away corner of the country than elsewhere, just as the catholic names for the vessels, such as "Jomfru Maria" (the Virgin Mary), "Sankt Peter" etc. were used right up to the war 1807-14.

In documents from the archives, the sand vessels were described by such a variety of type names as "galease", "brig", "slup", "krejert" and "skonnert". But this does not necessarily means that these sand vessels in size of hull and rig equalled the well known, but much bigger types from the provincial trade in the rest of the country. It could still have been the one masted vessel, supplied with one or two extra masts, e.g. with a smaller mast aft carrying a lateen sail (galease) or in the bow carrying a square sail (brig), or both with a small mast aft for a lateen sail and a similar mast carrying a square sail in the bow (krejert). This type of rigging is known from Sweden in the middle of the 17th century, the "roslagskute". A small 19th century fishing boat from Skagen with two masts carrying spritsails was called a "skawbrig". The term "slup" (sloop) and "skonnert" (schooner) show up later in the period. The slup appeared just after the war 1807-14, and was a special Norwegian phenomenon. These vessels, called "Danmarksslup" by the Danes and "Søgneslup" by the Norwegians, were mainly built in the area of Søgne in the towns Risør, Arendal etc., and in the same tradition as the sand vessels. They were small, clinker built vessels with oak planking, held together by treenails of juniper, frames of oak and fir. They were built with an overhang aft and were "sluprigged" (Fig. 21.10a).

In Denmark, this term meant a fore'n aft rig with one mast in two parts. It used to have a gaff – or mainsail, forestaysail, yard topsail, 2-3 different kinds of jibs and finally sometimes a flying jib or jib topsail.

One such vessel is preserved to this day, as the Danish National Museum is the owner of a "Danmarksslup". She was built 1854 in Svinør, Norway, especially for the "skudehandle", the trade between the two countries, and named "Familien" (the Family). The main dimensions were: 40 feet long, 18 feet wide and 6 feet deep. She had at that time a tonnage of $4^1/2$ kommercelaest. All these ships were built at or below this tonnage, in order not to have to take a pilot upon arriving in the Norwegian ports. Today, the tonnage is registered as 19.99 tons, as 20 tons is an important limit for a number of rules, including the required qualifications for skipper and crew.

In 1888 she was sold to Denmark and went into the common provincial trade. In 1898 she had a major refit at Rudkøbing, Langeland, and the old clinker planking was replaced by a new carvel planking, but she still kept her old slup-rig. The vessel had her first engine installed in 1918. After that she had several other engines – each bigger than the previous ones – and a proportional reduction of the sail area.

Over the past 45 years she was used in the packet-trade on Limfjorden. Through all these 45 years she had only one skipper – and her name was "RUTH".

Today "RUTH" is under restoration in a shipyard in the Western part of Limfjorden to serve in the future as a museum ship along with the other old ships in the collection of the National Museum, illustrating different aspects of Danish coastal trade in the 19th and early 20th century (Fig. 21.10b).

REFERENCES

Aagaard, K., 1802. Physisk, oeconomisk og topographisk Beskrivelse over Thye beliggende i Thisted Amt, Aalborg Stift. Viborg.

Carlsen, D.H., undated. Skudehandel Thy-Sydnorge. Klitmøller 1750-1800. Et eksempelstudie i entreprenøraktivitet. Specialeafhandling, Københavns universitet.

Gøthche, M., 1980. Sluppen "Ruth" - rapport om restaureringen af Nationalmuseets slup. Maritim Kontakt I. Kontaktudvalget for dansk maritim historie - og samfundsforskning. København.

Hvitfeldt, J., 1935-36. Skudehandelen i det 17. aarhundrede. Jyske samlinger 5. rk. II bind, København.

Klitgaard, C., 1943. Nogle selvejer - og skudehandlerslaegter fra Han herrederne. Historisk Aarbog for Thisted amt.

Krogh-Jensen, G., 1956. Sandskuden "Jomfru Maria" af Klitmøller. Historisk Aarbog for Thisted amt.

Krogh-Jensen, G., 1967. Den thylandske skudefart. Et tilbageblik i anledning af indvielsen af første del af Hanstholm havn. Thisted.

Møller, A.M., 1974, Skibsmålingen i Danmark 1632-1867, Handels- og Søfartsmuseets Aarbog.

Møller, A.M., 1981. Fra galeoth til galease. Studier i de kongerigske provinsers søfard i det 18. århundrede. Esbjerg.

Rasmussen, A.H., 1974. Skudefart og Limfjordshandel. Esbjerg og Thisted.

Skjødsholm, A., 1971. Skudehandelen mellem Vendsyssel, Han herred, Thy og det norske Sørland. Løkken.

Vigeland, N.P., 1936. Danmarksfarten fra Sørlandet. Oslo.

Fig. 21.1:   "Skuder" (jagt) on the shore at Løkken.   In the
foreground boats with a flat bottom, used for loading and
unloading the vessels, which were anchoring near the shore.
Horsedrawn carriers brought the loads up on dry land. Woodcarving
after drawing by Carl Neumann.   Illustreret Tidende, 1866).

Fig. 21.2:   The presumed "sandskude" (sand
vessel), painted on a Grandfather-clock, located
in Vester Vandet church.   The clock was donated
by the skippers in Klitmøller 1754.   Photo: The
Danish National Museum.

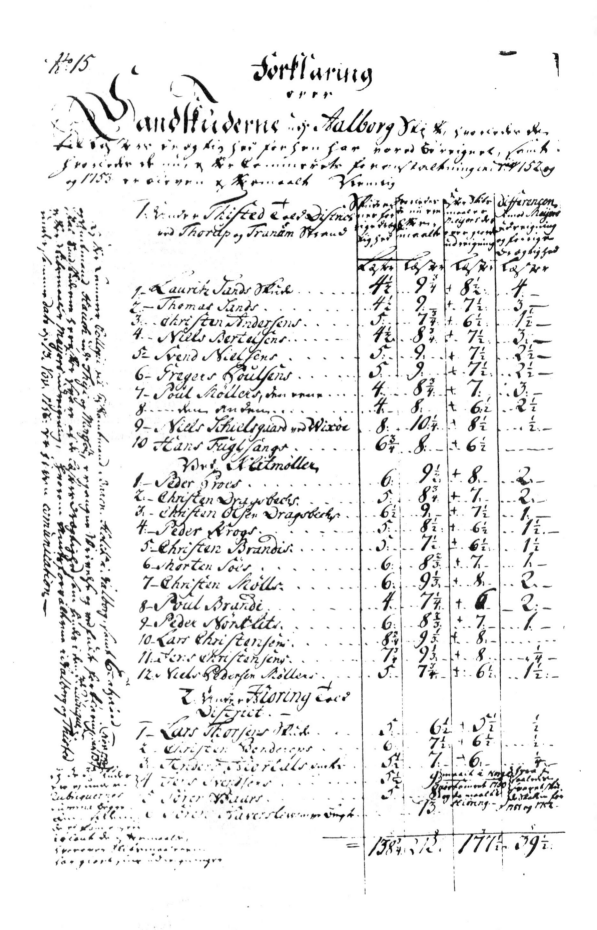

Fig. 21.3:   A document from the case of remeasuring in 1750–54.   The
first column shows the "kommercelaest" of the sandvessels before
remaesuring.   The second column after measuring and the third column shows
the adjusted tonnage.   The fourth column shows the difference between the
former and the adjusted tonnage.

Fig. 21.4: Parts of the wreck of a vessel washed ashore in 1976 on Klim Strand. About 65% of the vessel is preserved and the oak was in very good condition, without any decay. Photo: The Limfjordsmuseum.

Fig. 21.5: The measuring-table, a very important instrument for the recording of the wrecks. Photos by the author.

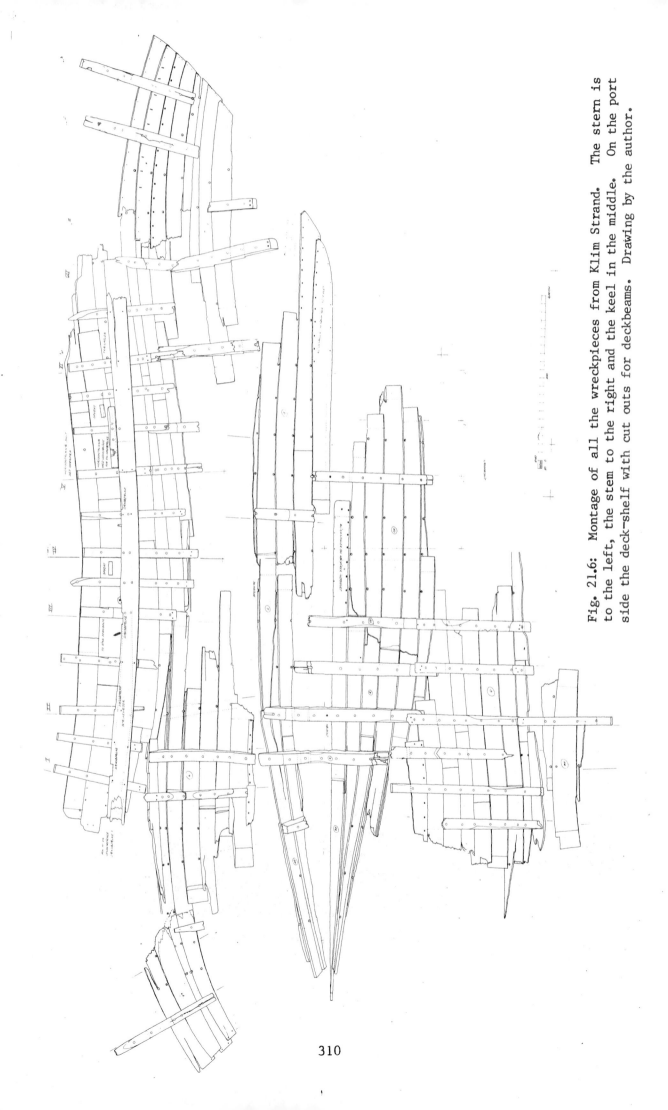

Fig. 21.6: Montage of all the wreckpieces from Klim Strand. The stern is to the left, the stem to the right and the keel in the middle. On the port side the deck-shelf with cut outs for deckbeams. Drawing by the author.

310

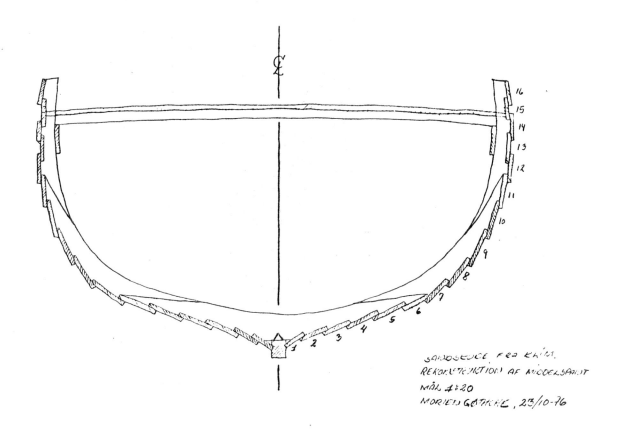

Fig. 21.7: Preliminary reconstruction of midship section. The sketch shows the principle of the construction with the first twelve planks in clinker and the last four in a peculiar "one on two" construction. The original vessel had a less pronounced rise of the bottom than shown here. Sketch by the author.

Fig. 21.8

Fig. 21.8:   "Familiens Lykke" of Lønstrup.
Copy of painting by Chr. Mølsted, 1886, showing
a double-ended, clinker-built hull with a jagt-
rigging, standing on the beach.

Fig. 21.9a

Fig. 21.9a-c: Wreck of a carvel built vessel at the shore of
Løkken. Photo: The Danish National Museum.
b: Stem- or sternpost of a wreck from the same place. Photo: The Danish
National Museum.
c: Parts of a wreck found in 1981 at Nors Å, just North of
Klitmøller. A clinker-built vessel with a newer carvelplanking nailed to
the outside surface. Photo: Henrik Bygholm.

Fig. 21.9b

Fig. 21.9c

Fig. 21.10a: The "Danmarksslup" "Raketten" of Svinør.
Drawing by I. Klysner, 1852. (Andorsengården, Mandal By-
museum, Norge. Bessesens samlinger).

Fig. 21.10b: The slup "RUTH", owned by the Danish National
Museum, under restoration 1982 in a shipyard at Vest Vildsund
in the Western part of Limfjorden. Photo: Danish National
Museum.

22. RECENT BOATS IN THE RHINELAND

Hans Walter Keweloh

On the occasion of the discovery of three old ships in eastern Prussia and Pommerania in 1894, 1895 and 1897, which attracted great public interest, ethnologist Albert Vob, then curator at the Museum of Ethnology in Berlin, wrote an essay on the finds. The essay discussed the importance of a documentation of local fishing boats and other small working craft for the history of ship building and ship archaeology (Voss 1899, 45–47). The idea prompted the German Society for Anthropology, Ethnology and Prehistory, together with the museum to start an inquiry entitled "On the investigation of old boat types on the inland waters and coasts of Germany and it's neighbouring countries".[1] For this reason they had developed a questionnaire to detect and describe those craft of a most simple structure and equipment, which are still customary or have been in use.[2] Asking for a description of outer appearance, equipment, employment of the boats etc., it was sent to persons in the German Reich, but also to those in German speaking neighbouring countries such as, for instance, Switzerland. This inquiry was quite successful. It had the usual difficulties of this kind of investigation: on the one hand it was not easy to recruit enough respondents for each region, on the other hand the specialized knowledge of the volunteers varies widely. So the information recieved is diverse in quantity and quality.

Nevertheless, it took extensive efforts to obtain information on the local boats and ships in the German-speaking countries.[3] During the period 1928–1933 Germanist Walther Mitzka made a new attempt to record those craft in the same area. He was interested in find the connection between words and the objects they describe. Doing his own field work he tried to collect the recent types of local peasant – and fishing boats (Mitzka 1932). Mitzka never intended nor did he achieve a complete documentation including exact plans of the boats as was done for example by Hans Szymanski on the smaller traditional sailing boats.

Except for Kurt Schwarz, who tried in 1926 to depict the development of the types of vessels on the Rhine up to the nineteenth century by pictorial and written source material, (Schwartz, undated) these represent the only extensive research done on different boat types on the inland waters in the territory of the Federal Republic of Germany.

In February 1979, the Deutsches Schiffahrtsmuseum in Bremerhaven, sponsored by the Deutsche Forschungsgemeinschaft, started its research project, the purpose of which was to document all recent preindustrial wooden boats in the river basin of the Rhine. Each year from April to October I have systematically looked for relevant objects all over the waters of our research area. In addition we receive a large number of tips from the general public who have been informed about our project through articles in regional newspapers or have heard about it on the radio.

In 1979 we documented the boats of the Lower Rhine between the Dutch frontier and Bonn; in 1980 of the Middle Rhine from Bonn to Mayence and in 1981 and 1982 of the Upper Rhine up to Lake Constance. We are still working in this region today. Of course we examined all tributaries too. There are for instance Ruhr, Mosel, Main and Neckar.

To document the boats we take measurements, and from these we draw plans showing top-view, side-view, cross-sections and special constructions in detail. We do the same for the boat equipment.

Besides that I have worked out an extensive questionnaire asking for age, place of origin, kind of wood, dialectal terms of parts of the boats etc.,.

If there are several craft of one type, we fully document one example only. For the others we need a short questionnaire which notes length, beam and height at fixed places as well as the measurements of the fittings.

Besides this documentation, we interview boat-builders, fishermen, ferrymen, peasants and boatsmen, all those who can give us detailed information on the use of the boats and equipment, on their operating ranges, durability and the crew. We also ask for the sequence of operation when building a boat and for the vocabulary of fisher- and boatsmen. For these interviews we use our extensive questionnaire as a kind of guide. This allows our interlocutors to give a free account without being continuously interrupted by questions. And we can keep him from straying from the point. Later on it allows a better and more systematic analysis of the conversations. We rarely used tape recorders, as tape recording is quite distracting for the interviewer when speaking on a boat or in a boat-builder's workshop. We only used a recorder for interviews at home with already well-known informants, who were not bothered by it.

We decided not to analyse the written source material in the archives at this time, because time was too short to work on source material and original objects simultaneously. We preferred recording boats from the entire field because of the danger of boats and informants gradually vanishing. The sources can still be used at a later time.

Spot-checks at some archives[4] showed, however, that a comparison between the material collected by field-work and the written sources highly improves our knowledge of boats and their use (E.g. Rudolph 1966).

When we arrive at Lake Constance in October, we will have finished work on the last part of the German Rhine basin. So I can strike a first balance: altogether we have catalogued about 1000 boats, "volkstümliche Kleinboote" as W. Rudolph has called them (Rudolph 1966,9). Greater ships as "Aaken", "Bönder", "Samoreusen" etc. (Schwarz, undated) customary on the Rhine in former times, no longer exist throughout the region.[5]

The 1000 or so boats are distributed as follows:

Lower Rhine – 240

Middle Rhine – 140

Upper Rhine – 600 to 650 boats.

Up to now, 162 of them have been measured in detail. They have been, or will be drawn at a scale of 1:20. Individual details of construction as well as some equipment will be drawn at a scale of 1:10, 1:5 or 1:2.

I'll now show some examples of this material, and how the different types and their most distinctive features have been determined by the conditions of building, use, propulsion system and the waters.

The conditions of building of the local boats on the Rhine constitutes one of the most important differences: while north of Karlsruhe the craft are only built of oak, south of this town up to the Lake Constance they are usually made of softwood - pine, fir or spruce.

Today oak is too expensive for boat-builders, since oak furniture has become fashionable. That's the reason why boatbuilding north of Karlsruhe has died out. So the boats documented at the Lower and Middle Rhine are the last examples of an old tradition.

South of Karlsruhe boatbuilding still continues, although on a much smaller scale. There are still a few full-time boat builders, often combined with a joiner's workshop. But most of them build boats in their spare time to earn extra money. Although the future of boatbuilding is uncertain, I'm convinced that it will survive. Recreational fishing is becoming more and more popular and many of the "dead-end" Rhine channels and other areas under investigation are ideal fishing waters. The "dead-end channels" are, at the same time, good fishing grounds for professional fishermen, all of whom are users of wooden boats. The anglers in particular seem to prefer wooden boats to those of metal or fibreglass, probably for reasons of nostalgia.

The type of wood used partly determines the sequence and kind of operations employed when building a boat. If planks of oak are used the bottom of the boat is mounted on a special harness, the "Gelege". The bottom of the boat is pierced and screwed onto girders (Fig. 22.1). Another beam fastened on the inside protects the bottom from damage. Only after it is completed is the craft taken from the girder. The holes in the bottom are now sealed using wooden plugs.

If softwood is used, the bottom of the boat is simply placed on sawhorses. During the work, the craft can always be moved.

Apart from this, the methods of hogging are different in these regions, too. If you build a boat out of oak, the planks and the bottom can only be hogged by means of fire (Fig. 22.2).

Often the fire is lit on a metal plate which is pushed under those parts to be heated. To prevent the wood from catching fire it is always kept wet. For this purpose a birch-broom, a rope's end or a rag is used. The bottom and strakes are usually hogged with a winch into the desired form (E.g. Timmermann 1957). For hogging the strakes some boatbuilders also use a weight, to pull them down.

When hogging softwood, a winch is also used but no fire. It is not necessary to enhance the flexibility of the wood. Boatbuilders call this technique 'cold hogging' ('Kalt biegen').

A bottom of a boat consisting of more than two boards is not always finished at first. Often the centre-piece is kept open until all floor timbers, ribs, thwarts, bulkheads and other fittings are fastened. Right at the end, the boat is set up and the centre-piece is closed from the down side. The advantage of this method is that greater pressure can be exerted on the outer planks, so that the boat becomes more water tight (Fig. 22.3).

At the Main river an extreme version of this method was employed. According to a shipbuilder of that region the entire bottom of the Main ships were left uncompleted until the very end. Until then only the two outer bottom-planks were laid, connected by the ribs and floor timbers. The side planks were already attached to the ribs, additionally held by special supports. After the wood had dried, the remaining bottom planks were inserted.

An important factor in determining the construction and appearance of the boats is the propulsion system.

Lower and Middle Rhine craft are propelled by two oars; the oarsman sits with his back to the direction of travel. Today the oars are usually attached to the gunwale by means of a pin. In former times they were loosely placed between two thole pins. Except on Lake Constance, little fishing boats on the Rhine above Mayence and on Mosel, Main and Neckar are not propelled in this way. The oarsman in the boats on these last-named rivers sits at the stern facing the direction of travel. The shorter hand rudder is loosely directed over the ship's side with both hands without any attachment to the boat. If the water allows it, the boat is poled. The poling man stands at the stern, using the pole to one side. In contrast on the Neckar River in Tübingen, the poling man stands on a platform in the stern of the boat propelling it by pushing the pole into the riverbed.

Above Karlsruhe these craft are powered by means of a poling-rudder, a combination of pole and rudder, by one man standing at the stern. The blade of this special rudder is much the same as a normal blade, but at it's ends are two spikes of about 3 cm length on the edges (Ellmers 1969,92, Fig. 8B and Rudolph 1966, 49, Figs. 41, 42). On the narrow "dead-end channels" of the Rhine this can be used for poling and pulling. The two spikes prevent the blade from slipping. They are also utilized to push off from trees in confined locations.

In contrast to boats which are propelled by hand rudder or pole, those which are propelled by oars have gunwales, and on the Lower Rhine, they also incorporate deck edges. The position of the thwarts is different too. On pulled boats the thwarts are spaced closer together. The rudder bench is to be found at the first third of the total length. The narrowness of the thwarts handicaps fishing by nets, so casting-nets never have been used in those boats.

Where boats are driven by poles or hand rudders, you find the thwarts at both ends of the boat. The middle part is free for working with nets and weirs. On the river Main the thwarts in the bow are supporting a cover plate on which the fisherman stands when hurling his casting-net (Fig. 22.4).

On the Upper Rhine, the fishing-boats have no other fittings apart from ribs and floor timbers. The fisherman can move and work with his fishing gear without hindrance (Fig. 22.5).

Some further examples shall show different constructions of boat bottoms, ends and boards, all determined by location and use. Almost all measured boats are flat bottomed except the sloops used by the pilots at the Binger-Loch in former times. A local ferryman told us that they had specially been constructed as pilot-boats by a native boat-builder of St. Goarshausen. Apparently he was inspired by the waves produced by the former paddle-steamers, but I think that he was inspired by boat design seen elsewhere.

These sloops have been built up on a sole 20 cm wide. This sole has no rabbet and is attached by six clinker-laid strakes on either side. These are riveted. At the front the planks end in a wooden block, in which they are lashed.

Clinker-built boats are as unusual in the Rhine basin as round-bottomed boats, except for Lake Constance. There, especially on the isle of Reichenau, fishing-boats are flat-bottomed and clinker-built. Fastened to a curved stem at the bow, the planks are nailed to a little transom at the stern. The three planks are riveted. The ribs, which were formerly made out of naturally bent wood, are steamed and bent into shape. Meanwhile iron ribs have also been used, but unsuccessfully because they have been too stiff compared to wooden ones, as the boat-builder told us.

Apart from the Lower Rhine, fishing-boats in the other parts of the Rhine-basin are flat-bottomed craft with only one side-plank (Fig. 22.6). Because of new legal provisions, which often prescribe a higher freeboard now, some boats are fitted with a second plank serving as a so called 'wind-board'.

Formerly the bottom as well consisted of only one plank, but today you don't find wood of sufficient width.[6] Therefore, the bottom is now constructed of two or more boards. The boat-builder is extremely careful to use wood from the same tree. If he can he takes one board from the one side and one from the opposite side, each the same distance from the axis of the trunk. Both planks are now said to warp in the same way, because they have grown under equal conditions. The stern and bow of these boats are ogged. The design of the ends shows regional differences. On the Upper Rhine they are quite broad with a bow of about 80 cm, and stern about 60 cm on boats 7 or 9 m in length. The closings are formed by blocks of oak, 3 to 6 cm thick and about 20 cm long. The side planks are fastened to these blocks.

The further north you travel the smaller the boat ends are. On the Middle Rhine, the Main and the Mosel, stern and bow are nearly equal in breadth. The block, fastened to the bottom, equals in height and length that of the Upper Rhine, but here higher ones - 15 to 16 cm high are not uncommon. Another method of closing the ends is to nail a small board, a so-called 'head-board' (Kopfbrett), to the stern and bow. These boards, 3 or 4 cm thick, can easily be replaced, if they should rot.

On the Lower Rhine this type is unknown, because it isn't suitable for this region.[7] Here the 'Nachen' has been used for fishing, a boat-type which is used in other regions as transport or working craft only (E.g. Ellers 1976, 39f and 43).

The side boards of the 'Nachen' consist of two planks with a characteristic joint coupling. Whereas the lower board slopes outwards, the upper one is straighter, both forming an angle. The nails are driven through the upper plank straight into the lower one.

You can easily differentiate between the 'Nachen' of the Lower and of the Middle Rhine by the angle of the side planks. On the Lower Rhine vessels the upper board even runs inwards, so that the widest part of the boat is not to be measured over the edges of the board but at the angle between the two side-planks (Fig. 22.7a). The upper-board on 'Nachen' boats of the Middle Rhine angle slightly outwards or sometimes straight up, so that the greatest width is at the edges of the board (Fig. 22.7b).

Besides the boats described here, many other types have been found, as I have mentioned in the beginning, some of them very local in design and not wide-spread.

The first stage of our work will be completed in October 1983 with reports and drawings of all the boat-types we found. This work is to be published as a handbook, in the same manner as that of Wolfgang Rudolph, which deals with the popular boats in eastern Lower Germany (Rudolph 1966).

NOTES.

1). The German title of the inquiry is: "Zur Forschung über alte Schiffstypen auf den Binnengewässern und von den Küsten Deutschlands und der angrenzenden Länder".

2). German title of the questionnaire: "Fragebogen zur Ermittlung und Beschreibung der noch im Gebrauch befindlichen oder ehemals gebräuchlichen Schiffsfahrzeuge einfachster Bauart und Einrichtung".

3). This material is to be found now in the archives of the Museum of Ethnology in Berlin-Dahlem. Only a little essay has been published out of this material (See Brunner 1917).

4). In the Staatsarchiv Wertheim I have, for example read lists of soccage, which notes all types of ships and boats being used in compulsory work.
In addition we could collect archive material of some fisher guilds.

5). Up to now we only have one drawing of a boat of 24 m length, which had been built for the WSA Freiburg at the beginning of this century.

6). On Middle and Upper Rhine these boats are therefore called 'Dreibord' (Three plank).

7). One boat, built on the Middle Rhine, which came to the Lower Rhine by chance, was called 'cockle shell' by the new owner.

REFERENCES

Brunner, K., 1917.   Die volkstümlichen deutschen Schiffsfahrzeuge. Festschrift Eduard Hahn zum 60.   Geburtstage: 292 – 307.

Ellmers, D., 1969.   Keltischer Schiffbau.   Jahrbuch des Römisch-Germanischen Zentralmuseums Mainz 16: 73 – 122.

Ellmers, D., 1976.   Kogge, Kahn und Kunststoffboot.   10000 Jahre Boote in Deutschland.   Führer des Deutschen Schiffahrtsmuseums Nr 7. Bremerhaven.

Mitzka, W., 1932.   Deutsche Bauern – und Fischerboote.   Grundfragen aus einem Sachkreis der Volkskunde.   Heidelberg.

Rudolph, W., 1966.   Handbuch der volkstümlichen Boote im östlichen Niederdeutschland.   Berlin.

Schwarz, K., undated.   Die Typenentwicklung des Rheinschiffs bis zum 19.   Jahrhundert. Köln.

Szymanski, H., 1929.   Die Segelschiffe der deutschen Kleinschiffahrt. Pfingstblätter des Hansischen Geschichtsvereins 20.   Lübeck.

Timmerman, G., 1957.   Kahnbau in Hitzacker.   Neues Archiv für Niedersachsen.   Vol. 9.1: 67 – 71.

Voss, A., 1899.   Zu den Schiffsfunden.   Nachrichten über deutsche Altertumsfunde 10 (13): 45 – 47.

Zimmermann, W., 1976.   Schiffsbau und Schiffsbauer in Heilbronn. Historischer Verein Heilbronn.   Jahrbuch 28: 243 – 255.

Fig. 22.1:   Boat-building at the Main river.   The so-called "Gelege" with a boat screwed on.

Fig. 22.2:   An oak board is being hogged by fire.

322

Fig. 22.4: Fishing at the Main river with a casting-net, hurled from the platform in the bow of a fishing-boat.

Fig. 22.3: A nearly ready built ferry-boat with open centre-piece at the bottom.

323

Fig. 22.5:   Fishing-boat from the Upper Rhine.

Fig. 22.6:   Flat bottomed fishing-boats with one side-plank on
the river Main.

Fig. 22.7a: Nachen of the Lower Rhine with the upper board running inwards.

Fig. 22.7b: Nachen of the Middle Rhine. The upper board goes straight up.

23. THE DEVELOPMENT OF FOLK BOATS IN POLAND FROM THE EXAMPLE OF STRUCTURES USED ON THE SAN AND THE BUG RIVERS

Jerzy Litwin

Poland has a relatively dense river network, of which the two largest rivers – the Vistula and the Odra – are basins for numerous tributaries flowing into the Baltic. A few smaller rivers whose sources are in Pomerania also flow into this sea. Apart from the rivers, quite a large area of Poland is covered by numerous lakes.

The abundance of inland waters has played a significant role in the history of water transport in Poland. The development of water transport was also favoured by rich forests, gentle slope of the rivers and accessible banks along which river ports, settlements and towns were located (Fig. 23.1).

The largest rivers, and especially the Vistula and its tributaries, played a key role in the transporting of Polish merchandise through Gdansk, mainly agricultural and wood products, which were exported to many countries in Europe.

Both along the larger rivers as well as along the seacoast, as early as the early Middle Ages an organized and highly technical production of floating craft took place. This is proved by many written sources, works of art and archaeological findings. A number of papers discussed these problems, but not all the problems have been thoroughly investigated and published.

Studies on the history of boatbuilding in Poland have been for some time now carried out by staff of the Polish Maritime Museum in Gdansk. After completing studies on early medieval shipbuilding, investigations have for several years been centred on two main problems – the history of inland boatbuilding in old times (this problem is investigated by the director of the museum doc. dr. hab. Przemysław Smolarek), and the cataloguing of relics of traditional boatbuilding which is the subject of the present work. This work is nearly finished and has progressed to the point where synthetizing the collected material is possible. An attempt at such a synthesis is presented below. It concerns traditional boatbuilding along two rivers – the San and the Bug – the largest tributaries of the Vistula. Only later it was found that the Bug flows into the Narew and the latter one into the Vistula, and not as it was thought before that the Narew flows into the Bug.

There are quite a number of riverside communities in Poland in which interesting types of water-borne craft are still built. Very often Polish folk boats resemble the dug-outs and rafts which form their prototypes. Judging by numerous findings of dugouts this type of boat was formerly the main means of communication. It may be supposed that at the same time rafts were built, but up to this time none have been found by archaeologists. Rafts played an important role in the history of inland transport on Polish rivers, they were also the origin of a whole family of ships from which they evolved.   Rafts for transporting merchandise were used in Poland as late as the beginning of the XXth century, and even today on some Polish rivers one may see timber floated in rafts.

Interesting and very representative for the general development of Polish shipbuilding are boats built in communities along the San and the Bug rivers.   At the beginning these rivers flow nearly parallel to each other and the distance between them is about 130 km.   Further on, the distance grows reaching about 270 km at their outlets.   The San and the Bug are decidedly different in character.   The San flowes form its source in the Bieszczady Mountains and over much of its length bears the character of a piedmont river.   It has a quick current and a shallow and hard bottom. The Bug has its sources in the Podolian Plateau in USSR and on its 189th kilometer enters Poland.   The river flows through flat country and is a typical lowland river with soft river bottom.

Traditional boatbuilding along the San river

The oldest information about navigation on the San indicate that the basic type of floating craft was the dugout.   Also rafts, ferries and more advanced, larger wooden ships were used on this river.   Today, besides boats, no other forms are used and the last dugouts were made before 1939. Simultaneously with the disappearance of dugouts was the arrival of plank boats, whose technical characteristics and shape are reminiscent of their original forms − the dugout and the raft.

I think that the developing trend of boats which many years ago predominated along the San be reflected by an interesting relic − a fisherman's dugout made in 1933 by Tadeusz Kowalik from Majdan Zbidniowski near Stalowa Wola.   During the September campaign in 1939 this boat was used by retreating Polish soldiers for crossing the San.   Then in order to thwart enemy pursuit, the dugout was cut in half.   During repairs, the owner cut the dugout along its axis of symmetry and inserted a 14 cm wide plank to widen the bottom.   Next he strengthened the shell of the boat with two bulkheads and a few frames (Fig. 23.2).

The most common method of expanding the dugout during the repair may reflect the idea of enlarging the dugout inherent in the fisherman's mind − in the horizontal plane.   It could have been similar centuries ago, when dugouts, which were the main means of locomotion by water, were supplanted by plank structures with technical characteristics taken over from the dugout but also transferred from rafts.   Characteristics of rafts seem to dominate todays boats from the San.   First of all these are such characteristics as: flat bow and stern, alternation of inserted strengthening pieces or the use of floors only, moving the widest parts of the boats towards their stern (or even to the stern itself) and the use of moss as sealant which was pressed down with special laths.   (It should be mentioned that moss was traditionally used here for piedmont cottages made of tree trunks and this method was probably transferred from such land structures to floating craft).

In today's folk boatbuilding on the San one meets exclusively boats which are an example of the "horizontal" trend of boat forms.   However, I know of no cases of connecting together a few dugouts to make a raft, though such a method has been used on other piedmont rivers − the Dunajec and the Poprad.

There are many and differentiated examples of the "horizontal" trend of building boats along separate parts of the river, which may be grouped into four versions.

Version I - boats from the Upper San

Navigation on the San becomes possible below the Solina dam where it reaches 40 and more metres width. And there, in Srednia Wieś interesting boat forms are used. These boats have a nearly rectangular bottom, single-strake sides and flat endings of bow and stern. Looking at the bottoms of these boats one may see an analogy with a raft built of tree trunks, the bow end of which was the narrower as one used to place the top ends of the trees there while the other end was formed by the root ends, which made it wider. Also transverse stiffeners - floors which do not reach to the side planks are reminiscent of a raft. The sides of these boats are single-straked and perpendicular to the bottom. These simple boats are sealed with tarred string instead of moss that was previously used, pressed inside the gaps. These craft are used for crossing the river to the fields lying on the other side of the river. The boats are propelled by poling (Fig. 23.3 and 23.12).

Version II - the fishing boats from the middle San

Along a large part of the San there are many boats used for fishing, recreation and communication. These constructions have a lot in common, differing slightly by their technical characteristics. Called some years before near Sanok the "squat boats", these boats were presented in ethnographic literature in 1932, and though near Sanok in 1979 I saw no such craft. One of the peasants in Zasławie showed me a few roots collected by him to build a boat. The name of the boat - "squat boat" - may suggest that at the time lighter - smaller boats, possibly dugouts were used?

From descriptions in the above mentioned ethnographic literature and from the accompanying photographs it might appear that the craft of today do not differ from the ones used in those days.

Fishing boats from the middle San may be represented by a specimen recorded in the village Słonne near Dubiecko. This boat was made from four pine boards, of which two formed a curved bottom, and the remaining ones the boat sides. A characteristic feature of the boat was that the side planks extended far outside the bottom plane, in order to protect the bottom against damage in case of striking an underwater obstacle. The bow and the stern were made of thick planks and often were additionally strengthened by planks covering "from outside" the main bonds. The boats were stiffened transversely with alternately arranged roots, and their "congestion" may be observed in the middle part of the boat. The boats are at present sealed with oakum or impregnated cord pressed down by steel wire fixed with wire staples. Formerly, moss was used pressed down by juniper strips, fastened with tin staples. These boats are propelled by poling, using a pole or an oar (Fig. 23.4 and 23.13).

Version III - sand dredgers

In very small numbers, and only in Jarosław, one may see boats which formerly were commonly used for excavating gravel from the river bottom.

Now they are becoming extinct, because gravel is excavated by industrial methods, using special excavators.

Now, the last sand dredgers' boats are used in Jarosław for recreation only, mainly angling. Technically, they are characterized by a bottom built of two wide planks and side planks, slightly deflected outwards. The ends of these boats are flat and relatively thick. Because of their application, rather strong transverse stiffeners are used. The middle part – the "hold" – is delimited by two bulkheads. On these bulkheads benches are fastened and between them are affixed two to three pairs of L-shaped frames made of naturally grown roots. In some boats positioning of the frames continues into bow and stern. The gravel boats, similar to fishing boats on the middle San, have side planks extending a little outside the bottom contour. The method of connecting the planks with the stem, used on most of the boats, is also interesting. The joint has the character of a two-stage key. As the boats mentioned earlier, the sand-dredger boats are sealed with impregnated cord held down by steel wire and staples. One of the boats preserved in Jarosław still carries a characteristic block in the place on the side where the sand-dredger's shovel was supported while gravel was being excavated from the river bottom. The boats were propelled by poles or elegant pole-cars (Figs. 23.5 and 23.14).

Version IV – fishing boat from Ulanow

On the lower San, and in particular near Ulanow, a small town known for its raftsman traditions, the developed plank boat dominates. This structure has several features similar to the boats used on the upper San. It is also the last boat form, since down to the river's outlet to the Vistula no other native version appears, while on the Vistula decidedly different types of craft dominate.

The boats from Ulanow have a bottom made of two or three planks and fairly high, double-strake sides. A technical detail of some interest is the "packet" method of making bottom and side planking curvatures. The method consists of putting together four planks which are given identical curvatures by shaving. This is quite important during connecting the lower side planks with the bottom. The result is an attractive boat. For connecting the bottom planks staples are used; then the frame roots are fixed. The external shape of the frames is corrected early on using frame moulds and a special device called "smiga". After fastening the side planks, the stem is slightly sharpened. The stern plank is higher and, on its sides, above the boat's sides it has two semi-circular notches – rowlocks. These holes, used at present as stern rowlocks, formerly could have been used for supporting the rods of a fishing net called "suwata". Such a solution, as I was informed by one of the older fishermen living on the middle San, was often used on fishing boats. The typical feature of the Ulanow boats is the double-strake side with double bevel. The side strakes are carvel-laid connected to avoid the noise of wave splashing, which is unavoidable in case of clinker joints. This method of connecting the side strakes is popular all along the whole San, and its origin also can be traced to raftlike structures, which as a rule had square jointed sides. Boats used on the lower San even today are sealed with marsh moss, which is dried before pressing between the strakes. The sealing is held down with juniper strips which are fixed from the outside with steel staples – cleats. A finished boat is impregnated with carbolineum, sometimes with wood tar. The boats are propelled by oar-poles. It may be added that a similar boat to that described here was used later by fisherman T. Kowalik instead of the earlier mentioned modified dugout (Figs. 23.6 and 23.15).

Conclusions

Contemporary boats from the San seem to be quite different in shape, though they have a number of common features. These are the following:

1. flat bottom, curved to differing degrees (along the upper San nearly straight – as in a raft bottom, along the middle and lower San the bottom is curved – as in dugouts),

2. flat and nearly perpendicular to the waterline at the bow and stern,

3. single-strake sides, or double-strake sides made of carvel-laid planks,

4. stiffenings of naturally-grown roots, alternately arranged,

5. bottom planks connected with staples,

6. no oarlocks – the boats are propelled by paddling or by poling,

7. sealing – formerly moss, at present modifications are adapted to maintain the traditional method of holding down the sealing.

Folk Boat Building on the Bug

As the San, the Bug also played an important role in the history of Polish inland navigation and boats of diverse types were built along this river.

The problems of navigation and fishing on the Bug were investigated by many researchers, hence scientific literature concerning water-transport problems is by far richer than in the case of the San.

From the point of view of traditional boatbuilding, and particularly the construction of small forms, publications concerning the Bug are more comprehensive and valuable. From these papers, published also in the beginning of this century, emerges that the most popular type of craft was the dugout. Even today quite a number of dugouts are used on the Bug and, if need arises they are still built. In effect, the Polish part of the Bug, represents a unique review of boat structures which are consecutive evolution stages of dugouts, illustrating the "vertical" development of the dugout. The "vertical" direction in which they were enlarged, is clearly visible in developed plank boats used on the middle and lower Bug.

There are several types of local boats which will not be presented here. These structures are simply adaptations of craft used on neighbouring lakes or they have been built by people with no special "maritime" traditions.

Version I - Fishing Dugout from the Upper Bug

Unique craft are used on the Bug below Włodawa in Kuzawka and Hanna two villages where a few fishermen make a living systematically catching fish in the Bug (Fig. 23.16). The boats they use are the true one-man dugouts, tested through years of use and still built today. These boats are most often hollowed out of willow trunks, sometimes from poplar or pine trunks. They have a light, slim fore part and a fuller after part in which is located the fisherman's seat. Inside each of these dugouts two natural bulkheads are made - one nearly at mid-length, the other slightly aft. These bulkheads form a fish bin without the auger holes often used in plank fishing boats, partly covered by loosely placed planks. On the after bulkhead is placed a plank extending aft - a sort of apron to prevent water from entering the boat. The apron plank is curved on the after side so that it fits the fisherman's body when he is kneeling or sitting, paddles with one hand steering the drifting boat. In this position, with the other hand, the fisherman operates a trawl type net, in co-operation with another fisherman. The characteristic position ensures relative stability of the boat and at the same time enables all necessary activities to be carried out. To keep from growing tired while fishing in the kneeling-sitting position, a bench is used and some dry hay is put under the knees to cushion them (Fig. 23.17).

Dugouts from around Włodawa have nearly identical hull proportions and interior arrangements (Fig. 23.7). Their equipment is also identical. An interesting detail is the shackle-ring fixed in the after part and used for holding this heavy oval part of the boat.

If asked why they use this type of boat instead of plank types, the users of dugouts answered that only dugouts can be safely transported to the fishing sites. On the Bug the fish are caught by a pair of fishermen drifting downriver operating one net between them. Because of the fishing technique used - drifting downriver - the boats must be transported upriver. Usually the fishermen transport their dugouts in the evening by horse-drawn waggon, some 20 km upriver and during the night drift to the selected place.

As the boats drift and the fishermen work together clearing the net, the boats lie side to side, connected with the shackle. This device is used also during drifting through fishless parts of the river. Connecting the boats in this manner allows one of the fishermen a short rest, while the other one does the steering.

Using traditional methods, it takes about 7 days to make a dugout, two days of which are taken up by finishing work - smoothing the surfaces. Lately, newer methods of hollowing have been used in Kuzawka and Hanna. The dugouts are made of willow trunks, on which initially mechanical saws are used with linearly working knives (chain saws) and with rotating disks (circular saws). With the chain saw the boat's profile is roughly made, and then with a hand circular saw the so called "air holes" are cut out, which are next removed manually from the interior of the fiture boat. After this is done, hand tools are used, i.e. axes, adzes and chisels. A finished boat is sealed with carbolineum and even painted with oil colours. A well maintained dugout which has been kept on land may be used for up to 20 years, a not so well maintained one, only 6 to 8 years.

Version II - Plank Boat Modeled on a Dugout

It may be supposed that the dugouts from the Bug described above will become extinct in the near future, and that in their place newer constructions will appear. Dugout users asked me if there are any workshops in which plastic boats similar to the dugouts could be made. A symtom of the coming changes are the attempts to pattern plank boats in Kuzawka on the dugout. I recorded one of these boats. It was made of four planks. In shape and structural detail it is reminiscent of the traditional dugout. However this boat isn't very popular among the fishermen and is rarely used.

A characteristic feature of this boat is that transverse strengthenings - floors - appear in the structure, and that there are no side frames.

The only transverse stiffenings are the two fish bin bulkheads. Like the dugouts, this boat is propelled by poling with an oar or by sculling with the oar inserted vertically into the water (Figs. 23.8 and 23.18).

Version III - Plank Boat Modeled on the Dugout

Fishermen from Kuzawka travelling far down the river said that their nearest neighbours use exclusively boats made of nailed planks. However, they still remembered the times when there was more dugouts on the Bug. A large number of such boats are used by fishermen from Krzyczew and Pratulin. The shape of these boats is original, unique to each one. They are examples of adopting a form derived from the dugout. In these boats the names of the structural elements are identical with those in dugouts.

The boats from Krzyczew and Pratulin are nailed together from three wide pine planks. The single strake bottom is strongly curved and extended at the bow with a massive, wide block into the side cut-outs of which the side strakes are inserted. The after part is closed by a wide five-sided transom leaning backwards. The only transverse stiffenings, and at the same time structural elements giving required flare midships, are formed by two bulkheads situated in the same parts of the boat as in natural dugouts. Also here the fish bin is filled with water poured in from above. The after bulkhead is higher and forms the base of a modified apron of the dugout. The apron which prevents water from dripping into the boat from the net is made of narrow planks, fixed to the upper sides of the hexagonal after bulkhead. In structures of this type there are no channels leading water to the fish bin, the water flowing over the boat's side. The position of the fisherman and the propelling technique are identical to those in the dugouts (Figs. 23.9, 23.19 and 23.20).

Version IV - Developed Plank Boat

Starting from the point at which the Bug enters Poland also on its right bank, many more types of water communication means are seen, and fishing boats form only a very small percentage of them. The most dominant craft by far are those used by peasants for crossing to the other bank to their fields. A large group is formed by recreation boats, specially made for angling.

Craft catalogued downriver from Niemirow, the first village on the right bank have a wide bottom, most often made of two planks. Also, boats with the bottom made of one or three planks appear. The sides of these boats are of clinker type and deflected in two stages from the bottom plane. The bottom and the sides are connected at the bow by a characteristic oak stem. This element is much smaller - lighter than in the boats from Krzyczew and Pratulin, and in its upper part is often obliquely undercut or circularly grooved. This stem focus is a reminder of the older method of building hollowed-out boats, although today builders of the boat cannot explain the sense of these decorations (Figs. 23.10, 23.21 and 23.22).

The transom of the plank boat is relatively wide and in most cases leans slightly backwards.

A characteristic feature of the boats with double-strake sides is the developed system of transverse stiffenings. These stiffenings are frames made of naturally grown oak crooks placed in pairs. Bulkhead planks are used only in fishing an angling boats, as fish bin walls (Fig. 23.23).

Plank boats from the middle and lower Bug have in most cases slightly higher sides obtained by adding a narrow cuppen to the second side strake. These cuppens protect the side strakes against damaging during paddling or hauling in the nets.

A few boatbuilders operate along the lower part of this river, because of larger demand for boats, while on the upper Bug the fishermen themselves build boats. The "workshops" of both are situated in open air.

Building of a boat begins from marking out straight lines on pine planks transported from the sawmill (if planks of even width are not cut out at the mill). For the marking out, a rope covered with soot is used. The rope is stretched between two selected points. After making the rope taut and lifting it up with a finger, it is released, striking the plank's surface and leaving a mark - a straight line. Two parallel planks are prepared for the bottom, and are placed on trestles and wedged. Next, the special moulds, the curves of the after and fore part are drawn. Excess material is cut off with a saw or axe and evened off with a plane. Scarfing of side edges is made with a plane with a guide and sloping runner. During the scarfing, the planks are fixed in wooden pincers, the lower ends of which are driven into the ground.

After the bottom strakes have been prepared for assembly, they are again placed on the trestles, wedged, and the strips connecting separate elements are nailed. Next the fore and after parts are curved upwards. To immobilize the bottom, before bending it holes are made in a few places through which are passed screws fixing the bottom to the foundation, i.e. to the assembly bench. Short, specially matched pegs pressed in between the bottom planks and the bench surface are used for bending the bottom. The side plank rake is determined with frame moulds and with a "smiga" (two strips fixed at one end, which can rotate around a common axle). After nailing down the first, i.e. the lower side strakes, the boatbuilder inserts into the shell some of the frames prepared for mounting in the boat. These frames are made of naturally grown crooks. Next, the strakes of the upper side strip are mounted in such a way that they overlap the lower strip. When the strakes are nailed down, the stem block and the transom board are fitted in. The stem block and the transom are most often oak. When all these procedures have been finished the boat is unfastened from the assembly bench, the strips connecting the bottom strakes are removed, and the remaining pairs of frames are put into the boat. Most often, they are situated in the places in which the screws fixing the boat's bottom to the assembly bench were placed. The holes left by the screws are stopped with pegs. Sometimes these pegs are used for fastening the frames. Finally, the cuppens are nailed and the boat is sealed by pressing impregnated string into the slits.

Conclusions

Analyzing the above types of boats used on the Bug, it may be stated that here, as perhaps nowhere else in Europe, an amazing, exceptional state of technical differentiation of floating craft have survived until today. On one river as we move downriver from its sources we may observe different stages of development of boats, starting from a dugout, through intermediary forms, to a plank boat. At the river mouth, features of other schools of boatbuilding are observed, which slowly penetrating upriver could influence the boatbuilding on the middle and lower Bug to such an extent that technically developed structures very much recall the boats from the lower Narew - the river into which the Bug flows - and boats from the middle Vistula. In the light of such evident development stages of the Bug boats, their dugout origin and "vertical" development trend are clearly visible. It is very difficult to find the "horizontal" trend in boats from the Bug, in opposition to the earlier presented boats from the San.

Similar as for the San boats, several common features may be singled out in case of the boats from the Bug. The more important are the following:

1. flat bottom, in profile showing an analogy with the shape of the dugout's bottom,

2. block ending of the bow, often grooved on the inside, reminiscent of the dugout's bow,

3. wide after part closed with a transom board,

4. single- or double-strake sides made of clinker planks,

5. stiffenings made of bulkheads or of pairs of frame crooks,

6. no oarlocks - the boats are propelled by paddling or poling, (Figs. 23.24a and b),

7. caulking made of oakum or strings.

FINAL REMARKS

Comparing the common features of boats from the San and the Bug it may be suggested that on Polish territory the proto-type of floating craft was the dugout, which depending on the type of environment was developed in a "horizontal" or "vertical" direction. In case of development in the horizontal plane, which took place along piedmont rivers, the technical feature of rafts were borrowed and adapted. Along lowland rivers the dugout was developed in the "vertical" direction.

Basing on the examples of the San and the Bug boatbuilding, a division into two boatbuilding environments may be carried out (Fig. 23.11). The boundary between these environments lies at the foot of the mountains. Along nearly the entire length of the Vistula, which has the character of a lowland river, up to this day boats of uniform type appear, differing in small structural detail only. Boats from the Bug are very much like the Vistula boats, while boats from the San are decidedly different. This proves that the direction of boat development was decided mainly by the conditions in which the boats were to be used.

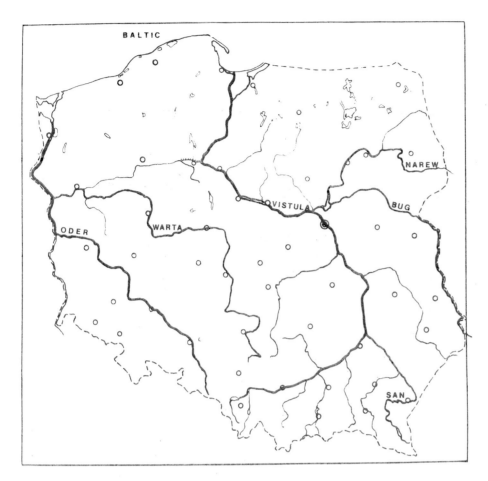

Fig. 23.1:   Map showing the main Polish rivers.

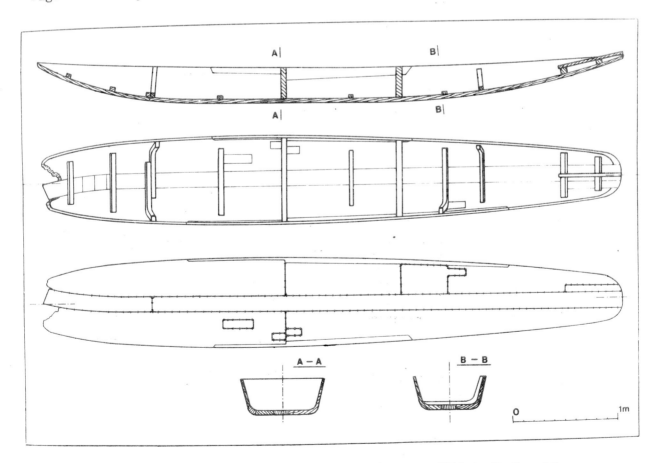

Fig. 23.2:   The repaired and expanded dugout used until 1940 by T. Kowalik from Majdan Zbidniowski on the San river.

337

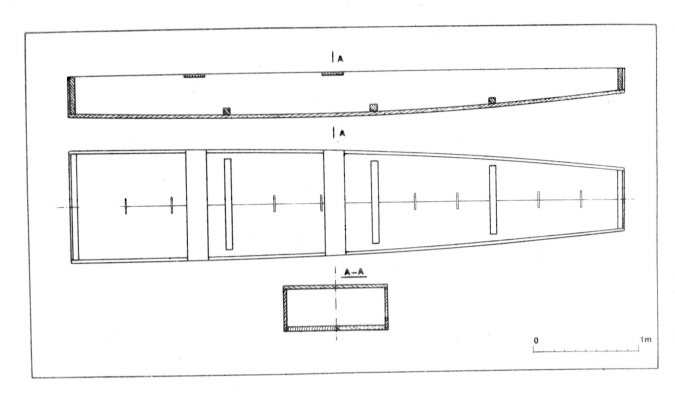

Fig. 23.3:   The typical upper San boat – boat plan.

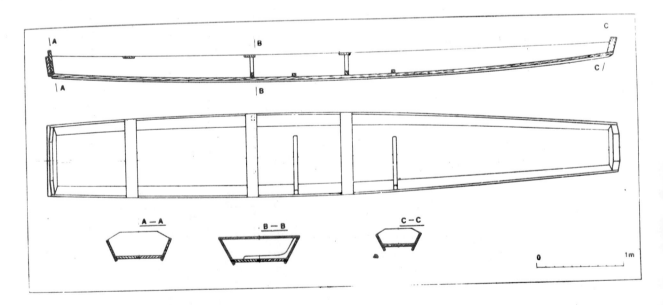

Fig. 23.4:   The fishing boat from Słonne – boat plan.

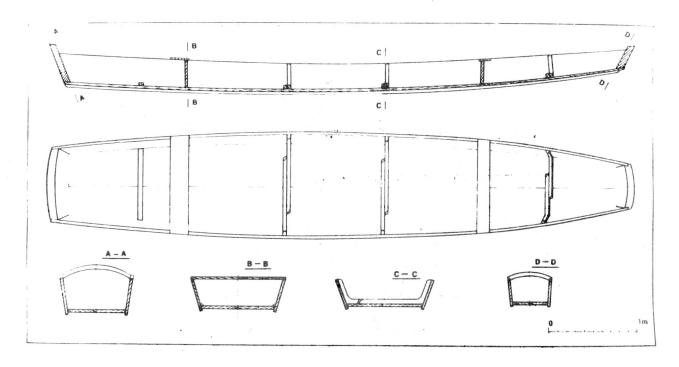

Fig. 23.5:   The sand-dredger's boat from Jarosław – boat plan.

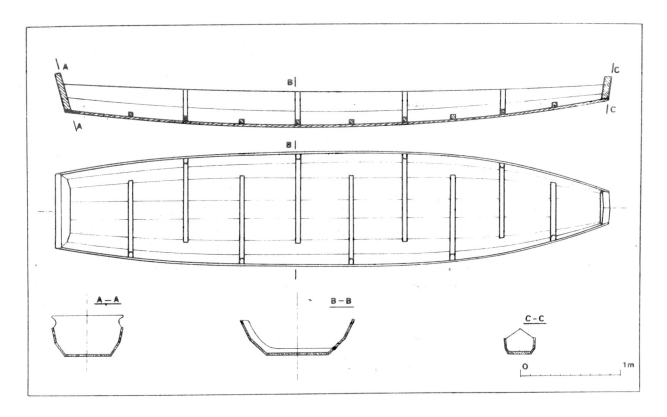

Fig. 23.6:   The fishing boat from Ulanow – boat plan.

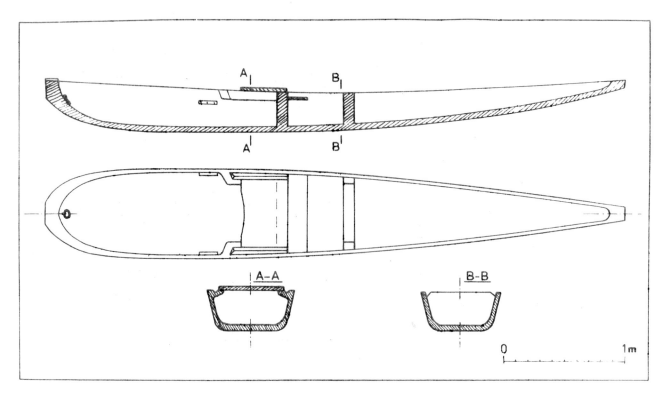

Fig. 23.7:   The fishing dugout from Kuzawka - boat plan.

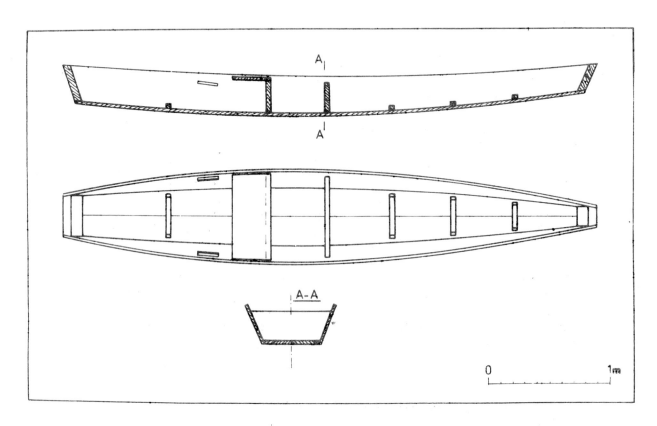

Fig. 23.8:   The plank boat modeled on a dugout from Kuzawka - boat plan.

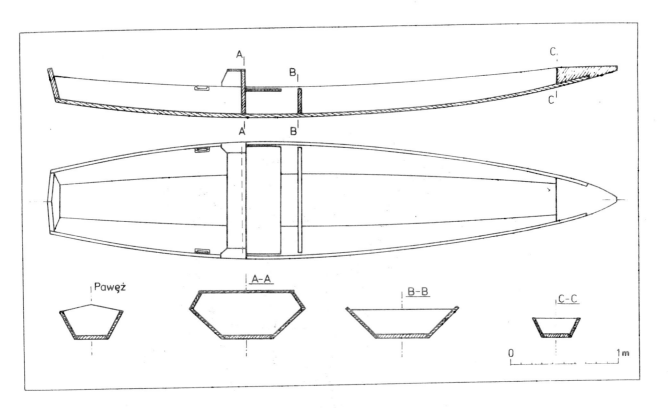

Fig. 23.9:   The plank boat modeled on the dugout from the village of
Krzyczew - boat plan.

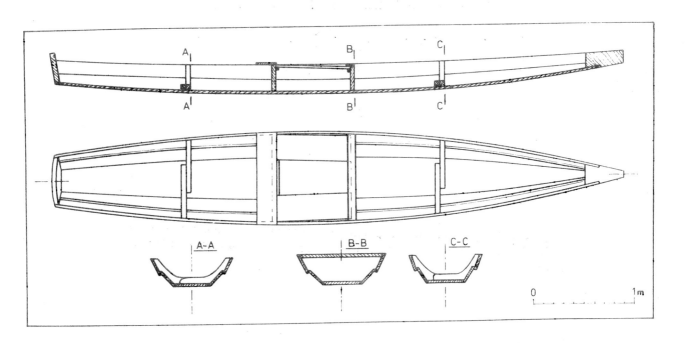

Fig. 23.10:   The plank boat from Brok - boat plan.

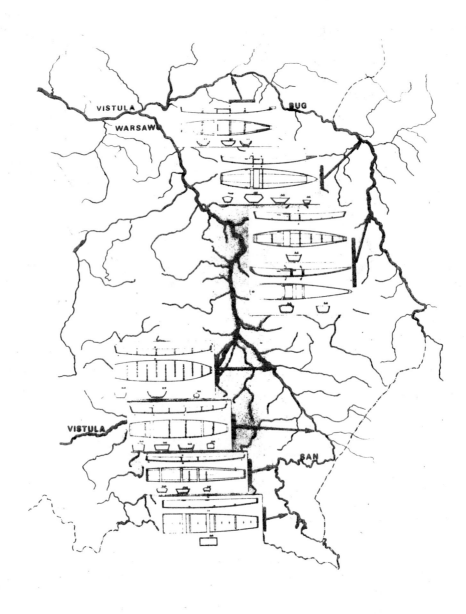

Fig. 23.11: Maps showing the development of folk boats in Poland – examples of crafts and areas where they are still in use.

Fig. 23.12:   Simple boats on the upper San in Srednia Wies.

Fig. 23.13:   Fishing boat from the middle San, village of
Słonne.

343

Fig. 23.14:   Three dredger boats on the middle San, town of
Jaros*l*aw.

Fig. 23.15:   Fishing boat from lower San, Ulanow.

Fig. 23.16: One-man dugouts on the upper Bug in Kuzawk village.

Fig. 23.17: Fishing dugout in Kuzawka – dry hay was placed under the knees during fishing in the kneeling-sitting position.

Fig. 23.18:   Plank boat and its dugout prototypes - Kuzawka.

Fig. 23.19:   Popular plank boat modeled on the
dugout - village of Pratulin.

Fig. 23.20: Plank boats modeled on the dugout in fisherman's farmhouse - Krzyczw.

Fig. 23.21: Developed plank boat from the lower Bug - village Brok.

Fig. 23.22:   The stems in many boats on the
lower Bug are obliquely undercut or circularly
grooved.

Fig. 23.23:   Typical communication boats used on the lower Bug,
village of Nur.

Fig. 23.24 a and b: Fishing dugouts are also used on the lower Bug,
village Kamienczyk - a fisherman demonstrates two methods of propelling -
A/ poling, B/ sculling.

24. BOATS OF THE SOUTHERN BALTIC

Wolfgang Rudolph

In 1958, an ethnological inventory of boats, implements and all other objects concerning maritime culture on the beach between the Bay of Wismar and the mouth of the river Oder was started in the German Democratic Republic. Inventory leader was Reinhard Peesch from the Institute of Ethnology at the German Academy of Science at Berlin. The initiator of maritime research was the institute's chairman, professor Wolfgang Steinitz, well known as a linguist and ethnographer. From his former fieldwork among the coastal Lapps and other arctic fenno-ugristic peoples in Northern Siberia he acquired a very good knowledge of the water craft's importance for beach dwellers in litoral cultures. In addition, Steinitz was connected in friendship with three of the illustrous initiators of ethnological boat-research in Scandinavia: with Ernst Klein from Stockholms Nordiska Museet, and with the great Finnish scientists Ilmari Manninen and Toivo Itkonen.

The subject of our systematic survey work were all types of working water craft, including landing sites, and all the boatyards and various kinds of other maritime workshops: those of sailmakers, of anchor smiths and of locksmiths for boat-engines, and so on, along our coastline and in its adjoining country districts between the river Elbe and the Oder-river, northward from Berlin. In this terrain we explored, during a ten year period, village after village, shipyard after shipyard, and each and every boat. Literally. The investigators were Reinhard Peesch and Wolfgang Rudolph, both ethnologists, and the shipwright, engineer Kurt Kühn. For our fieldwork we made use of a small former Danish fishing boat. Sailing along the coast we worked onboard every year from April until the end of November. Of great importance for our ethnological field investigation was the fact that of the investigators each was familiar with all the different localities, and able to speak the Lower German dialects of the coastal region, and likewise familiar with the maritime world of work. Rudolph was formerly a master mariner in the coastal trade, and Kühn was employed before the war and during the war as engineer at the famous Schichau-shipyard at Danzig and Königsberg. In this way we had at all times excellent contacts with the fishermen and sailors, and we enjoyed the cooperation of coastal dwellers.

The final stage in our ethnological field inventory was the analysis of all kinds of literature from the southern Baltic coasts, as well as the analysis of all kinds of old pictures with value for maritime history. During all the years of our investigation we had close cooperation with linguistic experts in Balto-Slaw languages and with specialists for the several lower German coastal dialects as well. In many cases this cooperation has given us the precise evidence for the Slavonic origins of some boatbuilding methods of the dark ages.

Ten years of research work produced a great corpus of material covering equally all the coastal regions from west to east. It was a collection of photographs and technical drawings, of descriptions and records from informants, a fundus of historical pictures, bibliograhies, archive excerpts and, last not least, a collection of original objects, boats and so on, destined for the future use in the museums at Straslund and at Berlin.

Our intention was to publish the results of this inventory as soon as possible. Indeed, we did produce, between 1966 and 1969, two monographs about the inshore fishing craft of our region, besides several papers in scientific periodicals. More catalogued material is open to scholars in the archive of Zentralinstitut für Gjeschichte, Wissenschaftsbereich Kulturgeschichte/Volkskunde, on the Academy of Science of the GDR, which contains the bulk of the photogaphs in black and white and in colour, and more technical drawings too. Summing up, one can reflect that this ethnological inventory of boats and boatbuilding on the Southern Baltic should be seen as a last minute piece of salvage work. Today, after little more than ten years, the bulk of objects then registered, particularly all the small cargo coasters, are lost for ever, because of the industrialization of our ports and the change in the living conditions in our villages.

The inventory's results revealed a broad spectrum of variety of regional and local boat constructions. Therefore it was a stringent necessity to classify this variegated material. We worked out at first a preliminary "home spun" typology of boats, with regard to the essential characteristics of their of the boat bottom, and of the stem and stern constructions. In this way we gradually drew up a nomenclature of scientific technical terms of boatbuilding elements, the use of which is mandatory in our institute. We published both in the Handbuch der Boote, in the year 1966. In 1974 the National Maritime Museum at Greenwich published our typology in monograph no. 14, about the Inshore Fishing Craft of the Southern Baltic.

But because the characteristics of a boat type are not in any case unique and well defined, and will be used by scholars very often controversially in international discussion, we are of the opinion that it could be more useful for a general survey of the regional stock of boats to employ the widely published system of boatbuilding methods, very often published by Olof Hasslöf, the grand Old Man of boat research. Hasslöf's technology should serve as a good source for attempting to solve the urgent historical and genetic problems inherent in tracing boat evolution in the Southern Baltic.

At the commencement of the 20th century the position as regards the production of indigenous vessels along the southern coasts of the Baltic was characterised by the coexistence of decidedly different techniques of production. For example around the year 1900, it was common, in large port towns of the region, such as Rostock, Stettin and Danzig, for carpenters to be building wooden ships at wharves and yards that lay adjacent to some of the most modern and famous steel ship-building yards in the world at the time like Neptun, Vulcan and Schichau. And even more startling that these carpenters, working in sight of the gigantic four funnel steamers and candidates for the blue ribbon race, were masters of four different techniques for the production of vessels, of which no less than two of the procedures clearly showed themselves to be relics of the prehistoric development of lcoal craft in the region between Belt and Curonian lagoon.

The oldest technique (I) on a relative time-scale and in regard to genetics, namely the binding up of rushes to make rafts, had by then been wholly reduced to the realm of children's games, authenticated by carpenters' oral traditions since the middle of the 19th century (Fig. 24.1). In this guise however it has in some places, for example on the lagoon of the mouth of the river Oder, been actively preserved even today. It is well known that children's traditional use of old-time tools, which are descended from the world of adults in the past, is very common, particularly in the sphere of fishing and hunting. Historic or archaeologic evidence of rafts of rushes no longer exists, but we have clear evidence of the use of prehistoric log rafts as manifested by a find made recently in the area of the river Warnow, which flows into the Baltic at Rostock. This find is dated to the first half of the fifth century.

Two further boatbuilding techniques (I and II) rely on the principle of hollow-shell construction. As a consequence of technology (II) vessels evolved incorporating a keel and stem timbers and with side planks meeting at a pointed stern. But it is noteworthy that in different parts of our region the laying of side planks was handled in two ways. Along the coast between Jutland in the West and the Finnish Bay between Finland and Estonia in the North-East, and from the Baltic coasts adjoining to the river Havel, flowing through Berlin, boats were built with clinker laid strakes. South and east of this area vessels were being built with flush-laid side planks, but in a true shell construction, fitting the ribs after the shell was built or partly built up.

The area in discussion here is one of the oldest cultural borders in Europe – the border between the area of the nordic clinker boatbuilding tradition and the area of the pontic-mediterranean tradition. Strictly speaking we cannot observe a clear and continuous frontier line, but only a broad belt of cultural contact. The main impact of the flush-laying method was felt along the great rivers, Oder, Weichsel, Memel and Düna, from the inland to the Baltic. The lagoons and bays on the mouths of these rivers either were flush-laying areas or areas in which both techniques were intermixed. Everywhere along the Baltic coasts clear evidence of clinker building can be seen. In general, all these boats were built "by eye" without the use of any aids.

In the experience of technology (III), the characteristic of which is a combination of hollowing-out and constructional methods, there arose transitional forms between the single-part logboat and the multiple-part plank-constructed boat of clinker or carvel construction, with flat bottom often gouged out of one longitudinal half of a tree trunk, and with several local variants of stem and stern-post forms, often with block stems hollowed out from log sections cut in half and fitted horizontally or vertically on top of the bottom shell or of the bottom plank (Fig. 24.2-24.4). Even today, we can find no less than six variations of such local stem and stern forms, in this region (Fig. 24.5-24.13 and 24.15-24.16).

For vessels built according to technique (II) the general, and customary popular term in the German language is 'Boot'. But for the craft built according to technique (III) a profusion of local designations includes in addition to German terms, many vestigial words deriving from the Baltic-Slav, or Baltic, languages of the coastal dwellers here, who since around 1300 have undergone a process of Germanisation. Beside the indigenous terminology there was once another distinction between techniques (II) and (III). Characteristics of construction such as keels, stems and sternposts, and a differentiated system of frames and stringers belonged to the working world of urban shipyards, organized in guilds.   On the other hand, the old-fashioned characteristics in hollowing and gouging techniques, together with the preferred use of simple, natural-grown knees and forked tree branches, was common to the realm of rural and local construction, practised by people who had not undergone either professional apprenticeship or any particular training, but who had built boats and small cargo vessels only periodically, dividing their time with other seasonal activities such as seafaring, fishing or lumbering work.   This tradition was characterised by a strictly regional terminology.

Summing up, technique (III) must be regarded as a relic of the 'true' logboat production which came to an end here in the late half of the 19th century.   Prehistoric or medieval logboats are found in growing numbers each year, with 60 finds registered in our wreck register.   The recent use of logboats in fishing has been documented to date as late as the years around 1920.

The fourth technique (IV), based on the principle of frame or skeleton construction, with a 'skin' or flush-laid strakes clothing the framework consisting of keel, stems and ribs, had been practised here as an urban shipbuilding craft ever since the 15th century, with centres in the Hanseatic port towns Lübeck and Danzig.   In the year 1962 a shipwreck was found of skeleton construction in shallow water off the isle of Hiddensee. Wood from this wreck was dated by radiocarbon techniques to about the year 1590 ± 100 years.   Traditional rural boatbuilding in the Southern Baltic region was for a long while influenced by the new skeleton building principle in a few places, namely around the port of Stralsund in Pomerania, formerly a Swedish protectorate and since the 17th century it had been a centre of shipbuilding for the Swedish navy and for Swedish postal communication by sea, between the Scandinavian homeland and the Swedish possessions on the continent.   We know that the famous Swedish shipwright, Fredrik Henrik af Chapman, worked at Stralsund's yard c. 1750.   Resulting from the professional training of carpenters in the Royal Stralsund dockyard it may well have been that the practice of building boats and small coastal trade vessels following the skeleton technique extended into some yards in the villages of the former isles of Darss and Zingst, northwest of Stralsund.   We have archival evidence that after 1760 the village carpenters built ships, called Yachts, in the carvel manner.   Moreover, we find in the neighbourhood around the port of Stralsund a local form of special stern construction for small fishing boats, strictly limited still today, namely double-ended keel boats with clinker-laid strakes but with a transom on the sternpost (Fig. 24.14).   The same construction can be found along the coast of the Swedish county of Blekinge, on Swedish fishing boats around the former navy dockyard of Karlskrona.   However, the skeleton technique in general was only adapted for rural boatbuilding in the Southern Baltic from 1850 onwards, as a result of the structural change in boatbuilding.   From that point, we see a gradual transition from discontinuous, seasonal working to year-round, specialised artisanship along urban lines, henceforth including theoretical training by way of school and literature.   For the bulding of cargo vessels, for deep sea fishing boats too, then a novelty in the Baltic, and for recreational sailing yachts built in carvel manner, village carpenters began to use moulds, but not drawn plans.   It is noteworthy that an intermediate method of building was often practised here by merging shell and skeleton principles.   We have certain evidence that carpenters built boats with flush-laid strakes, the planks being fastened with iron rivets, and then above the water line changed to laying planks in the clinker manner.   Moreover, we have records that people were building the underwater part clinker—laid, while the strakes above the waterline were carvel nailed.

Let me come to some final observations. I will point out three main particulars of the Southern Baltic coasts. Firstly, the clear continuity in shell construction's clinker technique for the building of cargo ships. We can trace a line of regional continuity from the prehistoric wrecks of Nydam, Haithabu, Ralswiek, Stettin and Danzig, all from the 4th to 11th century, to the wrecks of Warnemünde and of Prora, during the 17th and 18th centuries, up to the present times and clinker—built coastal craft. In the same way I contend that one can trace this same continuity from the old pontic—mediterranean manner of shell construction with sides of flush—laid strakes, fastened by means of spikes or by means of treenails and cramps. The coastal region of the Southern Baltic is the juncture where both these methods of boatbuilding met and overlapped.

Secondly, we have evidence of a definite regional development of rural boatbuilding methods based on the simple log boat or dugout made of oak or of pine, frequently still encouraged here in the 20th century. We cannot see any clear evidence of another tradition of extending soft—wooden log hulls by means of physical or chemical processes, a practice which began Eastward of the Bay of Riga, and from there spreading over the northern Eurasiatic zone of forests to the Siberian coasts of the Pacific.

Here on the Southern Baltic the progressive evolution that led to craft of higher quality for the villagers water transport followed two different lines of development from the simple log boat: 1) by way of bottom shell boats with one, two or three side planks, and 2) by way of three or more part bottom plank boats were shaped so as to resemble closely the form of the proto—type oak—tree dugout. Specimens of old—fashioned transitional types displaying both building methods still exist in many different localities. As one of the finest relic—types still we can see the bottom shell boat of Rostock. Rural boatbuilding processes of this kind evolved largely autonomously, remaining uninfluenced by advanced merchant cargo ship constructional methods, even as late as high medieval times, when the Slav or Baltic coastal dwellers had begun to fuse with the German immigrants and when their autochthonous designations entered the linguistic field. This is attested by many Slavic Baltic relic words in German coastal idioms, mostly technical terms of the primary characteristics of boat construction, namely boat ends, boat bottom and sides.

Because the rural development was autonomous and widely uninfluenced by the advanced shipbuilding methods of the higher social classes of the inhabitants of great shipping ports, the great profusion of local boat forms and types of rural water craft is apparent today. This is evidence that the coastal region of the Southern Baltic in medieval times formed part of the zone of cultural contact between the tribes of Danes and of Germans, the Baltic Slavs and the Balts. Another determining factor in the situation was the constant and lively maritime cultural interchange with the Swedes and with the Baltic Finns. It was thus that long term and far—reaching contacts arose between societies of different national background and of different socio—economic structure. Conditions of this kind favoured the general process of evolution of the Baltic coastal civilization as we see it today, presenting essential traits of a unified nature, yet retaining relics of the singularly varied and multiform array of boat types which characterise the traditional folklife.

Fig. 24.1: Rush-bundle raft from the Oder Lagoon (Oderhaff). The photos in fig. 24.1-24.6 have been exposed by the author.

Fig. 24.2-24.4: Bottom shell boat (Kahn) from Rostock.

356

Fig. 24.3

Fig. 24.4

357

Fig. 24.5: Block stem from the River Trave.

Fig. 24.6: Block stem from Darss.

Fig. 24.7: Block stem from the Oder Valley.

Fig. 24.8: Flat bottom boat from the Bay of Wismar.

Fig. 24.9-10: "Heuer" (a flatner) from the Oder Lagoon (Oderhaff).

360

Fig. 24.11: Boat (Kahn) with plank stem and sternpost, from the River Havel.

Fig. 24.12: Boat with ends closed without stem by joining the ends of the vertically fitted strakes, from the Leba Lake.

Fig. 24.13: · Boat with keel and conventional stem and
sternpost, from the Wismar Bay.

Fig. 24.14: Keel boat with transom-stern, from the Isle of Rugia. (10)

362

Fig. 24.15:   Flat bottom boat (Kahn) with thwartships-laid bottom planks, from the Isle of Rugia.

Fig. 24.16a: Detail of the stern of a boat (Waltelle) with inside stem and sternpost, from the Curonian Lagoon (Kurisches Haff).

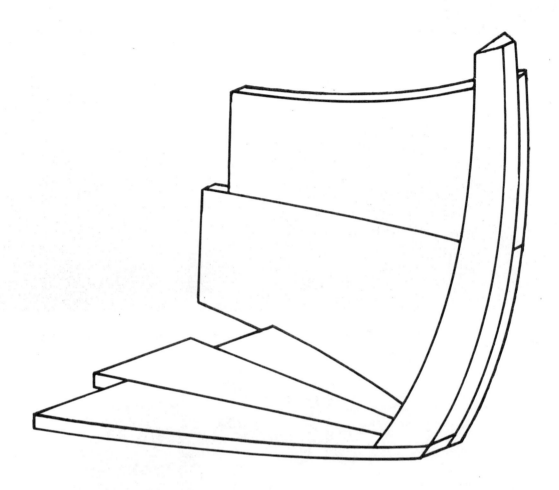

Fig. 24.16b: Perspective drawing of the construction of an inside
stern as shown in Fig. 24.16a.

25. NEW FINDS OF BOAT-GRAFFITI

Peter von Busch

I have been asked to make a brief presentation on the earliest form of boat graffiti - in fact it's so fresh that the ink of my sketches has not dried yet and the stereometrical photos have not yet been developed.

We have to collect and record information about older ships wherever we can find it. I will present information about the recording of graffiti on the church walls of the island of Gotland, about which very few people have known. This knowledge has passed into different hands throughout the last decades and only now has it been brought to light.

The picture of a medieval "kaupship" on the northern wall of the main aisle of the church of Fide was described and examined in the 50s by experts from the Swedish National Maritime Museum and the results have been published (Jonsson 1941).

Graffiti of signs, animals, figures, labyrinths and runes, construction of details of the church and even of some ships have also been discovered in this church and until a month ago we knew about 30 ships.

Under the supervision of Dr. Lagerlöf, from the Central Office of National Antiquities in Stockholm, who is in charge of the documentation of the churches of Gotland, a group including Sibylla Haasum and a photographer and a conservator, started a systematic investigation and documentation of 20 churches in order to find the best way to document the boat-graffiti found there. The photographer worked with stereometrical recording wherever it was possible for him to do so while the conservator made moulds of plasticine which were afterwards stabilized in plaster. The rest of us recorded the graffiti with the aid of drawn tracings on transparent sheets of plastic placed over the graffiti (Fig. 25.1 and 25.2). With the help of light we tried to find and pick up the details of the ships. Whenever the graffiti were vague and different interpretations had to be made, we used different colours to mark out the possible variations. Over a period of five days we investigated 20 churches, most of them in the middle part of Gotland. We made descriptions of more than 60 boat-graffiti-pictures of various shapes in 10 churches. In total there are nearly one hundred churches on Gotland, many of them medieval, so there is still a lot of search, survey and recording work to be done in this area.

Almost all of the pictures are located in the west part of the churches - in the bellroom on the whitewashed walls at eyelevel. It will probably be possible to date them to different periods between the 14th and 17th centuries. The dating is based on the details of depicted ship constructions, and masting and rigging. Also, the different layers of the white wash can be dated, which will be of further help in dating the graffiti (Fig. 25.2-25.4).

We all know that during the period just mentioned the seafaring farmers of the island of Gotland, either as owners or part-owners of ships, travelled extensively carrying trade goods of tar, furs, hides, lime and funts. Maybe the boat-graffiti are symbolic. The sea-faring farmers may have been trying to put the fate of one's ship, crew and cargo into the hands of our Lord when one made a picture of it on the holy walls of the church.

In Sweden although boat-graffiti are found especially in the churches in the island of Gotland they also occur elsewhere. Boat-graffiti have also been found in other Scandinavian countries as well as in England, France, Italy and Germany.

I hope that these drawings made by hand on the walls of churches by people who knew ships and shipping, can add some further information about the shape and structure of the ships, as well as of the rigging in earlier periods.

REFERENCES

Jonsson, Gunnar, 1941. Kaupskip i Fide. Gotländskt Arkiv: 45-50.

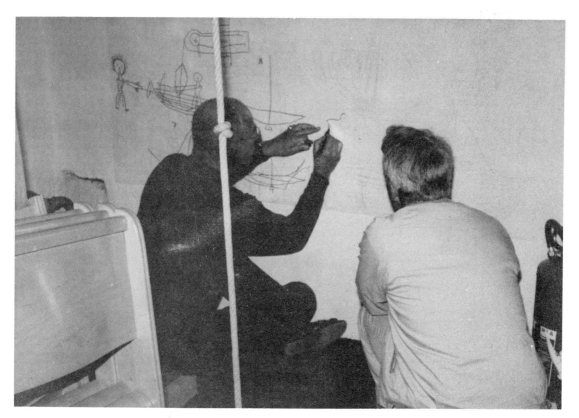

Fig. 25.1: The performing of a tracing on a sheet of plastic of one boat graffiti.

Fig. 25.2: Example of one tracing of two ship pictures on the wall of the bellroom in Lye church, Gotland.

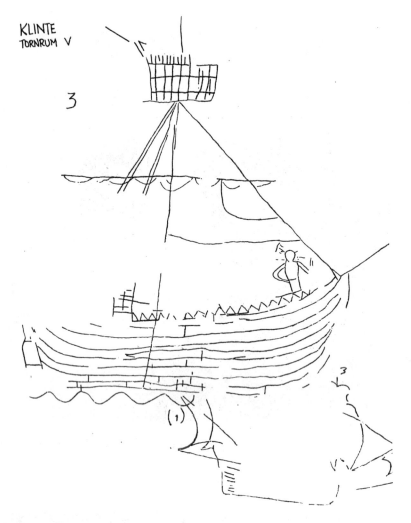

KLINTE
TORNRUM V

3

Fig. 25.3: Graffiti in the bellroom of Klinte church, Gotland, showing a onemasted, square-rigged vessel.

BUNGE
TORNRUM S   1   2

Fig. 25.4: Graffiti in the bellroom of Bunge church, Gotland, showing two bigger ships with two or more masts.

26. THE WRECK OF A SMALL BOAT FROM PORTØR

Arne Emil Christensen

During small-scale dredging work for a pleasure harbour at Portørenga near Kragerø in Southern Norway, fragments of a boat were found. The owner notified the local museum, which in turn sent the message on to the Norwegian Maritime Museum (Norsk Sjøfartsmuseum) and the University Collection of National Antiquities (Universitets Oldsaksamling). Under the Norwegian Ancient Monuments Act, the wreck is the responsibility of Norsk Sjøfartsmuseum, but as I had other fieldwork nearby, the first visit to the site was made by myself. The fragments salvaged were from a small clinker-built boat, mainly of oak. As the wreck lay beneath 1 m. of mud, it could have been of considerable age, so I strongly recommended that the NSM excavated it. Director Svein Molaug later visited the site, and agreed that it was well worth an excavation. As an academic experiment we decided to document the finds independently, and work out separate reconstructions. The boat was excavated during the period 9 - 12/10 - 1981 by Trygve Skaug and Bjarne Ims Henriksen from NSM and A.E. Christensen from U.O. as a joint enterprise. We had hoped to lift the boat intact, but this proved impossible, so it was dismantled carefully under water. Each fragment was drawn as it came ashore, and stored wet (Fig. 26.1). Later, the fragments were moved to NSM for conservation. Svein Molaug has published a report on the find in NSM Årbok 1981, with a preliminary reconstruction based on his recording of the fragments. I am still at work on a reconstruction model and drawing, but it is clear, even at an early stage of the work, that my reconstruction will differ from that published by Molaug.

The boat has been dated by the laboratory for Radiocarbon dates, NTH, Trondheim. The date given was AD 1575 ± 65. This was later changed to AD 1465 ± 45 years, after a revision of the standard values in one of the counters in the laboratory. As the strakes of the boat bear sawmarks, and the mast twarth is placed rather far forward in the boat, indicating a fore and aft rig, the revised date seems historically too early. The boat is east-Norwegian in character, but shows features that resemble West- and North-Norwegian practice, and which must be characterized as archaic in a boat found east of Lindesnes. It is of course impossible to pinpoint the building-place of a small empty wreck, and it may be far from the place where the vessel was found. However, the general shape of the boat indicates an East Norwegian building site, as do the materials used: oak, some spruce in the ribs, and juniper treenails.

The boat has five strakes, all of oak, like the keel and stem and sternpost. The keel has a T-shaped cross section, and the stem and sternpost are unrabbeted (Fig. 26.2). The planks are scarfed. In more recent boatbuilding in eastern Norway, one would expect a rabbet in the keel and stem and sternpost, and butt joints with butt-blocks in the planking. West-Norwegian boats are generally built like their Viking age ancestors, with a crossbeam above the floor-timber as transversal stiffening, and loose twarths above the beam, while the boats of East Norway generally have no beams, but twarths permanently fastened with knees. Our boat has no cross-

369

beams, as should be the case in an East Norwegian boat, but the only twarth found rests loose on the rib, with no knees, even though it has a hole for the mast, and should supposedly be securely fastened.   This curious mixture of details makes the boat somewhat of a missing link in the evolution of East Norwegian boats, from a common type used all along the Norwegian coast in the Viking age, to boats more like those used in Denmark and Western Sweden, while Western and Northern Norway still use boats very little removed from the Viking age types   (Fig. 26.3).

At this early stage, the find creates more questions than it answers, but it is no doubt that it deserves a thorough study, including reconstruction as a model and on the drawing board, and possibly a full-scale reconstruction of the boat itself after conservation.

REFERENCES

Molaug, S., 1981. Båten fra Portør. Norsk Sjöfartsmuseum. Årsberetning: 89-94.

Fig. 26.1: Fragments of the port side aft temporarily reassembled.

Fig. 26.2: Stem (uppermost) and sternpost with small fragments of the keel.

Fig. 26.3: Detail of thole with alternative hole for one tholepin. The illustrations of this paper have been photographed by Bjarne Ims Henriksen, Norsk Sjøfartsmuseum. (10)

27. SHIP-ARCHAEOLOGY IN DENMARK 1979-1982

Ole Crumlin-Pedersen

At the ISBSA· Symposium in Bremerhaven 1979 I reported on the archaeological investigations carried out in Denmark up to that time on medieval cog finds. Here a brief survey of excavations, investigations and experiments related to ship archaeology in Denmark over the last three years will be given (Crumlin-Pedersen 1980 and 1981).

On logboats the following news can be reported: at Tybrind vig on the island of Fyn a 10 m long Mesolithic logboat was excavated and raised by divers in 1980 during excavation of a sunken settlement which yielded many well preserved wooden objects, including an ornamented paddle (Andersen 1980 and 1982; Dal 1981). At the island of Barsø in Lillebaelt a 3.65 m long logboat was raised for the museum in Haderslev in 1982. The boat is of beech and was dated by C-14 to AD 940 ± 65, (K 1040, corrected) (Andersen 1983). The boatgraves at Slusegård, Bornholm, excavated 20-25 years ago, are now being prepared for publication in 1984. The 44 graves with traces of whole boats or parts of boats, all expanded logboats, are dated to the Roman Iron Age (AD 100 to 250) (Klint-Jensen 1978).

The area where the 7th century Gresetedbro ship was found in 1945 was searched in 1982 with seismic equipment (Crumlin-Pedersen 1968). A distinct anomaly in the layers in the river bank has been located, but a trial excavation is needed to show if this represents the remains of the ship.

Another river bank investigation is that at Maglebraende on the Fribødre river at the island of Falster. Here remains from shipbuilding activities around AD 1100 have been found in considerable quantity (Fig. 27.2). Evidently ships have been broken up here to supply the shipbuilders with planks and beams for new ships, whereas the frames and knees have been thrown into the shallow water by the building site (Skamby Madsen 1983).

The Fotevik-wreck in Scania, Sweden, reported on by Catharina Ingelmann-Sundberg of Malmö, was found in 1981 by Danish divers taking a course in underwater archaeology conducted by the author in cooperation with representatives of the Danish Sport Divers Union. The excavation of this wreck in 1982 and the mapping of the blockage (with parts of four other wrecks) was carried out as a joint project by Swedish and Danish museums and amateur divers. This is part of a larger fieldwork project on this archaeological complex, combining elements of land- and underwater archaeology (Hårdh 1983 and Ingelman-Sundberg & Söderhielm 1982).

The Viking Ship Museum also assisted at the harbour excavation at Hedeby (Haithabu) at Schleswig in North Germany in 1979. The parts recovered of the Haithabu ship and other ships' parts from the harbour area will be recorded and published in conjunction with the building of a new museum for the Haithabu finds, planned to be opened in 1985 (Crumlin-Pedersen 1969 and Schitzel & Crumlin-Pedersen 1980).

A 16 mm film (20 min.) "Historien om et vrag" (Story of a Wreck) by
Leif Stubkjaer showing the raising of the Vejby-ship in 1977 is now
available (Crumlin-Pedersen et. al. 1979). It is expected that parts of
this wreck, a cog, built around 1350 and wrecked in 1375-80, will be
exhibited in the future at the Viking Ship Museum in Roskilde together with
the 110 gold coins and the fragments of the cargo found with the ship. The
same may be the case with the Kollerup-cog of the 13th century, excavated in
1978 and recorded in detailed plans of all parts in 1980-81 in the museum in
Thisted, North Jylland (Jeppesen 1978, 1979a and b). After having
investigated the possibilities of conserving and exhibiting this ship
locally, the Thisted museum has asked the National Museum to take over full
responsibility for this wreck. Except for the forward section and
sternpost, the ship will be transferred to a long-term underground storage
(in sand under the ground water level) near Copenhagen. The two
aforementioned parts will be, it is hoped, conserved and exhibited in
Roskilde in the future.

Even some post medieval wrecks have been investigated in recent years.
At Vejle the bottom-part of a ship, probably of Dutch tradition of ab. 1580,
was excavated in a rescue operation in 1980 (Fig. 27.3a and b; 27.4a and b).
All parts of the ship have been carefully recorded by the local museum. A
17th century brickloaded wreck has been investigated at Lundeborg (Skaarup
1979-80) and a number of similar wrecks have been located elsewhere in
Danish waters, including the 19th century Lyngså-wreck of a small jagt
loaded with a main cargo of tiles and a small extra cargo of what seems to
be the personal belongings of a nobleman, wealthy merchant or royal official
(pewter plates, parts of a chariot etc.) (Teisen 1982 and 1983). Larger
wrecks of 18th century cargo ships have been investigated at Balka, Bornholm
(Vensild 1981), and at Laesø. Even a late 19th century schooner "Livlig",
wrecked in the Sound in 1898, has been investigated by amateur divers, and
their finds have been recorded and published (Teisen 1980).

In Denmark a number of replicas of Viking ship finds have been built
over the last 20 years by interested amateurs. New ships were also added
to the fleet in 1981 and 1982 by this "grass-roots movement" of replica-
builders and veteran ship restorers in Denmark. Taking advantage of the
experience in wood technology, ship handling etc. gained by these groups,
the Viking Ship Museum in Roskilde in 1982 initiated the ROAR-project. The
aim is to build a full scale replica of the 14 m long Skuldelev 3-coaster,
using the original types of materials and tools, and to conduct intensive
trials with the ship in order to establish its capacity, speed,
seaworthiness, flexibility etc. Construction will be carried out from 1982
to 1984 at the boatyard at the Viking Ship Museum, and launching is
scheduled for the summer of 1984 (Olsen & Crumlin-Pedersen 1968 and 1978).

REFERENCES

Andersen, S., 1983. En vikingebåd fra Barsø. Sønderjysk
Månedsskrift 6.

Andersen, S.H., 1980. Tybrind Vig. Foreløbig meddelelse om en
undersøisk stenalderboplads ved Lillebaelt. Antikvariske Studier: 7 f.

Andersen, S.H., 1982. Sunket i havet. Skalk 4: 10 f.

Crumlin-Pedersen, O., 1968. The Grestedbro Ship. Acta Archaeologica,

Vol. 39, Copenhagen: 262–267.

Crumlin-Pedersen, O., 1969. Das Haithabuschiff. Berichte über die Ausgrabungen in Haithabu. Bericht 3, Neumünster.

Crumlin-Pedersen, O. et. al., 1979. Koggen med Guldskatten. Skalk 6: 9 f.

Crumlin-Pedersen, O., 1980. Danish Cog Finds. The Archaeology of Medieval Ships and Harbours in Northern Europe. BAR Int. Series 66: 17–34.

Crumlin-Pedersen, O., 1981. Skibe på havbunden. Vragfund i danske farvande fra perioden 600–1400. Handels- og Søfartsmuseet på Kronborg, Arbog: 28–65.

Dal, H., 1981. Tybrind Vig. Sportsdykkeren nr. 5: 19 f.

Hårdh, B., 1983. Foteviken – handelsplats eller ledingshamm? University of Lund, Inst. of Archaeology. Report series No. 16.

Ingelman-Sundberg, C. & Söderhielm, P., 1982. Vikingaskepp Foteviken. Marinarkeologisk undersökning 1982 (preliminary report, Malmö).

Jeppesen, H., 1978. Nordenfjords. Skalk 5: 27.

Jeppesen, H., 1979a. Kollerupkoggen, et vragfund i en ralgrav. Handels og Søfartsmuseet på Kronborg, Arbog: 65 f.

Jeppesen, H., 1979b. Ummelandsfarer. Skalk 4: 3.

Klint-Jensen, O., 1978. Slusegård-gravpladsen I and II, Arhus (The boat-graves will be published in vol. III or IV of the same series).

Olsen, O. & Crumlin-Pedersen, O., 1968. The Skuldelev Ships (II). Acta Archaeologica, Vol. XXXVIII, 1967, Copenhagen.

Olsen, O. & Crumlin-Pedersen, O., 1978. Five Viking Ships. Copenhagen.

Schietzel, K. & Crumlin-Pedersen, O., 1980. Havnen i Hedeby. Skalk 3: 4 f.

Skaarup, J., 1979–1980. Et 1600-talsvrag ved Lundeborg. Fynske Minder: 63 f.

Skamby Madsen, J., 1983. Et skibsvaerft fra sen vikingetid/tidlig middelalder ved Fribrødre å på Falster. Hikuin, Arhus.

Teisen, M., 1980. 2 Handelsskibe på Øresunds bund. Handels- og Søfartsmuseet på Kronborg, Arbog: 102 f.

Teisen, M. 1982. Det bette vrag ved Lyngså. Vendyssel Nu og Da: 60 f.

Teisen, M., 1983. Det bette vrag. Maritim Kontakt nr. 6.

Vensild, H., 1981. Fra Bornholms Museum, 8.

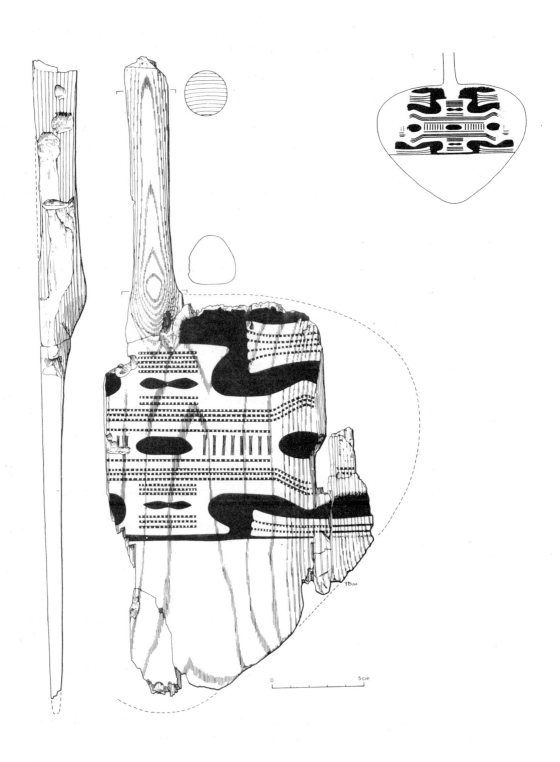

Fig. 27.1: An ornamented paddle found during excavation of a c. 6000 year old settlement site at Tybrind Vig, Fyn, Denmark. Forhistorisk Museum, Mosegård. Drawing by Fl. Bau.

Fig. 27.2: Parts of broken-up ships of the mid 11th century found 1982 in
the bank of the river Fribrødre å at <u>Maglebraende</u>, Falster, Denmark.
Planks and beams have been reused for the construction or repair of other
ships, but knees and frames were so specialized in shape that most of these
were just thrown away into the river alongside the shipbuilding site.
Photo: The Viking Ship Museum, Rostilde.

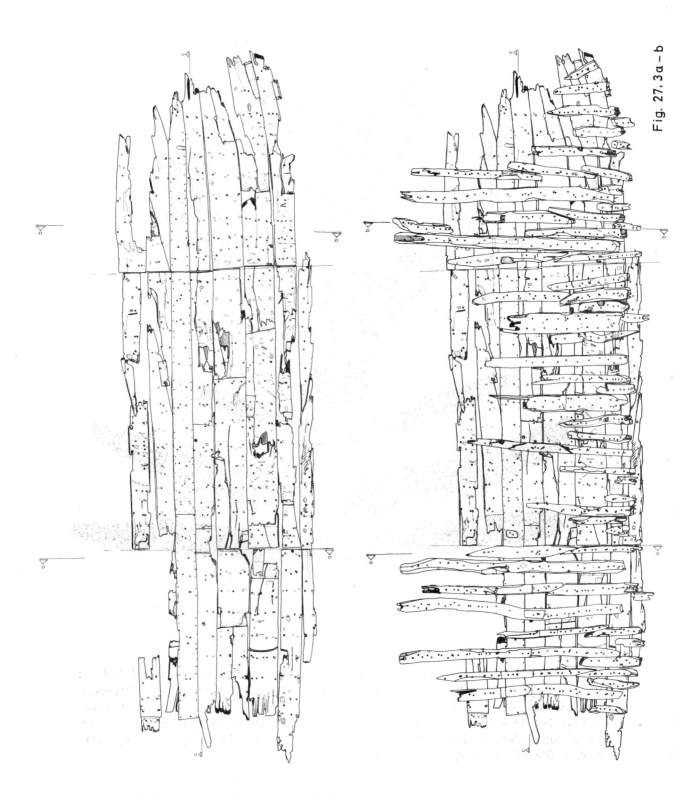

Fig. 27.3 a – b

Fig. 27.3 a and b and Fig. 27.4 a and b: Plans and sections of the Vejle wreck of c. 1580, based on detailed 1:10 measured drawings of the wreck: Fig. 27.3a: Planking seen from the inside; Fig. 27.3b: Planking with frames; Fig. 27.4a: Complete wreck with planking, frames and ceiling; Fig. 27.4b: Sections. Drawings by A. Wiggers, Vejle Museum.

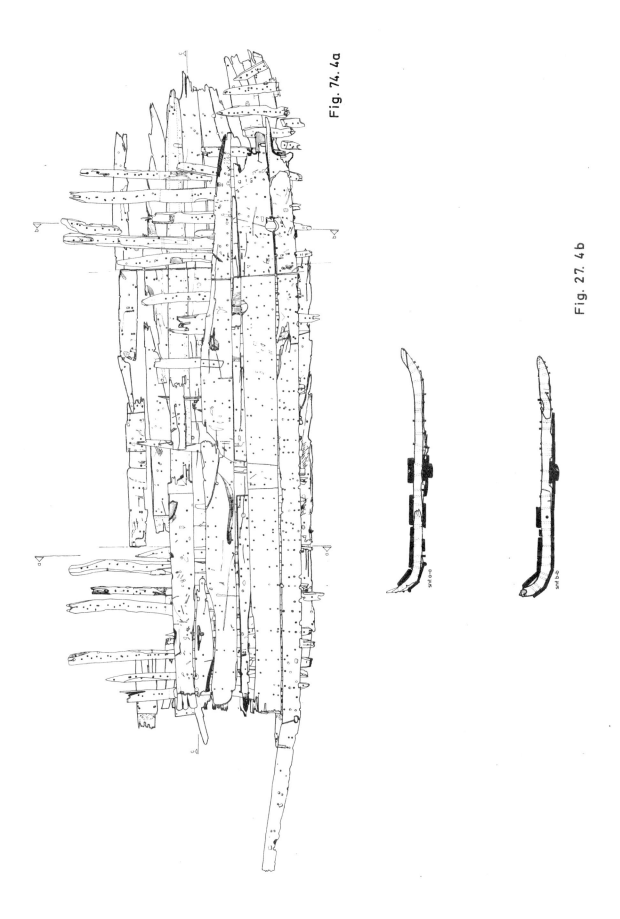

Fig. 74. 4a

Fig. 27. 4 b

snit a-a

snit b-b

379

28. SHIP AND BOAT ARCHAEOLOGY IN BRITAIN 1979-1982

Martin Dean

Since the last ISBSA in 1979 the number of wrecks of archaeological interest known in Britain has increased considerably but only five additional sites have been designated under the Protection of Wrecks Act, 1973. This difference is probably due to amateur and semi-professional divers finding sites which they either do not want scheduling, often for reasons which one suspects are financial and on the limits of legality, or because they are unaware of the site's archaeological importance.

The majority of known wrecks are of post-medieval date and were discovered because of the presence of cannon, which are obvious indicators of many wrecks, particularly where biological activity has removed all surface traces of the wooden structure. With the increased use of electronic detection equipment, it is to be expected that well-preserved vessels will be discovered in the sediments which cover much of the seabed around Britain. Some have already been found, the best-known examples are the Mary Rose and the Amsterdam, but others have been recently investigated, particularly HMS Invincible, sunk in the Solent 2 kms from the Mary Rose in 1758, and HMS Stirling Castle lost on the Goodwin Sands in 1703. The Admiralty chart of the area indicates a depth of four metres on the site of the Stirling Castle but commercial extraction of massive amounts of sand some five kilometres to the south has probably been the cause of large-scale sand movement in recent years which at one time left the Stirling Castle exposed in eighteen metres of water. At the present time it is not possible to be sure whether the ship is uncovered or not as the sand is continually on the move. Interestingly, the site was found at the start of a systematic survey of the area organised by local divers, the local archaeological society, and an enthusiastic local fisherman who had careful notes on more than two hundred net 'fastenings'. The first nine of these obstructions on the bottom revealed, surprisingly, three of the four naval vessels lost in the Great Gale of 1703, the other six being comparatively recent iron wrecks.

Only two of those sites, protected by the Historic Wreck legislation, predate the 15th century and they are the Bronze-Age sites at Dover, Kent and at Salcombe, Devon. As yet there has been no evidence for boat structure on either of these sites, but extensive Bronze-Age boat remains were excavated by Sean McGrail at Brigg in Lincolnshire and this has recently been published by the National Maritime Museum.

At least five probable Roman wreck sites are known to exist in British waters, four of them are suggested by pottery dredged up in fishermen's nets the fifth, located by divers at St. Peter Port in Guernsey, has not yet been surveyed but work is expected to start in the near future.

The earliest known ship whose structural remains survive in British Waters is the Grace Dieu, burnt at its moorings on the River Hamble, near Southampton in 1439, and now preserved in the estuarine muds. No large-scale investigation has taken place in recent years but the Archaeological

Research Centre of the National Maritime Museum is planning to record the remains in detail in the future. An aerial photograph of the ship taken at very low tide indicated the presence of another vessel fifty metres downstream and the Museum recently investigated this with probes, and the presence of solid timbers some 1.7m below the surface of the mud were detected.

16th century vessels are represented by the Mary Rose and the Cattewater Wreck both of which are featured elsewhere in the Symposium, and a handful of other wrecks, none of which have been excavated on any scale, although on some sites numerous finds seem to have been collected during so-called 'pre-disturbance surveys'. 11 vessels of the 17th century have been protected by legislation and they include HMS Dartmouth, sunk near the Isle of Mull in 1690, where coherent structural remains were recorded by the Institute of Marine Archaeology at the University of St. Andrews.

Apart from the Dartmouth and the Amsterdam, few of the other 17th century sites have reported evidence of hull remains, so recording has largely been limited to plotting the distribution of finds and seabed mapping. The standard of this recording is not always adequate, although as far as one can judge from the drawings produced, some of the groups seem to be operating to a responsible archaeological standard without the benefit of professional archaeological advice.

18th and 19th century wrecks have been found in the last decade with considerable structural remains surviving but, unfortunately, the attraction of the finds which inevitably abound on these well-preserved ships prove too strong for many of the divers without archaeological training, and recording of the important hull remains has not taken place. A good example of this is the Stirling Castle where minimal diving time was spent on measuring the approximate overall length and beam of the vessel, the bulk of the effort underwater being used to find and raise artifacts. Other comparable examples are the South Edinburgh Channel Wreck of c. 1790, the Restoration and the Northumberland, sister ships to the Stirling Castle, and the Catharina von Flensburgh, lost in Plymouth Sound in 1786 with a cargo of reindeer hides, many of which have been recovered from her hold.

It is possible to see then that, apart from the Mary Rose, the pattern of work on wrecks in Britain during the last few years has been for all types of diving groups, whether amateur, institutional or semi-professional, to spread their efforts over a wide variety of sites using comparatively restricted resources. The reasons for this are threefold; the nation as a whole cannot adequately fund more than one major excavation at a time, so large-scale underwater investigations will probably have to wait until the Mary Rose is raised and conserved; secondly, no single group has the resources to do anything other than comparatively limited investigations, and this applies equally to amateur groups, national institutions and those private organisations whose project funding comes from the sale of archaeological finds from the sites they work on; and lastly, there is the fascination divers seem to have for objects rather than information, and which they find they can retrieve from scattered wreck sites with the minimum amount of time being spent on recording yet still satisfy their archaeological peers.

Thinly spread resources and lack of archaeological discipline has resulted in variable quality of the underwater work in ship and boat archaeology in Britain in the past. It is to be hoped that there will be a change in emphasis in the future with fewer piecemeal investigations and more systematic surveys of the seabed around the British coast.

It is therefore pleasing to hear that plans are in hand to continue the survey of fishermen's net fastenings on the Goodwin Sands, particularly as the area has already indicated what potential there can be in such work. Also welcome is the newly-formed Nautical Archaeology Society which recently co-operated with the National Maritime Museum in supplying manpower for an underwater survey close to the important Iron-Age trading centre at Hengistbury Head, Dorset. Hopefully this type of work will set the pattern for the future, particularly where both sports divers and professional archaeologists can co-operate in systematic and detailed study of the seabed. It is only in this way that the extent of Britain's submerged maritime heritage can be fully assessed before embarking on further major projects of Mary Rose proportions.

29. CANADIAN SHIP AND BOAT ARCHAEOLOGY

Dan G. Harris

Before presenting this report, I would like to thank Mr Anders Franzén for his discovery of 'Wasa' which has given great impetus to the interest in marine archaeology – without his discovery in the subsequent work of the Royal Swedish Navy and of Dr. Per Lundström and his associates, we would probably not be meeting here today.   It is a great pleasure to present this report on behalf of Canada in Dr. Lundström's museum which has been a prototype for many of our naval and marine museums.   By way of a personal note, I have been acquainted with the Stockholm museum for some forty-four years.

I begin at our West Coast – British Columbia, and will work eastwards covering a territory in a few minutes over which a '747' usually takes seven hours to fly.

The Maritime Museum of Vancouver acquired in 1978, the former American sailing cutter 'Bayard' which served from 1913 as a light vessel on the British Columbia coast.   'Bayard' the last of her type in existence, was built in 1880 without drawings as a pilot cutter.   She is being restored to her original condition by volunteer labour as funds allow.   The three photographs attached show 'Bayard':

    1. In state when acquired (Fig. 29.1).

    2. Undergoing restoration (Fig. 29.2).

    3. The planned appearance after restoration (Fig. 29.3).

The Vancouver Museum has arranged for a seventy-three year old boat builder to demonstrate his skills by building small pulling boats on the museum premises.   He is assisted by interested members of the younger generation and we hope that his skills will thus be passed on.

In Winnipeg, the Provincial Museum has been restoring a York boat, the type of craft used for moving goods and persons on the Canadian waterways in the 18th and early 19th centuries.

On our way East, we diverge to the North West territories.   No activity has taken place at the Marble Island, the site of the Knight expedition ships of 1720.   The location is too remote for any display centre to be arranged.   An American proposal to raise a whaler of 19th century vintage, lying in the same location, has been dropped.   A broader survey is planned of H.M.S. Breadalbane, lying in the Eastern Arctic, by the Department of the Environment – Parks Canada Branch – the hull was surveyed in the winter of 1981/82 by a joint Anglo-Canadian team, financed in part by Alberta Gas Trunk Lines Limited. May I refer you to the July issue of the Royal Canadian Geographical Journal for the full report?

Here are particulars of the activities within the Province of Ontario. On Lake Huron, restoration of the old 19th century British Navy base has been completed by the Provincial Government. The store house and other buildings have been rebuilt. Conservation work is very necessary on the hulks of H.M.S. Tecumseth and the ex-U.S.S. Scorpion, which were pulled to the surface by the Royal Canadian Navy in 1953.

On Lake Ontario, the main event has been the transfer by the U.S. Navy Department of the title to the sunken armed schooners U.S.S. Hamilton and Scourge of the 1812 war period to the Provincial Crown. The two ships were surveyed by Commander Cousteau of France during the Spring of 1982. Discussions continue with the Ontario Government about raising one of the two vessels, but no decision is expected for some time.

There are many technical and financial problems still to be solved. At the eastern end of the Lake, the Marine Museum of the Great Lakes at Kingston reopened in June 1982 by Her Majesty's representative, the Lieutenant Governor of Ontario. The buildings are now almost complete but the restoration of the 19th century engine room of the old dry dock has yet to begin. The Institute of Professional Engineers have offered to carry out this work. The Museum has established a collection of all types of boats used on the Great Lakes. Some surveys have been made of a 19th century Lake schooner, a very distinctive type of vessel, lost off Kingston in the 1870's. It is the only example discovered so far on the Canadian side of the Great Lakes. She is in an upright position and her cargo has been found to be coal. One project proposed, is to move this wreck into the Kingston dry dock and use it as a school for divers. In addition to the hulls of H.M.S. St. Lawrence, of about 3,000 tonns, and the other frigates of the Royal Navy lying off Kingston, there is a very interesting site containing the hull of a vessel which was propelled by a Boulton and Watt type beam engine-driving paddle wheels. Further investigation of this site will be carried out because the discovery of the existence of a beam engine for marine use may be unique. Sailmakers tools and shipbuilders tools from the early 19th century Garden Island shipyard have been recovered for the Kingston Museum.

The Department of the Environment of the Federal Government has decided that the display centre for the Restigouche finds will be located on the Quebec side of the Campbell River, but the design of the centre has not been completed owing to present finanical restrictions. There are also some conservation problems to be solved. Some of you may recall, that a presentation of two films pertinent to the salvage was made at this museum - the naval museum Karlskrona (Sweden), in Helsinki (Finland), Copenhagen (Denmark) and in London (England) some ten years ago. There is particular interest in the 18th century frigate which was originally built in Quebec and converted to a warship in France in 1759.

In Halifax, Nova Scotia, the Maritime Museum has at last obtained suitable premises. It has taken over the survey ship Arcadia which served on the East Coast from 1913 to 1969. A ship's figure head is being carved by a staff member in the display area of the museum.

In Newfoundland, a site at Port aux Basques was found to contain a wreck in which coins of 1683 were found and a 350 year old astrolabe. The curator of the British National Maritime Museum gave great assistance in the identification of the astrolabe. Work on the site continues. The Bay of Bulls project has been completed by the Department of the Environment. As regards the Basque whaling vessel discovered at Red Bay, Robert Grenier has been able to come here after all and will later give you a separate detailed report.

Fig. 29.1:   The former American sailing cutter Bayard under tow by the 66 years old Charles H. Cates III.   Photo Vancouver Maritime Museum.

Fig. 29.2:   The Bayard under restoration in Vancouver in 1981.   Photo Vancouver Maritime Museum.

Fig. 29.3: A painting of Thomas F. Bayard as launched in 1880 for service as a pilot boat in Delaware Bay. Photo Vancouver Maritime Museum.

30. THE FOTEVIKEN INVESTIGATION, SCANIA, SWEDEN

Catharina Ingelman-Sundberg

Foteviken south of Malmö, is a narrow bay and one of the very few natural harbours along the western coast of Öresund (Fig. 30.1). Finds from such different periods as the stone, bronze, and iron age as well as the viking and early medieval periods, show the importance of the area throughout history.

In the late viking period and early medieval times, Foteviken was under Danish rule, and was a trading centre for ships from the north, south, east and west. A market place near Foteviken is mentioned in the Danish Chronicle "Saxo Grammaticus" from about 1200, and it is believed that it could have been the forerunner to Skanör-Falsterbo, one of the most important trading markets in Northern Europe in medieval times.

A huge barricade of poles and stones in the mouth of the bay, shows Fotevikens importance in the late viking period and early medieval times. It is about 350 m long, 2-7 m wide and rises about 1 m above the seabottom. It would not have been built had there not been a strong power to demand it and enough people to build it. Remnants of two ring walls on land nearby the bay give further interest to the area.

In the 11th and 12th centuries the Danish king assembled his fleet in certain sheltered harbours in Denmark. This organization was called the "ledung" and served as a system of defence along the Danish coast which at the time included the southern parts of todays Sweden. In these harbours, the king could easily gather his fleet in case of threats or if he himself planned an attack.

One of these harbours is Vordingborg on the west coast of Själland, Denmark. Here, archaeologists have found a watch tower, a market place, a 900 year old blockade and a wreck from the early medieval period. Because of its similarities to Foteviken, the question arose as to whether Foteviken was part of the Danish defence system and if so, whether the blockade in the mouth of the bay could in fact be from the same period as the defence system of Vordingborg.

In August 1981 a Danish team of marine archaeologists from the Vikingaskibshallen at Roskilde, made a preliminary investigation of Foteviken. The discovery of a 900 year old ship near the stone wall, lead to a combined land and marine archaeology investigation of the bay and surrounding area in the summer of 1982. The aim of the project was to excavate and salvage the ship as well as determine the perimeter, width and construction of the stone wall. The marine archaeological work was carried out by the Maritime Museum of Malmö and the Vikingaskibshallen at Roskilde.

THE FOTEVIKEN WRECK

At a depth of 2 m a 8.4 m long and 2.5 m wide heap of stones was found. Underneath there were found planks, ribs and two knees (Fig. 30.2). A carbon-14 sample dated the ship to 1060 $\pm$ 65 years. It was the oldest plank-built ship ever having been found off the Swedish coast. It was decided to have it salvaged and put on display at the Maritime Museum in Malmö, Sweden.

EXCAVATION TECHNIQUES

As it is planned to display the wreck and its surroundings as it was found after 900 years underwater, the whole site was carefully documented on photographs and drawings before anything was unearthed. Photomosaics were made of the wreck both horizontally and vertically in stereo and the stone assemblage was measured in three dimensions before it was raised.

The stones were salvaged with the help of a mobile raft with an underwater platform attached to it. They were registered according to their location on the wreck, put on the platform and lifted on board the diving vessel by crane. The site was then cleaned with a water dredge and the wreck measured.

The precise position of the wreck was established using a Kern theodolite (DKM 2-AE) from land, and four fix points A - D were placed under water. Measuring tapes were fastened to these points and each point measured on the wreck was located with three of the four measuring tapes. Two measurements gave the two dimensional location of an object, the third was a control measurement. Three dimensional measurements were taken with a depth gauge.

THE RAISING OF THE SHIP

The wreck was so fragile that it could not be raised in one piece. Instead, each plank was raised separately. The planks were carefully loosened from each other by hand and brought to the surface on specially constructed slates of masonite (Fig. 30.3 a and b). In this way the whole wreck was salvaged in a day and a half.

THE ORGINAL SHIP

The Foteviken ship had been built of oak and by the time it sank it was old and worn out. Signs of repairs to stop the ship from leaking can be seen near the keel. The garboard strakes have been strengthened and an extra piece of timber put on the keel at the stern.

About 35% of the wreck is left. The port side of the ship, part of the keel and one starboard strake are preserved, whereas the rest of the starboard side, the stems, the maststep and a 1.5m^2 area in the middle is missing (Fig. 30.4 a and b).

Originally the ship was about 12 m long and the lightweight, low hull with a distance of 80 cm between the ribs suggests that the ship once was a small warship. Its construction is similar to that of Skuldelev ship no 5 at the Vikingeskibshallen at Roskilde, dated to 960 ± 100 years.

No artefacts have been found inside the ship. Its worn-out state, the number of stones inside the ship, its closeness to the blockade as well as a huge cut through one of the strakes near the keel, indicate that the ship was scuttled to be used as part of the defence system.

THE INVESTIGATION OF THE BLOCKADE

Foteviken is a shallow natural harbour between Hammarsnäs and the Scanian mainland. Its about 2 km long and carries from 200 to 1000 m in width. The blockade is situated in the mouth of the bay. The entire structure is 370 m long and 2-7 m wide. Today it lies in 0.5 to 1.7 m of water. The position of the stone wall was established using the Kern theodolite and cross sections were taken every 25 m. Test excavations were carried out with the help of a water dredge in four different places. Only the uppermost parts of the stone wall were investigated in this way.

OTHER WRECKS IN THE BLOCKADE

As a result of the work on the blockade, four more wrecks were found. Three of the wrecks were in a bad state of preservation, and no salvage of these ships is planned. The ships were sunk as part of the blockade and like the Foteviken wreck, they were most probably warships.

The fifth wreck had been sunk in the middle of the blockade where there was a passage about 7 m wide. It was found at a depth of 1.4 m under 1.5 m of sand. From the typology point of view this ship, a warship, has been dated to the first part of the 11th century. A stringer from the side of the ship was found and as the main part of the wreck has sunk in sand, it is hoped that a good deal of the ship's structure might still be preserved.

SUMMARY

The preliminary investigation at Foteviken has shown that the area is not only of local interest but also of interest from a general archaeological and historical point of view in Scandinavia. The huge blockade dated to late viking/early medieval time and built to prevent enemies from entering the bay, attests to Fotevikens importance in those days. It was most likely the site of a market place which could have been a forerunner to the important trading market at the "twin" towns of Skanör and Falsterbo in the medieval days. The blockade could have served to shelter the inhabitants from attacks, as well as the King's fleet which might have had a base there.

So far we have found strong indications as to the important role of Foteviken in the 11th and 12th centuries. However, further excavation on land and underwater is needed to determine whether Foteviken could have been a place of importance equal to that of Birka in Sweden and Hedeby in Denmark.

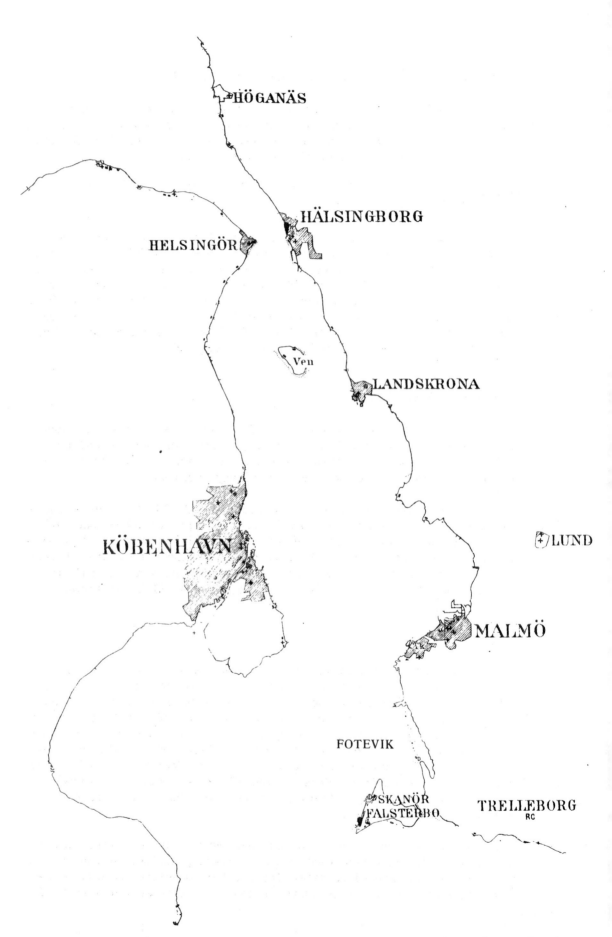

Fig. 30.1: Fotebviken is one of the few natural harbours along the western coast of Öresund. Five wrecks from the late viking/early medieval period were found as part of a blockade in the mouth of the bay.

Fig. 30.2: When first found the wreck could be seen as a heap of stones on a sandy bottom. When some of the stones were removed, the structure of a 900 year old wreck was discovered. Photo The Maritime Museum in Malmö.

Fig. 30.3a and b: The raising of the hullplanks from the wrecksite. Note the foamrubber tied over the plank in order to keep it in position. Photo: The Maritime Museum in Malmö.

FOTEVIK 1982
VRAK 1

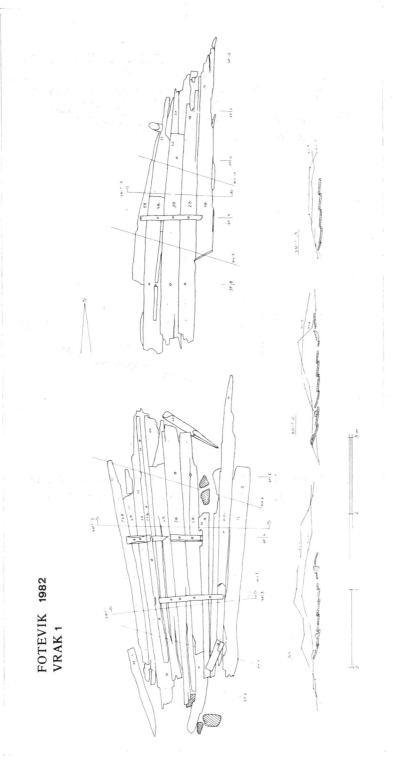

Fig. 30.4a: Plan and sections of the site of wreck 1 at Foteviken.
Almost all of one side of the ship is preserved except for the stems and an
area in the middle of the ship. Stones and poles under the ship indicate
that it has been part of a blockade.

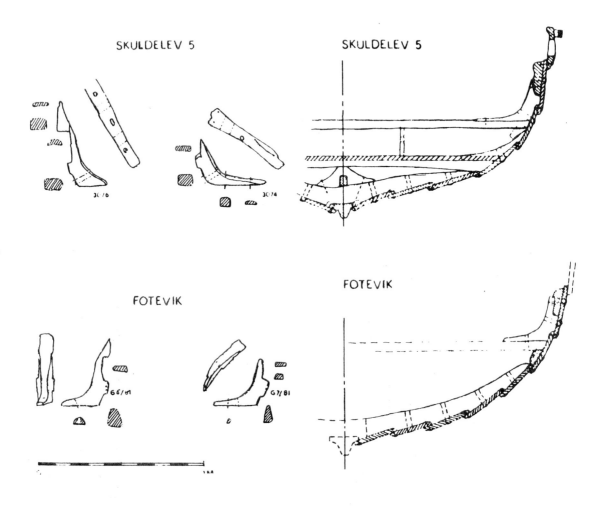

Fig. 30.4b: Projection drawings of bite knees of the wreck Skuldelev 5 and Foteviken 1. Note the similarities between the bite knees.

31. RECENT DEVELOPMENT IN SHIP AND BOAT ARCHAEOLOGY IN THE NETHERLANDS

Reinder Reinders

In the Netherlands, archaeological investigation of ships is concentrated to the IJsselmeerpolders, where to this date, 350 ships have been found, of which 150 have been systematically investigated. In 1942 the Noordoostpolder, the second polder in the former Zuiderzee, was drained, exposing shipwrecks in the former seabed (Fig. 31.1). In 1982 it was forty years ago that the first ship was excavated by P.J.R. Modderman.

Apart from the IJsselmeerpolders, two other areas claim the investigators' interest: the river area in the centre of the Netherlands and, recently, the coastal waters. In the beginning of the seventies, interest in the investigation of shipwrecks along the Rhine and other rivers was given a boost by the discovery of ships near Zwammerdam, dating from the Roman period. In the last few years, new finds have continuously been uncovered in connection with construction and sand excavation work in this area.

Unlike the investigation of shipwrecks on land, little direct action, so far, has been undertaken in the area of underwater exploration of ships. During the last decade, however, amateur and professional divers have visited the wrecks with growing frequency and one can only guess, what the results of those visits may be.

PROTECTION OF SHIPWRECKS IN SITU

During the last four years, the character of the activities in the IJsselmeerpolders has changed, resulting in greater interest in the protection of shipwreck sites. Before the new polderland was put into its final use, usually as many shipwrecks as possible were excavated and the rest were left for later investigation. The major drawback, however, was that by then large parts of the wrecks had rotted away, because excavation took place long after the draining of the polder.

The excavations in Zuidelijk Flevoland revealed that many ships have remained in good condition thanks to the fact that they have sunk in a thick layer of clay that constitutes the former seabed. When a polder is drained, two changes in environmental conditions severely affect the oak, that most of the ships are made of: first, the soil surface subsides, and second, the groundwater-table is lowered. The reclamation of Zuidelijk Flevoland, however, is still far from complete. It is true that the soil surface has subsided by about 50 cm, but over large areas the groundwater-table has not yet dropped to a great degree. The soil is saturated with water and its condition is very much like that of the former seabed. Under these almost anaerobic conditions, the wood has stayed virtually intact.

In 1978, an experiment was carried out to determine whether the wood could be prevented from decaying under the conditions described above. A shipwreck was surrounded by a vertical plastic foil sheet, preventing the water around the ship from escaping (Fig. 31.2). The thick layer of clay on which the ship rested was also leak-proof, so that the water couldn't escape in that direction either. In this tub, the groundwater-table is higher than the original surface of the surrounding land. So an anaerobic environment has been created where wood cannot be affected by aerobic micro-organisms, that cause rapid decay (Reinders 1982).

Six ships underwent this treatment in 1979 and 1980 and five more will follow in the autumn of 1982 (Table 1). In addition, all fragments of a cog, excavated in 1981, have been stored below groundwater level in situ. It is generally assumed that under these conditions the wood will take much longer to be affected. On some lots, the groundwater-table was lowered many years ago, exposing the wood to aerobic conditions. As it is unknown whether the protecting measures will result in a return of the anaerobic conditions, groundwater samples will have to be taken in order to establish the content of oxygen, acid etc.

EXCAVATIONS IN THE IJSSELMEERPOLDERS

The programme for the following years consist in collecting, by means of trial trenches, the greatest possible amount of data concerning the 100 ships that have not yet been excavated. Usually, protection of these shipwrecks is impossible because they are situated in a permeable sand-layer or because building activities necessitate excavation. Other ships are of little interest and not worth the cost and trouble of protection. They will just be covered with an extra layer of soil to give them the best possible protection until the moment of excavation. Although in the period following the Bremerhaven symposium much time has been spent on prospection, as many as 13 ships have been excavated (Table 2). This paper presents some preliminary information about these vessels and their significance to the investigation carried out in IJsselmeerpolders.

Cogs

Four years ago at the Bremerhaven symposium, I hesitated to use the word cog when talking about the medieval boat finds in the Netherlands (Reinders 1979). Excavations of the last four years have shown, however, that some of these vessels indeed deserve the name cog.

It had always been expected that the Noordoostpolder would be the best place to find cogs, as this polder is situated between the mouth of the river IJssel, with several important Hanze towns along its borders, and the Wadden- and North Sea. During the last few years, however, four medieval ships were found in Zuidelijk Flevoland, not far from the southern coastline of the former Zuiderzee, between Hardewijk and Muiden. One of the vessels had stayed reasonably intact, embedded in a relatively thick layer of clay, enabling us to protect it in 1980. The remaining ships seemed to have got stuck in the pleistocene sand and subsequently to have been beaten to pieces. On the top of the sandy subsoil, a fairly thin layer of clay had been deposited so the ships were lying just beneath the surface and the wood of the upper parts had already started to decay.

At lots NZ 42 and NZ 43 two small cargo-boats were found, one of which

TABLE 1: Protection of shipwrecks in the IJsselmeerpolders

Year of protection	polder	lot	category or type of vessel	approximate date of wreckage
1944	Noordoostpolder	M 107	cargo vessel (excavated)	1400
1979	Zuidelijk Flevoland	KZ 47	fishing vessel, waterschip	1575
1980	Zuidelijk Flevoland	AZ 79	fishing vessel, waterschip	1600
		NZ 13	fishing vessel, waterschip	1550
		HZ 9	fishing vessel, waterschip	1625
		LZ 5	cargo vessel	16th century
		NZ 3	cargo vessel	15th century
		OZ 43	cargo vessel (excavated)	13th century
1982	Zuidelijk Flevoland	AZ 89	cargo vessel, tjalk	1785
		AZ 114	cargo vessel	1625
		GZ 13	cargo vessel	1550
		LZ 1	cargo vessel	1550
	Oostelijk Flevoland	C 60	fishing vessel, waterschip	17th century

TABLE 2: Excavations in the IJsselmeerpolders, 1979-1982.

Year of excavation	polder	lot	category or type of vessel	approximate date wreckage
1979	Zuidelijk Flevoland	NZ 42	fishing vessel, waterschip	1575
		NZ 42	cargo vessel with bricks	15th century
		NZ 43	cargo vessel	14th century
		NZ 44	fishing vessel, waterschip	1525
		QZ 18	cargo vessel with coal	1890
		MZ 41	fishing vessel, botter	1850
		PZ 33	cargo vessel	1750
1980	Zuidelijk Flevoland	OZ 71	cargo vessel	1700
		PZ 37	cargo vessel	1750
	Oostelijk Flevoland	B 71	cargo vessel, beurtschip	1625
1981	Zuidelijk Flevoland	OZ 43	cargo vessel, cog	13th century
1982	Zuidelijk Flevoland	NZ 74	fishing vessel, waterschip	1500
		nZ 74	fishing vessel, waterschip	1500

still carried part of the load: bricks. Both ships showed the characteristics of construction seen in virtually all the late-medieval IJsselmeerpolders-wrecks: flush-laid bottom planks, overlapping side planks, twice-bent nails and a caulking of moss, lath and sintels (Reinders 1980). Yet, the ship of lot NZ 43 also showed some unexpected characteristics. In the first place, it had a rounded bottom and in the second place it lacked a mast step above the keel. It did have a heavy wooden chock with a square hole, fastened against the port-side between two ribs. The greater part of the starboard-side was gone, with the exception of a heavy rib in which holes had been bored at an angle. Undoubtedly, these holes served for fastening a wooden chock by means of treenails comparable to the construction on the portside (Fig. 31.3). This type of construction had never been found in the Zuiderzee-area. Ellmers pointed out the movable mast of the 'Steinhuder Käne' (Salemke, 1968) and Crumlin-Pedersen the pictures of vessels showing an elevation for the driving of piles in harbours. Yet I wouldn't preclude the possibility of an A-mast. Does the seal of Kuinre offer an example of this construction (Ewe, 1972)?

Older excavations too produced relatively small ships, none of which matched the Bremer cog. In most cases, there was not enough evidence to call those ships predecessors of the cog. But in 1981 we were luckier. At lot OZ 43 a medieval ship that lay scattered on a sand-layer was excavated. The sides were bent outward, stem and stern were mostly gone and fragments of the frames were scattered around. Only the bottom had stayed more or less intact thanks to the heavy floor-timbers (Fig. 31.4).

Despite its wretched condition, many parts of the vessel had been preserved, enabling us to spend more time than usual recording data. First, stereo-photographs were taken in order to get an overall picture, and cross-section were drawn. Then, the scattered fragments of the frames were adjusted and measured in order to get an impression of the ship's shape. Recording of the hull, as practised by Crumlin-Pedersen (1979) and McKee (1978), had never been done in the IJsselmeerpolders, but it seemed appropriate to do with this ship. Thus, every plank has been measured and drawn, using, for practical reasons, scale 1:10.

With the aid of the measurements, a provisional model was made to get an impression of the ship's shape and to test the method used. Initially, the model was given a straight keel, but it later turned out that the planks of the bottom wouldn't fit unless in combination with an upwards-bent keel, fore and aft. According to the model, the cog must have had the following dimensions (approximately):

- length of bottom   13.20 m

- overall length   16.40 m

- height of stem   4.20 m

- height near the mast   3.00 m

- beam   5.90 m

It is clear that these dimensions are modest in comparison with the Bremen cog, but the two vessels have some characteristics in common; even the number of bottom and side strakes probably was the same. Although the sides had square holes in two places, no beams have been found that protruded through the hull. The frames in the front part of the ship had cross-beams, but these had been fastened to the ribs by means of knees, as had the lower cross-beams of ship 1 of Kalmar (Åkerlund, 1951). The construction of the remains of the stem and stern revealed that the four lower strakes fitted into a rabbet in the lower part of the stem and stern posts, whereas the upper strakes overlapped the inner stem post. No indications of a heavy outer stempost, as with the Bremen cog (Ellmers, 1979) have been found; so we assume that there was only a narrow outer stem post. The seal of Harderwijk may be an example of this stage in the development of the cog. This seal, and the dating of several potsherds, make it likely that the ship of lot OZ 43 dates from the 13th century.

During the excavation of the cog at lot OZ 43 in 1981, another medieval ship was found at a short distance from the one just described. The first fragment that turned up in the trial trench was a heavy beam with a notch at both ends, one of the beams that protruded through the hull.

'Waterschepen'

The 'Waterschip' was by far the most common type of fishing vessel of the former Zuiderzee (Reinders, 1982). During the past four years, the investigation of 'waterschepen' has been one of the leading projects of the Ketelhaven museum. In the Noordoostpolder and Oostelijk Flevoland six of these vessels had been excavated and the site of several more was known. In Zuidelijk Flevoland their number turns out to be much higher. Until now, at least 12 ships have been found; five of which qualified for protection. Judging from the artefacts found during excavations and reconnaissance, we are dealing mostly with ships dating from the period 1500-1650.

The majority of 'waterschepen' that were excavated in the past years date from the end of the 15th and the beginning of the 16th century. Bottom and sides had overlapping planks, as in a 'waterschip' found at lot MZ 22 (Reinders 1979). Although in some cases only very little remained, our knowledge of this type of vessel has increased considerably, especially in the field of inventory, weight and origin of ballast stones, and construction details. In one of the 'waterschepen' excavated in 1982 it was possible to establish the place where two provisional moulds had been.

A 16th century 'beurtschip'

Unlike the shape of the cogs - V-shaped in section fore and aft - the 'waterschepen' had a full bow and were V-shaped at the rear. Both types of vessels are very distinct from the well-known flat-bottomed cargo vessels, bluff fore and aft that were in use in the Netherlands from the 17th century on. Therefore, it is most interesting that during the past years several ships dating from the 16th century have been found. Just like the 'waterschip', these vessels had a full bow and a V-shaped stern. Three ships qualified for protection, among them a large cargo-vessel; one of its boards had remained intact up to the bulwarks.

One of these typical 16th century cargo vessels was found during the construction of a canal in Lelystad in 1980. The starboard side as well as the bottom had remained reasonably intact, but with the exception of a large fragment, the port side was missing. The ship had an overall length of 18 m and a beam of 5.5 m (Fig. 31.5). There are indications that this vessel was equipped with a spritsail and lee-boards. Lee-boards came into use in flat-bottomed vessels in the second half of the 16th century to reduce leeway.

The ship transported scythes, a case containing several hundred chicken eggs, three new bronze cooking pots, a barrel holding about 100 pewter objects and three leather bags. Judging from the nature of these artefacts, the ship probably was a so-called 'beurtschip', a vessel that operated a regular service between two towns bordering ther Zuiderzee. Thanks to some coins found in the living quarters, we know that the ship must have sunk around 1620. Repairs and the poor condition of the ceiling indicate that the ship had been in service for quite some time.

SHIP AND BOAT FINDS ALONG RIVERS AND IN COASTAL WATERS

Not far from Zwammerdam, along the 'Oude Rijn', is situated the town of Woerden where, in 1978, embankments from Roman times were excavated. While investigating the area, the Instituut voor Oude Geschiedenis en Archeologie (Institute for Ancient History and Archaeology) of the Nijmegen University, found a ship in the river bed. Unfortunately, only part of the ship (about 10 m) was lying in the trench, so only a partial archaeological investigation was possible (Boagers 1979). The vessel strongly resembled those found near Zwammerdam. The bow of the Woerden ship had remained in good condition. Living quarters for the crew were near the mast as evidenced by a fireplace, shoes, a dish and pots found there.

Along other Dutch rivers, ships and fragments of ships have been found as well: a fragment of hull planking used as sheet-piling in 's Hertogenbosch, and fragments of vessels - probably medieval - in Kessel and Hattum. In Hellendoorn, archaeologists of the Ketelhaven Museum have investigated a small river boat, found during the construction of a barrage in the Regge (Vlierman 1981). The vessel's bottom consisted of two planks, the sides of one plank. Its length was about 6 m and its width 1.12 m. It shows characteristics generally accorded a 'punter' (Fig. 31.6).

The situation with respect to the investigation of shipwrecks in coastal waters and outside the territorial waters is somewhat confusing. The activities of amateur divers and professional salvors, give rise to unwanted situations that in other countries have already been dealt with. The problems are partly of a judicial nature and belong to the field between ius praedae and the monuments act. Besides, there are also some practical difficulties in the Netherlands that interfere with underwater exploration, such as poor visibility and strong currents near the coast. Knowing the problems of ship excavation on land, one will find it difficult to imagine that underwater exploration of ships in Dutch coastal waters at this moment is technically and financially feasible. It is also doubtful however, whether a scientifically accurate investigation can be performed without raising an entire vessel.

In several cases, investigation is carried out in cooperation with an archaeological institute or a museum. Amateur divers from Sliedrecht and Amsterdam have raised parts of a logboat from a sand-pit near Tiel. Under the auspices of the 'Rijksdienst voor het Oudheidkundig Bodemonderzoek' and with the collaboration of the Ketelhaven musem, they have also attempted to trace a fragment of the ship that was found in a former bed of the Rhine near Meinerswijk (Arnhem) (Reinders, 1979). Another example is the investigation of the VOC ship ''t Vliegent Hart' in the coastal waters near Vlissingen, where Cowan and Rose collaborated with Kist (Rijksmuseum, Amsterdam).

An inventory of the issue underwater exploration (Maarleveld, 1981) by order of the Ministry of Culture may lead to a centralized approach to underwater archaeological exploration, the main requirement of which is a complete registration of the objects.

ARCHAEOLOGICAL BOAT-FINDS AS MUSEUM OBJECTS

At the Stockholm symposium, much attention has been paid to the Wasa, so that it might be useful to finish with a survey of vessels that, after excavation, have been added to museum collections and are now exhibited. Very few museums in the Netherlands have boat finds in their collection at this moment.

The collection of the Ketelhaven museum comprises four vessels from Zwammerdam: fragments of a logboat, a well-boat and two barges. The third barge from Zwammerdam is destined to go to the Maritime Museum Prins Hendrik in Rotterdam. At the moment, only the conservation of the logboat and a well-boat has been completed. The Ketelhaven collection further includes five vessels of medieval times and four post-medieval vessels.

It is clear that the storage of such a great number of ships poses a problem; there was no room left for the wood belonging to the medieval ships found at lots NZ 43 and OZ 43, forcing us to sink these vessels below groundwater-level as had happened in 1944 to a 14th century ship (Modderman, 1945).

The number of vessels poses not only a storage problem; their conservation would entail considerable expense. The search for methods to treat waterlogged wood has, in several cases, resulted in the decision to dry the vessels in Ketelhaven. A fragment of a 17th century mud-barge, excavated in 1972, was left outside to dry in all types of weather and has remained outside under a cover until 1975. At an exhibition about the conservation of waterlogged wood, many were amazed at the more than acceptable result of the drying process, which led to the decision to treat the wreck of a 17th century merchantman that was kept under a sprinkling installation in Ketelhaven by the same method. Before, it had been ascertained that the wood was still in good condition (de Jong, 1981).

After three years of drying, a start has been made with the finishing (Oosting, 1982). After the drying process, the seams between the planks had widened to 1-2 cm; in most places, this is not at all conspicuous. At the surface, a crackle layer of 1-4 mm had appeared, giving the vessel a drab appearance; this layer has been scraped off. Where necessary, countersunk steel bolts have been used as strengthening. Despite the gaping seams, the cracks and the added steel bolts, the result of the 'operation' is satisfactory. In the future, the wood will receive an additional treatment to prevent further decay; this is not expected to raise any problems, now that the wood is dry. It goes without saying that this kind of drying process is disastrous to small objects which require preservation of the original surface.

TABLE 3: Archaeological boat-finds as museum objects.

Location	museum	type of vessel	reference	provenance	approximate date of wreckage
Amsterdam	Nederlands Scheepvaart Museum	logboat	Jaarverslag 1975	Spaarndam	8th century AD
Assen	Provincaal Museum	logboat	Van Zeist 1957	Pesse	6300 BC
Ketelhaven	Museum voor Scheepsarcheologie	logboat	De Weerdt 1977	Zwammerdam	2nd century AD
		merchantman		Noordoostpolder	1650
		mud-barge	Reinders 1981	Lelystad, B 19	1675
	excavation site	'De Zeehond'	Reinders 1982	Lelystad, F 3	1886
Utrecht	Centraal Museum	Utrecht ship	Ellmers 1972	Utrecht	8th century AD

SUMMARY

Between 1979 and 1982, a method was developed in the IJsselmeerpolders to protect shipwrecks by raising the groundwater level within a vertical plastic enclosure. Today, ten ships are being protected this way.

Among the numerous finds, the investigation of a 13th century cog took an important place. Despite the deplorable condition of the wreck, its shape and structure could be established. In 1980, during the digging of a canal in Lelystad, a 16th century 'beurtschip' was found that had been wrecked around 1620. The starboard side of this vessel was still intact, offering us a welcome source of information on 16th century shipbuilding.

Outside the IJsselmeerpolders, the excavation, in 1978, of a flat-bottomed vessel from Roman times near Woerden drew attention. The vessel, found in a former Rhine-bed, bears similarities to the ships found in the Zwammerdam area, not far from Woerden. In Hellendoorn a small boat was excavated in the former course of the Regge; it dates from the late Middle Ages and shows some characteristics of a 'punter'.

Two museums added archaeological boat-finds to their collections. The Nederlands Scheepvaart Museum, of which the new accommodation opened in 1981, exhibits a logboat found near Spaarndam. In Ketelhaven, a logboat from Zwammerdam and an Amsterdam mud-barge were prepared to be exhibited. A 17th century merchantman that had been under a sprinkling installation for ten years in the museum, was gradually dried over a period of three years. Despite cracks and gaping seams, the result is satisfactory.

REFERENCES

Bogaers, J.E., & J.K. Haalebos, 1979. Archeologische Kroniek van Zuid-Holland over 1978. Holland, 11: 313-339.

Crumlin-Pederson, O., 1979. Some principles for the recording and presentation of ancient boat structures. Sources and Techniques in Boat Archaeology. BAR, Supplementary Series 29.

Ellmers, D., 1972. Frümittelalterliche Handelsschiffahrt in Mittel – und Nordeuropa. Neumünster.

Ewe, H., 1972. Schiffe auf Siegeln. Bielefeld.

Jong, J. de, W., Eenkhoorn & Wevers, A.J.M., 1981. Controlled drying as an approach to the conservation of shipwrecks. ICOM Committee for Conservation, 6th Triennial Meeting, Ottawa.

Maarleveld, T.J., 1981. Notes and news. International Journal for Nautical Archaeology, 10: 156-157.

McKee, E., 1978. Recording details of the hull. The Graveney Boat. BAR, British Series, 53.

Modderman, P.J.R., 1945. Over de wording en de beteekenis van het Zuiderezeegebied., Groningen.

Oosting, R., 1982. Restaurieplan voor de E-81. Werkdocument R.IJ.P., 1982-98 Abw.

Reinders, R., 1979. Medieval ships: recent finds in the Netherlands. Medieval Ships and Harbours in Northern Europe. BAR, International Series, 66: 35-43.

Reinders, H.R., van Veen, Vlierman, K. & Zwiers, P.B., 1980. Drie schepen uit de late middeleeuwen. Flevobericht 166. Lelystad.

Reinders, R., 1981. Mud-works, dredging the port of Amsterdam in the 17th century. International Journal for Nautical Archaeology, 10: 229-238.

Reinders, R., 1982. Shipwrecks of the Zuiderzee. Flevobericht 197. Lelystad.

Vlierman, K. & van Dijk, L., 1981. Een laat-middeleeuws bootje, gevonden bij Hellendoorn. Werkdocument R.IJ.P., 1981-98 Abw.

Weerdt, M.D. de, 1977. Römerzeitliche Transportschiffe und Einbäume aus Nigrum Pullum/Zwammerdam (Z.-H). Studien zu den Militärgrenzen Roms 2: 187-198.

Salemke, G., 1968. Die alten Kähne vom Steinhuder Meer in Niedersaschsen. Das Logbuch 4.3: 3-6; 4.4: 13-14.

Zeist, W. van, 1957. De mesolithische boot van Pesse. Nieuw Drentse Volksalmanak: 4-11.

Åkerlund, H., 1951. Fartygsfynden i den forna hammen in Kalmar, Uppsala.

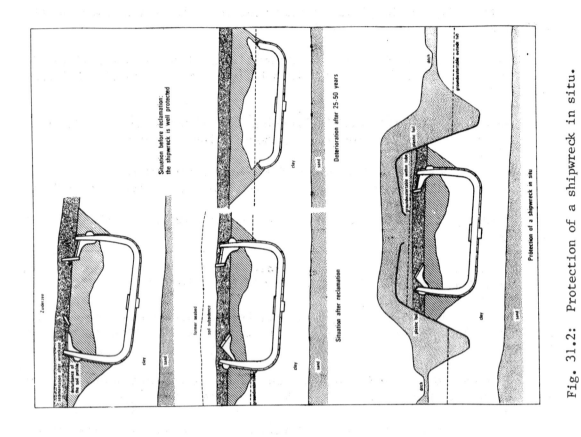

Fig. 31.2: Protection of a shipwreck in situ.

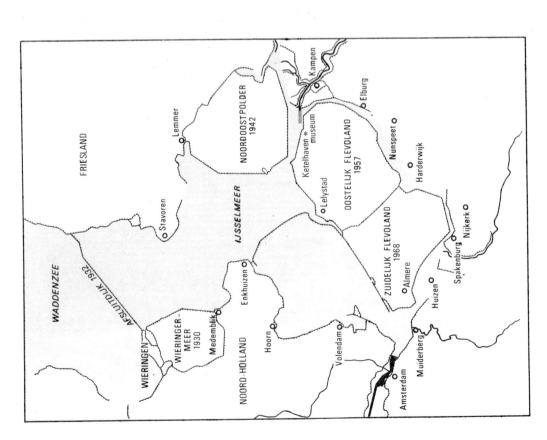

Fig. 31.1: Polders in the former Zuiderzee.

410

Fig. 31.3: Excavation of a medieval cargo vessel at lot NZ 43 (Fig. 31.3-6: Photo Rijks dienst voor de IJsselmeerpolders).

Fig. 31.4: Excavation of a 13th century cog at lot OZ 43.

Fig. 31.6: Excavation of a late medieval boat near Hellendoorn.

Fig. 31.5: Excavation of a 16th century 'beurtschip' in the centre of the town of Lelystad.

32. RESEARCH ON NAUTICAL ARCHAEOLOGY AND TRADITIONAL BOATS IN FRANCE

Eric Rieth

In recent years, French research on traditional boats and nautical archaelogy has undergone a revival.   Before reviewing the main areas covered by the present research teams, it may be useful to list some institutional changes which are meant to help future developments.

The new Ministère de la Mer[1], created in May 1981 and later on transformed into a Secrétariat d'Etat, has not forgotten the study of the past.   A Comité d'Action Culturelle Maritime[2], created with the aim of defining priorities met for the first time in Paris, July 1982.   Among the different topics[3] which were covered, it was noted that the traditional coastal boats were not considered as monuments historiques by the administration in charge of the protection of historic remains. As a result it was decided that the boat scrapyards, numerous in Brittany, should be protected by the Inspection des Sites.

Another good sign was a recent agreement between the Ministère de la Culture and the Ministère de la Defense for underwater archaeology programmes centered on post medieval sites almost untouched in France[4].

Teaching is an important sector where some progress has been made, at least in Paris at the Unité d'Histoire de l'Art et d'Archéologie de l'Université de Paris I[5] and at the Ecole des Hautes Etudes en Sciences Sociales[6]. This has led to the organisation in June 1982 of the Premières Journées d'Archéologie Navale which were held at the Musée de la Marine.

The Secondes Journées d'Archéologie Navale jointly organised by the Ecole des Hautes Etudes en Sciences Sociales and the Musée de la Marine[7] should be held in June 1984.

As regards museums, it should be noted that the Musée de la Marine is presently undergoing rearrangement.   But the most ambitious programme under way is at the future Musée des Sciences et de l'Industrie (Parc de la Villette, Paris) to be opened in 1986.   The archaeology section will exhibit a reconstruction of the wreck of the Roman ship from Madrague de Giens along with various associated presentations. At Marseille, the salvaging of the wreck from La Bourse has been followed by lyophilisation treatment and a presentation at the Musée d'Histoire.   The same museum also has a partial reconstruction of the antique wreck from Laurons on display.

Each of the developments represents a step towards better coverage of the numerous tasks to be undertaken.

1.   Traditional Boats

After the Second World War, J. Poujade[8] and R. Y. Creston[9] launched studies of maritime anthropology but they had no followers and it is only

413

since 1970 that the movement has started again.

The first work to be quoted in this respect is the study of the Bateau de Berck made by François Beauduoin[10]. This work established a method and showed that even a modest boat could be exhaustively analyzed: shape, size, structure, and all other characteristics of a boat are determined by geographic, historic and economic factors.

This study was a thesis presented in the Ecole des Hautes Etudes en Sciences Sociales, but most of the following research has taken place in a non-academic framework. Present-day developments as well are centred in the coastal regions. Britanny is that region where research projects are the most numerous whether the work has proceeded in isolation, J. Le Bot[11], or in a team, Ar Vag[12]. These two project-types differ in their approach; the first is mainly technical while the second starts with a detailed technical analysis but also attempts to assess the changes in boat types according to the socio-economic requirements. Brittany is the first region which has tried to build up a research framework outside the academic world through the Fédération Régionale pour le Patrimoine Maritime now transformed into a Fédération Régionale pour la Culture Maritime[13].

This society facilitates contacts between researchers and concentrates much of its resources on dissemination of the results, especially in the form of exhibitions. In Normandy[14] and Saintonge[15], similar but less systematic developments have taken place. The Mediterranean is lagging behind in spite of efforts by private societies like the Fondation de Collioure[16] which has done interesting research on the barques catalanes and sailing techniques using a lateen sail. Outside France, it is only in the islands of St. Pierre et Miquelon[17] that a programme of research is being currently carried out.

Another problem is to protect the last remains of the regional maritime past. Often such efforts are undertaken by local societies where independent research workers cooperate with professionals wishing to preserve traces of past or vanishing techniques.

It is difficult to draw up a comprehensive list of all traditional boats which have been protected[18] but it can be said that this kind of activity has been most successful. Britanny comes first in this respect. It is unfortunate to note that the project built up by the Association pour le Musée de l'Atlantique[19] towards a museum where local boats would have been gathered and exhibited seems to have been abandoned[20], at least as regards the museum which was to be created at Port Louis off Lorient in Britanny.

But many local boats have already vanished and only reconstructions can be tried.

To experiment with the boats themselves is an obvious follow-up to all these different activities. This has been the case for Eliboulane[21], an open boat derived from a shallop for sardine fishing at Douarnenez. The shallop has been built by local shipwrights with research workers who could check the information they had gathered, orally or in archives, by direct experiments. On the Mediterranean coast, at Collioure, two barques catalanes have been preserved and equipped to reconstruct lamparo fishing of sardinal and for lateen sail manoeuvering.

There is a strong incentive towards the local dissemination of the knowledge derived from all those research efforts. Although in recent years, maritime museums, in spite of rather rich collections[22], have not allocated much space to traditional boats, numerous small museums have been organized as part of or as the result of research programmes. This movement is encouraged by the authorities in the framework of the Centres de Culture Scientifique et Technique which are not solely museums but have a role towards further research.

As regards publications, it is indispensable to mention the Chasse Marée[23], a high class magazine devoted to maritime anthropology and to traditional boats. It is the successor of the Petit Perroquet edited by the same Bernard Cadoret which was founded about ten years ago.

A number of less ambitious publications, occasional or periodical, are locally produced in various places by independent research workers. It is reasonable to hope that the encouragement given by the authorities will improve upon some of these ventures which are at times somewhat amateurish in character.

2. Nautical Archaeology

It is fortunately possible to be more precise in the field of nautical archaeology than in that of traditional boats. The excavations, which are costly and subject to government authorization[24], are few in number and easily documented. In France, the most important efforts concern the Antiquity.

a) La Madrague de Giens[25] (Var)

This is the wreck of a Roman cargo ship which has been under excavation since 1972 by a team from the Centre National de la Recherche Scientifique (CNRS) under the leadership of P. Pomey and A. Tchernia. The last excavation work was done during the summer of 1982 and if final conclusions cannot as yet be drawn it is nevertheless possible to describe the main aspects of this important ship dated 50 B.C. which was carrying amphorae from Terracina, Italy.

Different computations lead to a tonnage[26] which was at least 350 tonns and might have been as high as 500 tonns with a carrying capacity of between 300 and 400 metric tons. Therefore it is a ship as big as the last and biggest medieval boats, e.g. the nave from Genoa or Venice from the early 15th century.

The analysis of the structure[27] reveals that the shell-first technique was used with planks being linked to one another by tenons and mortises following a technique which is now well-documented, having been found in numerous antique wrecks. It seems that some "skeleton" elements may have been used in the building process before the "shell" was completed, but this does not necessarily mean that some sort of combined shell and skeleton technique has been utilised. A detailed analysis of the material will be necessary before arriving at an acceptable record of the actual building process[28].

On the contrary, the profile of the boat is already precisely known with a long curved stern and an inserted stem terminating in a cutwater, the first of that kind to be discovered. The shape of the sections seems very sophisticated and further study should give interesting information on the sailing qualities of such boats.

It is also very interesting to note that this shape corresponds very closely to the symmetric type of boats as shown on certain well-known mosiacs from Ostia (Italy), and Themetra (Tunisia). Such a close relationship between archaeological findings and iconographic opens the way for important research as well as on rigging.

b) The wreck from La Bourse (Marseille)[29)]

This wreck has been discovered at the site of the Antique harbour which is at present located on land. The remains, which are ca 19.20 m long and 7.50 m wide, were excavated by J.M. Gassend. The researcher, together with J.P. Cuomo, a shipwright, concluded that it was a skeleton-first type of construction with floor-timbers and frames attached first, although in several steps, the planking being laid afterwards.

This technical reconstrution is another new solution, based on the fact that the conically-shaped treenails should have been pushed in from the outside of the hull. But the evidence presented by J.M. Gassend has until now met more scepticism than approval. More material would be necessary.

c) The wreck from Laurons, Golfe de Fos (Bouches du Rhône)

This wreck dated to the 2nd century AD was also excavated by J.M. Gassend, a project which came to an end in September 1984. The original must have been c 15 m long, 4 m wide and 1.50 m deep. The most interesting aspects of this wreck are two: an important part of the deck was preserved and one of the steering oars has been found as well as the structure for holding and manoeuvering it. But such remains are creating problems as yet resolved: for example, there is a square section in the upper part of the steering oar which does not fit the system of ropes by which the oar was most likely attached.

d) The wreck Bay of Saint-Gervais II, Golfe de Fos (Bouches du Rhône)[30)]

This wreck was excavated by Miss M.P. Jézégou in 1978-79. The preserved part of the hull is only 9.50 m long and 4.50 m wide. It is dated to the first quarter of the 7th century AD, the only example in France of a wreck from an early medieval time[31)].

The most interesting characteristics are that the floor-timbers are fixed to the keel and in between half frames, and that the planks were nailed to the frames from outside; all of which indicates a skeleton-first technique. But several planks have widely spaced mortises and some have none at all. This is therefore an example of skeleton-first construction with some remaining details of shell-first. Other examples from the same or neighbouring periods would be necessary before drawing any conclusions.

Although regional research and maritime societies may have been neglected for too long in France, the movement is now well underway, part of the support coming from amateurs who study traditional boat building and try to save the remains of such boats.

On the contrary, nautical archaeology belongs to the research performed by universities and the administration. Important results have been obtained, which generates the hope that gradually the enormous task will eventually be completed.   In the future for example it is likely that the priority assigned to Antique wrecks will not prevent the excavation of wrecks from other periods: a 16th century wreck recently found at Villefranche is an example of the type of work which, just begun, should be pursued.

What remains is further to refine chronology, verify certain hypotheses, and to broaden our axes of thinking in the study of keel forms. A further task that remains is to make a major effort to disseminate what is known, both at the teaching and the museum level.

Translation from the French language: Paul Adam and Keith Bradfield.

NOTES

1. In previous Septennates, France had a Secrétariat à la Marine Marchande, but its sphere of competency was more limited that that of the present Ministère de la Mer.

2. This Committee has its registered office at the Ministère de la Mer, 3 Place de Fontenoy, 75700, Paris. Tél.: 567 55 05. All questions should be directed to its executive officer.

3. The FIAM budget (FIAM = Fonds d'Intervention et d'Action Maritime).

4. An essential body in this context is GRAN (GRAN = Groupe de Recherche en Archéologie Navale). This association, set up under the Act of 1901, is run principally by officers of the Marine Nationale. Cf. René Guillemin, "Naissance et projets du Groupe de Recherche en Archéologie Navale", Cols Bleus, March 1982, No. 1701, pp. 7-9.

5. This instruction is provided, within the framework of the Certificate in Mediaeval Archeology (Licentiate level), by Eric Rieth. The theme selected for 1982-83 is "The contribution of archaeology to our knowledge of the means of water transport in Mediaeval Europe".

6. This annual seminar, run by Jean Boudriot (the author of "Le Vaisseau de 74 canons") has for 1982-1983 the title: "An attempt at a typology of military and commercial buildings: XVIIth-XIXth centuries".

7. The records of these "Days" will be published in the course of 1983. The next Days will be held in 1984. For all information, write to the Museé de la Marine, Journées d'Archéologie Navale, Palais de Chaillot, 75116, PARIS.

8.   Jean Poujade is best known as the author of <u>La route des Indes et ses navires</u>, Paris, 1946. He also founded the publication <u>Les Documents d'Ethnographie Navale</u>, Paris, Gauthier-Villars, which led an all too brief existence. Cf. the introductory section 1948 for his excellent "ethnographic questionnaire" for boats, pp. 26–41.

9.   René–Yves Creston was for a number of years Secretary General of the Comité International d'Ethnologie Maritime.

10. François Beauduoin, <u>Le bateau de Berck</u>, Paris, 1970. We would also quote his famous <u>Bateaux des côtes de France</u>, Grenoble, 1975. This work has played a truly revelationary role in France.

11. Jean Le Bot, <u>Les bateaux des côtes de la Bretagne Nord</u>, Grenoble 1976; <u>La bisquine de Cancale et de Granville</u>, Grenoble, 1979.

12. Edited by Bernard Cadoret, <u>Ar Vag – Voiles au travail en Bretagne Atlantique</u>, Vol. 1, Grenoble, 1978; Vol. 2, Grenoble, 1979. Volume 3 is currently being produced by l'Estran, Douarnenez.

13. This Federation has its office at the Musée de la Pêche, Ville Close, 29 110, Concarneau. The Federation and the Ar Vag group have published a plate in connection with the Year of Patrimony: <u>Pour le Patrimonie Maritime de la Bretagne</u>, Quimper, 1980.

14. Cf. for example Pierre–Henri Marin, <u>les Hirondelles de la Manche, Pilotes du Havre</u>, Paris, 1981. A study on a much larger scale is now being performed by François Renault. One aspect of this research has been presented by him in "Cordiers du Cotentin: les Bautiers de Barfleur", <u>Le Chasse-Marée</u>, No. 2, 1982, pp. 2–16.

15. L'Association des Bateaux Traditionnels d'entre Loire et Gironde, which has its office at the Museum d'histoire Naturelle, 17000, La Rochelle, organized in 1981 an exhibition presenting the initial results of its research. Cf. <u>Bateaux traditionnels d'entre Loire et Gironde</u>, supplement to the <u>Annales de la Société des Sciences Naturelles de la Charente-Maritime</u>, April 1981.

16. La Fondation de Collioure, Chateau Royal, 66190, COLLIOURE, apart from being in process of establishing a museum of the Catalane coast, performs ethnographical research, and arranges exhibitions and other activities. It also publishes <u>Les Cahiers de Collioure</u>. Issue No. 3, October 1980, is devoted entirely to a reconstruction of Sardine fishing.

17. Cf. Jean Chapelot, Aliette Geistdoerfer, Eric Rieth, <u>Les iles Sainte-Pierre et Miquelon, étude archéologique, historique et ethnographique,</u> Paris 1980. Two other volumes are in process of publication.

18. It is impossible, within the framework of this article, to give a complete list of all the salvage operations recently undertaken. Also, it is difficult to establish in any precise way the exact number of protected objects. One of the roles of the <u>Comité D'Action Culturelle Maritime</u> set up by the Ministére de la Mer will be to centralize this type of information, and disseminate it as widely as possible.

19. The Association pour le Musée de l'Atlantique has its office at the Musée de la Marine, Palais de Chaillot, 75116, PARIS. The Association publishes an information sheet.

20. The original intention was to create, in and around the citadel of Port-Louis, near Lorient (Morbihan) a sort of French counterpart to the Mystic Seaport. At present, this project appears to have been abandoned.

21. Cf. the account of this experience given in Le Chasse-Marée, No. 2, 1981, pp. 55-74.

22. The Musée de la Marine Paris has in storage an important collection of French fishing boats from the second half of the 19th century, a collection partly acquired by Admiral Pâris.

23. Le Chasse-Marée, 4 issues a year since 1981. Address: Abri de Marin, 29100, Douarnenez.

24. No drilling operation or excavation is permitted on the French shore other than by a request addressed to la Direction des Recherches Archéologiques Sous-Marines, Fort Saint-Jean, 13100, MARSEILLE, Cedex 02. It can be added that this body registers all underwater finds (both isolated objects and homogeneous sites) and maintains an exact card-index file.

25. The basic work in this context is André Tchernia, Patrice Pomey, Antoinette Hesnard, L'épave romaine de la Madrague de Giens. (Var), 34ème supplement to Gallia, Paris, 1978. This first volume deals with the excavations of 1972-1975. A second volume is currently being produced.

26. Cf. above all Patrice Pomey, André Tchernia, "Le tonnage maximum des navires de commerce romains", Archaeonautica, 2, 1978, pp. 233-251.

27. Cf. the remarkable synthesis by P. Pomey in P. Alfredo Gianfrotta, Patrice Pomey, Archeologia subacquea, Milan, 1981, above all pp. 260-266.

28. The recent article by Richard Steffy, "The reconstruction of the 11th century Serçe Liman vessel. A preliminary report", IJNA, 1982, II, I, pp. 13-34, shows very clearly that in the 11th century the procedures of construction were far from having been mastered. In these circumstances, one must be prudent and retain the concept of relativity concerning this period of technological transition.

29. Jean-Marie Gassend, L'épave de la Bourse, Musée d'Histoire, Marseille (in process of publication). At the time of writing, we have been able to study only samples of this important work.

30. The excavation of this wreck is the subject of an advanced thesis of the 3rd cycle to be held by Marie-Pierre Jezegou at the end of 1982 at the University of Provence (Aix-en-Provence).

31. It should be emphasized that other sites from the late Middle Ages are known in France, but have not been the subject of serious excavation. Cf. Alain Visquis, "Premier inventaire de l'épave des jarres à Agay",

Cahiers d'Archéologie Subaquatique, II, 1973, pp. 157-167; from the same author: "Présence sarrasine en rade d'Agay au Xème siècle", Compte rendu de la recontre d'Archéologie SousMarine de Fréjus Saint Raphaël, December 1974. Cf. also JeanPierre Joncherav, "L'épave sarrasine du Bataiguier", Archéologia, 85, 1975, pp. 4248. And, in addition, Serge Ximénes, "Etude préliminaire de l'épave sarrasine du rocher de l'Estéou", Cahiers d'Archéologie Subaquatique, V, 1976, pp. 139-150.

33. THE DEVELOPMENT OF THE ARCHAEOLOGY OF BOATS AND SHIPS IN POLAND

Przemysław Smolarek

The archaeology of ships is not very old as a specialized science in Poland.

It is a fact that various wrecks and remains of old boats and ships have frequently been found in lakes, rivers, port canals, or coastal sea waters, mainly during peat digging, or whilst carrying out water, drainage, hydro-engineering and dredging jobs. The wrecks discovered during such undertakings occasionally proved something of a sensation, a "curio from the past", recorded in learned books already in the 18th century, but as long as there were no scientists or museums interested in the problems, no attempts were made to protect and describe the finds in the proper manner. Even when the first museums began to open their doors to the public and archaeology was taking shape as a discipline of science, information about the remains of old boats or ships did not always, or not always on time, reach the museums and archaeologists; or sometimes, it simply failed to arouse their interest. In consequence, a wreck found by chance was often dismantled by villagers, to be used as fuel.

For example, such was the fate of the boats found in the years 1840-1850 in the marshland near Rumia (a village not far from Gdynia) and the perfectly preserved wreck of a Mediaeval ship discovered in 1870, when a dock was being built in the Port of Gdansk.

The last six years of the 19th century witnessed some stir of interest in boatbuilding relics, when a number of early Mediaeval boats was found during drainage work being carried out along the Pomeranian Baltic coast: first in 1894 in meadows near Dierzgon, later in 1895 in the vicinity of Frombork on the Vistula Lagoon, then, in 1896 at Charbrow on Lake Łebsko and in 1905, near Mechlinki on Puck Bay.

This growing interest in the relics of old Pomeranian boatbuilding was the result - as in various other European countries - of earlier discoveries of significant relics of boatbuilding in Scandinavia, mainly in Nydam, Gokstad and Oseberg. To own such a valuable exhibit, or even something similar, became the ambition of many archaeological museums. When the Pomeranian museum learned about the wrecks found at Dierzgon, Frombork, Łeba and Mechlinki, the boats - as the first plank-built in the region - were recovered, transported to museums, and examined. The interpretation of such wrecks usually followed similar lines everywhere. The influence of romantic sagas and legends about the Vikings, as well as the superb beauty and magnificence of the widely-popularized Scandinavian boats, was so strong, that almost every larger boat from the early Middle Ages which was later found in any European country within range of the Nordic influence and expansion, was said to be of Viking origin. The boats found in Pomerania were also classified as belonging to this group.

For quite a long time, some Polish scholars also suffered from this

"Viking psychosis", although here and there, more and more critical voices could be heard, as to the cultural identity of the Pomeranian wrecks, as well as those which were later found in the region, including those at Orunia near Gdansk and near Czarnowsko on Lake Łebsko, etc.

It must, however, be stressed that the "Viking ships" appeared, for some time, to be much more attractive than, for example, old types of Polish boats and ships used in inland shipping - uninspiring, as they were, in appearance, similar to the ordinary-looking craft still used on Polish rivers and lakes.

For whole decades, remains of such "domestic" types of boats still failed to excite interest. Neither were serious attempts made to recover or preserve the wrecks found in sea waters, though at least some of them - of great historical value, such as the wreck discovered whilst dredging the port in Gdynia in 1928, and dated as 17th century, or another, assumed to be 16th century, found off Rozewie in 1938 - could have been retrieved at a relatively minor investment in labour and money.

There is no doubt that one of the main reasons for such a situation in Poland, was the lack of a proper museum, a maritime museum I should add, and lack of researchers specializing in the history of ship building.

"Ship archaeology" was still to be born as a separate discipline. As a rule, boatbuilding problems were studied by archaeologists, for whom boatbuilding constituted one of the many aspects of material culture, which is their domain. This general picture cannot be changed by the attempts made to establish a Maritime Museum in Szczecin (in 1946), nor the appearance of one or two men who took up studies on boatbuilding as their main line of interest.

The efforts and achievements of those early pioneers finally bore fruit, with the situation beginning to improve gradually, and in time, the problems of the history of boatbuilding were more frequently to be found in scientific periodicals, or even daily papers. Of great significance here, were the studies on the origins of the Polish state, initiated after World War II and conducted in among other places such important Baltic ports as Gdansk, Kołobrzeg, Szczecin and Wolin, or inland, in Opole and Wrocław on the River Odra. These investigations provided much valuable information on early-Mediaeval boatbuilding. Relics of this and dug-out boats predominated in the archaeological material collected in Polish museums.

No museum in the country, however, could boast a substantial number of constructional elements of ships (not to mention whole wrecks) from the Middle Ages or later. A similar situation was observed in the relics of inland boatbuilding. The best collections were those of contemporary, domestic-produced fishing boats, or those used by peasants, and the greatest amount of information was of boat and raft-building, thanks mainly to the activities of ethnographic centres in Torun and Łodz.

The starting point for systematic research on ship archaeology was the establishment, in 1960, of the Polish Maritime Museum (CMM) in Gdansk.

In drawing up its long-term general programme of activities, the CMM defined its plans also in the discipline in question. The general thrust of the plans was a comprehensive description of the history of shipbuilding in Poland. The studies of the development of the building techniques used for wooden boats and ships, i.e. "ship archaeology", were to constitute one of the elements of this undertaking.

We assume that the means of achieving our goal should be:

a) to search for and preserve, appropriately selected relics of boatbuilding — by underwater exploration, land excavation and field research of a maritime ethnographic character.

b) archival and field studies, for the purpose of gaining written and linguistic material which would throw some light on the development of boatbuilding.

c) to collect material of an iconographic and documentary character (copies of illustrations, pictures, etc., as well as technical drawings of old boats and ships).

It is impossible within the time limit allowed for this report, to discuss all the undertakings — organizational and thematic — carried out within the framework of the programme mentioned in the years 1960 - 1982. I shall, of necessity, confine myself to a concise presentation of some recent ventures in underwater exploration, land archaeology, excavations and work in maritime ethnography.

Let us start with underwater research. Ventures of this kind, undertaken in Poland before the CMM was established, were limited rather to sporadic operations on lakes or rivers and did not possess the attributes of specialized marine archaeological studies. The CMM, on the other hand, intended to take up underwater explorations in the Baltic, these to become a regular form of activity. In this sense, they pioneered this type of research in our country. We thus set out to develop the conceptional and technical bases of the programme.

In the first phase of the research planned, the implementation of the programme was to follow two parallel courses:

a) the creation of organizational and technical bases,

b) underwater explorations to prepare an "inventory chart" of the Polish coastal waters.

It was planned to take up systematic investigations of the most interesting finds located during inventory explorations, in the second phase.

As to the organization and technical base, the aim was to create a special Centre for Underwater Research in the CMM. The Centre was to comprise its own research vessel, a specially-trained team of researchers, a chemical laboratory, conservators' workshop etc. Incidentally, I would like to add that this project has already been implemented to a large extent.

The introduction to inventory reconnaissance in the Baltic became archival studies, the aim of which was to establish a sui generis "register" of accidents and catastrophies in Polish coastal waters. The register, together with the reports and information submitted to the Museum by fishermen and hydro-engineering enterprises, concerning discoveries of new wrecks - and later supported by the materials concerning wrecks and collected by the Gdansk Maritime Office and Polish Ship Salvage Co., were to become the starting point for our inventory work in the Baltic.

Underwater research began in Puck Bay, in 1969.   In the years 1969-1981 it was mainly concentrated in the waters of Gdansk Bay.

Wrecks found during underwater surveys are entered into the inventory chart and designated W-1, W-2, etc., (wreck No. 1, wreck No. 2) (Fig. 33.1). Documentation of the preliminary investigation of each new find consisting of, for example, a fisherman's report of a discovery, the position of the wreck as defined by our team, characteristics of the site and find, drawings and photographs, etc., is filed in the records of the Department of Underwater Research.

So far, about 30 wrecks of historical value, worth further systematic investigations have been entered into our chart.

Despite the fact that the inventory-taking is far from complete and although, according to the original decisions, systematic investigations were to commence on its completion, extraordinary circumstances forced us to introduce slight alterations in the adopted scheme.

During the construction of the North Port in Gdansk, technical units of the port authorities encountered several wrecks of historical value whilst investigating the future anchorage.   As they were found in the anchorage area, they might have suffered damage when the port opened.   Under the circumstances, the CMM decided to investigate and protect them.   The most interesting wrecks examined were the W-5, W-6, W-20 and W-24.

Wreck W-5, discovered in the summer of 1969, was found 54°27'94" N and 18°42'65" E, at a depth of about 16 m.   After having prepared the necessary documentation under water, it was raised in 1975 (Figs. 33.2-33.4).

The ship remains consisted of the keel, stern-post, part of the starboard planking from the stern-post to the midship frame, together with the cargo adhering to the planking.   The ship, of which only the wreck remained, might have been about 25 m. long.   Dated by the C-14 method as 15th century, she was built by the shell method, of overlapping planks. She sank just after leaving the Port of Gdansk, where she had taken on cargo, the remains of which included slabs of copper, bundles of iron bars, more than a hundred barrels (in varying state of repair) containing, among other things, tar, iron ore, potash and wax, as well as oak staves for making barrels, so-called splintered oak, etc.   Altogether, the preserved cargo weighs over 10 tons.   All the barrels retained the merchants' marks, signifying that they belonged to merchants from Torun on the Vistula.

Wreck W-6 lay in position 54°28'N and 18°42'E, at a depth of 18 metres. Systematic investigations carried out by the CMM in the years 1969-1981 showed that all that remained of the wreck was the bottom filled with ballast stones, the stem, and the stern-post.   19 cannons cast at the end of the 16th century and beginning of the 17th century lay on the ballast stones and in the vicinity of the wreck.   Among the stones and around the wreck, several thousand other objects were found, e.g. seamen's personal effects, Swedish coins, remains of small fire-arms and side arms, galley utensils, etc.   After investigating the wreck, it was concluded that it was the remains of the Swedish warship "Solen" which had been sunk in the battle between the Polish and Swedish fleets off Oliwa in Gdansk Bay, on 27th November 1627 (Figs. 33.5-33.6).

Again near Gdansk, but further to the south-east, several hundred metres off the shoreline, where the seabed was being dredged for a future dock in the North Port, several wrecks were encountered in the sand 2-8 metres below the sea floor. They originated mostly from modern times (18th to 19th centuries).

As a rule, only the bottom parts of the wrecks discovered in shallow waters remained. Wrecks found at depths below 25 m. were in an incomparably better state of repair. Wreck W-20 discovered in 1973, 54°29'31" N and 18°52'51" E during hydro-engineering work may serve as an example. It lies at a depth of about 55 m. According to the notification submitted to the Museum, it is in very good condition. The hull appears to be undamaged, only the masts being broken, but still in their steps and clamps. The whole wreck is covered with a thick layer of fishing nets. This will be the object of investigations by the CMM in the near future. It would seem to date to the end of the 18th c.

The CMM carries out land archaeological excavations as well and I would like to mention here two sites, as examples.

In 1973, the remains of a wreck were found near the Wisłoujscie fortress, at a distance of about 400 m inland from the shore of the bay, 8 m. below the surface of the ground: the C-14 method dates them as 13th century. Not much is left of the wreck itself: fragments of four strakes and eight frames. All the elements were made of oak. The planking was clinker-built of planks about 30 cm. wide. The seams, caulked with animal hair, were joined with iron nails driven in at 20-30 cm. intervals. The tightly fitted frames were of characteristic cross-section, measuring, on average, 18 x 13 cm. They were joined to the planking by wooden pegs 3.5 cm. in diameter.

The investigations near Tolkmiko, a small fishing village on the Vistula Lagoon, would seem to be very promising. In 1971, during drainage work in the meadows not far from the village, an excavator picked up some constructional elements of an old ship from a dredged ditch. The discovery was reported to the CMM which, unfortunately, could only undertake preliminary investigations as late as the summer of 1980, to be followed by systematic investigations. When this report was being written, the work was still in its initial phase. I will therefore limit myself to a brief introductory outline of the find.

Up to the present day, it has been established that there are at least four wrecks in the meadows. They lie at a depth of 50-200 cm. in layers of loamy mud, about 100-200 m. from the present shore of the Vistula Lagoon. The area was probably once a small bay.

The final chronology of all the wrecks has not yet been established. The Tolkmicko I appears to be the oldest, while the Tolkmicko II, according to C-14 tests, is dated to about the year 1500.

The state of preservation of the wrecks varies.

The Tolkmicko I and IV, laying close to each other, have been uncovered only partially and it is impossible, at this stage, to say how many of their elements are still under the ground. We know, however, that the remains of wreck No. 1 include at least the fore-part of the ship, the keel with a stem, 3.25 m. long along the chord, rectangular in cross-section and attached to the keel by a vertical scarf. Six portside strakes, five starboard strakes and several frame timbers are joined together. The planking is overlapping, the seams caulked with animal hair and joined with iron nails tightened on the inside with rhomboid washers. The distances between the nails measured on the uncovered garboard strake are, e.g. 19-21-22.5-22-18-17.5 cm. The three uncovered ribs are about 9 cm. high and 16 cm. wide, spaced every 102-105 cm. They are joined to the planking with wooden pegs, 3.2 cm. in diameter (Fig. 33.7).

Of the Tolkmicko III, only a fragment of side planking about 6 m. long and 1 m. wide remains (Fig. 33.8).

Of the Tolkmicko IV, probably 1/3 of the hull has been uncovered so far - the bow or stern parts.

There is no doubt that the wreck Tolkmicko II is in the best condition. So far, the part uncovered is 18 m. long 3 m. wide. The ship remains include the keel and at least 5-6 strakes on the port side, with as many on the starboard. The planking is overlapping, caulked with animal hair and joined with iron nails. The high (about 13 cm.) and narrow (about 9 cm.) ribs are tightly and regularly spaced, more or less ever 48-50 cm. Ceiling planks rest on the floor timbers. There is no stem found, the stern probably being closed with a transom (Fig. 33.9).

Pottery found in the wreck dates from about the year 1500, but it cannot yet be ascertained whether this can be associated with the wreck.

Although the information on the construction of the four Tolkmicko wrecks is only preliminary in character, it can be presumed that the find may yield a substantial quantity of interesting material concerning regional boatbuilding.

I would also like to mention one of our undertakings in marine archaeological ethnography - a large-scale inventory project covering types of Polish boats - both those used on inland waters and those in coastal waters. Advancing industrialization and other social and economic factors, will soon result in the artisan boats being sought after not by ethnographers, but archaeologists. Standard, mass-produced and "plastic" boats are becoming more and more frequent in Polish waters. Some types, so characteristic for centuries, have been lost forever. The craft of the artisan boatbuilding is also dying out. Despite this, types which constitute a continuation of the ancient boatbuilding technology of the Polish cultural area can still be encountered in various regions.

Generally speaking, our inventory project follows two courses:

1)   The preparation of drawing-photographic, technical and descriptive documentation of boats built and employed in various regions, and the compilation of a kind of catalogue of types popular in different parts of Poland.

2)   The accumulation - based on the inventarisation fieldwork of a collection of the most interesting types of Polish artisan boats. Such collections we already established at Hel and Tczew.

We have a branch - the Fishery Museum, at Hel, a small fishing town on the peninsula of the same name (Fig. 33.10). There we have collected types of fishing boats used along the Polish coast, from the Vistula Lagoon in the east to Szczecin Lagoon in the west. The most interesting types preserved here are the square-rigged "barkas" from the Vistula Lagoon, the "połbarkas" "zakowka" and so-called "pomeranka" from the central coastal area, the characteristic "czolen" from Lake Łebsko and the so-called "chojar" from the Szczecin Lagoon.

In the second of our branches, called the Vistula Museum at Tczew, a collection of inland boats built throughout the country, from the Beskidy Mountains in the south to the Cashubian district in the north, is being prepared. The most conspicuous craft include a raft built of dug-outs and used on the Dunajec River, a "galar" from the region of Basuna on the Vistula, and, particulary, a ferry from Janowiec on the Vistula, which is a direct descendant of the "szkuta" - and the "dubas" type - employed on the Vistula in olden days.

Let us say that the inventory project was followed by studies for the purpose of preparing a monograph on Polish artisan boat-building of the 20th century.

Now some more about the future plans of the CMM. We intend to continue our efforts in all the fields mentioned, i.e. underwater investigation, land archaeological investigations and ethnographic field research. Special emphasis will be placed on the studies of Polish river boats. Such research has already been undertaken by the Museum.

From time immemorial to the railway era, rivers played a highly important role, as the main trade routes, in the development of communication and transport in Poland. With the passage of time, specific types of ships developed, these being adapted to river shipping, the organization of shipping, type of cargo, etc. So far, the craft so typical of Polish cultural area have not been the subject of papers, apart from short articles - no larger, specialized monograph. Thus, Polish boat-building remains unknown not only to the foreign reader, but also the Polish. The CMM wishes to change this situation.

Our primary aim is to concentrate on searches for wrecks of old Polish river craft and in consequence, create a source base for studies of their building technology. We have a fairly rich collection of written, archival sources, and even some iconographic documents, but we still suffer from a lack of material relics of those ships in Polish museums.

I dare say that if we manage to recover the wrecks already reported to the CMM, we shall probably have a good deal of interesting material for the discussion on the history of boat-building in this part of Europe.

Although my report focuses on the work carried out by the CMM, I would like to conclude it with some interesting undertakings, similar in character, by other institutions.

To begin with, it should be noted that boat-building relics obtained by Polish museums, are usually the result of chance discoveries reported to these museums. Dug-outs prevail, plank built boats are rarer. Among the latter, one of the most interesting was a boat found during drainage work in the fields near Czarnowsko, on the Łebsko Lake and reported to the

Archaeological Museum in Gdansk, in 1962.

Incidentally, this is one of four wrecks discovered in this region and has been named Czarnowsko II. Constructionally, it resembles the earlier wrecks encountered on Lake Łebsko in the years 1896–1931. The Czarnowsko II is built on a T-shaped keel and has overlapping planking. The seams are moss-caulked, joined with wooden pegs driven in from the outside and wedged on the inside. Of special interest is the joining with the stern-post, which is of a type not noted so far in boat-building material from the southern coast of the Baltic, also a distinct hollowing in the horizontal part of the keel. At present, we know the boat only from some fragments. The C-14 method dates the wreck to the 9th century. Systematic excavation of the find is foreseen.

Recently, work of a marine archaeological character has been taken up by various institutions. I think that in this context, mention should be made of underwater investigations inland. After World War II, underwater archaeological searches inland were recommenced in the mid-50s. Initially, they were limited – as I have already mentioned – to fairly sporadic operations on lakes and rivers and were mainly secondary or fortuitous to normal land excavations. They were not meant as long-term, specialized maritime research. They did not produce any important boat-building relics, with the exception perhaps, of a 10th century dug-out found in Lake Lednickie. For some time, a scientific centre has been taking shape at the Nicholas Copernicus University in Torun, which specialized in, among other things, the field under discussion. It can be assumed that regular lectures on underwater archaeology and field-work, will contribute to the growth of interest in the archaeology of ships and boats inland.

The Archaeological Museum in Gdansk has been carrying out systematic excavations at Gniew, a town on the Vistula (about 60 km to the SE of Gdansk). This museum is mainly interested in the genesis and development of the town. As Gniew was an important centre of the Vistula trade, searches were taken up to locate the port there. The CMM was invited to participate. Last year, investigations ended in the finding of the first fragment of port facilities. It can be assumed that further efforts will afford some knowledge as to the genesis of the port, its structure and later development. Written sources mention collisions near Gniew, hence it would be logical to expect to find one of the wrecks.

During investigations on the old port of Puck on Puck Bay, the wrecks of several boats were encountered, the oldest of these supposedly being from the 6th century and the youngest – the 13th. The results of the studies carried out by the local museum, with the help of divers from Łodz, have not yet been published in scientific periodicals, so we are only able to mention the undertaking.

Summing up, it can be said that the establishment of the CMM created the basis for systematic investigations on the technology of wooden ships in Poland. The work of the Museum has a visible effect – directly or indirectly – on the growth of interest in this problem by other institutions in Poland.

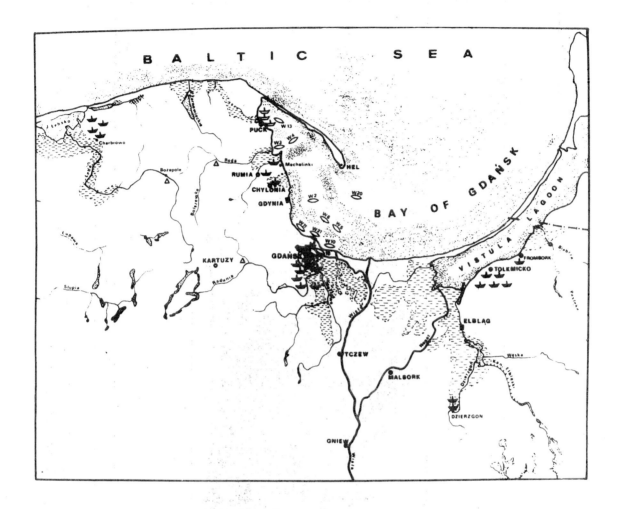

Fig. 33.1:   Map of the Bay of Gdansk with indications of some located wrecks.   (The plans and photos here have been produced by the Polish Maritime Museum in Gdansk).

- some of wrecks discovered in the Bay of Gdansk,

- wrecks excavated in dry land,

- single constructional elements of boats or fragments of their equipment, found accidentally,

- greater concentration of constructional elements, parts of equipment of boats etc., discovered during systematical archaeological investigations,

- Vistula Lagoon, waters and marshes before the year 1300.

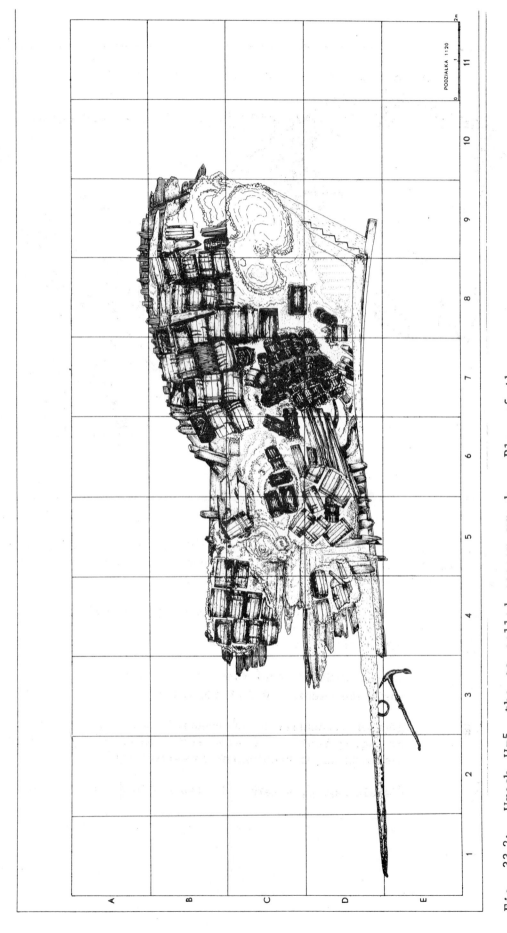

Fig. 33.2: Wreck W-5, the so called copper wreck. Plan of the remains of the hull with cargo of barrels, slabs of copper and bundles of iron bars.

430

Fig. 33.3: Wreck W-5, part of the stern on the starboard side. After recovering and removing most of the cargo. The rest of the cargo and part of a cross-beam are visible in the photo.

Fig. 33.4: One end of a crossbeam from the hull of the wreck W-5.

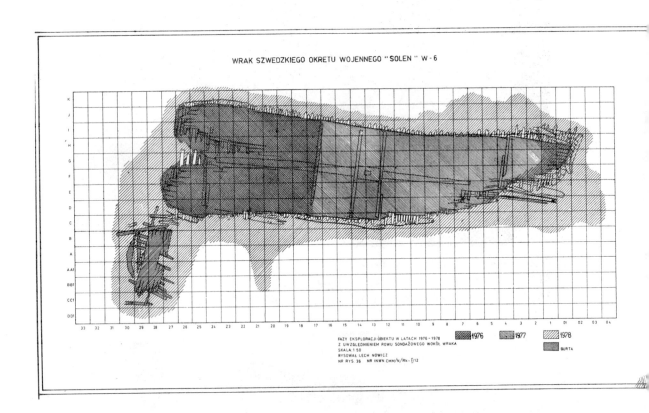

Fig. 33.5:   Plan of the site of wreck W-6, the Swedish warship
Solen,   sunk in battle in 1627.

Fig. 33.6:   Knight salvaged from the wreck of the Solen (W-6).

Fig. 33.7:   The wreck Tolmicko I.   The photo shows the fore part of the hull.

Fig. 33.8:   The wreck Tolmicko III.   The photo shows the fore part of the hull with a hole in one of the frames.

Fig. 33.9:   The wreck Tolmicko II.   The aft part of the hull.

Fig. 33.10:   The Fishery Museum at Hel.   In the background "barkas" from the Wisła Bay.

34. MEDIEVAL SHIPS FROM THE CENTRE OF STOCKHOLM

Björn Varenius

One of Sweden's largest archaeological excavations ever, the Helgeandsholmen excavation in front of the Parliament building in Stockholm, was fairly recently brought to an end. The fieldwork lasted from June 1978 until October 1980. Many important contributions to the knowledge of early Stockholm were made, notably to the maritime sector as the remains of eleven boats and ships were found. The vessels are dated, mainly on a stratigraphical basis, from the first half of the 14th century to the 17th century. Treatment has been concentrated on the older ships and therefore I have chosen to talk about them.

Time does not permit but a brief summary of the ships. Among the more spectacular finds was boat V, a long, narrow and low clinker-built ship with a preserved length of 18.2 m (Fig. 34.1). She is now reconstructed and measures 22.5 m in length with a beam of 3.4 m. The ship was propelled by 16 rowers and she also bore traces of a rig — one mast with a square sail. Obviously she was an exponent of the viking ship-building tradition. One could see it in the general shape of the hull as well as in details. Worthwhile noting are the double decoration-grooves on the keel, the hull planking and the frames.

The main building material was pine. She belongs to the 14th century, most likely the middle of it. A full-scale replica of the ship is presently being built.

Another, contemporary, but totally different ship, was encountered not very far from the above described. Its main features were sturdiness and strength, and it was entirely built of oak. The frames were closely fitted, distance between centres approximately 50 cm. The hull planks were heavy, too, especially in the bottom where the first three strakes were laid edge to edge, not overlapping. Unfortunately, one could not determine the shape of the stems, but with great probability this was the remains of a cog (Fig. 34.2). Certainly, that is a very rare find in this region.

As I mentioned in the beginning, eleven boats were encountered during the excavation. Ten of them were of pure clinker technique, the only exception the cog with its strange combination of edge to edge and overlapping strakes.

Boat III of Helgeandsholmen was apparently a 15 m clinker-built vessel, quite tightly framed but of a lighter dimension than the cog. The mast has been stepped in a three-piece keelson. Two loose oarlocks were found, and in the aft part of the ship a wooden box, (1 x 1 m) filled with fine clay was resting on the frames, probably not in its original position (Fig. 34.3). Its function must be assumed, since there were no traces of fire, to have been that of a hearth. Fires could be lit without going ashore. Like the other two ships described here, she is stratigraphically dated to the 14th century. This kind of ship has, without doubt, been of great importance to the economic structure and transporting system during the middle and latter part of the middle ages.

Fig. 34.1: The aft starboard side of boat V was fairly well preserved. She was probably a guardian ship in Stockholm harbour in the 14th century. (The photos in the figures have been produced by the Central Office of National Antiquities, Stockholm).

Fig. 34.2: A medieval cog, boat II, in front of the Parliament building. The aft part is covered by the city-wall of 1530.

Fig. 34.3:   A wooden box filled with clay was found in the aft
part of boat III.   It may have been a hearth.